DEBT
MANAGEMENT

Financial Management Association Survey and Synthesis Series

DEBT
MANAGEMENT

A Practitioner's Guide

John D. Finnerty
Douglas R. Emery

Harvard Business School Press
Boston, Massachusetts

05 04 03 02 01   5 4 3 2 1

Library of Congress Cataloging-in-Publication Data

Finnerty, John D.
    Debt management : a practitioner's guide / John D. Finnerty, Douglas R. Emery.
        p. cm. -- (Financial Management Association survey and synthesis series)
    Includes bibliographical references and index.
    ISBN 0-87584-617-3 (alk. paper)
    1. Corporate debt. 2. Debt. 3. Corporations--Finance. I. Emery, Douglas R. II. Title. III. Series.

    HG4028.D3 F53 2001
    658.15'26--dc21   2001016792

The paper used in this publication meets the requirements of the American National Standard for Permanence of Paper for Publications and Documents in Libraries and Archives Z39.48-1992.

Text design by Wilson Graphics & Design (Kenneth J. Wilson)

To our families with love and appreciation

Louise and William • *Cindy, Ryan, Lacey, and Logan*

Contents

Preface

*T*his book provides a comprehensive approach to managing debt. We have written the book for corporate treasurers and chief financial officers who must regularly deal with debt management issues. It will also interest academics who teach corporate finance and wish to incorporate practical material into their courses.

There are two phases to debt management: (1) design decisions made before the debt is issued and (2) managerial decisions made afterward. The first set of decisions, called the new-issue-design decision, concerns how to design a debt issue to meet the issuer's financial objectives within the constraints imposed by the capital market. The issuer must select the debt's maturity, interest rate features, redemption features, and the market in which to sell the debt, as well as decide whether to include a conversion or other specialized features, among other things. We discuss the important process of financial innovation and when innovation adds value, and we explain a rich variety of fixed-income innovations and how the features of these securities were designed to reduce the issuer's cost of debt.

The second set of decisions, called the refunding decision, concerns debt redemptions and repurchases, and in particular, how much debt to retire, when to retire it, and how to do it most cost-effectively. For example, an issuer can retire a callable bond early by exercising the attached call option. However, it must then forgo the opportunity to wait and call it later. Among other things, we describe how to evaluate opportunities to refund debt, call sinking-fund bonds, make sinking-fund prepurchases, and optimize the value of the call option.

Chapters 1 through 4 provide an overview of debt management and describe the global capital market environment within which debt management takes place. Chapter 1 describes the various sectors of the U.S. bond market and the important changes taking place. Chapter 2 discusses short-term financing and other aspects of commercial debt financing. Chapter 3 describes the markets for longer-term debt financing, including the U.S. public and private markets and the international debt market. Chapter 4 explains the special aspects of the high-yield debt market.

Chapter 5 covers the basic bond features. We review recent research concerning corporate debt provisions and provide some practical insights into how an issuer can select the right mix of debt features. We address the important tax and accounting issues involved in debt management decisions in chapter 6 and explain how the current tax code encourages refunding high-coupon debt, whereas current accounting rules discourage it.

Derivatives play an increasingly important role in finance. The growing use of interest-rate-derivative products, such as swaps, swaptions, caps, floors, and collars, has spawned new techniques for debt management. Chapter 7 contains a comprehensive discussion of fixed-income derivative products and how they are used in debt management. We also describe how complex fixed-income products can be analyzed by identifying their attached options. For example, a callable bond is really just a bond with an attached interest rate option. We explain how a firm can synthetically create callable bonds by issuing noncallable bonds and buying an appropriately structured interest rate call option. We also explain how an issuer of callable bonds can realize an embedded call option's time premium by selling a swaption. These and other examples illustrate the growing usefulness of derivatives in debt management.

The rapid pace of securities innovation over the past two decades has spawned dozens of new fixed-income products. Some are truly innovative, whereas others are but tweakings of existing product designs. We survey a broad range of debt innovations in chapters 4 and 8, preferred stock innovations in chapter 14, and convertible securities innovations in chapter 15. We identify those that have truly benefited shareholders and explain the reasons.

In the design of a new debt issue, it is often useful to have a valuation model to measure the impact of proposed design changes on the debt's value. Similarly, in deciding when to call a debt issue, debt managers increasingly rely on sophisticated option-based valuation models. Implementing synthetic bond strategies also requires sophisticated valuation technology. To address this need, we devote all of chapter 9 to bond valuation methodology. We illustrate how to use the model to value call options in chapter 10, to reach decisions concerning when to refund in chapters 10 and 11, and to manage sinking-fund prepurchases in chapter 12.

We address more specialized topics in the remaining chapters. Chapter 13 deals with five special cases of bond refunding. Chapter 14 applies the basic debt management approaches to preferred stock, a security that is fundamentally very similar to debt. Chapter 15 discusses convertible securities and the special role the conversion option plays in debt management. Chapter 16 provides some concluding comments on where we believe debt management is headed.

As the title indicates, we wrote this book with practitioners in mind. The material is presented in a way that is in keeping with the most current thinking in finance but minimizes complex mathematics. For example, the presentation of the valuation model in chapter 9 uses a binomial tree approach in order to simplify the discussion. We illustrate each of the analytical techniques with a real-world example to demonstrate its usefulness to practitioners.

We hope you enjoy reading the book and learning more about the fixed-income market. As you manage your firm's debt, we wish you falling interest rates, successful innovations, and profitable refundings.

John D. Finnerty
Douglas R. Emery

Acknowledgments

We thank our many friends and colleagues for their support and encouragement during the process of writing this book. We are especially grateful to Martin S. Fridson, managing director of Merrill Lynch High Yield Research, who graciously provided data and other information on the high-yield debt market that were especially helpful in preparing chapter 4; Stephen B. Land, Esq., partner at Linklaters & Alliance, who read the sections of the book dealing with tax issues and offered numerous helpful suggestions particularly for chapter 6; Lawrence A. Darby III, Esq., partner at Kaye, Scholer, Fierman, Hays & Handler, who provided guidance on several important corporate finance legal issues; David M. Lukach and P. Woodbridge Wallace, partners at PricewaterhouseCoopers LLP, who were very helpful with the accounting issues discussed in chapter 6; Thomson Financial Securities Data, especially Mark Lerch, president, Peter Marney, Mary Burke, Sylvia Figel, Keyur Amin, and Robert Carr, who provided the new-issues data for tables 8-1, 14-1, and 15-1; and Andrew J. Kalotay and Francis X. Farrell, who coauthored a predecessor book on liability management with John Finnerty (also part of the Survey and Synthesis Series).

We are grateful for the comments we received from four anonymous reviewers; their very specific comments and suggestions were much appreciated and the finished product benefited greatly from their guidance.

John Finnerty thanks his partners at PricewaterhouseCoopers, especially Steven Skalak and Ted Martens, and his colleagues at Fordham University, especially Dean Ernest J. Scalberg and professor Marek Borun. Doug Emery thanks his colleagues at the University of Miami, especially Dean Paul K. Sugrue for his support and encouragement.

We thank the Financial Management Association International, especially Jack S. Rader, executive director, and professors Kenneth M. Eades, Arthur J. Keown, and Philip L. Cooley, editors of the Survey and Synthesis Series, for letting us contribute to the Series.

Lastly, many thanks to Harvard Business School Press, especially our senior editor Kirsten D. Sandberg, our editorial coordinator Erin Korey, our manuscript editor Amanda Gardner, and Nancy Benjamin of Books By Design, for helping us turn our concept into this book.

Chapter *1*

Overview of Debt Management

In July 1995, Santa Fe Pacific Corporation repaid an issue of 100-year bonds.[1] A predecessor company, the Atchison, Topeka and Santa Fe Railway Company, had issued the bonds in 1895 when it emerged from bankruptcy for the second time. The bonds promised to pay 4 percent interest (hence, they are referred to as the *4s of 95*), but the bond contract permitted the issuer to skip interest payments during the first five years if it lacked sufficient earnings and to defer interest payments thereafter for an indefinite period. In today's parlance, the bonds were *deferred interest debentures*, and the issuer's financial condition qualified them as *junk bonds*, bonds with credit ratings that are below investment-grade.

Over the years, the value of these bonds fluctuated as the railroad prospered and suffered and as interest rates rose and fell. The low was $285 (per $1,000 face), reached in August 1896. In fact, the bonds never reached their face amount until November 1934. With improved railroad business, the bond's value peaked at $1,312.50 in 1946. Value fell thereafter, and when interest rates soared in 1981, the price sagged as low as $305 in October. With declining interest rates and maturity approaching, bond value marched upward to $1,000 in July 1995. All the while, bondholders collected a meager 4 percent interest each year. At maturity, the bondholders got the $1,000 for each bond that the original bondholders had been promised way back in 1895. But by then inflation had eroded the value of the $1,000 payment to about $5.54.[2]

The saga of the Atchison, Topeka and Sante Fe 4s of 95 illustrates a number of important bond characteristics. A *bond* is a contract for

1

borrowed money. It represents a promise to pay *interest* periodically and repay the borrowed money (the *principal*) on terms that are specified in the contract (the *bond indenture*). The indenture is a legal contract between the issuer and the bondholders, which specifies certain remedies, such as bankruptcy, if the issuer fails to make each promised payment or violates any of the other contract provisions (the *covenants*). The indenture also indicates when early redemption is possible and on what terms.

Most bonds require interest payments, such as the 4 percent per year in the case of the Atchison, Topeka and Santa Fe, although *zero-coupon bonds* do not make any cash interest payments before maturity. Bonds issued in the United States must have a stated maturity in order for the issuer to be able to deduct interest payments for income tax purposes. Any fixed maturity will suffice.[3] One-hundred-year bonds are unusual, although several such issues have been sold since 1993.

There are many types of bonds. This book is mainly concerned with *corporate bonds,* which are issued by corporations. They are *senior* to the corporation's equity securities. The choice of *capital structure* (debt-equity mix) is an important issue but is not addressed in this book. We focus on how to manage debt so as to maximize shareholder value, taking the corporation's capital structure as a given.

The Goal of Debt Management

The goal of debt management is to maximize shareholder wealth by minimizing the firm's after-tax cost of its debt. Therefore, a firm should choose the set of after-tax interest and principal payments with the smallest present value.

Debt management consists of two phases: (1) design decisions made before incurring the debt and (2) managerial decisions made afterward. In the first phase, the issuer must decide on the debt type, the terms, and where to borrow. The design must meet the issuer's financial objectives within the realities of the capital market. We refer to this activity as the *new-issue-design decision.*

In the second phase, the issuer should minimize the cost of the outstanding debt. The issuer should actively seek opportunities to redeem and replace, that is, *refund,* outstanding debt that will increase shareholder wealth by reducing the cost of the debt. Such decisions include which debt to redeem, how much of it to retire early, when to redeem it, and how to redeem and replace it most cost-effectively. We refer to this activity as the *refunding decision.*

The two phases of debt management are related, of course. If a firm wants to be able to redeem bonds at its option prior to maturity, the bond indenture must include a *call option*. Because the call option is costly, a benefit-cost analysis is needed.

Both phases include looking for positive-net-present-value (positive-NPV) opportunities, that is, opportunities that are worth more than they cost. For example, a design that attracts a class of bond investors who are willing to pay more (accept a lower coupon rate) than they would for an otherwise identical conventional bond issue is a positive-NPV opportunity.

Debt Versus Equity

Debt is a contract to pay interest and repay principal; it is thus a legal obligation and is enforceable in court. Failure to comply with the contract can lead to bankruptcy. Debtholders have first claim on the firm's cash and any cash derived from the sale of other assets. Equity is a form of ownership. The equity holders are the residual claimants; they get what is left after the debtholders have been paid. The bond indenture (contract) has the information needed to value a bond.

Debt offers investors a more predictable and hence less risky pattern of cash flow and a less variable rate of return than equity securities. The debt's required rate of return (*required return*) depends on the yields available on other debt of identical risk and characteristics.

Debt has an important tax advantage over equity: Interest on debt is tax deductible, but dividend payments are not. Therefore, securities that qualify as equity for certain purposes, such as bank regulatory capital requirements, but have tax deductible interest payments are sought after. Such hybrid securities show that in practice, the distinction between debt and equity sometimes gets blurred. In fact, the Internal Revenue Service (IRS) has tried several times to impose a well-defined tax boundary between debt and equity. Each time it has encountered stiff opposition to the proposed regulations and has withdrawn the proposal.[4]

Debt accounts for most of the short- and intermediate-term external financing for U.S. firms and approximately 80 percent of long-term funds. Equity accounts for the remainder, with new issues of common stock being about 14 percent and preferred stock accounting for about 6 percent of the long-term external funds. U.S. firms typically issue more than $500 billion of new long-term debt annually.

Types of Long-Term Debt

There are four main classes of long-term corporate debt: secured, unsecured, tax-exempt, and convertible. We cover the first three here and examine convertible debt in chapter 15.

Secured Debt

Secured debt identifies specific assets as collateral, which reduces the lenders' risk and therefore the bonds' required return. However, the issuer sacrifices flexibility. The assets can be sold only with the secured debtholders' permission or with suitable replacement collateral. The most common types of secured debt are:

- *Mortgage-backed securities,* which have a lien on specific assets identified in the contract (*mortgage*). If the issuer defaults (fails to comply with the contract), lenders can seize and sell the specific assets to pay off the debt obligation.

- *Collateral trust bonds,* which are similar to mortgage bonds except that the lien is against securities, such as common shares of one of the issuer's subsidiaries, rather than against tangible property such as plant and equipment.

- *Equipment trust certificates and conditional sales contracts,* which are often issued to finance the purchase of aircraft or railroad rolling stock. The borrower gets title to the assets only after it fully repays the debt.

Unsecured Debt

Unsecured long-term debt consists of *notes* (unsecured debt with an original maturity of ten years or less) and *debentures* (unsecured debt with an original maturity greater than ten years). Notes and debentures are secured only by the strength of the issuer's general credit. A bond indenture specifies their terms. If the issuer goes bankrupt, note holders and debenture holders become general creditors.

Debentures may have different levels of seniority. *Subordinated debentures* rank behind more *senior debentures* in claims on the firm's assets in the event of bankruptcy. This subordinated position exposes lenders to greater risk, and therefore raises the required return relative to the senior debt of the same firm.

Tax-Exempt Corporate Debt

Under certain conditions, firms can issue tax-exempt bonds, whereby bondholders do not pay federal income tax on their interest. Congress grants tax-exempt bonding authority to encourage specific investments. The Tax Reform Act of 1986 sharply reduced the list of activities that qualify for tax-exempt financing. Activities that still qualified following that act include solid waste disposal and hazardous waste disposal facilities.

The tax exemption lowers the required return relative to otherwise comparable taxable debt. In general, making maximum use of such financing maximizes shareholder wealth.

The U.S. Bond Market

The U.S. bond market is the largest in the world. Among the entities that issue bonds in addition to U.S. corporations are the U.S. government, federal agencies, state and local governments, foreign firms, foreign governments, and international agencies. Figure 1.1 shows the size and composition of the U.S. bond market as of June 2000. Corporate bonds make up the largest sector, and U.S. government bonds, called *Treasury securities*, make up the second largest sector. Federal agency securities have been the fastest-growing sector in recent years.

Figure 1.1 Size and Composition of the U.S. Bond Market, June 2000 (billions of dollars of par value)

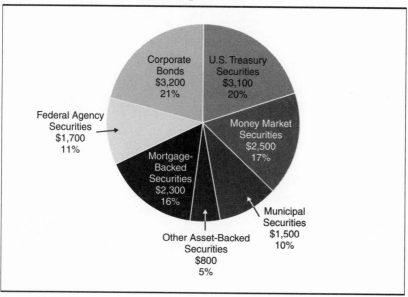

Sources: Federal Reserve System, U.S. Treasury.

The corporate bond sector includes mainly debentures and mortgage bonds, but also encompasses medium-term notes, tax-exempt corporate bonds, and bonds issued by foreign corporations (referred to as *Yankee bonds*). Corporations also issue asset-backed bonds backed by assets other than mortgages, such as credit card receivables, auto loans, and home equity loans, which are reported separately in figure 1.1.

Figure 1.2 shows the volume of new issues of U.S. corporate debt between 1975 and 1999. Volume grew from $43 billion in 1975 to $924 billion in 1998, a twenty-fold increase, before declining in 1999. Volume got a boost between 1996 and 1998 when interest rates dropped sharply and corporations refunded their callable high-coupon debt.

The size of corporate debt issues also seems to be increasing. As of this writing, the largest corporate debt issue occurred in June 2000. Deutsche Telekom International sold $14.6 billion (dollar equivalent) in bonds, consisting of $6.9 billion of five-year bonds, $3.7 billion of ten-year bonds, and $4.0 billion of thirty-year bonds. (The previous record was the $8.0 billion issue by AT&T Corp. in March 1999.) The Deutsche

Figure 1.2 Volume of New Issues of Corporate Debt in the United States, 1975–1999 (billions of dollars of proceeds)

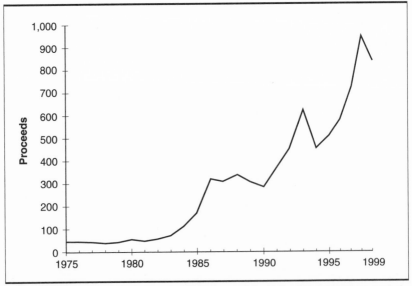

Source: Federal Reserve Bulletin, Board of Governors of the Federal Reserve System, Washington, D.C., various issues.

Telekom offering had four components, which were denominated in four different currencies.[5]

Treasury and Federal Agency Sectors

The U.S. Treasury issues bills, notes, and bonds that are backed by the full faith and credit of the U.S. government. *Treasury bills* are *discount notes,* which have only one payment at maturity; most have an initial maturity of three months, six months, or one year. *Treasury notes* and *bonds* make periodic coupon (interest) payments and a maturity payment; notes have an initial maturity of ten years or less, and bonds have longer maturities.

The U.S. Treasury uses public auctions. Three- and six-month bill auctions take place weekly. Longer-term Treasury securities are issued less frequently. The Treasury auctions the notes to a group of *primary dealers,* who also promote an active *secondary market* for Treasury securities. Trading volume is about $200 billion per day, making the Treasury sector the world's most liquid securities market.

Several federal government agencies and *government-sponsored enterprises* issue debt securities to finance public policy objectives, such as education, home ownership, and farming. These include the Federal Home Loan Mortgage Corporation (FHLMC), the Federal National Mortgage Association (FNMA), and the Government National Mortgage Association (GNMA), all of which purchase and *securitize* residential mortgage loans; the Student Loan Marketing Association; the Federal Farm Credit System and the Federal Agricultural Mortgage Corporation; the Small Business Administration; and the Tennessee Valley Authority, which operates a large electric power generating system in the rural South. The debt of government-sponsored enterprises does not carry the full faith and credit of the U.S. government; however, the perception is that the U.S. government would be loath to let them go bankrupt.

Information about FHLMC, FNMA, and GNMA, and their securities, appears in the financial news, such as the *Wall Street Journal,* almost daily. For the most part, in such reports, these agencies are referred to by their respective nicknames, Freddie Mac, Fannie Mae, and Ginnie Mae. We will follow that convention and also refer to them by their nicknames.

Treasury and federal agency securities are traded worldwide by a wide range of investors, including pension funds, insurance companies, commercial banks, mutual funds, state and local governments, foreign investors, and, to a limited extent, individual investors.

Mortgage-Backed and Asset-Backed Sectors

Mortgage-backed and asset-backed securities sectors include bonds backed by portfolios of mortgages and portfolios of other asset classes, respectively. Mortgage-backed securities are securitized mortgages. The vast majority are issued by Freddie Mac, Fannie Mae, and Ginnie Mae, but there are also several "private label" mortgage securitizers that are frequent issuers. The mortgages are securitized by packaging them into different types of securities, principally *mortgage pass-through securities*, which pass interest and principal payments received on the underlying mortgage portfolio through to investors, and *collateralized mortgage obligations* (CMOs), which repackage the cash flows in ways that appeal to investors. Mortgage-backed securities allow lenders to move mortgages off their balance sheets. They sell mortgages and use the proceeds to make new loans.

Mortgages were the first assets to be securitized. But the concept was quickly extended to a variety of other asset classes, notably credit card receivables, auto loans, and home-equity loans. Because of their strong credit quality, mortgage-backed and asset-backed securities appeal to the same types of bond investors as do Treasury and federal agency securities.

Municipal Securities Sector

The municipal sector consists of debt securities issued by more than 50,000 state and local governments and their agencies. Such bonds finance a wide range of public projects, such as schools, highways, hospitals, and low-income housing.

Municipal bonds are typically exempt from federal income taxes.[6] They are of two types: *general credit bonds*, backed by the issuing government's taxing authority, and *revenue bonds*, backed only by the revenues from the project being financed. Understandably, projects that benefit only their users, such as bridges and highways, are typically financed with revenue bonds and repaid from user fees.

When the federal income tax was introduced in 1913, the interest on municipal bonds was excluded from federal income taxation, and it has remained so. Because of the federal income tax exemption, investors are willing to accept lower yields, and tax-exempt municipal bonds carry a lower rate of interest than similarly rated taxable bonds. Individuals hold about 75 percent of all municipal bonds. The rest are owned primarily by mutual funds, banks, and insurance companies. Because pension funds are themselves tax exempt, they do not own municipal bonds; they can earn a higher return on taxable debt.

Other Bond Market Participants

Along with the issuers, investors, underwriters, traders, professional money managers, and regulators are also participants in the bond market.

Investors

In addition to the thousands of institutions, corporations, agencies, and foreign investors, millions of individual investors own bonds either directly or through their ownership of bond mutual funds or pension plans. The growth of self-directed profit-sharing plans and 401K plans has undoubtedly given a boost to individual bond ownership.

Figure 1.3 shows the percentages of outstanding bonds owned by each class of investors in the United States. Insurance companies are the largest class of bond owners, with 18 percent of the outstanding bonds. Mutual funds and foreign investors, chiefly foreign central banks, are next, with 15 percent each.

Underwriters

Most corporations use underwriters to issue bonds, although some frequent issuers sell directly to investors. The underwriters, which are also securities dealers that trade outstanding bonds in the secondary market, purchase the bonds and resell them at an agreed-on markup. The underwriters provide a form of insurance by guaranteeing the

Figure 1.3 Bond Ownership Breakdown

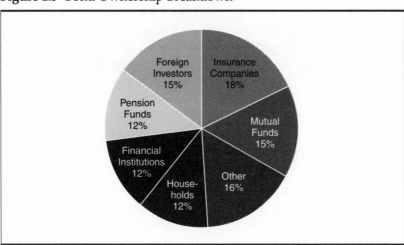

Source: Bond Market Association.

price. The markup, called the *gross underwriting spread,* covers the insurance premium and the underwriter's direct costs.

Alternatively, corporations can sell debt directly to investors in the *private placement market.* A securities dealer may assist by serving as the *placement agent.*

Traders

The vast majority of bonds trade in the over-the-counter (OTC) market. National and regional securities dealers maintain the OTC market. Some domestic bonds are listed on the New York Stock Exchange, and some Eurobonds are listed on the Luxembourg Stock Exchange. Individual investors find such listing attractive because they can track bond prices conveniently. However, even with listed bond issues, most of the trading takes place in the OTC market.

Traders "make" markets by offering to buy or sell bonds. The difference in the bid and offer prices at which holders can sell or buy a bond compensates the dealer for the cost and risks involved in market making.

Professional Money Managers

Professional money managers invest in bonds on behalf of the customers, owners, or beneficiaries of financial institutions, such as mutual funds, insurance companies, and pension funds. Such managers also work for private firms and what are called hedge funds, which are private investment funds.

Professional managers can develop expertise and a comparative advantage over other types of investors. For example, professional bond portfolio managers have devised specific strategies to appeal to specific risk-return investor preferences. Also, managers specialize in particular market sectors, such as Treasury securities or mortgage-backed securities.[7]

Regulators

The securities industry is regulated at both the national and state levels. The U.S. Securities and Exchange Commission (SEC) is the federal government agency that oversees securities regulation in the United States. Among its activities, it licenses brokers, broker-dealers, and mutual fund managers; administers the registration of securities for public trading; and monitors federal security law compliance. In addition, every state has a regulatory body that enforces its securities laws.

The National Association of Securities Dealers (NASD) is a dealer-created organization that monitors and enforces its members' compliance with the securities laws. The other exchanges also regulate and monitor their members to ensure their market's integrity. Because the vast majority of bonds are traded in the OTC market, the exchanges play a more active role in the equity and commodity markets than in the bond market.

Obtaining Bond Information

Suppose you wanted information about a publicly traded bond. One source is the *Wall Street Journal*, which has bond quotes similar to the list shown in table 1.1. The Coca-Cola bond quote (highlighted in the table) provides the following information:

- *Coupon rate.* Coca-Cola pays a coupon rate of 6 percent on these bonds, or $30.00 (one-half of 6.00 percent of $1,000) every six months.

- *Maturity year.* Assuming the bonds do not have a sinking fund, Coca-Cola will pay owners $1,000 per bond at the bond's maturity in 2006 (indicated by the *06*).

- *Current yield.* The bond's current yield is 6.6 percent, which is the annual coupon payment divided by the closing dollar price.

- *Trading volume.* Forty-nine of these bonds were traded the day before this quote appeared.

- *Closing price.* The *closing price*—the price of a financial security in the last trade before the market closed—for this bond the day before this quote was published was 90¼. Bond prices are quoted as a percentage of the par value. The Coca-Cola bond was selling for

Table 1.1 Hypothetical Bond Quotes

Bonds	Cur Yld	Vol	Close	Net Chg.
Caterplnc 9⅜ 10	9.4	30	99½	−1½
Chryslr 9.95s 17	8.8	37	113½	...
Citicp 6½ 08	6.8	2	95½	+⅛
ClevEl 7¾ 09	7.7	10	101⅛	−⅝
Coca-Cola 6 06	6.6	49	90¼	+½
CrayRs 6⅛ 11	cv	31	79½	−¾

90¼ percent of its face value. The quote indicates a dollar price of $902.50 (90.25 percent of $1,000) excluding accrued interest.

- *Net change in price.* The closing price is $5 (½ percent of $1,000) higher than the previous day's closing price.

A variety of additional symbols and notations can provide further information. For example, the Cray bond in table 1.1 has *cv* for its current yield. The *cv* denotes a convertible bond, which can be exchanged at the bondholder's option for a given number of shares of Cray common stock.

Bond Guides

A *bond guide,* such as those published by Moody's or Standard & Poor's, provides more information about this and other bonds than the newspaper does. For example, you can determine the exact date a bond pays interest, its maturity date, and how the principal is to be repaid. Table 1.2 illustrates information from a hypothetical bond guide. From the highlighted quote, you know the following information:

- Coca-Cola pays interest on January 15 and July 15 each year.
- Coca-Cola's 6 06 bonds mature on July 15, 2006.
- Coca-Cola has $150 million worth of these bonds outstanding.
- This bond issue does not include a sinking fund provision.

Current Yield

The *current yield* equals the annual coupon payment divided by the closing dollar price. It is a measure of the rate of income from the coupon payments. However, it ignores any capital gain or loss between the purchase price and the principal repayment. The yield to maturity is the appropriate measure of the return, because it measures the *total* return from owning a bond, including changes in market value. Given that current computer and information technology could easily provide the yield to maturity, there is little need for the bond quote to include the current yield. It seems the current yield is still given because of tradition.

Trends Affecting the Bond Market

The buoyant U.S. economy has produced federal budget surpluses, which have reduced the Treasury's borrowing needs. Traditionally the

Table 1.2 Excerpt from a Hypothetical Bond Guide

CUSIP	Issue	Rating	Amt. Outst. Mil.$	Interest Dates	Current Price		Yield to Mat.	1995 High	1995 Low	Current Call Price	Call Date	Sink Fund Prov.	Issued	Price	Yield
126117AC	CNA Financial Corp. nts. 6.25 2003	A3	250	M&N 15	99⅛	bid	6.38	99⅛	83⅛	N.C.	—		11-9-93	99.82	6.28
126117AE	deb. 7.25 2023	A3	250	M&N 15	99⅛	bid	7.31	99⅛	78⅜	N.C.	—		11-9-93	99.68	7.28
12613BAA	CNC Holding Corp. sr. sub.nts. 13.00 2007	B3 r	188.6	M&S 1	—			—	—	104.87 to	9-1-97	Yes	N.A.	0.00	
190348AC	Coast Fed. Bank FSB cap.nts. 13.00 2002	Ba2	50.0	MJS&D31	113¾	bid	10.20	113¾	108½	105.57 fr	12-31-97		12-18-92	100.00	13.00
19039MAA	Coast Savings Fin., Inc. sr.nts. 10.00 2010	Ba2	58.0	M&S 1	—			—	—		—		4-1-93	100.00	10.00
19041PAA	Coastal Bancorp, Inc. TX sr.nts. 10.00 2002	B1 r	50.0	MJS&D30	—			—	—	100.00 fr	6-30-00	No	6-23-95	100.00	10.00
190441AN	Coastal Corp. sr.nts. 8.75 2009	Baa3r	150	M&N 15	104	bid	7.38	104	101⅛	N.C.	—		5-13-92	100.00	8.75
190441AJ	. sr.nts. 10.375 2010	Baa3	250	A&O 1	112⅝	bid	7.18	111½	109¼	N.C.	—	No	9-25-90	99.88	10.40
190441AL	sr.nts. 10.00 2011	Baa3	300	F&A 1	111¾	bid	7.20	111¾	111¾	N.C.	—	No	1-29-91	99.50	10.08
190441AQ	. nts. 8.125 2002	Baa3	250	M&S 15	109	bid	6.45	108½	95¼	N.C.	—	No	9-11-92	99.62	8.18
190441AM	. deb. 9.75 2003	Baa3r	300	F&A 1	113⅛	bid	7.45	112⅞	103⅛	N.C.	—	No	7-30-91	99.44	9.83
190441AH	sr. deb. 10.25 2004	Baa3r	200	A&O 15	118⅛	bid	7.40	117½	108	N.C.	—	No	10-3-89	99.85	10.27
190441AF	. sr. deb. 11.75 2006	Baa3r	400	J&D 15	105¾	sale	10.81	109⅛	104⅛	103.92 fr	6-15-96	Yes	6-24-86	100.00	11.75
190441AK	sr. deb. 10.75 2010	Baa3	150	A&O 1	118⅛	bid	8.56	120	107	N.C.	—	No	9-25-90	99.59	10.80
190441AP	sr. deb. 9.625 2012	Baa3r	150	M&N 15	108	bid	8.69	108⅞	106	N.C.	—	No	5-13-92	99.34	9.70

(continued)

Table 1.2 (continued)

CUSIP	Issue	Rating	Amt. Outst. Mil.$	Interest Dates	Current Price		Yield to Mat.	1995		Current Call Price	Call Date	Sink Fund Prov.	Issued	Price	Yield
								High	Low						
190441AR	. deb. 7.75 2035	Baa3	150	A&O 15	106⅜	bid	7.25	—	—	N.C.	—	No	10-16-95	99.96	7.75
191098AB	Coca-Cola Bottling Consol nts. 6.85 2007	Baa3r	100	M&N 1	103½	bid	6.42	103½	99⅛	N.C.	—	No	11-1-95	100.00	6.85
191175AB	Coca-Cola Bottling Group sr.sub.nts. 9.00 2003	B2 r	140	M&N 15	100¾	bid	8.86	100¾	87½	104.50 fr	11-15-98		11-8-93	100.00	9.00
191216AB	Coca-Cola nts. 7.75 2006	Aa3r	250	F&A 15	100¼	bid	5.50	101⅛	100⅛	N.C.	—	No	2-12-91	100.00	7.75
191216AC	nts. 7.875 2008	Aa3r	250	M&S 15	105⅞	bid	5.45	105⅞	98⅞	N.C.	—	No	9-9-91	99.69	7.93
191216AD	nts. 6.625 2002	Aa3	150	A&O 1	104¼	bid	5.84	104¼	90⅞	N.C.	—	No	9-30-92	99.32	6.71
191216AE	nts. 6.00 2006	Aa3r	150	J&J 15	100⅜	bid	5.93	100⅜	86½	N.C.	—	No	7-15-93	99.81	6.03
191216AF	deb. 7.375 2093	Aa3	117	J&J 29	110⅝	bid	6.66	110⅝	86⅜	N.C.	—	No	7-22-93	98.93	7.46
191219AR	Coca-Cola Enterprises nts. 6.50 2007	A3 r	300	M&N 15	101⅞	bid	5.42	101⅞	95½	N.C.	—		11-12-92	99.63	
191219AT	nts. 7.00 2009	A3 r	200	M&N 15	104½	bid	5.68	104½	94⅞	N.C.	—		11-12-92	99.31	
191219AM	nts. 7.875 2002	A3	500	F&A 1	109¾	bid	5.92	109¾	97⅛	N.C.	—	No	1-29-92	100.00	7.87
191219AN	nts. 8.50 2012	A3	250	F&A 1	118¼	bid	6.63	118¼	99⅝	N.C.	—	No	1-29-92	100.00	8.50
191219AB	deb.5.75 2005	A3 r	153.3	F&A 2	100¾	bid	5.89	103	98⅝	§104.89 to	3-31-96	Yes	1-29-76	98.83	7.98
191219AV	zero cps.nts. 2020	A3		N.P.	–			—	—	N.C.	—		5-9-95	12.93	
191219AP	deb. 8.50 2022	A3	750	F&A 1	122⅛	bid	6.69	122⅛	98½	N.C.	—	Yes	Ref.fr. 4-1-97 @ 104.08		

actively traded Treasury securities, referred to as the *on-the-run Treasuries,* have served as the benchmarks for pricing other debt securities because of their liquidity and absence of default risk. As Treasury borrowing volume decreases, other debt issuers have introduced benchmarks. Fannie Mae's is called the Benchmark Notes program, and Freddie Mac's is called Reference Notes. Ford Motor Credit Company's is called Global Landmark Securities. Others are likely to follow. Becoming a benchmark note can lower the bond's required return because it increases the bond's liquidity.

Trends in Debt Issuance

If total federal debt continues to decline, the composition of new debt issues is likely to continue shifting away from Treasury securities. Figure 1.4 shows recent trends in the issuance of Treasury debt, federal agency debt, corporate debt, municipal debt, mortgage-backed securities, and asset-backed securities since 1992. Treasury issuance is below what it was in 1992 and is down significantly from its 1996 peak. All of the 1997, 1998, and 1999 new issues only repaid maturing debt, and in the prior five years, less than 10 percent was net new borrowing.

Municipal debt issuance in 1998 and 1999 was below its 1993 peak, although it was up sharply from the relatively low 1994 and 1995 volumes. In contrast, all of the other sectors had rising trends through 1998, although only federal agency debt issuance continued to increase in 1999. The drop in interest rates between 1996 and 1998 stimulated mortgage, municipal, and corporate refinancings, which led to an increase in new issue volume, especially in 1998.

The Future of the Bond Market Sectors

Based on the trends in figure 1.4, here are some of the possibilities for the future:

- Treasury borrowings will decline to the extent that budget surpluses are used to reduce the federal debt. Nevertheless, the Treasury will issue new bonds to refund a substantial proportion of the maturing debt. The Treasury's outstanding debt exceeds $3,100 billion, which cannot be repaid quickly.

- As the economy expands, federal agencies will continue to borrow to fund growth in the markets they serve. In addition, if interest rates drop, borrowers will refinance their debt, which will increase the volume of new securities.

Figure 1.4 Trends in Debt Issuance, 1992–1999

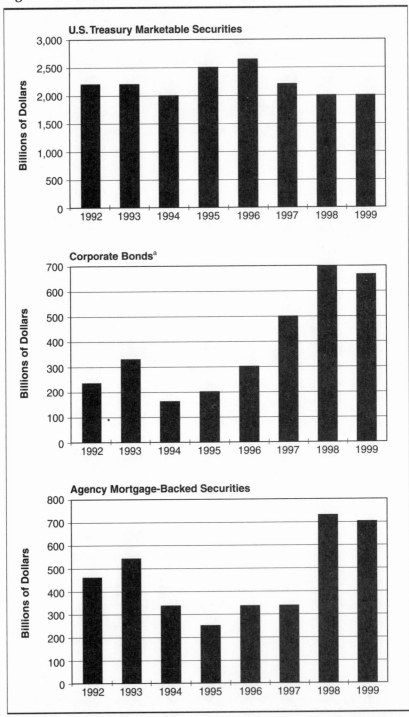

[a]Includes all nonconvertible debt and Yankee bonds but excludes all medium-term notes and Treasury and agency debt.

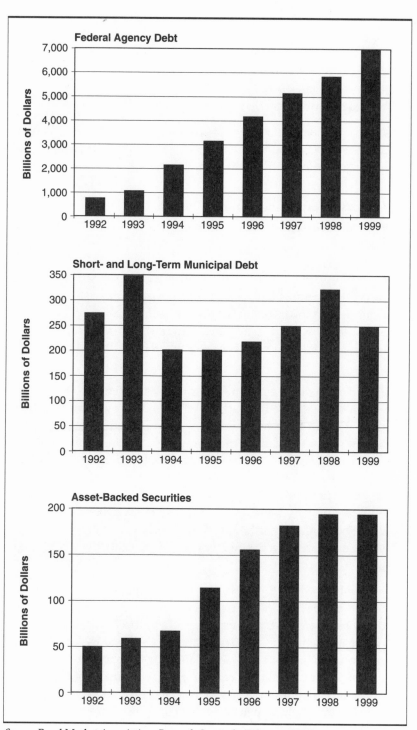

Source: Bond Market Association, *Research Quarterly* (February 2000).

- As the economy expands, corporations will continue to borrow to fund their growth; if interest rates drop, they will refund existing debt. Corporations will also seek new opportunities to securitize assets that have predictable cash flows. As a result, the asset-backed securities market is likely to grow more quickly.

- A drop in interest rates would stimulate municipal refundings, as happened between 1996 and 1998. In addition, municipal debt issuance is affected by political decisions.

Factors Stimulating Market Growth

Several other factors have stimulated the expansion of the global debt market:

- New international bank capital rules increased the incentive for banks to securitize loans.[8] Securitized loans, such as asset-backed loans, have a lower *risk weighting* than otherwise equivalent direct loans, such as auto loans, and they are also more liquid. As a result, bank debt is relatively more expensive than a public debt issue.

- The creation of the euro on January 1, 1999, effectively merged the eleven separate credit markets of the adopting countries. Since then, the European bond market has continued to evolve.[9] In the first four months of 1999, the volume of euro-denominated corporate bonds was more than four times the comparable 1998 volume in those countries.[10] The combined market can handle very large issues. In June 1998, Philip Morris sold a $1.12 billion bond issue in Europe. In 1999, issuers of euro-denominated bonds sold more than $600 billion worth, and these bonds accounted for a larger share of international bond issues (45 percent) than U.S. dollar bonds (43 percent).[11]

- In the late 1980s, the U.S. government sponsored the so-called Brady bond plan, which allowed banks to exchange illiquid defaulted loans to emerging-market countries for publicly traded bonds whose principal repayments were secured by U.S. Treasury zero-coupon bonds. The Brady plan securitized more than $100 billion of previously illiquid emerging-market bank debt. Until 1999, no country had missed a payment on its outstanding Brady bonds, which had attracted pension funds and insurance companies to invest in these bonds.[12]

- The high-yield (junk bond) bond market reopened in 1991. Mutual fund sponsors formed several new junk bond funds that attracted huge pools of funds.

- The market for emerging-country debt, both sovereign (government) and corporate issuers, grew rapidly over the 1990s. Occasional crises, such as the Russian debt moratorium in August 1998 and subsequent default, have led investors to reassess the risks posed by this bond market segment and caused new-issue activity to cease for a while. But each crisis has proved only temporary, and the market continues to develop.

- Various initiatives have been announced that should reduce information asymmetries and transaction costs in the U.S. bond market. Bonds are traded in the OTC market. There is no central exchange or composite tape as there is in the stock market. Reliable bond price data have been difficult to obtain, but that situation appears to be changing. Vendors such as Bloomberg, Bridge, and Reuters gather real-time pricing data for the most actively traded bonds and complement these data with a combination of daily prices on less actively traded bonds and model-generated prices for certain other debt issues. Also, a group of major bond dealers recently formed a global electronic interdealer broker, BrokerTec Global LLC, to service U.S. Treasuries and euro-denominated sovereign debt, which should improve the availability of bond pricing information to large bond investors and reduce transaction costs.[13] BrokerTec is an online interdealer brokerage initially dealing in government securities and euro-denominated sovereign debt. It expects to expand into other segments of the bond market and into bond futures eventually. Finally, in April 1999, the Bond Market Association created Corporate Trades I, which electronically facilitates the reporting of actual trades involving investment-grade corporate bonds.[14] These initiatives should further improve the efficiency of the bond market, which reduces investment risk, thereby stimulating greater investment in bonds.

- The Internet is creating new trading opportunities.[15] Several large securities firms formed TradeWeb LLC in 1998, which permits large investors to trade Treasury securities with eight broker-dealers directly over the Internet. Trading volume exceeds $2 billion per day.[16] In April 1999, Ford Motor Credit Company became the first firm to sell securities directly to investors online in hopes that the ease and lower cost of transacting would attract new bond investors to its debt securities.[17] Also in 1999, New York City sold $250 million of bonds over the Internet through MuniAuction.[18] Finally, Cantor Fitzgerald and the New York Board of Trade have introduced the first twenty-four-hour exchange that trades Treasury futures online.[19] The system displays bids, offers, and recent transaction prices. Electronic trading speeds execution and reduces transaction costs.

The Role of Technology

Technology is reshaping the bond market. We note briefly two important developments here and discuss several others in later chapters.

Valuation Technology

Increasingly, both phases of debt management rely on sophisticated option-based valuation models, especially when implementing synthetic bond strategies. To address this need, chapter 9 develops a bond valuation methodology and illustrates its use in both new-issue design and refunding decisions.

Derivatives

The growing use of interest rate–derivative products, such as *swaps, swaptions, caps, floors,* and *collars,* has spawned new techniques for debt management. For example, a callable bond is really just a "straight" bond with an embedded interest rate option. Chapter 11 explains how an issuer can synthetically create callable bonds by issuing noncallable bonds and buying an appropriately structured interest rate swaption. It also explains how a callable bond issuer can realize the value of the embedded call option without calling the bonds, by selling a swaption.

Derivatives create opportunities for debt issuers and investors to manage their risk exposures more efficiently. Chapter 7 describes the main fixed-income derivatives and how they can be used for risk-management purposes.

All of these changes and evolution create an exciting and highly competitive environment.

Chapter 2

Commercial Debt Financing

*F*irms can borrow money in a number of different ways. They can borrow from other firms or from institutions such as banks, insurance companies, and pension funds. In addition, borrowing can take an assortment of forms, such as loans of various types, privately placed debt securities, trade credit, and leasing.

Most commercial debt financing involves short-term and intermediate-term funds. These phrases refer to the original maturity of the debt obligation. *Short-term funds* are debt obligations that are scheduled for repayment within one year of issuance. *Intermediate-term funds* are to be repaid in from one to perhaps as many as ten years of issuance, and *long-term funds* typically mature ten or more years after issuance.

Trade credit is the largest source of short-term debt. Commercial banks are another major source of short-term debt. Commercial paper is an alternative source of short-term debt, but only for the largest and best-established firms. Insurance companies and commercial banks are the major sources of intermediate-term financing for the general needs of smaller firms and the specialized needs of larger ones. Insurance companies and pension funds are the major sources of long-term debt for smaller firms without ready access to the public bond market. Long-term debt for such smaller firms can be in the form of traditional loans or unregistered debt securities that will be privately held.

Another useful distinction in connection with commercial debt is where the funds will come from to repay the debt. Firms typically arrange short-term debt to finance seasonal or temporary needs. Short-term lenders are mainly concerned with the firm's working capital position and its ability to liquidate current assets—collecting on receivables and selling inventories according to seasonal patterns—to

21

generate cash to meet the firm's current obligations. Intermediate-term and long-term lenders are more concerned with the profitability of the firm's operations.

Trade Credit

Trade credit is credit extended by one firm to another. Businesses routinely grant trade credit on the sales of their goods and services. Purchasers of raw materials, manufactured products, and services are generally permitted to wait until after the goods or services are delivered to pay for them.

Trade credit is effectively a loan from one firm to another, but the loan is tied to a purchase, as it is with financing offers to consumers from automobile manufacturers. The product and loan (credit) are bundled together.

This bundling controls financial contracting costs that are created by market imperfections. By using trade credit, both participants may be able to lower the cost or risk of doing business for the following reasons:

- *Financial intermediation.* The loan price can benefit both participants by being lower than the customer's alternative borrowing costs but higher than short-term investment interest rates available to the supplier. A successful transaction makes the supplier a convenient and economical "bank" for the customer and makes the customer a reliable short-term investment for the supplier.

- *Collateral.* Repossessed collateral is more valuable to a supplier than to a bank because the supplier has expertise in producing, maintaining, and marketing it.

- *Information costs.* A firm accumulates important information about its customers in its normal business relations, which may be enough to make an informed credit-granting decision. If a bank wants to lend to this same customer, it must incur the cost of gathering the information, which gives the supplier a cost advantage over a bank.

- *Product quality information.* If a supplier is willing to grant credit to its customers, that credit provides a type of product-quality guarantee. If the product is acceptable, the customer pays the trade credit on time. If the product is unacceptable, the customer ships it back and refuses to pay.

- *Employee opportunism.* A firm can reduce the chance of employee theft by separating the employees who authorize transactions, physically handle products, and handle the payments. This segregation of duties makes it much more difficult for dishonest employees to steal merchandise or money without being caught. Trade credit helps separate the functions.

- *Steps in the distribution process.* It is not practical to exchange payments at each step in the product distribution and delivery process. By granting credit to the ultimate buyer, the payments mechanism bypasses all of the agents in the distribution process, requiring only one payment from the ultimate buyer to the original seller.

Trade credit is the largest single source of short-term funds for businesses, representing approximately one-third of the current liabilities of nonfinancial corporations. Because suppliers are often more liberal than financial institutions in extending credit, trade credit is a particularly important source of funds for small firms.

With trade credit, the seller specifies when payment is due and often offers a cash discount if payment is made sooner. For example, the terms "2/10, net 30" are frequently encountered; this means that the buyer can take a 2 percent cash discount if payment is made within ten days (the *discount period*). Otherwise the full amount is due within thirty days (the *net period*)

Suppose a firm purchases $50,000 worth of supplies each day on terms of 2/10, net 30. The firm always pays in exactly ten days. Therefore, it will owe its suppliers ten times $50,000, or $500,000 (less the 2 percent discount). Its suppliers are providing a continuing loan of almost $500,000. If the firm instead paid at the end of thirty days, the trade credit loan amount would be $1,500,000 (30 × 50,000). Of course, the extra $1 million in financing comes at the cost of the 2 percent discount.

Cost of Trade Credit

With no discount offered or if payment is made soon enough to take the discount, there is no cost for trade credit. When cash discounts are offered but not taken, however, there is a cost. With a discount for early payment, the discounted price is the "real" price. That is, with a $100 invoice and a 2 percent discount, the "real" price is $98. If the firm does not pay its bill within ten days, it is effectively borrowing $98 and paying $2 interest.

The nominal annual percentage rate (APR) cost of the trade credit is

$$\text{APR} = \frac{\text{discount \%}}{100\% - \text{discount \%}} \times \frac{365}{\text{total period} - \text{discount period}}$$

Therefore, if a firm pays in exactly thirty days under 2/10, net 30 trade credit, its cost for the twenty extra days is 2.0408 percent (2/98), and with 18.25 (365/20) twenty-day periods in a year, its APR cost is 37.2449 percent ([2.0408][18.25]).

The APR cost is widely used, but it actually understates the true annual interest rate because it ignores the effect of interest compounding. The *effective annual percentage rate* (APY) cost is calculated by compounding the credit period for the number of periods in a year.[1] Continuing our example, the APY cost for a 2/10, net 30 trade credit that is paid off in exactly thirty days is 44.59 percent. This is the twenty-day cost of 2.0408 percent, compounded for 18.25 periods.

Stretching Accounts Payable

As the APY cost calculation shows, forgoing a cash discount can be expensive. Therefore, some firms stretch their accounts payable by postponing payment beyond the end of the net period. Such stretching lowers the true cost of the loan because it extends the life of the loan without additional charge.

For example, with credit terms of 2/10, net 30, paying in forty rather than thirty days lowers the APY cost from 44.59 percent to 27.86 percent. Stretching to ninety days drops the APY cost to less than 10 percent. Suppliers may tolerate delinquencies, particularly when the buyer has large seasonal funds requirements.

Stretching accounts payable is a good example of what is called a zero-sum game: what the credit-receiving party saves is a cost to the supplier. But because it is a repeated game within a continuing relationship, a buyer must be careful. Excessive stretching may create other implicit costs, such as a decline in credit rating and strained relations with suppliers. It can also lead to less favorable future payment terms and higher prices. Therefore, the total cost of trade credit, although difficult to estimate, should be carefully evaluated.

Effective Use of Trade Credit

Trade credit offers certain advantages as a source of short-term funds. It is readily available to most firms, and it is informal. If a firm has been paying its bills within the discount period, it can get additional credit simply by delaying payment—at the cost of forgoing the discount.

Trade credit is also more flexible than other means of short-term financing. The firm does not have to negotiate a loan agreement, pledge collateral, or adhere to a rigid repayment schedule. In particular, the consequences of delaying a payment beyond the net period are much less onerous than those resulting from failure to repay a bank loan on schedule. For these and other reasons, trade credit is particularly valuable to smaller firms, which may have difficulty obtaining credit elsewhere.

Short-Term Bank Debt

Commercial bank debt is second in importance to trade credit as a source of short-term financing. Commercial banks also provide intermediate-term debt. Banks provide loans in a wide variety of forms that are tailored to the specific needs of the borrower. They generally lend to their most creditworthy customers on an unsecured basis. But when a borrower represents a significant credit risk, the bank may ask it to provide some form of security, such as a lien on receivables or inventory. Finance companies also lend on a secured basis.

Short-term unsecured bank loans take one of three basic forms: a specific transaction loan, a line of credit, or a revolving credit. Such loans are generally regarded as self-liquidating: The lender expects that the assets the firm purchases with the loan proceeds will generate sufficient cash to repay the loan within a year. A promissory note specifies the amount of the loan, the interest rate, and repayment terms. Short-term unsecured loans typically bear interest at a *floating rate*.

Transaction Loans

Two examples of transaction loans are a bridge loan and a project loan. A *bridge loan* provides temporary funds between the time of initial expenditures and the time when sources of long-term funds will be put in place. Bridge loans usually require prearranged *take-out commitments* from a source of long-term debt or equity, which are precommitted to pay off the bridge loan.

A *project loan* requires the borrower to use the loan proceeds exclusively for a project, such as an oil well or shopping mall, that is expected to provide the cash to pay all interest and principal. If the loan is *nonrecourse* (or *without recourse*), interest and principal payments are covered exclusively by the cash flow from the specified project. If the loan is *with recourse* to the project's sponsor and the project fails to generate sufficient cash flow, the sponsor is charged to the extent required by the recourse provisions.

Line of Credit

A *line of credit* allows a bank's customer to borrow up to a specified maximum loan balance at any one time. Credit lines are normally for one year, with annual reviews and possible renewals.

Credit lines are not for long-term funds needs, so banks require borrowers to have a zero loan balance periodically for some specified amount of time (for example, thirty consecutive days each year). If a borrower does not, the bank may give a warning and insist that the firm secure additional long-term financing. Most credit lines are informal arrangements. If the prospective borrower's credit deteriorates, the bank is not legally obligated to advance funds.

Revolving Credit Facility

A revolving credit facility represents a legal commitment to lend up to a specified maximum amount any time during a specified period. In return for this legal commitment, the borrower must pay a *commitment fee*, typically between 0.25 percent and 0.5 percent, on the difference between the permitted maximum and the amount actually borrowed. This fee increases the firm's cost of borrowing and compensates the bank for committing itself to making extra funds available to the firm. Revolving credits are evidenced by short-term notes that usually mature in ninety days. The borrower can roll these over automatically as long as the notes mature no later than the date the revolving credit agreement expires. Revolving credits often extend beyond one year, and the borrower often has the option to convert the revolving credit to a term loan when the revolving credit expires.

Commercial Paper

The largest, most creditworthy firms are able to borrow on a short-term basis by selling *commercial paper,* an unsecured promissory note that has a maturity of from 1 to 270 days, although a longer maturity is possible if it is placed privately or else registered with the SEC. More than four thousand firms issue this form of security.

Commercial paper is sold either directly or through dealers. Large industrial firms, utilities, and medium-size finance companies generally sell their paper through dealers, which typically charge a commission of ⅛ of 1 percent on an annualized basis. Such dealer-placed paper typically has a maturity of between 30 and 180 days. Principal buyers are other business firms, insurance companies, pension funds, and banks.

Roughly 40 percent of all commercial paper is sold directly to investors. Large finance companies, such as General Motors Acceptance Corporation and General Electric Capital, typically sell their paper directly. They tailor the maturities and the amounts of the notes to fit the needs of investors, mostly other corporations investing temporarily excess cash. In contrast to most industrial firms, the large finance companies use the commercial paper market as a permanent source of funds by regularly issuing new commercial paper.

Issuers of commercial paper frequently obtain a *standby letter of credit facility*, which provides insurance for commercial paper holders if the issuer is unable to repay or refinance the debt. Banks generally charge an annualized fee of ¼ to ½ of 1 percent for such backup lines, which increases the cost. In some cases, a revolving credit facility may provide that a portion of its availability can be used as a standby letter of credit facility.

Cost of Commercial Paper

Commercial paper is issued on a discount basis, so the cost is higher than the stated rate because interest is paid in advance. As shown in figure 2.1C, a 10 percent discount loan has an APY (effective annual) interest rate cost of 10.66 percent. Allowing 0.25 percent for the cost of a standby letter of credit and 0.50 percent for legal and other out-of-pocket costs, the true annualized interest rate cost of this "10 percent commercial paper" would be about 11.41 percent.

Rating Considerations

Commercial paper is rated by agencies such as Moody's Investors Service and Standard & Poor's. The rating agencies use similar criteria. Moody's has two basic commercial paper rating categories: "Prime" and "Not Prime." The Prime category is subdivided into P-1 (highest quality), P-2, and P-3. Standard & Poor's has four basic commercial paper rating categories: A, B, C, and D. The A category corresponds to Moody's Prime category and is subdivided into A-1+ (highest), A-1, A-2, and A-3.

Figure 2.1 Cost Comparison of Four Types of Single-Payment Loans

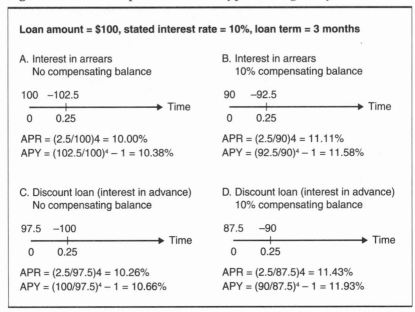

Loan amount = $100, stated interest rate = 10%, loan term = 3 months

A. Interest in arrears
   No compensating balance

100   −102.5
├──────┼─────────────→ Time
0   0.25

APR = (2.5/100)4 = 10.00%
APY = (102.5/100)⁴ − 1 = 10.38%

B. Interest in arrears
   10% compensating balance

90   −92.5
├──────┼─────────────→ Time
0   0.25

APR = (2.5/90)4 = 11.11%
APY = (92.5/90)⁴ − 1 = 11.58%

C. Discount loan (interest in advance)
   No compensating balance

97.5   −100
├──────┼─────────────→ Time
0   0.25

APR = (2.5/97.5)4 = 10.26%
APY = (100/97.5)⁴ − 1 = 10.66%

D. Discount loan (interest in advance)
   10% compensating balance

87.5   −90
├──────┼─────────────→ Time
0   0.25

APR = (2.5/87.5)4 = 11.43%
APY = (90/87.5)⁴ − 1 = 11.93%

The highest-rated paper, P-1/A-1+, has the lowest interest cost and the smallest chance of interrupted market access. At times the cost differential between paper rated P-1/A-1+ and P-3/A-3 has been more than two full percentage points. In market crises, the market for paper rated lower than P-1/A-1 can dry up. The market for commercial paper rated P-3/A-3 is very limited, and paper is rarely initially issued with a rating less than P-3/A-3. Some firms use an *irrevocable letter of credit* to obtain a higher rating.

Term Loans

A bank *term loan* is a loan for a specified amount that requires the borrower to repay it according to a specified schedule. A term loan generally matures in one to ten years, but banks permit longer maturities under special circumstances. Repayment is normally at regular intervals in equal installments.

In some cases the loan may provide for a larger final payment, called a *balloon payment*, or simply repayment at maturity in one lump sum, called a *bullet maturity*. A loan with a bullet maturity is like a typical corporate bond. The interest is paid periodically over the life of the loan, but the principal is repaid in one lump sum at the end.

Cost of Bank Financing

Term loans usually have a *floating interest rate*, which is reset periodically to reflect current market conditions. In most cases, the interest rate floats with the bank's *prime rate*, a benchmark rate that banks may use to price loans.[2] However, banks also use other benchmark rates, usually based on the bank's cost of funding the loan. For example, larger, more creditworthy customers might be able to select a basis of one of the *London Interbank Offered Rates (LIBOR)*, which are the rates prime banks offer one another on deposits in the London market, or the interest rate the bank pays on large certificates of deposit.

Commercial banks sometimes offer loans at *money market rates* that are below prime to compete with the commercial paper market. Banks charge less creditworthy customers a higher rate, usually expressed as a percentage over prime, depending on the customer's credit standing. For example, a bank whose prime rate is 8 percent might lend to a local manufacturing firm at prime plus 0.5 percent, or 8.5 percent, and to a local merchant at prime plus 2 percent, or 10 percent. If the bank raises its prime rate to 8.5 percent, the interest rate on the manufacturing firm's loan would become 9 percent, and on the merchant's loan it would become 10.5 percent.

A *compensating-balance requirement*, generally between 10 percent and 20 percent of the size of the loan, is in addition to interest charges. This requirement may be a minimum, but more commonly it is a required average deposit balance during the interest period. Such an average gives the borrower greater flexibility, because a high balance one day can offset a low balance on another day. Compensating-balance requirements are more common when credit is tight in the entire economy. A compensating balance adds a cost when a firm has to maintain a higher cash balance than it otherwise would.

Figure 2.1 summarizes the costs of four types of single-payment $100, three-month loans at 10 percent APR. The types are based on whether interest is paid in arrears (at the end of the year, cases a and b) or in advance (a discount loan, cases c and d) and on whether a compensating balance is required (cases b and d) or not (cases a and c). The figure shows how the loan's APY cost increases with compensating balances, and by paying interest on a discount basis.

Loan Security

Banks often require loan security. For short-term debt, the borrower may pledge liquid assets such as receivables, inventories, or marketable securities. It may be a floating lien against one or more classes of short-term assets. More commonly, the collateral is a detailed list. A firm can usually borrow between 70 percent and 90 percent of the face value of the receivables it pledges. With inventories that are easily sold, borrowing between 50 percent and 75 percent of the inventory's retail value is common.

For loans secured by receivables or inventories, the cost is normally the prime rate plus a premium of up to five percentage points. The premium depends on the bank's cost of processing the receivables and the quality of the receivables or inventory pledged. However, there are normally no compensating balances on such loans. Finance companies also make secured loans, but usually at higher rates than commercial banks.

By pledging, a firm can borrow more than it could on an unsecured basis. However, the firm incurs extra administrative and bookkeeping costs and sacrifices some control. In some cases, the borrower's customers pay the bank directly, or pledged inventories are physically separated and given special handling.

Comprehensive Credit Facility

Instead of negotiating a separate loan commitment in each category, a firm may arrange a *comprehensive credit facility* covering all of its loan requirements. Frequently this is a revolving credit facility that converts to a term loan after a few years. For large loans, the credit facility is usually provided by a *syndicate* of banks. The loan syndicator *underwrites* the loan by committing to lend the full amount. It then *sells down* portions of this commitment to other banks. The syndicator earns a fee for bearing the risk and cost of syndication. A comprehensive credit facility can often provide greater financial flexibility to both the banks and the borrower.

Certain institutional and legal considerations tend to encourage loan syndication. For national banks, the legal limit for investment in any one issuer's obligations is 15 percent of the bank's capital and surplus. In addition, banks normally have internal policy restrictions based on the borrower's credit strength, prevailing money market conditions, the types of facilities requested (shorter maturities are preferable to long-term loans), the borrower's financial leverage and its business and other risks, and the expected overall profitability of the bank's relationship with the borrower from providing loans, cash management, and other services.

Bank Capital Standards

The tighter capital standards that U.S. bank regulators imposed on commercial banks beginning in 1989 have made it more difficult to arrange large, syndicated bank loan facilities. Interest rate spreads widened, loan maturities shortened, credit standards became more demanding, and bank fees increased. Nevertheless, although bank loan financing slowed, it certainly did not stop. In recent years, the loan market has improved as banks have adjusted to the new capital standards. In addition, innovations, such as credit swaps, have enabled banks to cope with the stricter regulations.[3]

Bank Loans Versus Bonds

Although bank loans are higher in interest cost, they provide greater financial flexibility than bonds. A firm takes in a relatively large amount of cash when it issues bonds, and it must then manage that cash until it is needed. A term loan, bridge loan, or project loan often provides a schedule for the firm to obtain cash at the points it will be needed. Revolving credit facilities usually allow for multiple repayments and reborrowings (up to the total committed amount), so the firm can tailor cash flow to its circumstances.

Bank loans also provide greater refunding flexibility than bonds. Unlike bonds, a borrower from a bank can usually repay the loan without penalty at the end of any interest period.

Global Bank Loan Market

The global bank loan market has developed into one of the most dynamic financial markets in the world. It is not subject to national regulation and is therefore free to intermediate on a flexible basis between depositors and borrowers from different countries. Virtually all the major banks in the United States, Canada, the United Kingdom, Continental Europe, and Japan participate in this market. The U.S. dollar is the dominant currency. Other important currencies are the euro and the Swiss franc. Substantial growth occurred in the 1970s with the large inflow of deposits from the Middle Eastern oil-producing nations and in the 1980s as the United States continued to run enormous balance of payments deficits.

Important participants in the global bank loan market include the large clearing banks in the United Kingdom; large commercial and universal banks in France, Germany, Japan, and Switzerland; and, to a lesser extent, the consortium banks based in London. These banks lend through bank loan syndicates. The larger European or Japanese banks also arrange private placements of bonds with institutional investors.

Leasing

A *lease* is a rental agreement that goes on for a year or longer. Under a lease agreement, the owner of an asset (the *lessor*) grants another party (the *lessee*) the exclusive right to use the asset during the specified term of the lease in return for a specified series of payments. Payments are typically constant and made regularly, such as monthly, quarterly, or semiannually. However, there are alternative patterns, such as having lower payments during the early years before the asset reaches its full potential to generate cash flow.

Many lease agreements also give the lessee the option to renew the lease or purchase the asset. Sometimes the purchase option specifies a fixed price, but usually it is the asset's fair market value at the date the lessee exercises the option. If the purchase option is not exercised, the leased asset continues to belong to the lessor.

A firm must make its lease payments to continue using the asset. Otherwise the lessor can reclaim the asset (which it legally owns) and sue the lessee for the missed payment. Failing to make a lease payment is like failing to make a required debt payment. The lessor becomes a creditor and can force the lessee into bankruptcy.

Lease financing has expanded to cover just about every type of capital equipment, in part because capital equipment has become increasingly complex and costly and quickly obsolete. Firms in capital-intensive industries, such as railroads, airlines, and utilities, have been unable to use fully the tax deductions that result from asset ownership. Lease financing provides an effective way to transfer tax deductions from those who cannot use them to those who can.

Types of Leases

With a *full-service lease*, the lessor (owner) is responsible for maintaining and insuring the assets and paying any property taxes due on them. With a *net lease*, the lessee is responsible for these costs. *Operating leases* are short term and are generally cancelable at the lessee's option before the end of the lease term. *Financial leases* (or capital leases) are long term. They generally extend over most of the estimated useful economic life of the asset. Usually they cannot be prematurely canceled by the lessee. Financial leases that can be canceled generally require the lessee to reimburse the lessor for any losses.

Financial Leases

Financial leases represent an important source of long-term financing. Entering into a financial lease is like entering into a loan agreement. There is an immediate cash inflow equal to the value of the asset. The firm realizes this value, because it gets the exclusive use of the asset without having to purchase it. It realizes the same stream of economic benefits (other than tax deductions) that it would if it had purchased the asset.

The lease agreement calls for specified periodic payments, just like a loan agreement. Moreover, if the lessee fails to make timely lease payments, the lessee runs the risk of bankruptcy, just as it would if it missed an interest payment or principal repayment on a loan.

Thus, the cash flow stream associated with a financial lease is similar in financial effect to the cash flow stream of a loan. This suggests an appropriate starting point for analyzing a financial lease: Compare it to the alternative of borrowing to finance the purchase price of the asset and repaying this loan over the lease term.

Advantages of Leasing

Leasing offers a number of possible advantages:

- *Tax efficiency.* The main reason to lease is the lessor's ability to use the tax deductions and tax credits associated with asset ownership more efficiently than the lessee can.

- *Reduced risk.* Most leases are short-term operating leases that provide a convenient way to use an asset for a relatively short period of time. Cancelable operating leases, such as computer leases, relieve the lessee of the risk of product obsolescence. This risk transfer is efficient. The lessor, such as the equipment manufacturer, is usually in a better position to assume the risk. This motivation for leasing reflects the valuable cancellation option.

- *Reduced cost of borrowing.* Lessors of assets that can be sold readily, such as vehicles, usually do not have to perform credit analyses quite as detailed as those conducted by general lenders. They are also more likely to be able to use standardized lease documentation. Both factors reduce transaction costs and so can result in a lower cost of borrowing for the lessee, particularly a smaller firm that may face restricted access to conventional sources of funds.

• *Bankruptcy considerations.* In the case of aircraft and vessels, special provisions of the bankruptcy law give a lessor greater flexibility than a secured lender has to seize the asset in the event of nonpayment, because the lessor owns the asset. Suppliers of capital to smaller or less creditworthy firms, for which the risk of financial distress is greater, often prefer to advance funds through a lease rather than a loan. Because the lessor retains ownership of the asset, it can seize it if the lessee defaults.

• *An alternative source of financing.* Leasing provides yet another alternative financing method. It may or may not be a better source. Leasing has even enabled transactions that debt covenants did not allow using other methods.[4] However, investors have learned about such loopholes, and more recent debt contracts include leasing restrictions.

Disadvantages of Leasing

There are two principal disadvantages to leasing. First, the lessee gives up the depreciation tax deductions associated with asset ownership. Second, the lessee generally does not get the residual value. Prospective lessees should evaluate carefully the cost of losing these benefits. Only then can they decide if leasing is really cheaper than borrowing and buying.

Tax Treatment of Financial Leases

The IRS has established guidelines to distinguish for tax purposes true leases from installment sales agreements and secured loans. If the terms of the leasing arrangement satisfy the guidelines, the lessee can deduct for tax purposes the full amount of each lease payment, and the lessor is entitled to the tax deductions and tax credits of asset ownership.

Contracting Costs, Agency Costs, and Debt Maturity

A variety of factors affect a firm's choice of amount and mix of short-term debt as well as the overall maturity structure of the firm's debt: the cost of each source of funds, the desired level of current assets, the seasonal component of current assets, and the extent to which a firm uses the maturity-matching approach to hedge its debt structure. Beyond these basic factors, several contracting costs and agency costs also affect the firm's use of short-term debt:

- *Flotation costs.* The costs of issuing long-term securities like bonds and common stock are generally much higher than the costs of arranging short-term borrowings. Consequently, the firm issues these long-term securities only infrequently. In the interim, firms borrow short term from banks or issue commercial paper. As these short-term borrowings build up, they are eventually replaced with long-term securities.

- *Restricted access to sources of long-term capital.* Legal restrictions limit the types of loans that institutional investors can make. It may not be attractive for smaller firms, or larger firms whose debt would be rated below investment-grade, to sell long-term debt securities. They may have to rely on trade credit, bank financing, or finance company borrowing.

- *Less restrictive terms.* Bank financing does not normally carry penalties for early repayment, whereas bonds normally do have penalties. Such a penalty is simply the cost of the "hidden" option to refinance. Because of this cost, the more likely a firm is to want to repay early, the more attractive bank financing becomes.

- *Bankruptcy costs.* Bankruptcy costs create a bias in favor of longer maturities, because every time short-term financing comes due, there is the "hidden" option to default. Shareholders must decide whether it is worth it to "repurchase" the assets from the debt holders or to "walk away."

- *Firm's choice of risk level.* The firm's attitude toward risk affects its philosophy about financing its working capital and, more generally, its choice of short- versus long-term financing. Because of possible increases in interest rates, firms whose shareholders are not well diversified, as is often the case with smaller firms, frequently choose a relatively lower proportion of short-term debt financing.

Private Placements

The private debt market has generally been much more receptive to smaller issues and complex financings than the public market.

Privately placed securities are not registered for sale to the public, but by U.S. securities law must satisfy the restrictions on exemption from registration. These restrictions limit firms to selling (or reselling) unregistered securities only to those who qualify as *sophisticated investors*—for example, life insurance companies, property and casualty insurance companies, credit companies, pension funds, and wealthy individuals. Among these, life insurance companies hold the overwhelming majority of private debt. This limitation makes privately placed securities less liquid. As a result, with all else equal, investors require a higher interest rate for bonds that will be privately placed than bonds that will be publicly traded.

Life Insurance Companies

The major life insurance companies possess a high degree of investment sophistication, which allows them to make their own judgments about the risks in highly complex situations. Smaller life insurance companies have traditionally been influenced by the major life insurance companies and by debt ratings.

Life insurance companies have a relatively assured annual cash flow, which they can commit for *takedown* up to several years in the future. Understandably, insurance companies require a commitment fee for committing funds in advance. Subject to credit risk and overall loan security, life insurance companies seek the greatest return offered by competing securities.

Obtaining a large amount of funds privately from life insurance companies can be cost-effective from a borrower's perspective. Often it is necessary to approach only a few institutions to obtain the desired financing. This reduces the cost and time to arrange the loan.

Features of Private Debt

Privately placed securities generally have shorter maturities than comparable publicly traded debt securities. The growth of the managed money and guaranteed investment contract business has made life insurance companies enthusiastic buyers of intermediate-term debt, with a five- to ten-year maturity.

Security and restrictive covenants are important in private placements. Tighter covenants protect private lenders who face greater *agency costs* because the debt is not freely tradable. Private placements typically include limitations on indebtedness, limitations on liens, limitations on cash distributions, and net worth and working capital requirements.

Credit Ratings

Even with a private placement, obtaining a credit rating can be advantageous. There is a trade-off between the cost of getting a favorable rating and the benefit of access to a broader and more competitive market.

Life insurance companies are sensitive to the borrower's credit-worthiness because of capital regulations. The National Association of Insurance Commissioners (NAIC) has a six-category rating system for private placements. The amount of reserve a life insurance company must hold for a loan depends on the NAIC rating. Because of reserve requirements, life insurance companies much prefer investment-grade (NAIC-1 or NAIC-2) loans.[5] In recent years, only about 10 percent of the privately placed debt issues were rated below investment-grade (NAIC-3 or lower).

Table 2.1 shows the corporate bond rating systems for public and private debt used by the three leading corporate bond rating agencies: Fitch, Moody's, and Standard & Poor's (S&P). The top four categories are investment-grade and the others speculative-grade (or high-yield, or junk) debt. The rating agencies use + (better) or – (weaker) signs or numbers (1 being the strongest to 3 being the weakest) to subdivide each rating category below triple-A.

Private placements are a substantial source of commercial debt financing, especially for smaller firms without access to the public debt market. A private placement is also good for firms needing complex loans, such as project financing, and specialized debt forms, such as equipment financings and production payment loans.

Rule 144A Quasi-Public Market

In April 1990, the SEC adopted Rule 144A under the Securities Act of 1933, which relaxed the restrictions on trading unregistered debt and equity securities. Prior to this, private placement investors demanded an *illiquidity premium* in yield. Rule 144A allows large, sophisticated, *qualified institutional buyers (QIBs)* to trade unregistered securities with each other.[6] As a result, debt and equity securities issued under Rule 144A are much more liquid and are considered quasi-public securities.[7]

Table 2.1 Summary of Corporate Bond Ratings

Fitch	Moody's	S&P	Brief Description
Investment-Grade			
AAA	Aaa	AAA	Gilt edge; prime quality; provides maximum safety
AA+	Aa1	AA+	⎫
AA	Aa2	AA	⎬ Very high grade
AA–	Aa3	AA–	⎭
A+	A1	A+	⎫
A	A2	A	⎬ Upper medium grade
A–	A3	A–	⎭
BBB+	Baa1	BBB+	⎫
BBB	Baa2	BBB	⎬ Lower medium grade
BBB–	Baa3	BBB–	⎭
Speculative-Grade			
BB+	Ba1	BB+	⎫
BB	Ba2	BB	⎬ Low grade: has speculative quality
BB–	Ba3	BB–	⎭
B+	B1	B+	⎫
B	B2	B	⎬ Highly speculative
B–	B3	B–	⎭
Very Speculative; Substantial Credit Risk or Already in Default			
		CCC+	⎫
CCC	Caa	CCC	⎬ Substantial risk; in poor standing
		CCC–	⎭
CC	Ca	CC	Extremely speculative; may be in default
C	C	C	Even more speculative than those rated CC
		CI	CI = Income bonds; no interest is being paid
DDD			⎫
DD			⎬ In default
D		D	⎭

Benefits to Issuers

A Rule 144A private placement can be *underwritten.* The issuer can sell its securities to one or more investment banks, which then resell the securities to QIBs. This method of issuance is very similar to what occurs in an underwritten public offering, but without the extensive documentation being made public.

Rule 144A issues can generally be arranged more quickly than public offerings because they are not registered. Relative to privately placed securities, they are more liquid because of fewer trading restrictions, which lowers the required interest rate and reduces agency costs. Lower agency costs allow less restrictive covenants compared to private placements.

Investors

The principal buyers of Rule 144A debt offerings are large life insurance companies. They are most receptive to Rule 144A debt offerings that are rated investment-grade (e.g., Moody's Baa 3 or better or Standard & Poor's BBB- or better). The major rating agencies apply the same rating criteria to Rule 144A debt issues that they do to public debt issues.

Table 2.2 compares the commercial bank market, the private placement market, and the Rule 144A quasi-public market. The Rule 144A market permits the longest maturity and generally affords the greatest flexibility.

The Rule 144A market has matured. Volume has increased, liquidity has improved, and yields have moved much closer to those available in the public debt market. The Rule 144A market has thus become relatively more attractive for borrowers and, in particular, for foreign issuers that desire long-term fixed-rate debt but do not want to provide the extensive disclosures that a public debt offering would require.[8] They are willing to disclose sensitive business and financial information privately to prospective lenders, and a Rule 144A private placement lets them restrict the flow of information without having to bear the cost of the illiquidity premium that would result from a traditional private placement.

Rule 144A High-Yield Market

Rule 144A offerings are especially attractive to many non-investment-grade (i.e., junk bond) issuers that cannot qualify for shelf registrations. A traditional public debt offering can take up to six weeks to get SEC clearance. During this time, market conditions can change, causing the issuer to miss an attractive issuing opportunity.

The high-yield Rule 144A market has grown dramatically since 1995. Traditional junk bond offerings and Rule 144A junk bond offerings raised approximately equal amounts in 1995, but Rule 144A offerings now make up more than three-quarters of the high-yield market.[9] The illiquidity risk can be further reduced with *registration rights:* Issuers agree to register the bonds so that investors can freely trade them after as little as six months after issuance.[10]

Table 2.2 Comparative Analysis of Private Borrowing Alternatives

Feature	Commercial Bank Market	Private Placement Market	Rule 144A Quasi-Public Market
Maturity	Up to 15 years in special cases, but most maturities do not exceed 10 years.	Up to 20 years.	Up to 30 years.
Interest rate	Floating rate. Interest rate risk can be eliminated through an interest rate swap.	Fixed-rate or floating-rate debt can be placed.	Fixed-rate or floating-rate debt can be placed.
Prepayments	Permitted, subject to unwinding the interest rate swap, if any.	Requires compensation to make up for any lost future interest income (i.e., a "make-whole" provision).	Normally permits greater refunding flexibility than commercial bank and private placement markets.
Covenants	Comprehensive set of financial covenants, usually even more restrictive than private placement covenants.	Comprehensive set of financial covenants.	Usually less restrictive covenants than in the commercial bank and private placement markets.
Time to arrange	15 to 25 weeks	10 to 20 weeks	10 to 15 weeks
Rating requirements	None.	Generally requires at least an NAIC-2 rating.	Generally prefers investment-grade ratings from at least two major rating agencies but the Rule 144A market for high-yield debt has been growing.

Pension Funds

Pension funds are another important source of long-term debt financing.

Public Pension Funds

Public pension funds consist primarily of state and local government employee retirement funds that maintain substantial investments in debt securities. Public pension funds tend to be unwilling to commit to extend loans as far in advance as life insurance companies do. Among other things, the flow of funds into state and municipal pension funds depends on current legislation, the salary levels of state and municipal employees, and, in some instances, the cash management requirements of the sponsoring state or municipality.

Most public pension funds are credit-quality-sensitive investors, either by preference or by statute or regulation. Many are required by statute or policy to invest in securities that are rated single-A or higher. Many are also prohibited from buying securities of foreign corporate obligors. Other legal investment requirements, such as a minimum length of corporate existence or a minimum coverage of fixed charges, may also preclude certain public pension funds from purchasing the debt securities of a particular borrower.

Private Pension Funds

Private pension funds consist primarily of corporate pension funds. Many large corporations manage their own corporate pension funds, but the majority are managed by either the trust departments of commercial banks or private investment management firms. As with life insurance companies, a high percentage of the investable assets is managed by a relatively small number of institutions.

Private pension funds are normally not restricted as to the credit quality of the securities they may purchase. Therefore, the rating of a firm's bonds is a less important consideration than it would be for a public pension fund. In addition, private pension funds normally face few, if any, restrictions (other than the requirements of ERISA) on their ability to purchase securities issued by foreign corporations.[11]

Other Financial Institutions

Other classes of financial institutions are also important purchasers of privately placed debt. However, these institutions have diverse investment policies, so generalizations about this group's investment objectives are not possible.

Conclusion

Firms can borrow money in a variety of ways. Among the borrowing alternatives are borrowing from other firms like themselves through trade credit or issuing commercial paper, borrowing from banks, and selling debt securities directly to financial institutions through either a traditional private placement or a Rule 144A quasi-public offering. The next chapter discusses a source of funds that is popular among the largest most creditworthy firms: the public securities market.

Chapter **3**

Debt Capital Markets

*I*nvestment-grade firms increasingly are issuing securities instead of borrowing from banks because, among other recent capital market developments, stricter bank capital regulations initiated in 1989 reduced the availability of bank financing. Simultaneously, the growth of money market mutual funds broadened the market for commercial paper, and the development of medium-term notes (commercial paper–like notes that mature in between nine months and thirty years) and Euronotes (commercial paper and medium-term notes sold outside the United States) extended commercial paper to longer maturities and to foreign markets, respectively.

This chapter describes the public debt capital markets and compares them to private bond markets. We explain the debt issuance and investment banking processes and detail the costs. A firm must register the securities it issues with the SEC to be able to sell them publicly in a general cash offer. As detailed in the previous chapter, unregistered securities must be sold privately, mainly to institutional investors. Private placements have lower transaction costs, but even Rule 144A private placements are less liquid than public issues. Thus, a liquidity-issuance-expense trade-off determines which source of funds will be cheaper.

A firm must also decide on the geographical market in which to borrow, such as the U.S. market, the Euromarket, or a foreign currency–denominated debt market. Many international firms borrow in foreign currencies to hedge currency risk or get a tax benefit from international tax asymmetries.

Overview of the Corporate Bond Market

Larger firms usually issue debt securities by making a *general cash offer*, also referred to as a *registered public offering*. Alternatively, some

43

firms, particularly smaller ones, issue unregistered debt securities directly to investors through a *private placement*.

There are foreign markets for securities too. The *Eurodollar bond market* is the market outside the United States for U.S. dollar–denominated bonds. A similar market exists for Eurodollar bank loans. At times, the Eurodollar bond market provides more attractive terms on new issues than the U.S. market does.

Investors

There is an extensive long-term debt capital market in the United States, Europe, and Japan. The market includes financial institutions, such as life insurance companies and pension funds, which provide fixed-interest-rate financing, and commercial banks, which provide floating-interest-rate financing. There are also developing capital markets in many emerging nations, which can provide cost-effective financing for local subsidiaries or local projects. These regional markets consist of local institutions, which usually have a preference for floating-rate lending, especially when the country periodically experiences relatively high inflation rates.

Several factors affect investor willingness to lend:

- *Profitability of the firm.* As a general rule, lenders want to know how loan proceeds will be used, so they can assess the likelihood of default. They will not lend unless they believe the firm will generate enough cash flow to pay interest and principal on the debt.

- *Leverage.* Lenders want to know about the firm's other debt obligations that could contribute to default.

- *Assessment of risk.* Lenders insist on being fully compensated for all risks. Their assessment of each type of risk affects the rate of interest they are willing to accept.

- *Credit standing of the borrower.* As a matter of statute or policy, some lenders, such as many public pension funds, will not purchase corporate bonds that are not rated single-A or better by the major rating agencies (Fitch, Moody's, and S&P).

- *Liquidity of the debt securities.* The lack of liquidity inherent in privately placed, unregistered securities significantly affects the interest rate that lenders will accept. Nevertheless, younger firms are generally restricted to the private placement market because of their riskiness and the relatively small amounts of debt they want to sell.

- *Interest rate on the debt.* The interest rate must be high enough to compensate lenders for the perceived risk of default and illiquidity.

Growth of the Markets

Figure 3.1 shows the annual growth of the public and private placement bond markets since 1975. It is notable that the amount of debt placed privately has declined since the late 1980s while the amount of public offerings has virtually exploded. The public market offers investors greater liquidity and issuers more attractive loan terms and pricing.

Table 3.1 summarizes the relative sizes of the different segments of the long-term debt market as of June 30, 1995. Life insurance companies are the largest holder of debt.

Public Bond Market

Firms usually make general cash offers with the help of *underwriters,* middlemen who typically buy the securities from the issuer and then resell them to investors. In other cases, underwriters only market the securities. The investors in privately placed debt are also the main

Figure 3.1 Growth of the Public and Private Markets for Bonds, 1975–1998

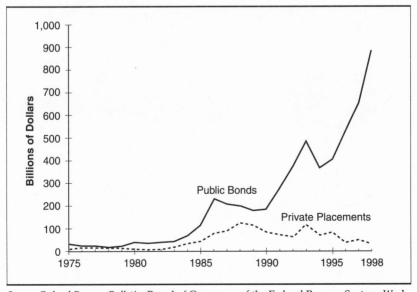

Source: Federal Reserve Bulletin, Board of Governors of the Federal Reserve System, Washington, D.C., various issues.

Table 3.1 Sources of Long-Term Debt, June 30, 1995

Segment	Total Assets (in billions)	Holdings of Corporate and Foreign Bonds	
		Amount (in billions)	% of Total Assets
Life insurance companies	$1,992.4	$818.5	41.1%
Other insurance companies	704.4	104.2	14.8
Public pension funds	1,316.3	280.4	21.3
Private pension funds[a]	2,610.4	318.2	12.2
Commercial banks	4,339.2	103.7	2.4

Source: Federal Reserve Board, *Flow of Funds Accounts: Quarterly Levels* (September 13, 1995).
[a]Includes the Federal Employees' Retirement System Thrift Savings Plan.

buyers of public offerings of debt securities (although not usually pension funds). Individual investors also purchase publicly offered debt, and in greater amounts than they used to because of the growth in individually directed retirement accounts.

General Cash Offers

A general cash offer has three steps:

1. *File the registration statement.*[1] The issuer files a *registration statement* with the SEC, which includes a *preliminary prospectus.*[2] (A preliminary prospectus is also called a *red herring* because of a legend warning that it is only preliminary, which must be printed on its cover in bold red letters.) The prospectus provides specific investment information to investors. The SEC reviews the registration statement and must authorize the offering to proceed.

2. *Determine pricing.* After the review process is complete, the issuer and the underwriters negotiate the terms of the offering and the underwriters' compensation. The issuer then files the final amendment to the registration statement with the SEC, which contains the *final prospectus.*

3. *Close the offering.* The offering *closes* three business days later. Corporate securities transactions customarily settle, or close, in the United States on the third business day following the transaction

date. At the closing, the issuer exchanges the securities for pay-ment, net of underwriter fees, and the underwriters deliver the securities to investors in return for payment.

Marketing to Individuals

From time to time issuers have designed debt issues to appeal to in-dividual investors. A popular technique is to offer small-denomination notes that provide for quarterly interest payments and market these notes through retail securities firms.

In November 1998, for example, AT&T Capital Corporation issued $500 million of 8.25 percent Senior Public Income NotES (PINES), due 2028, through a syndicate of securities firms with a strong retail clien-tele.[3] The issuer listed the PINES on the New York Stock Exchange. The PINES have a minimum denomination of $25, whereas corporate bonds usually have a minimum denomination of $1,000. They pay interest quarterly, whereas corporate bonds usually pay interest semi-annually, and they are callable beginning five years after issue.

The small-denomination notes provide a new clientele for corpo-rate debt securities, which may be willing to invest on more favorable terms to the issuer.[4] For example, individual investors may charge less for embedded options, such as a call provision or an option to defer coupon payments.[5]

Benchmark Notes

The U.S. Treasury has reduced its issuance of new Treasury debt and expects to reduce it further. Seeing an opportunity, Fannie Mae launched its Benchmark Notes program in January 1998.[6] It now raises about three-quarters of its funds through this program, an easily trad-able class of securities that it hopes will replace Treasury securities as the pricing benchmarks that bond investors use to price their bond portfolios. Fannie Mae believed it would be able to save between 2 and 5 *basis points* (hundredths of a percent) in yield on the benchmark notes.[7] After Fannie Mae's success, Freddie Mac introduced its Refer-ence Notes program, the Federal Home Loan Bank system launched its TAPS program, and Ford Motor Credit Co. introduced its Global Land-mark Securities program.[8]

Public Offering Versus Other Alternatives

Table 3.2 compares the characteristics of the bank loan, private placement, and public bond markets. The bank loan market tends to

Table 3.2 Comparison of the Characteristics of the Bank Loan, Private Placement, and Public Bond Markets

Characteristic	Debt Market		
	Bank Loan	Private Placement	Public Bond
Maturity	Short	Medium to long	Long
Interest rate	Floating	Fixed	Fixed
Severity of information problems posed by the average borrower	High	Moderate	Small
Average loan size	Small	Medium to large	Large
Average borrower size	Small	Medium to large	Large
Average observable risk level	High	Moderate	Lowest
Covenants	Many, tight	Fewer, looser	Fewest
Collateral	Frequent	Less frequent	Rare
Renegotiation	Frequent	Less frequent	Infrequent
Lender monitoring	Intense	Significant	Minimal
Liquidity of loan	Low	Low	High
Lenders	Intermediaries	Intermediaries	Various
Principal lender	Banks	Life insurance companies	Various
Importance of lender reputation	Somewhat important	Most important	Unimportant

Source: Mark Carey, Stephen Prowse, John Rea, and Gregory Udell, *The Economics of the Private Placement Market* (Washington, D.C.: Board of Governors of the Federal Reserve System, December 1993), p. 33.

prefer shorter-term floating-rate loans with relatively tight covenant restrictions. The public bond market is generally willing to accept longer maturities and larger issues with relatively nonrestrictive covenants. The private placement market falls in between the other two markets with respect to average borrower and loan size, covenants, collateral requirements, and intensity of monitoring. However, lender reputation is most important in the private placement market. Lenders in this market perceive that they have significant reputa-tional capital at stake when they make a decision to loan money. Con-sequently, the lending standards they apply tend to be rigorous.

Investment Banking and the Cost of Issuing Securities

A firm can market its securities itself (as the U.S. government does), but most use investment bankers. Table 3.3 shows the ranking of the fifteen leading debt securities underwriters in the United States and worldwide during 2000. The top five have a 63 percent U.S. market share.

Investment Bankers

Investment bankers offer advice about the type and terms of security to issue and which market provides the most attractive terms, help pre-pare documentation, agree on the security's price, and market and underwrite new securities issues. They also devote much time and energy to designing new securities that will reduce issuers' funding costs and increase investors' after-tax risk-adjusted rates of return.

Underwriting

There are two types of underwriting: (1) purchase and sale and (2) best efforts.

A true underwriting agreement involves a *purchase and sale*, in which an investment bank purchases the securities from the issuer at a fixed price and agrees to reoffer them to investors at a specified price less a specified commission. The securities dealer bears the risk that the entire issue may not be saleable at the initial offering price. If it is not, the securities dealer will sell the securities at the market-clearing price and bear the loss. A purchase-and-sale underwriting thus involves a form of insurance.

In a *syndicated public offering*, an underwriting group (syndicate) is formed to purchase the debt securities from the issuer and reoffer them to investors. The lead managing underwriter assembles a syndicate consisting of those securities dealers it believes can best market the bonds.

Securities issues sold through investment bankers are not always true underwritten offerings. In a *best-efforts* arrangement, an invest-ment bank commits to use its best efforts to market the bonds to investors. There is no commitment to purchase and therefore little

Table 3.3 Leading Managing Underwriters of Public Debt Securities Offerings, 2000

Rank	Manager	Amount ($ millions)	%	Issues
All U.S. corporate straight (full credit to book manager), January 1, 2000–December 31, 2000				
1	Merrill Lynch	208,276.8	17.7	2,404
2	Salomon Smith Barney	154,088.1	13.1	1,044
3	JP Morgan	149,849.4	12.8	1,051
4	Morgan Stanley Dean Witter	117,496.1	10.0	1,754
5	Credit Suisse First Boston	111,078.3	9.5	756
6	Goldman Sachs	90,746.4	7.7	486
7	BofA Securities	65,581.6	5.6	543
8	Lehman Brothers	61,442.4	5.2	358
9	Deutsche Bank	41,660.0	3.5	209
10	UBS Warburg	32,860.1	2.8	222
11	ABN Amro	23,239.1	2.0	530
12	Bear Stearns	22,211.0	1.9	233
13	First Union	20,874.3	1.8	269
14	Morgan Keegan	7,957.6	0.7	342
15	First Tennessee Bank	6,741.8	0.6	285
Eurobonds (full credit to book manager), January 1, 2000–December 31, 2000				
1	Deutsche Bank	83,457.8	9.7	343
2	UBS Warburg	68,945.2	8.0	343
3	Morgan Stanley Dean Witter	66,786.7	7.8	318
4	Merrill Lynch	66,036.6	7.7	269
5	Salomon Smith Barney	60,423.1	7.0	223
6	Credit Suisse First Boston	57,127.6	6.6	239
7	JP Morgan	54,264.3	6.3	226
8	Goldman Sachs	46,776.1	5.4	191
9	Barclays Capital	38,942.7	4.5	154
10	ABN Amro	38,346.5	4.5	157
11	Lehman Brothers	31,095.3	3.6	114
12	Dresdner Kleinwort Benson	28,529.6	3.3	106
13	BNP Paribas	26,642.1	3.1	137
14	HSBC Holdings	20,867.6	2.4	141
15	Nomura Securities	14,454.6	1.7	61

Source: Thomson Financial Securities Data.

Note: Includes all public debt and Rule 144A issues.

financial risk to the investment bank. Informally the securities dealer may be called a *best-efforts underwriter*, although it never owns the security. Most private placements are sold on a best-efforts basis, wherein securities dealers simply act as an *agent* for the issuer and help negotiate the terms of sale.

Some firms, including finance companies, may sell securities directly to investors to reduce issuance expenses. This is more likely when the issuer has a natural market, such as current bond holders.

In most cases, however, investment bankers have superior access to market information and channels of distribution as a result of their day-to-day securities dealing. Therefore, it is usually more economical to sell securities through an investment banker.

Underwriters' Compensation

Underwriters charge a *gross underwriting spread*, which is a percentage of the issue price. This spread has three components:

- The *management fee*, usually 15 percent to 20 percent of the spread, which compensates the managing underwriters for their assistance in designing the issue, preparing the documentation, forming the syndicate, and directing the offering process
- The *underwriting fee*, usually 15 percent to 20 percent, which compensates for underwriting risk
- The *selling concession*, generally the remaining 60 percent to 70 percent, which compensates for the selling effort

Underwriters' compensation represents a significant portion of the flotation expense. Table 3.4 provides a flotation expense breakdown for public offerings of various types and sizes between 1975 and 1999. It is generally most expensive to float a common stock issue and least expensive to float an issue of straight (nonconvertible) bonds. This reflects differences in underwriting risks. It is also due to the higher selling commissions required to distribute common stock issues, large portions of which are usually marketed broadly to individual investors. Note the significant economies of scale in issuing securities.

Negotiated Versus Competitive Offerings

A firm can offer securities publicly using either competitive bidding or a negotiated offering. Under *competitive bidding*, the issuer specifies the type of securities it wishes to sell and invites securities dealers

Table 3.4 Gross Underwriting Spread and Out-of-Pocket Expenses for Registered Public Offerings, 1975–1999[a]

Issue Size ($ millions)	Common Stock			Preferred Stock			Convertible Preferred and Convertible Debt			Bonds		
	Gross Under-writing Spread (%)	Out-of-Pocket Expense[b] (%)	Total (%)	Gross Under-writing Spread (%)	Out-of-Pocket Expense[b] (%)	Total (%)	Gross Under-writing Spread (%)	Out-of-Pocket Expense[b] (%)	Total (%)	Gross Under-writing Spread (%)	Out-of-Pocket Expense[b] (%)	Total (%)
Under 10.0	8.64	5.94	14.58	4.73	1.75	6.48	6.41	5.09	11.50	1.57	0.11	1.68
10.0 to 24.9	6.47	2.65	9.12	2.90	0.86	3.76	4.12	1.64	5.76	0.97	0.06	1.03
25.0 to 49.9	5.88	1.59	7.47	2.22	0.46	2.68	2.92	0.93	3.85	0.78	0.04	0.82
50.0 to 99.9	5.39	1.03	6.42	2.03	0.31	2.34	2.59	0.55	3.14	0.71	0.06	0.77
100 to 199.9	4.99	0.72	5.71	2.74	0.25	2.99	2.22	0.35	2.57	0.74	0.08	0.82
200 to 499.9	4.62	0.56	5.18	2.73	0.15	2.88	2.40	0.17	2.57	0.76	0.09	0.85
500 to 1,000	4.22	0.58	4.80	2.81	0.14	2.95	2.47	0.07	2.54	0.82	0.06	0.88
Over 1,000	3.28	0.78	4.06	2.88	0.27	3.15	2.36	0.05	2.41	0.83	0.07	0.90

Source: Thomson Financial Securities Data.

[a]Gross underwriting spread and out-of-pocket expenses are expressed as a percentage of the offering price for common stock issues and as a percentage of principal amount for preferred stock and bond issues.
[b]Includes legal fees, accounting fees, SEC filing fee, blue sky expenses, and printing, mailing, and miscellaneous out-of-pocket expenses.

to bid for the issue. It puts the securities up for bid, and the bidding process determines which investment bankers will market the issue and at what price.

In a *negotiated offering*, the issuer selects one or more securities dealers to manage the offering and works closely with them to design the terms of the issue and determine when to issue the securities. Many firms offer shelf-registered debt and preferred stock by competitive bid (except during periods of heightened market volatility) but generally sell common stock on a negotiated basis. Railroads frequently sell equipment trust certificates through competitive bidding.

Whether competitive offerings are cheaper has been a hotly debated question, and the evidence is inconclusive. However, recent studies suggest that the competitive process usually does not lead to significant cost savings, except perhaps during stable market periods that have strong bidding competition.

Competitive bidding generally results in lower underwriting spreads, but can have greater underwriting spreads during periods of greater market uncertainty. Moreover, the negotiated offering process provides greater design and timing flexibility. The issuer has not committed in advance to specific terms or a particular offering date.

A negotiated offering also gives securities dealers the opportunity to form the most effective selling group for the issue. Rather than splitting them into competing bidding groups, the negotiation process provides a stronger incentive for securities dealers to assess the demand for, and stimulate interest in, the issue prior to pricing. Since they know that they will have the securities to sell, they will not hesitate to begin the marketing activities. Competitive bidders, in contrast, would lose their marketing investment if they were not selected.

During normal market periods, an investment-grade issuer that plans to issue conventional debt securities is likely to achieve a lower cost of debt through competitive bidding. Non-investment-grade debt issuers or issuers of innovative debt securities are likely to find the negotiated offering process more cost-effective because offering such securities usually requires a more intensive marketing effort, and investment bankers may not be willing to undertake this process until they are assured of the issue.

Other Costs of Issuing Securities

In addition to the gross underwriting spread, there are out-of-pocket expenses, such as lawyers' and accountants' fees and engraving, printing, and mailing costs. Out-of-pocket expenses tend to be fixed expenses and are therefore a significant cost factor only in connection with small offerings.

Shelf Registration

The SEC's Rule 415, commonly known as *shelf registration,* allows a firm to register an inventory of securities and sell them whenever it chooses for up to two years. The securities are "on the shelf" until sold, which provides flexibility. A new registration statement is not needed for each securities sale, which reduces flotation costs. Securities can be sold within minutes. Also, a single shelf registration statement can cover many types of debt securities. This permits issuers to design the security at the time they sell it to exploit any special investor preferences.

Rule 415 has effectively extended competitive bidding to issues of securities by the roughly two thousand large firms that qualify to use shelf registration. Securities dealers and institutional investors can bid for securities that a firm has on the shelf. But the evidence is mixed on whether Rule 415 has had any impact on transaction costs.

Previous research concluded that firms could lower their debt issuance costs by using the (then newly available) shelf-registration procedure. However, it turns out that firms issuing debt using shelf registration had lower debt issuance costs before the procedure existed.[9] As a consequence, the previously reported lower issuance costs associated with shelf registration are explained at least in part by a self-selection bias.

In connection with a public offering, the investment banks conduct *due diligence,* that is, they investigate the affairs of the issuer on behalf of the investing public. Shelf registration may reduce the underwriters' ability to perform adequate due diligence. Research concerning equity offerings suggests that underwriters charge a premium as payment against the potential costs of future litigation or loss of reputation (or both) and, further, that this premium is positively related to a firm's expected due diligence liabilities.[10] In other words, it appears that underwriters believe that shelf registration diminishes their ability to perform due diligence adequately, and they price this risk accordingly. In addition, stock price reactions for firms using shelf registration do not differ from those of firms using traditional methods.[11] Therefore, aside from any other benefits, it does not appear that shelf registration provides a significant transaction cost savings over traditional offering methods.

Frequency and Timing of Borrowings

Economies of scale make large issues more cost-effective than smaller ones. However, the shelf registration process has increased the frequency and decreased the average size of corporate debt issues.[12] Larger issues should improve secondary bond market liquidity. Consequently, firms usually plan to issue long-term debt in large, discrete amounts and issue debt off the shelf opportunistically. However, because of capital market efficiency, gains from speculating on interest rate movements are highly unlikely.

A firm that plans to issue debt may obtain a modest reduction in the total cost of the transaction with short-term debt management. It should not issue debt when conditions look volatile or temporarily bad. For example, the supply of funds for non-investment-grade bonds tends to shrink during periods of tight money or particularly volatile interest rates. Also, a large U.S. Treasury financing can temporarily depress the debt market. Therefore, issuers should remain flexible with respect to timing in order to prevent temporary factors from adversely affecting their cost of borrowing.

Public Offering Versus Private Placement

An important issue is the relative cost of public versus private placement. Public offerings are typically underwritten by one or more investment banks that conduct due diligence, whereas in a private placement, securities are sold directly to institutional investors who conduct their own due diligence. The price and other terms of the new issue are established through direct negotiation between the issuer and potential buyers in a private placement.[13]

Announcement Effects

A wealth of evidence indicates that the announcement of a public sale of securities can elicit a significant negative stock price reaction.[14] This reaction is generally attributed to new information about the firm that the market infers from the announcement.

Reduced Information Asymmetries, Monitoring, and Certification

A private placement may allow investors access to private information, thereby reducing asymmetric information. With respect to monitoring, privately placed debt issues usually have more restrictive covenants than comparable public debt issues.[15] The tighter covenants improve monitoring efficiency (for reasons explained in chapter 5) but also create an opportunity cost in the form of decreased operating and financial flexibility. Finally, large, sophisticated institutional investors that purchase private debt render a quality certification with their purchase of a substantial amount of the firm's securities.

Private Placement Versus Public Offering Announcement Effects

In marked contrast to public offerings, research shows a consistently positive average stock price reaction to private issues for debt, equity, and combinations (convertible debt), with larger issues eliciting a more positive response.[16] These results are consistent with the notion that private placement leads to reduced information asymmetries, increased monitoring, and certification.

Reduced Cost of Resolving Financial Distress

Another possible benefit of private debt is that it might be easier than public debt to restructure because it generally involves fewer and more sophisticated investors. Consistent with this idea, financial distress is more likely to be resolved outside bankruptcy when more of the firm's debt is owed to banks but is less likely to be resolved outside bankruptcy when the firm has more than one public debt issue outstanding.[17] Similarly, firms with complex public debt structures more frequently undergo bankruptcy.[18] In addition, the capital market appears able to distinguish firms that are most likely to succeed at restructuring their debt outside bankruptcy (probably based on the composition of the firm's debt).[19]

Interestingly, banks, perhaps because of their typically very senior priority, do not play a significant role in resolving financial distress. Rather, relief from financial distress comes primarily from subordinated public creditors.[20] When senior creditors have a security interest in the debtor's assets and there is a significant amount of lower-priority debt, the senior creditors can generally force subordinated creditors, which have a great deal more to lose in bankruptcy, to make greater concessions to the debtor to avoid bankruptcy.

With public debt outstanding, the company's owners may have an incentive to continue some projects that would otherwise be abandoned.[21] This occurs because contracts for public debt cannot be based on an optimal liquidation policy for the firm; such a policy would depend on private information, which the firm would not want to share with its bondholders. If private lenders have access to better information about the value of the firm's assets, private debt contracts can lead to efficient liquidation policies. In that case, the firm may prefer to negotiate private debt contracts with its lenders.

The proportion of private debt is inversely related to the amount of the firm's outstanding long-term debt but is not apparently related to the potential costs of financial distress.[22] Of the two principal explanations offered for the use of private over public debt financing, reduced information asymmetries (coupled with increased monitoring and certification) appears to be more important than reduced costs of financial distress.

Transaction Costs

When interest rates are volatile and the costs of searching for the lowest-cost alternative are high, debt issuers are more likely to use private debt.[23] When interest rates are stable and search costs are lower, public debt is cheaper. Not surprisingly, firms that can choose between public and private debt can borrow more cheaply.[24]

Choice of Market: Some Practical Considerations

A private placement offers the following advantages over a public offering:

- *Lower issuance costs for smaller issues.* A private placement avoids the costs of registering the securities, printing prospectuses, and obtaining credit ratings. Also, a private placement agent's fee is generally considerably lower than the underwriting expenses for a comparable public offering and can be avoided altogether if the issuer negotiates directly with investors.

- *Quicker placement.* Issues can be placed more quickly for firms that do not qualify for shelf registration. Registering securities requires time to prepare the registration statement and have the SEC review it.

- *Greater flexibility of issue size.* The private market is more receptive to smaller issues. Issues of only a few million dollars each are not uncommon. Public debt and preferred stock issues of less than $50 million principal amount are usually more costly, because their small size decreases their liquidity and thus lessens their attractiveness to investors.

- *Greater flexibility of security arrangements and other terms.* Private investors are capable of analyzing complex security arrangements, and it is easier to tailor the terms of an issue to suit both sides of the transaction. It is also easier to obtain lenders' consents to a change in terms because the debtholders are sophisticated and there are fewer of them.

- *Lower cost of resolving financial distress.* Fewer and more sophisticated holders of private debt reduces restructuring costs, a conclusion supported by empirical research.

- *More favorable share price reaction.* As documented by empirical research, private placements reduce information asymmetries, improve monitoring efficiency, and provide certification.

A private placement has the following disadvantages relative to a public offering:

- *Higher yield.* To compensate for illiquidity, buyers require a yield premium on private debt.

- *More stringent covenants and more restrictive terms.* Private issuers are often not public firms and thus not subject to the reporting requirements of the securities laws. Private purchasers insist on tighter covenant restrictions to compensate for the greater agency costs. The covenants alert investors when something has gone wrong, such as a sharp reduction in firm value. Private lenders have also insisted on tighter protection against *event risk*—the risk that stockholders might initiate events such as a leveraged buyout that could expropriate bondholder wealth. These covenants can limit a firm's operating flexibility, possibly forcing it to pass up profitable investment opportunities.

International Debt Financing

Bond issues are regularly launched in New York, London, and Tokyo and traded almost immediately in every time zone. Increasingly, domestic debt issues (like domestic common stock issues) are sold overseas as well as in the United States, and foreign debt (and equity) issues are also sold in the United States. The capital markets have become global, and for this reason, financial managers need a global perspective when raising funds.

A firm that wants to borrow funds to finance a foreign capital budgeting project can (1) borrow U.S. dollars in the United States and export the funds to the foreign country, (2) borrow U.S. dollars in the Euromarket, (3) borrow in the foreign country, or (4) borrow in whichever currency and in whichever market seems to provide the lowest interest cost. The fourth strategy is particularly tempting but also very risky, as many *former* corporate treasurers will attest!

The international capital market is the market for debt securities that functions outside the national capital markets. Its existence reflects the accumulation of dollar and foreign currency balances by foreign investors and their willingness to invest in debt securities of issuers that are located outside the country that issued the currency. Such international markets are often referred to generically as the *Euromarkets*. There are Euromarkets for dollars (the Eurodollar market), British pounds (the Eurosterling market), Japanese yen (the Euroyen market), and so on.

A *Eurobond* is a bond issued outside the country in whose currency it is denominated. Firms headquartered in the United States issue dollar-denominated Eurobonds to investors in Europe (hence the prefix *Euro*) and other areas outside the United States. U.S.-dollar-denominated bonds often represent more than half the total Eurobond market.

Issuing bonds denominated in a foreign currency is an alternative to issuing Eurobonds. However, it involves a foreign exchange risk. The issuer must either realize foreign currency from its operations or purchase foreign currency to meet its future debt service obligations.

Dollar-Denominated Borrowing in the Eurobond Market

The Eurobond market developed during the 1960s when the U.S. government levied an interest equalization tax on the purchase of foreign securities by U.S. investors and imposed restrictions on capital exports by American firms. Large U.S. balance-of-payments deficits continued the outflow of dollar funds. The U.S.-imposed withholding tax on interest payments by domestic firms to foreign investors discouraged foreign investment of these funds in domestic bond issues. Instead, foreign investors avoided this withholding tax by buying Eurobonds issued by special-purpose subsidiaries of U.S. firms established in the Netherlands Antilles, which enjoyed a special status as a result of a tax treaty then in effect with the United States. The 30 percent withholding tax was eliminated in 1984, permitting U.S. firms to sell debt directly to foreign investors free of this tax. Nevertheless, the Eurobond market continues to thrive.

Characteristics of Eurobonds

Dollar-denominated Eurobond issues are as varied as domestic bond issues. Most are straight debt issues, but convertible Eurobonds and Eurobonds with warrants are not uncommon. Nevertheless, there are important differences between the domestic bond and Eurobond markets:

- The Eurobond market, a truly international market, is essentially unregulated. Hence, yields are somewhat less susceptible to government influence than are domestic bond yields. Nevertheless, arbitrage activity ensures that Eurobond yields normally track domestic bond yields fairly closely.

- Eurobond investors usually own assets denominated in several currencies. The relative attractiveness of dollar-denominated Eurobonds, and hence the relationship between bond yields in the domestic bond market and yields in the dollar-denominated Eurobond market, depends on U.S. dollar exchange rates. When the U.S. dollar is appreciating relative to the other major currencies, Eurobond investors tend to increase their purchasing of dollar-denominated Eurobonds (as well as other dollar-denominated assets). This activity can drive Eurobond yields below domestic bond yields and create an attractive borrowing opportunity for U.S. firms. This gives rise to a so-called *Eurobond market window*.

- Because of investors' exchange rate sensitivity, Eurobond maturities are usually shorter, and issue sizes generally smaller, than in the domestic market.

- Eurobonds are generally *bearer bonds.* Issuing bonds in bearer form makes it more difficult to refund them prior to maturity, because most buyers can be contacted directly only when they claim their interest payments from the paying agent.

- Eurobonds pay interest annually. Because domestic bonds generally pay interest semiannually, domestic bonds and Eurobonds must be compared based on their effective annual yields (or some other consistent method of calculation).

Table 3.5 presents the mix of domestic and international bond financing by U.S. firms from 1984 to 1999. The volume of Eurobond financing picked up sharply in 1985, 1993, and 1997, when the strength of the U.S. dollar and other factors led to a sharp increase in foreign demand for dollar-denominated bonds.

Table 3.5 Volume of Domestic and International Bond Financing by U.S. Firms, 1984–1999 (millions of dollars)

Year	Domestic[a]	International[a]	Total[a]	% Domestic	Trade-Weighted Dollar Exchange Rate[b]
1984	$ 81,153	$ 17,986	$ 99,139	81.9%	138.19
1985	165,759	37,781	203,540	81.4	143.01
1986	312,696	42,596	355,292	88.0	112.22
1987	301,525	24,308	325,833	92.5	96.94
1988	328,946	23,178	352,124	93.4	92.72
1989	297,104	22,851	319,955	92.9	98.60
1990	275,760	23,054	298,814	92.3	89.09
1991	361,860	27,962	389,822	92.8	89.84
1992	443,813	27,591	471,404	94.2	86.61
1993	608,255	38,379	646,634	94.1	93.18
1994	441,287	56,755	498,042	88.6	91.32
1995	496,296	76,910	573,206	86.6	84.25
1996	567,671	83,433	651,104	87.2	87.34
1997	708,188	103,188	811,376	87.3	96.38
1998	923,771	77,965	1,001,736	92.2	98.85
1999	818,683	122,615	941,298	87.0	97.08
Total	$7,132,767	$806,552	$7,939,319	89.8%	

Source: Federal Reserve Bulletin, Board of Governors of the Federal Reserve System, Washington, D.C., various issues.

[a]Includes convertible debt.
[b]Index for which March 1973 = 100.

Financing in the Euromarket

Long-Term Loans

From time to time, U.S. firms have found it advantageous to sell entire bond issues in the Eurobond market, rather than domestically, and to borrow in different currencies. A few years ago, the World Bank introduced *global bonds,* which are designed to qualify for immediate trading in the United States, Europe, Asia, and any other capital market in the world where it is lawful to trade them, and hence to reach the broadest group of investors. Global bonds make it possible for a bond issuer to enter the Euromarket and the domestic bond market simultaneously. This makes it easier for U.S. issuers to exploit an opportunity to raise funds in the Euromarket at a lower cost than what is available domestically.

For example, in March 1999, Citigroup Inc. issued $1.5 billion of global bonds, which it listed on the Luxembourg Stock Exchange.[25] The notes are registered in nominee name and are transferable only in book-entry form (the notes are registered in the name of Cede & Co., the securities clearing agent's nominee, and are not available in definitive paper form) through both the Depository Trust Company (the U.S. securities clearance system) and Cedelbank or the Euroclear System (the European securities clearance systems). The book entry system eliminates the need for physical movement of securities certificates, which facilitates global trading because the trades can be cleared electronically.

Short-Term Loans

Firms can borrow short-term funds in the Euromarket, with the interest rate usually tied to LIBOR. Most loans consist of *Eurodollars*, which are U.S. dollar deposits in banks outside the United States. But loans are also extended in other currencies. Most Eurodollar loans are overnight. The overnight rate is referred to as *overnight LIBOR*. But banks also lend each other Eurodollars for longer periods, such as for one week at *7-day* LIBOR, for one month at *1-month* LIBOR, and so on. There are similar interest rates for other Eurocurrencies, such as sterling (British pound) LIBOR, Euro LIBOR (referred to as *Euribor*), and so on.

Dollar LIBOR is important in the commercial loan market. Many dollar-denominated short-term loans, including in the United States, bear interest at a rate tied to LIBOR. For example, the interest rate on a loan might be stated as 3-month LIBOR plus 1 percent. Similarly, floating-rate Eurobonds usually have an interest rate that is tied to LIBOR.

Foreign Bonds

A *foreign bond* is issued by a foreign company or government in the country in whose currency it is denominated. For example, *Yankee bonds* are denominated in U.S. dollars and issued in the United States by foreign firms or governments. They differ from Eurobonds. A U.S. firm sells Eurobonds outside the United States; a foreign firm sells Yankee bonds in the United States. Other examples of foreign bonds are Bulldog bonds (issued in Britain), Matador bonds (Spain), Rembrandt bonds (Netherlands), and Samurai bonds (Japan). Foreign bonds often face tougher restrictions and disclosure standards than bonds sold by domestic issuers. As a result, the Eurobond market has grown more rapidly than the national markets for foreign bonds.

Credit Sensitivity

Although international investors are very conscious of security quality, historically they have generally not calibrated credit risks as finely as is done in the U.S. debt market. This situation is changing as credit ratings become more widely accepted in the Euromarkets. As a general rule, however, a borrower must be large and well known. Commitments made by major U.S. institutional lenders also provide strong endorsements for borrowers in the global capital market.

Maturity Choice

Even under very favorable market conditions, investors in the global capital market generally are not willing to accept debt maturities as long as those available in the United States. The typical maturity for long-term debt in the global capital market does not exceed ten years, although there have been longer-dated issues. Under weak market conditions, maturities of between five and seven years become prevalent.

Currency Conditions

The flow of funds to the Euromarkets is volatile, for several reasons. Most investors can also invest in their respective domestic capital markets, as well as in other national markets, and they move their funds from one market to another, primarily on the basis of the denominated currency's short-term outlook. Fluctuations in currency expectations can make borrowing in a particular national capital market more or less attractive. In the extreme, relative expectations have led to a mushrooming of one or more sectors of the global capital market and, simultaneously, the virtual closing of one or more other sectors.

Inflation is a major factor in currency expectations. In general, when one country has greater inflation than another, its currency is viewed as riskier, and hence less attractive, to international lenders. At the very least, the rate of interest will have to be sufficiently higher to compensate for the higher inflation rate. When all countries are suffering from very high rates of inflation, investors tend to reduce the amount they have invested in long-term fixed-interest-rate debt obligations. In addition, the investors' view of world stability and the political and economic stability of their respective countries will influence their willingness to invest in the Euromarkets. Investing funds outside the domestic market on a medium- or long-term basis requires investors to monitor political events that might alter the value of their investments.

Types of Investors

Historically, investors in the Euromarkets generally fall into two categories. The substantial majority are individuals buying for their own account through banks, frequently Swiss banks or other banks that provide client anonymity. The rest, fewer but growing in relative importance, are banks, insurance companies, pension funds, investment trusts, and certain government agencies in several countries that trade for their own account. These institutions buy private placements as well as public issues.

As with other investments, the attractiveness of a given Eurobond is relative. Withholding tax would reduce a bond's attractiveness as compared to a similar domestic bond, and yet withholding tax is commonly required on interest payments made to entities that reside outside the country in which the borrower is located. In reaction, in countries where there is a withholding tax, an offshore financing subsidiary is typically established in a jurisdiction without any withholding tax (or at least with a low withholding tax) to avoid this problem. Also, trust indentures usually require an issuer to gross up interest payments sufficiently to cover the withholding tax should such a tax be imposed after the bonds are issued.

Local Sources of Capital

Borrowing funds or raising equity in the local capital market is often a good way to hedge the political risk associated with a foreign project. Any event that harms the profitability of the project will affect the local lenders and investors in the project. This prospect tends to furnish a disincentive for the local government to take such actions. The strength of the disincentive depends on how much local investors and lenders have at stake in the project.

Despite its desirability, raising capital in the local market is not always feasible. Bank financing is often more readily available than bond financing. Funds availability in the emerging bond markets is limited, and maturities are short. In recent years, Brazil, Ecuador, India, Indonesia, Malaysia, Mexico, South Korea, Thailand, and Trinidad and Tobago all had viable corporate debt markets. But the Brazil market was mostly leasing company bonds maturing within eighteen months of issue. In Mexico, corporate debt maturities ranged up to seven years, but only about half had an original maturity exceeding one year. South Korea had the deepest corporate debt market of the nine countries mentioned above, but original debt maturities could not exceed five years. A notable exception was Trinidad and Tobago, where maturities of government bonds were up to twenty-five years and corporate bonds were up to fifteen.

As the emerging economies develop, so will their local capital markets. Where such markets exist, borrowers with investments in these countries should carefully consider raising at least some of the needed capital in those markets.

Conclusion

This chapter reviewed the main sources of debt capital. It is important to keep in mind that the world capital markets are becoming increasingly interrelated. At any time, one or another capital market may provide the lowest-cost funds.

There are many alternative ways to borrow funds, such as a bank loan or a public or private issue of bonds. A firm must weigh the costs and benefits of each and choose the least-cost alternative.

A borrower can sell bonds in the public market or the private market. It can sell them directly to investors or engage a securities dealer to act as an underwriter or a placement agent. The bulk of the debt securities issued by U.S. firms are sold in the domestic capital market in negotiated underwritten offerings.

The initial decision involves the form of borrowing and, if bonds are involved, what type of security to issue. Bank loans are usually at a floating interest rate, and bonds are usually fixed rate. Because issuance costs are proportionately lower for larger debt issues, it is impractical for a firm to sell bonds each time it needs to borrow funds. Bank financing is more cost-effective for small financings and offers greater drawdown flexibility. After deciding what type of security to sell, the firm must determine which market offers the most attractive terms. The private market is generally more attractive than the public market for debt issues that are small or have complex security arrangements.

A firm can borrow funds in its domestic debt market, the Euromarket, or some other country's capital market. The cost of funds for each alternative should be calculated after tax on a consistent basis, such as expressing each in terms of the same currency and using the same frequency of compounding. After calculating the costs of borrowing, the firm should select the lowest-cost alternative, taking into consideration any particular benefit from hedging foreign exchange, political, or other risks.

Chapter 4

High-Yield Debt

The high-yield debt market is a large global capital market providing capital to below-investment-grade borrowers. At year-end 2000, outstanding high-yield bonds totaled roughly $500 billion and made up about 20 percent of the universe of rated corporate bonds. This chapter describes the market and contrasts it with the investment-grade bond and bank loan markets examined in chapters 2 and 3.[1]

Market Overview

John Moody, founder of Moody's Investors Service, who played a crucial role in defining the high-yield debt market and developed the modern system of bond ratings, seems to have coined the term *high yield*. He used that term to describe lower-rated debt as early as 1919. In 1926, Arthur Stone Dewing of the Harvard Business School published a study concluding that the high yields are generally sufficient to cover the default losses on lower-rated debt.[2] Thus, the high-yield debt market has long been part of the U.S. capital market landscape.

Until the early 1980s, the high-yield debt market consisted mainly of bank loans to subinvestment-grade borrowers, so-called fallen angel bonds, and a small volume of original-issue non-investment-grade bonds. *Fallen angels* are bonds that were once investment-grade (Moody's Baa or better and Standard & Poor's BBB or better) but have deteriorated in credit quality. The low credit quality of high-yield bonds explains the frequently used term "junk bond" market.

The new-issue high-yield bond market began to expand rapidly in the early 1980s, fueled in part by issuance of bonds to finance leveraged buyouts (LBOs) and by relaxation in bank regulation that permitted thrifts to buy junk bonds. High-yield bond mutual funds, which had started to appear in the 1970s, also grew. The recession of 1990–1991 raised the default rate and temporarily halted the market's growth. Growth resumed in 1993 as the economy recovered from recession.

Driven by the capital needs of global telecommunications, media, health care, and technology firms and the growth of the emerging economies, the high-yield bond market tripled in size between 1987 and 1999 (see figure 4.1).[3]

The mix of debt has also changed. In the mid- to late 1980s, 40 percent of the new issues financed acquisitions and LBOs, whereas by 1990, LBOs accounted for just 4 percent of this volume. Capital expenditures (including acquisitions) and refinancings (including refinancing of high-yield bank debt) each currently account for nearly half of each year's high-yield debt financing.

Types of Securities

During the 1980s, issuers of high-yield bonds introduced a variety of innovative debt instruments to suit their needs and those of investors better. Recently issuers have gone back to basics and now mainly issue plain vanilla cash-pay, fixed-rate bonds. However, deferred-interest debentures, which do not pay cash interest (but accrue it and add it to principal) for the first few years, are still issued.

Figure 4.1 Growth of the High-Yield Bond Market, 1987–1999

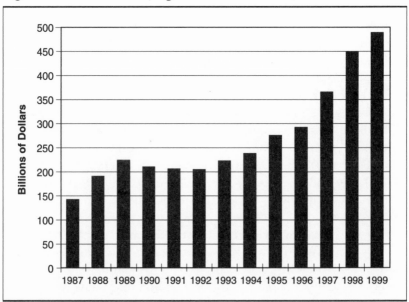

Source: Moody's Investors Service.

They are most common in the wireless telecommunications and other industries that have large capital needs but little or no operating cash flow during their development stage.

Conventional Fixed-Rate Bonds

Fixed-rate, cash-pay bonds are by far the most common instrument in the high-yield bond market, accounting for approximately 90 percent of high-yield bonds. The initial maturity is usually between five and ten years, and more than three-quarters of these bonds are callable. The call feature usually begins between three and five years after issue and enables the issuer to refinance the debt if its credit quality improves.[4] Sinking funds (i.e., periodic repayment of principal) are rare; fewer than 5 percent of high-yield bonds have them.

Innovative Securities

The high-yield debt market is responsible for several innovative debt securities (see chapter 8). For the most part, the high-yield innovations were designed for two purposes. First, many below-investment-grade firms were expected to have limited operating cash flow for a few years but greater cash flow in later years. Several debt securities were designed to fit this cash flow profile. Second, LBO financing accounted for a large percentage of the high-yield bonds issued in the early and mid-1980s. Some of the innovative debt instruments were designed to provide the initial financing and contained features intended to encourage prompt refinancing.

Five high-yield securities with innovative interest rate features are:

- *Split-coupon securities* and *deferred-interest debentures* pay zero cash interest for a few years; the interest accrues and is added to principal. They are issued at a discount to face value and give issuers time to build operating cash flow to meet their debt-service requirements.

- *Pay-in-kind (PIK) securities* give the issuer the option to pay interest in cash or in like-kind securities for several years after issue.[5] During the PIK period, these securities trade without accrued interest because the issuer can pay in kind rather than in cash. The PIK coupons are reflected in the security's quoted price.[6]

- *Step-up-coupon securities* have a low (nonzero) interest rate for the first few years, which steps up once on a specified date to a higher predetermined interest rate.

- *Increasing-rate notes* (IRNs) were developed in the mid-1980s to provide interim LBO financing. The coupon rate increases each quarter, usually by 25 or 50 basis points, which provides a strong incentive to refinance them with long-term debt before maturity.[7]

- *Extendable securities* and *reset securities* give the issuer the option to extend the maturity at designated times. If the issuer elects to extend, the terms of the security provide a mechanism for resetting the coupon rate to one that will make the securities worth a stated price (usually par or a slight premium to par).[8] Investors usually have a put option, which they can exercise if they find the new coupon unacceptable. The reset feature can benefit firms if their credit quality improves and protect investors if the firm's credit quality declines.[9]

Another class of innovative high-yield debt instruments consists of bonds with warrants to purchase the issuer's common stock. A holder could exercise the warrants by tendering bonds. The package of debt with warrants can be viewed as a *synthetic convertible bond* because both involve the exchange of bonds for stock of the issuer. (Convertible bonds are discussed in chapter 15.) Bonds with warrants, like convertible debt, are valuable in dealing with agency costs, and the agency costs that bondholders face tend to be more significant the poorer the issuer's credit quality.

High-Yield Bank Loans

The line between bank loans and bonds has blurred, especially in the high-yield market. Bank lenders' desires for liquidity and diversification of their credit-risk exposure, coupled with the standardization of bank loan documentation, have led to a growing market for trading below-investment-grade bank loans. Trading activity in the secondary bank loan market has increased dramatically since 1990. Also, a market has developed for *B loans,* which are longer-term bank loans with little amortization in the first few years, making them look similar to securities.

Significant differences remain between the high-yield bond and high-yield bank loan markets. Bank loans carry floating interest rates, have sinking funds, are callable at the end of each interest period without penalty, are usually secured by a lien on the borrower's assets, and have more restrictive covenants. Bonds are usually fixed rate, without a sinking fund, provide call protection, and are unsecured.

Figure 4.2 Investors in High-Yield Securities

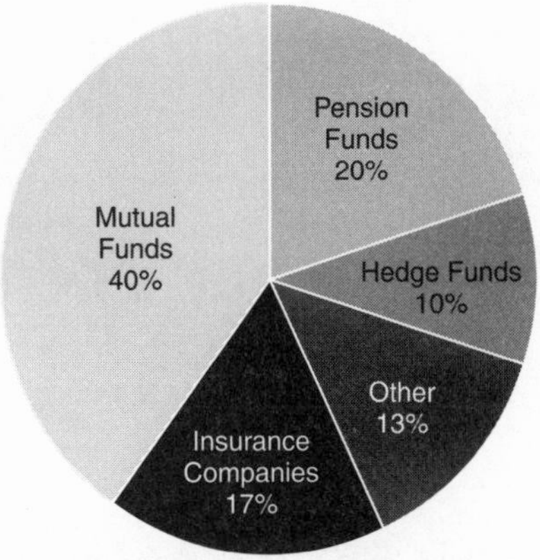

Source: Joseph V. Amato, "The High-Yield Bond Market," in Frank J. Fabozzi, ed., *The Handbook of Fixed Income Securities,* 5th ed. (Chicago: Irwin, 1997), p. 323.

Investors

Mutual funds are the dominant class of investors, accounting for about 40 percent of total high-yield investments (see figure 4.2). In the late 1980s, insurance companies were the largest class of investors, but their market share has fallen to 17 percent from 30 percent, and thrifts, which made up 15 percent of the market, have become an insignificant factor. As a result of the growing importance of mutual funds, the availability of capital is sensitive to high-yield mutual fund flows, which are closely correlated with high-yield bond returns.

Issuers

The volume of new issues of high-yield bonds tripled between 1995 and 1998 to more than $140 billion but fell to under $100 billion in 1999. More than half of the new issues are single-B-rated, more than one-quarter are double-B-rated, and the rest are below-single-B or unrated.

The overall credit quality of the high-yield market has improved because investors, especially mutual funds, have demanded higher-quality debt. Figure 4.3 illustrates the improvement in rating quality between 1989 and 1999. In 1999, double-B issuers represented 32 percent of high-yield bonds, up from 18 percent in 1989.

The issuers' industry concentration has also shifted. The media, cable, and telecommunications industries have accounted for a growing

Figure 4.3 Improvement in High-Yield Bond Rating Quality,
1989–1999

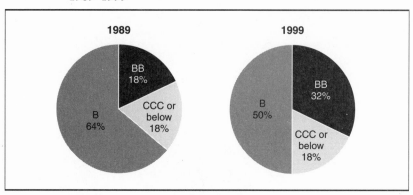

Source: Martin S. Fridson, *Extra Credit: The Journal of Global High Yield Bond Research* (New York: Merrill Lynch, January–February 2000), p. 39, and Joseph V. Amato, "The High-Yield Bond Market," in Frank J. Fabozzi, ed., *The Handbook of Fixed Income Securities,* 5th ed. (Chicago: Irwin, 1997), p. 316.

Note: Excludes defaulted issues.

portion of the volume of new issues. Bonds of U.S. issuers make up about 90 percent of the high-yield bond market.

Issuers in the high-yield bond market have increasingly relied on SEC Rule 144A. More than 80 percent of the high-yield bonds issued since 1997 have been sold with registration rights in reliance on this rule. Issuers privately sell unregistered debt securities to underwriters, which then resell them to QIBs under the safe-harbor resale provisions of Rule 144A.[10] This approach enables firms to lock in the rate of the new issue without having to wait for the securities to become registered. The issuer usually agrees to register them with the SEC within thirty to ninety days.[11] Investors have usually insisted on full-fledged "roadshows," in which the prospective debt issuer's management tours major U.S. cities to meet with investors and generate demand for the issue, before committing to invest. However, during robust periods like the late 1990s, some frequent high-yield issuers have been able to raise funds through "drive-by" deals without roadshows.

Interest Rate

High-yield bonds usually provide a premium in yield of between 200 and 550 basis points over the yield of comparable Treasury securities to compensate investors for default risk. Single-B-rated bonds usually yield about 200 basis points more than double-B-rated bonds. The default risk premium increases during recessions, such as 1990–1991,

Figure 4.4 Yield Spread for High-Yield Bonds, 1985–2000

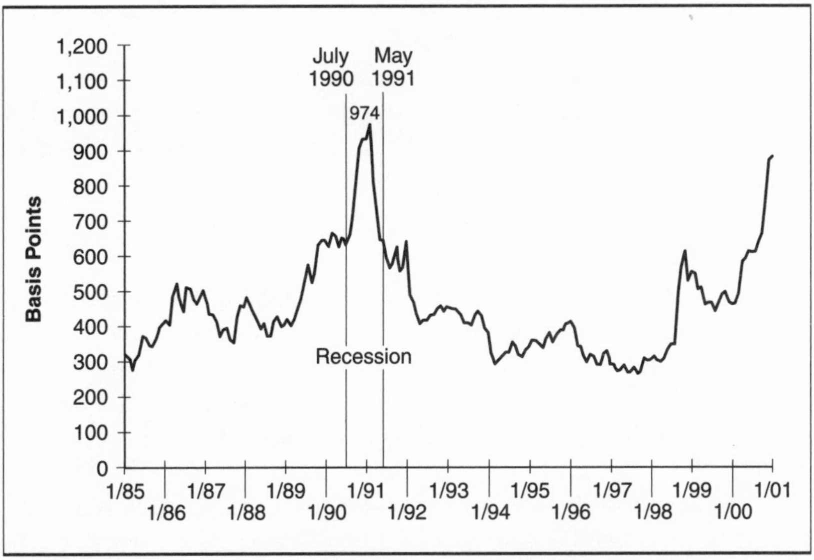

Source: Martin S. Fridson, Chief High Yield Strategist, Merrill Lynch. Reprinted by permission. Copyright © 2000 Merrill Lynch, Pierce, Fenner & Smith Incorporated.

Note: Based on the Merrill Lynch High Yield Master Index versus the 10-Year U.S. Treasury yield.

when the risk of default intensifies, as illustrated in figure 4.4. The average spread between high-yield bonds and Treasuries reached a peak of 974 basis points in January 1991.

Debt Ratings and the Risk of Default

As explained in chapter 2, the major debt rating agencies provide assessments of the issuer's credit standing and, especially important, the likelihood that the issuer will be able to make full and timely payment of principal and interest throughout the life of the debt. Their debt ratings serve as indicators of default risk, with the highest-rated bonds having the lowest risk. The highest four rating categories are known as *investment-grade ratings.* For Moody's, the investment-grade ratings are Aaa, Aa, A, and Baa. For Standard & Poor's, investment-grade ratings are AAA, AA, A, and BBB. Ratings lower than investment-grade are called *speculative-grade ratings* (Moody's Ba, B, Caa, Ca, and C; Standard & Poor's BB, B, CCC, CC, C, and D, meaning "in default"). The high-yield bond market consists of speculative-grade bonds.

Each debt rating agency distinguishes different levels of credit quality within each rating category below triple A. Moody's attaches the numbers 1 (high), 2 (medium), and 3 (low). Standard & Poor's attaches a plus sign for the highest and a minus sign for the lowest. For example, a medium-grade single-A credit would be rated A2 by Moody's and A by Standard & Poor's, and would be of somewhat higher quality than one rated A3 by Moody's or A- by Standard & Poor's.

Importance of Bond Ratings

Bond ratings indicate the likelihood of default. Bonds in the top three investment-grade categories are judged from "favorable" to "gilt edge." They have a capacity to pay interest that ranges from "strong" to "extremely strong." Bonds rated in the lower categories (Baa or BBB, or below) offer less protection and have a progressively greater risk of default.

The distinction between investment-grade and speculative-grade ratings is important because of institutional investment restrictions. To qualify as *legal investments* for commercial banks, bonds must usually be investment-grade. In addition, various state laws impose minimum rating standards and other restrictions for bonds to qualify as legal investment for saving banks, trust companies, public pension funds, and insurance companies. A firm's bond rating is very important to maintaining access to the capital markets on acceptable terms.

The NAIC has established six bond rating categories. The amount of reserves an insurance company must maintain for each bond investment depends on the bond's rating. Bonds rated NAIC-3 or below are speculative-grade and require significantly more capital. With the introduction of this new rating system and capital-maintenance standards, speculative-grade bonds have become much less attractive to insurance companies. The yields an insurance company requires to buy speculative-grade bonds are significantly higher, to compensate for the greater amount of capital they must maintain.

Debt Ratings and Financial Ratios

Debt issuers usually strive to maintain a particular (target) debt rating. The rating agencies use several criteria to rate a bond. For example, in the case of industrial firms, Standard & Poor's evaluates the following factors:

- Operating risk
- Market position

- Margins and other measures of profitability

- Management quality

- Conservatism of accounting policies

- Fixed-charge coverage

- Leverage (including off-balance-sheet debt) compared to the liquidation value of assets

- Adequacy of cash flow to meet future debt service obligations

- Future financial flexibility in the light of future debt service obligations and planned capital expenditure requirements

Each factor bears on the risk of future default. The rating agencies weigh their assessments of relevant factors and reach a decision; there is no all-purpose formula. In fact, several factors are difficult to quantify. Nevertheless, certain key credit statistics for comparable firms whose debt carries the target rating offer useful guidance.

Table 4.1 shows how the values of ten key credit ratios vary across the six highest rating categories assigned by Standard & Poor's; notice how all the ratios progressively improve with the firm's senior debt rating. Taken together, they go a long way toward distinguishing the degree of default risk as indicated by the credit rating.

Historical Returns on High-Yield Debt

Consistent with the risk-return trade-off in the capital market, high-yield debt provides higher average returns than investment-grade debt, but high-yield returns are more volatile. This volatility stems mainly from defaults, which vary over the business cycle and accelerate during recessions. For example, between 1989 and 1999, the Merrill Lynch High Yield Master Index provided an average monthly return of 0.82 percent versus 0.73 percent for BBB-rated bonds, with a standard deviation of 1.55 percent versus 1.31 percent for BBB-rated bonds.[12] However, high-yield bonds also provide a diversification benefit because their returns have relatively low correlations with Treasury and high-grade corporate bond returns.

Default Rates

The average annual default rate is the ratio of the par value of debt defaults during the year to the total par value of outstanding debt. It averaged 2.63 percent between 1971 and 1999 but varied between a low rate of 0.16 percent in 1981 and high rates of 10.14 percent and 10.27

Table 4.1 Senior Debt Ratings as Indicators of Credit Quality

Key Financial Ratios[a]						
Senior Debt Rating[b]	AAA	AA	A	BBB	BB	B
Interest coverage ratio	21.39x	10.02x	5.67x	2.90x	2.25x	0.74x
Fixed-charge coverage ratio[c]	6.96	5.31	3.42	2.22	1.62	0.85
EBITDA/Interest[d]	31.68	14.78	8.25	5.02	3.46	1.56
Funds from operations/Total debt	109.8%	75.4%	49.1%	30.3%	20.2%	9.8%
Free operating cash flow/Total debt	53.8	27.9	19.6	3.9	0.7	(1.7)
Pretax return on permanent capital	25.1	19.1	16.0	11.8	10.2	6.2
Operating income/Sales	21.2	17.1	14.6	12.3	11.9	8.7
Long-term debt/Capitalization	9.7	18.9	28.8	40.7	50.2	62.2
Total debt/Adjusted capitalization (including short-term debt)	22.6	28.3	36.7	45.3	55.6	71.4
Total debt/Adjusted capitalization (including short-term debt and 8x rents)	36.1	40.1	46.8	56.1	65.5	76.5

Source: Adapted from *Global Sector Review* (New York: Standard & Poor's, October 1995), p. 10. Reproduced with permission of Standard & Poor's Rating Services, all rights reserved.

[a]Median of the three-year simple arithmetic averages for the period 1992–1994 for firms whose senior debt had the indicated rating.
[b]As assigned by Standard & Poor's.
[c]Based on full rental charges, rather than the one-third of rental charges used in the SEC fixed-charge-coverage calculation.
[d]EBITDA = earnings before interest, taxes, depreciation, and amortization.

percent in the recession years of 1990 and 1991, respectively. Defaults during these years included numerous large, overleveraged LBOs. The rate rose to 4.15 percent in 1999, the highest default rate since 1991.[13] Studies have revealed that the default rate is higher for lower-rated issues and that the likelihood of default for a debt issue increases for about four years after issue, remains at a relatively high level for about three to five years, and thereafter decreases.[14]

Studies have also documented that when default occurs, investors recover about 40 percent of the par value on a present-value basis, but the percentage recovery depends on the seniority of the debt and whether it is secured, and the recovery rate varies from year to year.[15] For example, recoveries on defaulted issues averaged only 28 percent in 1999.[16] The greater the likelihood of default and the lower the expected recovery are, the higher the interest rate needs to be to compensate for the expected default losses.

Annual Returns and Risk of High-Yield Bonds

The overall interest rate environment, the condition of the economy, the condition of the issuer's industry, and regulatory factors affect high-yield debt returns. For example, restrictions that regulators imposed on insurance companies and thrifts in 1989–1990 reduced their investments in high-yield debt and created a severe supply-demand imbalance that reinforced the effects of the economic slowdown in forcing interest rates higher.

High-yield debt involves greater credit risk than investment-grade debt but less credit risk than stocks. Consequently, the annual returns high-yield bonds provide fall between those of higher-grade, less risky bonds and stocks, as illustrated in table 4.2. Similarly, B-rated bonds produce higher average returns but expose investors to greater risk than do BB-rated bonds, and bonds rated below B should provide higher average returns than higher-rated bonds. However, at least two studies have found that over extended periods, CCC-rated bonds have provided lower returns and involved substantially greater risk, primarily default risk, suggesting that investors tend to overpay for the lowest-rated bonds.[17]

Correlations Among High-Yield Debt and Other Security Returns

High-yield debt returns have relatively low correlations with the returns on high-grade corporate bonds and Treasury securities. For example, the correlation coefficient between the returns on ten-year

Table 4.2 Average Annual Returns and Risk, 1985–1999

Security	Average Annual Return	Standard Deviation
Large cap stocks[a]	18.60%	14.93%
Small cap stocks[b]	12.72	18.46
High-yield bonds[c]	10.92	5.27
High-grade corporate bonds[d]	9.60	5.27
Ten-year Treasuries	8.88	7.66
Three-month Treasury bills	5.88	0.48

Source: Martin S. Fridson, *Extra Credit: The Journal of Global High Yield Bond Research* (New York: Merrill Lynch, January–February 2000), p. 13.
[a]Standard & Poor's 500 Index.
[b]Russell 2000 Index.
[c]Merrill Lynch High Yield Master Index.
[d]Merrill Lynch High Grade Corporate Master Index.

Treasury securities and high-grade corporate bonds was 0.94 for the period 1985 through 1999; the correlation coefficient between the returns on high-yield bonds and ten-year Treasury securities was only 0.37.[18] High-yield bond returns are more closely correlated with stock returns than are high-grade corporate bond returns. This feature of high-yield bonds, which is consistent with their position between high-grade bonds and stocks in the risk-return spectrum, implies that adding high-yield debt (bonds or bank loans) to a portfolio of high-grade bonds can produce a diversification benefit.

Credit Analysis

High-yield debt differs from investment-grade debt in that credit-worthiness is relatively more important and changes in interest rates relatively less important in determining their value. The potential change in the issuer's credit standing is usually an important factor in assessing the prospective returns of high-yield debt. Also, the presence of nonsystematic, firm-specific risk means that much of the default risk associated with high-yield debt can be eliminated through portfolio diversification.[19]

A firm's bond rating indicates its credit standing. But often unrated bonds or bank loans must be valued. A *credit analysis* indicates how the debt would be rated. This is a key step in the valuation process for any unrated bond or loan and is especially important for high-yield debt because the degree of default risk is a major determinant of the investors' required return.

Using Key Credit Ratios to Assess Credit Risk

The values of selected credit ratios can be used collectively to gauge the credit quality of a bond or a loan. You can infer a credit rating by comparing the credit ratios for the bond or loan issuer to the credit ratios for firms whose debt has been rated.

The median values for a set of key credit ratios serve as a useful point of reference. Table 4.1 provides three-year median values for ten key credit ratios for various historical periods and the six top rating categories assigned by Standard & Poor's. The credit ratios in the table are among the most important ones on which Standard & Poor's relies in making credit risk judgments. Cash flow is particularly important because the firm must generate enough cash flow from its operations to service its debt. In addition, Standard & Poor's takes industry-specific factors into account. Thus, it is important when assessing a bond's credit quality to select comparable firms from the same industry as the issuer of the bonds or loan under analysis.

It is evident in table 4.1 why a firm's credit ratios can be helpful in determining within which rating category its debt would fall were the debt rated. For example, the interest coverage ratio becomes progressively lower as the credit rating falls from AAA to B. Similarly, fixed-charge coverage, EBITDA (earnings before interest, taxes, depreciation, and amortization) to interest, funds from operations to total debt, free operating cash flow to total debt, pretax return on permanent capital, and operating income to sales all decrease steadily as the credit rating falls from AAA to B. In each case, the lower the credit ratio is, the weaker is the credit standing and the greater the risk of default.

The last three credit ratios in table 4.1 serve as measures of leverage. The higher the leverage is, the greater is the risk of default. In each case, the median credit ratio is greater the lower the credit rating is. Taken collectively, the pattern of the credit ratios in table 4.1 makes them highly useful as indicators of credit quality.

Ratio analysis is somewhat imprecise because the rating agencies base their rating judgments on a variety of considerations. Although credit ratios are important, other factors also matter. These include:

- The agencies include their assessment of the quality of management, which can cause the credit rating to differ from what the credit ratios would otherwise seem to imply.

• The credit ratios are calculated from historical data. The agencies also base a credit assessment to a large degree on several years of projected credit ratios. If a firm's business situation, and thus its credit ratios, are deteriorating (improving), the appropriate credit rating may be lower (higher) than historical ratios would otherwise imply.

• Credit ratings are designed to be valid over the entire business cycle. Thus, a firm's credit ratios at a high (low) point in the cycle will generally be above (below) the median values for its rating category.

• Comparisons among firms in different industries are potentially misleading. For example, a firm with relatively liquid tangible assets, such as an oil and gas producer, can use more leverage than a firm of similar size and profitability with mostly intangible assets, such as patents, trademarks, and goodwill. Systematic differences across industries make it imperative that the comparable firms be chosen from within the same industry.

• Cross-border comparisons can be very misleading. The credit ratios may not be comparable due to differences in accounting principles, national economic conditions, financial practices, and other factors.

• Care must be taken to adjust each firm's reported figures for the impact of nonrecurring items, such as special one-time charges, gains or losses on sales of assets, and one-time accounting changes.

Credit Analysis Example

Suppose we wish to determine the credit quality of Pogo Producing Company's senior debt. Pogo has rated debt outstanding, so we can use the Moody's and Standard & Poor's ratings to check our assessments.

Table 4.3 contains the credit analysis. A comparison of Pogo's credit ratios to the median values for the most recent period in table 4.1 suggests a rating somewhere in the Ba/BB range. Pogo explores for, develops, and produces oil and gas in the United States and internationally, so oil and gas producers with debt rated in the Ba/BB category were identified. The credit ratios for each firm were calculated based on data available for the latest twelve months ended June 30, 2000, and displayed in table 4.3.[20]

Comparing Pogo Producing's credit ratios to those of the other oil and gas producers in table 4.3 confirms the initial judgment that the firm

Table 4.3 A Comparative Credit Analysis for Pogo Producing Company

Company	Senior Debt Rating[a]		Pretax Interest Coverage[b]	EBITDA/ Total Debt[c]	Free Cash Flow/ Total Debt[d]	Total Debt/ Total Capitalization[e]	Total Debt/ Market Capitalization[f]	Debt/ Reserves[g]	Reserve Life[h]
	Moody's	S&P							
Pogo Producing	Ba3	BB+	2.88x	63.3%	18.2%	45.2%	23.7%	$2.58	9.3
Gulf Canada Resources	Ba1	BBB–	2.26	43.7	13.0	57.8	41.4	4.51	9.1
Barrett Resources	Ba1	BB+	3.32	43.9	NM[i]	50.7	24.6	2.05	10.9
Ocean Energy	Ba1	BB+	3.96	52.6	6.1	55.3	30.0	3.07	7.9
Pioneer Natural Resources	Ba2	BB+	1.34	29.5	6.6	67.9	54.3	2.81	11.8
Vintage Petroleum	Ba2	BB+	4.77	77.1	7.8	48.9	25.0	1.02	18.8
Average			3.13	49.4	8.4	56.1	35.1	2.69	11.7
Newfield Exploration	Ba2	BB	13.80	143.1	NM[i]	26.7	9.9	2.12	5.2
Nuevo Energy	Ba2	BB	1.02	30.1	NM[i]	51.7	51.1	1.26	14.0
Belco Oil & Gas	Ba2	BB–	NM[i]	28.9	NM[i]	80.8	56.8	3.55	10.6
Swift Energy	Ba3	BB	4.64	49.2	NM[i]	54.8	23.2	3.17	10.6
Average			2.83[k]	62.8		53.5	35.3	2.53	10.1

(continued)

Table 4.3 (continued)

Company	Senior Debt Rating[a] Moody's	Senior Debt Rating[a] S&P	Pretax Interest Coverage[b]	EBITDA/ Total Debt[c]	Free Cash Flow/ Total Debt[d]	Total Debt/ Total Capitalization[e]	Total Debt/ Market Capitalization[f]	Debt/ Reserves[g]	Reserve Life[h]
Forest Oil	Ba3	BB–	1.87	40.1	NM[i]	54.4	31.8	3.36	8.1
HS Resources	Ba3	BB–	2.06	28.5	3.4	76.1	49.8	3.19	15.2
Houston Exploration	Ba3	BB–	3.04	58.1	NM[i]	46.1	26.9	3.07	7.6
Stone Energy	Ba3	BB–	8.77	150.8	29.9	25.0	8.5	1.55	6.6
Bellwether Exploration	Ba2	B+	2.32	41.4	NM[i]	73.5	55.1	3.66	7.3
Danbury Resources	Ba2	B+	3.15	50.4	1.8	60.2	28.0	2.47	9.9
Range Resources	Ba2	B+	0.91	27.9	8.3	62.4	66.5	4.00	9.2
Average			3.16	56.7	10.9	56.8	38.1	3.04	9.1

[a]The implied senior debt rating when the firm only has subordinated debt outstanding. Senior debt is rated two notches above subordinated debt (e.g., Ba1 for senior implied by Ba3).

[b]EBIT (Earnings Before Interest and Taxes) divided by total interest (i.e., including capitalized interest).

[c]EBITDA = Earnings Before Interest, Taxes, Depreciation, and Amortization.

[d]Free cash flow = cash flow from operations minus capital expenditures and minus also the increase in working capital.

[e]Total capitalization equals total debt (both long and short-term) plus the book value of total equity.

[f]Market capitalization values the common equity at its market value.

[g]The ratio of total debt to the amount of oil and gas reserves (expressed as the number of equivalent barrels of oil).

[h]The ratio of the firm's oil and gas reserves to the annual oil and gas production (each expressed as the number of equivalent barrels of oil).

[i]Not meaningful because EBIT is negative.

[j]Not meaningful because free cash flow is negative.

[k]Average of pretax interest coverage for Nuevo Energy and Swift Energy.

has a Ba/BB credit rating. Pogo's interest coverage is about average, its leverage is below average, and its ratio of cash flow to debt is above average. Its debt-to-reserves ratio is consistent with the stronger Ba/BB credits, and its reserve life is consistent with the weaker Ba/BB credits. The last two ratios highlight the importance of asset quality in determining a firm's credit standing. On balance, Pogo is a Ba2/BB credit.[21]

Distressed Debt

Many fixed-income investors shy away from *distressed debt*, the debt of firms that are either operating in bankruptcy or headed in that direction. Distressed debt is one of the riskiest sectors of the high-yield market, but consistent with the risk-return trade-off, it also offers investment opportunities that can reward careful analysis with attractive risk-adjusted returns.

Chapter 11 of the Bankruptcy Code enables reorganized firms to get a fresh start. When a firm files for Chapter 11, investors who are uncomfortable with the bankruptcy process bail out, and the prices of its securities usually plummet. The securities prices recover—and the most senior debt may even return to par value—if the firm can reorganize successfully. The challenge for analysts is to distinguish firms that will be able to reorganize successfully from those that will not.

Valuing distressed debt requires a basic understanding of the bankruptcy process.[22] Filing for Chapter 11 triggers the *automatic stay* provisions of the Bankruptcy Code, which preclude attempts by creditors to collect on the debt the firm owes or to interfere with the property or operation of the firm's business. The firm becomes a *debtor-in-possession*, which operates under the Bankruptcy Court's supervision while it attempts to work out a *plan of reorganization* or, if it is in the best interest of its creditors, formulates a plan of orderly *liquidation*.[23] The amounts that creditors ultimately recover depend on whether the firm reorganizes, continuing to operate but under a new business plan, or liquidates, in which case all its assets are sold and the proceeds distributed to claim holders in order of strict priority. Administrative expenses come first, priority claims such as those arising from the debtor's business while it is in bankruptcy come next, then secured debt claims, unsecured senior debt, subordinated debt, preferred stock, and last come common stock claims.

Strict priority is not always observed in reorganization, and the bankruptcy process can take years.[24] The plan of reorganization is negotiated among the debtor and the various classes of claimants, and how effectively each class negotiates also determines its recovery. The court must approve the ultimate distribution of value, embodied in the plan of reorganization.

Valuing the debt of a bankrupt firm requires assessing the value of the debt's claims on the debtor. The type of debt is very important. Secured debt has a lien on specific assets and can accrue postpetition interest during bankruptcy if there is adequate collateral value in the assets. Different classes of debt can have significantly different values.

If the debtor has proposed a plan of reorganization, the *disclosure statement* distributed to its creditors contains the information needed to value its debt. If no plan of reorganization has been proposed, a greater level of analytical sophistication is required. A class of investors, called *vulture funds*, specializes in investing in the debt of bankrupt firms and negotiating a plan of reorganization with the debtor, often earning very attractive returns for the effort expended and risks assumed.

Emerging-Market Debt

The international emerging markets encompass all of Latin America, the Middle East, Africa, Central and Eastern Europe, and Asia (other than Japan). Emerging-market debt includes sovereign and corporate bonds, traded performing bank loans, local currency debt instruments, and Brady bonds. The volume of new issues averaged about $75 billion per year between 1997 and 1999. Emerging-market yields have exceeded U.S. high yields by between 200 and 400 basis points, but the yields vary significantly by country.

Sovereign Credit Risk

Sovereign (government-issued) debt instruments account for most of the trading in emerging-market debt. The prices of corporate debt reflect sovereign risk, and there tends to be a high correlation between the prices of corporate and sovereign debt. In some cases, corporate debt ratings are constrained by a sovereign debt ceiling. Attractive investment opportunities can result because corporate debt can have better credit quality than the country where the firm is located. For example, if a firm earns a high percentage of its external debt service needs through hard-currency exports and this cash flow is protected against foreign exchange controls, the firm's debt can have lower risk than the government's. Valuing corporate debt therefore requires analyzing sovereign risk based on foreign exchange reserves, the balance of payments, economic growth prospects, and other factors and the extent to which sovereign risk affects corporate debt issuers in that country.

Brady Bonds

Brady bonds are sovereign bonds issued by developing countries in exchange for their defaulted bank loans. They were developed in 1989–1990 to restructure Mexico's bank debt.[25] Seventeen countries have participated in the program, issuing $170 billion of Brady bonds. Many Brady bond issues are large and liquid. In December 1999, yields ranged from 8 to 30 percent. No Brady bonds defaulted until Ecuador missed an interest payment on September 30, 1999.[26]

Brady bonds come in a variety of types.[27] There are often three or more classes of bonds issued in exchange for a country's defaulted bank loans. Discount bonds (or principal-reduction bonds) pay a market rate of interest but require the banks to forgive a substantial amount of debt. Par bonds (or interest-reduction bonds) do not require any reduction in principal but pay a below-market interest rate. Both have twenty-five- to thirty-year maturities, par call, and bullet maturities and include full collateralization of principal in the form of zero-coupon U.S. Treasury bonds plus a collateralized rolling guarantee of eighteen months' interest. Noncollateralized Brady bonds may have a fixed or floating interest rate and usually amortize principal and have a relatively short maturity.

Market participants value discounts and pars differently from the noncollateralized Brady bonds. They value the fully collateralized principal and the collateralized rolling interest guarantee separately from the remaining cash flows because of their lower risk, and then add the values of these two components to the value of the risky interest stream.[28]

Conclusion

The high-yield debt market includes high-risk-and-high-return debt, both bonds that are rated below investment-grade and bank loans of comparable credit standing. It is a global market, although it is located mainly in the United States. The high-yield market has matured within the past decade and has expanded outside the United States.

High-yield debt poses greater default risk than high-grade debt, which makes high-yield debt harder to value. Two sectors of this market, distressed debt and emerging-market debt, are the riskiest but also appear to offer the greatest opportunities for above-average returns because market imperfections and information asymmetries often give rise to pricing inefficiencies that an astute trader can exploit whenever it finds them.

Chapter **5**

New Issue Design

A firm that wants to borrow money by selling bonds has several decisions to make:

• Should the interest rate be fixed or variable?

• When should the debt mature?

• Should there be a sinking fund that will retire the debt in installments?

• Should it retain a call option to redeem and refund the bonds? Or should it give bondholders a put option to redeem the bonds if interest rates rise?

The issuer's choices are usually made in consultation with investment bankers and are guided by how much investors will pay for particular packages of features.

Basic Bond Features

The debt contract specifies the basic features of the debt. The contract for a public debt issue is called a *bond indenture*. A trustee, as agent for the bondholders, monitors contract compliance. For a private issue, the contract is called a *bond agreement* or *note agreement*.

Maturity

Bonds issued in the United States have a *maturity* date, which is the date by which the borrower must repay the money borrowed. When a bond is issued, the length of its life is its *original maturity*. Virtually any original maturity is possible, but most U.S. corporate bonds issued in recent years have had original maturities between five and thirty years. The bond's *remaining maturity* (simply called its *maturity*) is the amount of time remaining until the maturity date.

A bond's maturity is important for three reasons:

- During this time, the bondholder expects interest (coupon) payments, and at the end of the period, the bondholder expects principal repayment.

- The bond's yield depends on it.

- The volatility of a bond's price depends on it; the longer the maturity is, the greater is the price volatility.

Generally original maturities of ten years or less are called *notes*. Longer-term corporate borrowings are called *bonds*. Notes with a maturity of up to five years are considered *short-term*. Those with a maturity between five and twelve years are considered *intermediate-term*, and those with a maturity greater than twelve years are *long-term*.

Par Value and Coupon Rate

A bond's *par value* (or *face value*, or *principal*) is the amount to be repaid by the maturity date. Most U.S. corporate bonds have a par value of $1,000.

The *coupon rate*, which is quoted as a rate per year unless stated otherwise (e.g., a quoted rate of 10 percent means 10 percent per year), sets the bond's interest payments. The total annual interest cost is the coupon rate times the par value. For example, a bond with an 8 percent coupon rate and a $1,000 par value will pay $80 yearly. U.S. corporate bonds usually make two semiannual payments—in this example, $40 every six months.

Most coupon rates are fixed (constant), although *floating-rate bonds* pay a coupon rate that resets periodically according to a formula stated in the contract. The formula is usually based on an interest rate benchmark, such as a financial index, although some have been based on a nonfinancial index, such as a commodity price.

Zero-coupon bonds do not make interim payments. The single par value payment at the maturity date covers all interest and principal repayment. The bond's interest is the difference between the price paid and the par value.

A bond's *yield to maturity* is the APR earned if the bond is bought for its current price, held to maturity, and all promised payments are made in full on time.

Early Redemption Provisions

There are two types of early redemption provisions. One conveys the option to redeem up to the entire issue prior to maturity. The other imposes an obligation to retire a substantial portion of the issue in stages prior to maturity.

Optional Redemption (or Call) Provision

Many corporate bonds can be redeemed by the issuer before maturity. Issuers must pay for this call option because it is disadvantageous to the bondholder. The cost, which depends on the terms, is typically a combination of a repayment premium over the par value, a somewhat higher coupon rate, and a grace period before the call provision goes into force. For example, a thirty-year bond with a 10 percent coupon rate might have a five-year grace period and a call price of 107.5 percent of par value for the sixth year. Table 5.1 illustrates such a redemption schedule, wherein the call premium (excess over 100 percent)

Table 5.1 Optional Redemption Price Schedule for a Thirty-Year Bond Issued February 1, 2000

The Debentures are redeemable at the option of the Company at any time, in whole or in part, upon at least 30 but not more than 45 days' notice, at the following redemption prices (expressed as percentages of principal amount) in each case together with interest accrued to the redemption date. If redemption occurs during the 12 months beginning February 1, the redemption prices are the ones indicated in the following table. If redemption occurs on February 1, 2020 or thereafter, the redemptive price is 100%. However, prior to February 1, 2010, the Company is not permitted to redeem any of the Debentures pursuant to this option, directly or indirectly, from or in anticipation of the proceeds of the issuance of any indebtedness for borrowed money that has an interest cost of less than 10% per annum.

Year	Price	Year	Price
2000	110.00%	2010	105.00%
2001	109.50	2011	104.50
2002	109.00	2012	104.00
2003	108.50	2013	103.50
2004	108.00	2014	103.00
2005	107.50	2015	102.50
2006	107.00	2016	102.00
2007	106.50	2017	101.50
2008	106.00	2018	101.00
2009	105.50	2019	100.50

declines by equal amounts each year to zero in year 21 and the nine years thereafter. The first year's call price is usually the coupon plus the par value (110 percent in table 5.1).

With a call provision, the issuer can call the bonds in whole (the entire issue) or in part (a portion). When a portion is called, the bond contract specifies how the bonds to be called will be chosen. Public bond indentures usually require that they be chosen randomly. Private bond indentures usually require pro rata redemption.

A bond that is *noncallable* cannot be redeemed.[1] However, a bond that is *nonrefundable* can be redeemed, provided it is not redeemed using proceeds from a lower-cost debt issue that ranks senior to or on a par with the refunded issue. The redemption provision in table 5.1 includes an example of a nonrefundability clause.

The *make-whole call provision* is an indexed bond call option. The strike price is indexed to the yield on a comparable Treasury bond. For example, the Engelhard Corporation 7⅜ percent notes due August 1, 2006, specify a call price equal to the greater of par value and the present value of all remaining principal and interest payments discounted at the comparable Treasury yield plus 10 basis points (hundredths of a percent).

Mandatory Redemption (or Sinking-Fund) Provision

When repayment of a bond's principal will be made entirely at maturity, it is called a *bullet maturity*. Repaying principal in multiple installments (usually annually) is called a *sinking fund*. A sinking fund effectively shortens the debt's maturity because some of it is repaid before maturity. This reduces the bondholders' credit risk exposure. Bonds can be called and redeemed[2] for cash (usually at par value), or bonds selling below par value can be purchased in the open market. When a debt issue has a sinking fund, the final payment (at maturity) is called the *balloon payment*.

Usually the sinking-fund payments are the same each period, although some corporate bonds include the option to redeem additional bonds. This is referred to as an *accelerated-sinking-fund provision*. For example, an issuer might have a *double-up option*—the option to redeem up to twice the minimum sinking-fund payment.

Put Provision

A *put provision* is a bondholder option to sell the bond back to the issuer for par value on designated dates. This feature benefits investors and therefore increases the bond's value. If interest rates rise, thereby reducing a bond's value, investors can sell the bonds for par value and reinvest the proceeds at the higher prevailing interest rate.

Conversion Feature

A *convertible bond* gives bondholders the option to convert the security into stock by exchanging the bond for a specified number of shares of the issuer's common stock. This feature allows bondholders to benefit from an increase in the value of the issuer's common stock.

An *exchangeable bond* allows bondholders to exchange each bond for a specified number of common shares of an affiliate of the issuer or of some other corporation whose stock the issuer happens to own.

A convertible bond can be viewed as a package consisting of a straight bond and a nondetachable call option.[3] The presence of embedded options makes bond valuation complex.

Protective Covenants

Covenants are designed to protect bondholders by restricting the borrower. The covenants often spell out financial tests that must be met before the borrower can do the following:

- Take on more debt (*debt limitation*)
- Use cash to pay dividends or make share repurchases (*dividend limitations*)
- Mortgage assets (*limitation on liens* or *a negative pledge clause*)
- Borrow through one of its subsidiaries (*limitation on subsidiary borrowing*)
- Sell major assets (*limitation on asset dispositions*)
- Merge with another firm or sell substantially all its assets to another firm (*limitation on merger, consolidation, or sale*)
- Sell assets and lease them back (*limitation on sale-and-leaseback*)

Events of Default

Bond contracts also specify *events of default*. If the borrower fails to pay interest or repay principal promptly, defaults on another debt issue, or fails to adhere to one of the covenants, the lender can demand immediate repayment of the debt. Often, however, bondholders will try to negotiate, because they usually do not want to take ownership of the firm.

Bond Investors' Required Return

A bond's value is based on its coupon rate and the investors' required return. The required return is based on the risks investors face, especially the degree of default risk; the higher the risk is, the higher is the required return.

Risks Associated with Investing in Bonds

Bonds have at least seven types of risk:

- *Interest rate risk.* The value of a bond changes in the opposite direction from a change in interest rates. As interest rates rise (fall), the price of the bond falls (rises). Such price fluctuation is referred to as *interest rate risk* (or *market risk*). Interest rate risk is caused by several factors, primarily changes in expected inflation, changes in the riskiness of the firm, and changes in the supply and demand for funds.

- *Reinvestment risk.* When a coupon payment is made, there is the risk that the payment must be reinvested at a lower interest rate. This *reinvestment risk* is greater for longer holding periods and for bonds with relatively large coupon payments, such as high-yield bonds.

- *Call risk.* If interest rates drop and the issuer exercises its call option, investors risk having to reinvest their money at a lower interest rate.

- *Default risk.* *Default risk* (or *credit risk*) refers to the risk that the bond issuer might default. Defaults are of two types: *payment default*, which occurs when the issuer does not make a required interest or principal payment, and *technical default*, which occurs when some other provision is violated. A technical default may be a warning of a possible payment default. Bond or credit ratings provide a measure of default risk. Corporate bonds have a higher required return than comparable Treasury bonds, primarily because of default risk. Naturally, the differential increases with default risk.[4]

- *Inflation risk.* *Inflation risk* (or *purchasing power risk*) occurs because the value of a set cash flow amount falls as the rate of inflation rises. For all but floating-rate bonds, there is inflation risk because the coupon rate is fixed. Floating-rate bonds have lower inflation risk to the extent that their interest rates track changes in inflation.

- *Liquidity risk.* *Liquidity risk* (or *marketability risk*) depends on the ease with which investors can sell bonds at or near their intrinsic value. A useful indicator of liquidity is the spread between the bid price and the ask price. The wider the spread is, the lower is the liquidity. Liquidity risk is less important to investors who plan to own the bonds until maturity.

- *Foreign exchange risk.* A bond whose payments are denominated in a foreign currency has uncertain U.S. dollar cash flows. The risk that the foreign currency will depreciate relative to the U.S. dollar is referred to as *foreign exchange risk* (or *currency risk*).

It is important in designing a new issue to determine how much investors will charge for risk bearing and adjust the new issue's features to achieve an acceptable cost of funds.

Base Interest Rate

Bond investors use the yields on the *on-the-run Treasury securities* (the most recently auctioned three-month, six-month, two-year, three-year, five-year, ten-year, and thirty-year Treasuries) as *base interest rates* for expressing the yields on non-Treasury bonds. Some investor services also provide the yields of other actively traded Treasury securities as benchmarks. The base rate is the yield to maturity on the most actively traded Treasury security with the closest maturity to the average life of the targeted non-Treasury bond. For example, the base rate for a ten-year non-sinking-fund corporate bond on June 30, 2000, was 6.78 percent.

Risk Premium

Suppose the yield to maturity on a ten-year corporate bond is 7.78 percent and the yield on the ten-year on-the-run Treasury is 6.78 percent. The *yield spread* is 100 basis points. This spread is a *risk premium*, which reflects the additional risk, chiefly default risk, of owning the corporate bond rather than a comparable Treasury security. Thus:

Corporate bond yield = Base interest rate + Premium

Six main factors determine the risk premium:

- *Type of issuer.* There are several bond market sectors (see figure 1.1). Some sectors are further subdivided because of differences in risk. For example, the corporate sector is subdivided into utilities, transportation companies, industrials, and banks and finance companies. Sectors and subsectors are generally perceived to have different types of risk.

- *Default risk,* which is the risk that the issuer might fail to make timely payments of interest or principal.

- *Remaining maturity,* which is the amount of time remaining until the maturity date.

- *Embedded options.* The presence of an embedded option affects the size of the risk premium. An embedded option that is unfavorable to the investor (e.g., a call option) increases the spread. An embedded option that is favorable to the investor (e.g., a put option or a conversion option) decreases the spread. In fact, an option can be so favorable that the spread becomes negative, and the bond's yield is less than that on a comparable Treasury security.

- *Tax status of the interest payments.* Tax exemption can lead to a negative spread. Yields on municipal bonds are routinely less than those on comparable Treasuries.

- *Liquidity,* which is the risk that the investor will not be able to realize a bond's full intrinsic value if it has to sell the bond quickly.

The Yield Curve

The relationship between yield and maturity for a given credit quality is called a *yield curve.* The Treasury yield curve is the most basic. Figure 5.1 shows the yield curve for A-rated industrial corporate debt on June 30, 2000. A yield curve can be drawn for each rating category within a sector or even subsector to reflect the required returns for the grouping. The yield curve can accurately predict the required return for a prospective new bond of a particular grouping and maturity. For example, using figure 5.1, a ten-year new issue would require a 7.78 percent nominal annual yield, and a thirty-year new issue would require an 8.13 percent yield.

Financial Contracting

The modern corporation is exceedingly complex, in large part because there are so many contractual relationships. *Financial contracting* describes the business world in terms of both explicit and implicit contracts. One exceptionally important set of contracts are those between a corporation and its bondholders. Financial contracting provides numerous useful insights about bondholder risk and why bond contracts are structured the way they are.

Figure 5.1   Yield Curve for A-Rated Industrial Corporate Debt
on June 30, 2000

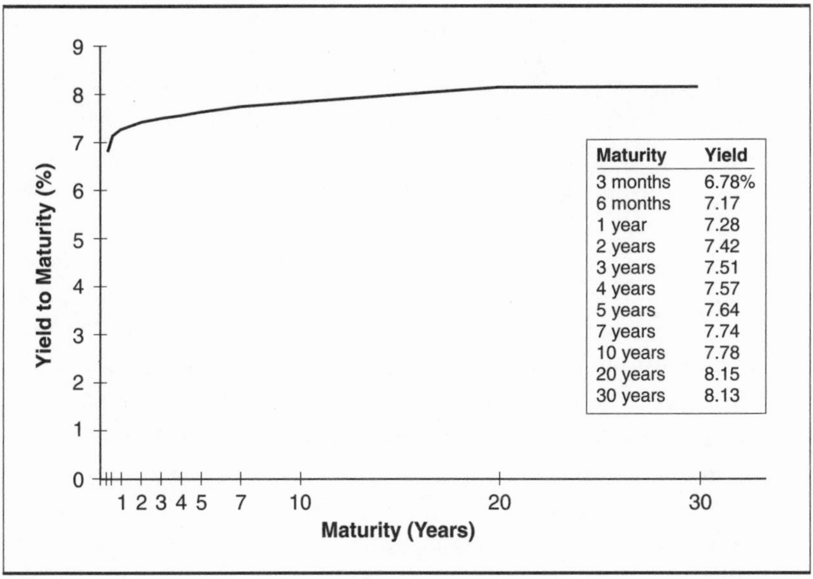

Maturity	Yield
3 months	6.78%
6 months	7.17
1 year	7.28
2 years	7.42
3 years	7.51
4 years	7.57
5 years	7.64
7 years	7.74
10 years	7.78
20 years	8.15
30 years	8.13

Source: Bloomberg L. P.

The main issue in financial contracting is how to minimize the costs of having the agent make decisions that affect the principal. The answer lies in (1) creating incentives, constraints, and punishments; (2) having reasonable monitoring procedures; and (3) identifying and using contracts that minimize the possibility of conflicts of interest at the outset.

Principal-Agent Relationships

A firm can be viewed as a set of contractual relationships among its stakeholders. This view uses *agency theory,* which is the analysis of *principal-agent relationships,* wherein an agent is making decisions that affect a principal. Stakeholder relationships can be described as principal-agent relationships.

Some of the more visible examples of explicit principal-agent relationships are money managers, lawyers, and agents of real estate, travel, and insurance. Many other situations can be described in the principal-agent framework as though the two parties were principal and agent even though one party is not literally an agent for the other. For example, most employees are not classified as an agent for their employer, but do act as an agent at some point.

Agency Problems

A potential conflict of interest between an agent and principal is an *agency problem*. Such conflicts can be as simple as the agent's not putting forth "full effort." Because agents may put their own self-interest ahead of those of the principal, an agent's decision making is more suspect when the interests of the agent and principal diverge.

Agency problems occur because of asymmetric information. If the principal knows everything an agent does, the agent would never be able to misbehave. Thus, if it were possible and not unreasonably costly to monitor the agent's actions perfectly, there would be no agency problems. But perfect monitoring, even if possible, is exorbitantly expensive. It's easier to do it yourself than constantly monitor. Without perfect monitoring, there is the problem of *moral hazard*, because agents can take actions for their benefit and to the principal's detriment. Moral hazard exists whenever agents can take unobservable actions.

Monitoring

The more monitoring there is, the harder it is for an agent to misbehave—but the extra monitoring costs money. Not all agents will take self-interested actions to the detriment of the principal, so spending too much on monitoring is wasteful. Therefore, there is a trade-off between the resources spent on monitoring and the possibility of agent misbehavior.

If a contract paid agents in perfect accord with the best interests of the principal, there would be no need for monitoring. When the agents acted in their own best financial interest, they would also be acting in the principals' best interest. But our world is not characterized by perfect accord or perfect information. Consequently, we need to search for better contracts—ones that minimize the possibility of conflicts of interest.

Agency Costs

Monitoring, constraints, incentives, and punishments are designed to push agents to act in the principals' best interests, but they are costly. These extra costs of having an agent act for a principal—those in excess of what it would cost the principals to "do it themselves"—are called *agency costs*. The costs are like friction in a machine: the more there is, the less efficient the machine is and the more energy is wasted.

Agency costs are of three types:

- Direct contracting costs, which include transaction costs for setting up the contract, such as the selling commissions and legal fees of issuing bonds; opportunity costs due to constraints that preclude otherwise optimal decisions (e.g., missing a positive-NPV investment because of a bond covenant); and incentive fees to encourage good agent behavior, such as employee bonuses

- The costs of monitoring the agent (e.g., auditing costs)

- The loss of wealth from agent misbehavior in spite of monitoring, such as wasted time

The *optimal contract* minimizes the relationship's total agency costs and transfers the decision-making authority in the most efficient way, thus providing the smallest waste. In most cases, the optimal contract entails some attention to each of the three component costs.

Debtholder-Stockholder Conflicts

In a general sense, the stockholders can be viewed as having an option against the debtholders (bondholders). The stockholders have *limited liability,* the option to default. There is always some possibility (even if extremely small) that corporate debtholders will not get the full amount promised on or before the specified due dates.

The stockholders are viewed as agents in their relationship with the debtholders (principals). There are incentive conflicts that give rise to at least three types of problems—asset substitution, underinvestment, and claim dilution—whereby shareholders may expropriate value from the debtholders. In fact, these problems can even cause a negative-NPV investment to *increase* stockholder wealth.

Asset-Substitution Problem

Firms routinely substitute assets—for example, using cash to buy materials. However, because of limited liability—the option to default—the *asset-substitution* problem occurs when stockholders replace a significant portion of the firm's existing assets with riskier assets, thereby expropriating value from the debtholders.

The total firm value is the market value of all the firm's assets. The debtholders' claim is a fixed promised amount, which is secured by this value. The debtholders will never get more than their claim, but they will get less if the firm defaults, and the chance of default increases if the risk of the firm's assets increases. A greater chance of default lowers the value of the debt. The debt value decline is a windfall for the stockholders because they are the residual claimants.

A Simplified Illustration   A firm worth $1,500 owes its debtholders $1,000. There is a 99 percent chance the debt will be fully repaid on time and a 1 percent chance the firm will default and the debtholders will get absolutely nothing. The expected value of the debt repayment is $990 (1000[0.99] + 0[.01]), and the stockholders' value is the residual $510 (1,500 − 990). If the firm substitutes its current assets for riskier assets (with the same $1,500 value), there is now a 90 percent chance of full debt repayment and a 10 percent chance of default. After the substitution, the expected value of the debt payment is only $900 (1,000[0.9]), but the stockholders' residual value has increased to $600. Here, there was no change in the firm's total value. However, even if the new assets have lower value, the stockholders gain provided it is not more than $90 lower.

Real World Example: The Green Canyon Project   Several years ago Placid Oil Co., owned by trusts of the three Hunt brothers of Dallas, sons of the legendary H. L. Hunt, defaulted on its bank loan agreement following a plunge in oil prices. Subsequently it filed for bankruptcy, hoping to stretch out its loan payments and fund its Green Canyon project, a highly risky $340 million project that was a desperate effort to find oil and gas in the Gulf of Mexico and save the business— even though Placid had not been in the drilling business. The drilling area was a hostile operating environment. In fact, the project set a world water-depth record for drilling. Also, the company used an untested technology, a one-of-a-kind floating drilling and production system. The Hunts were betting the ranch on one of the world's riskiest ventures. Understandably, the banks went to extraordinary lengths to stop the project.

Consider the situation in terms of the default option. When the firm's assets are worth less than its debt obligations, the stock is not worth much because it is like an out-of-the-money call option. The stockholders' situation is like a lottery ticket: They have a lot to gain but not much to lose. This is the essence of the asset-substitution problem in a financially distressed firm. The asset substitution (replacing an oil products distribution business with an oil exploration business) increases risk, which increases the value of the option (the firm's common stock). Certainly it was a gamble, but Placid was already bankrupt and would not be worse off if it failed and would be way ahead if it succeeded.

Eventually all three Hunt brothers' trusts and two of the Hunt brothers and their wives wound up in bankruptcy as their financial woes mounted. The Green Canyon project did not pay off, and Placid finally abandoned it. The banks did not come out as badly as they might have; they got back their principal and even some of their interest.

It could have turned out differently. Winning this big gamble would have provided enough for everyone. The problem, of course, was that the debtholders put up all the money for the gamble—even though they did not want to. The stockholders chose the gamble, without putting up any additional money. Perhaps more of us would play the lottery if we could get other people to purchase the ticket for us!

Underinvestment Problem

Underinvestment is the mirror image of the asset-substitution problem. With risky debt outstanding, the stockholders may lose value if the firm makes a low-risk investment, even if the investment has a positive NPV. As we saw in the asset-substitution problem, the stockholders gain with an increase in risk. Logically, under the same conditions, the stockholders will lose with a decrease in risk.

With underinvestment, the firm refuses a good (positive-NPV) but low-risk investment so as not to shift wealth from the stockholders to the debtholders. Despite the loss from such a risk change, stockholders can gain from an investment if it has a sufficiently large positive NPV. However, if the decrease in stockholder value from lowering the asset risk outweighs the positive NPV of the investment, stockholders will refuse to undertake the investment.

Claim Dilution

Claim dilution can occur when dividend payments or additional borrowing reduce the value of the debtholders' claims.

Claim Dilution via Dividend Policy   Paying out a large cash dividend may dilute the existing debtholders' claim because it reduces both the firm's cash and its owners' equity. Cash is a zero-risk asset, so the reduction in cash increases the average risk of the firm's remaining assets. At the same time, the equity reduction enlarges the firm's proportion of debt financing, thereby increasing the risk of the debt and reducing the value of its claim even further.

This is simply a different form of asset substitution. The substituted assets are the same except for having a smaller amount of cash. Because cash is a riskless asset, removing some of it (paying it out to stockholders) raises the average risk of the remaining assets. The increase in risk will decrease the value of the firm's outstanding debt.

Claim dilution via dividend policy is why many bond issues (and virtually all junk, or high-yield, issues) have some form of dividend restriction. Typically it limits cash dividends to a fraction of earnings or cash flow. In some cases, it may prohibit the payment of cash dividends altogether until long-term debt is repaid to some specified level.

Claim Dilution via New Debt   A substantial increase in debt may also dilute the existing debtholders' claim on the firm's assets. As with asset substitution, the increased risk (caused by dilution) decreases the value of the firm's outstanding debt.

Real World Example: RJR Nabisco's Leveraged Buyout   Several years ago RJR Nabisco's LBO increased the firm's outstanding debt from about $5.7 billion to about $23.2 billion. Following the announcement of the bid, existing RJR Nabisco bonds plunged roughly 20 percent in market value. Although the preexisting debt contract did not restrict new debt, investors had not expected any significant policy change. However, investors were rudely confronted: the firm constrained its actions only by the *explicit* debt contract.

Following the RJR Nabisco LBO, there was near turmoil in the high-grade bond market, but investors had learned an important lesson. Since then, corporate bonds routinely include debt restrictions to protect investors against such "event" risk.

Asset Uniqueness

In general, unique assets are riskier than generic assets because they are less liquid if they need to be sold. Therefore, all else equal, unique assets have a higher required return. Said another way, the collateral provided by unique assets is of lower value. Of course, assets might be highly sought after because of their uniqueness, but they also might become worthless. Using unique assets is simply a risk-return trade-off.

Working Within Contractual Relationships

There are other practical considerations that bond contracts must deal with.

Financial Distress

Financial distress can intensify goal divergence. For example, firm decisions are constrained by the bond contract. But financial distress increases incentives for asset substitution and underinvestment dramatically. It is hard to imagine Placid Oil Co. engaging in asset substitution by doing the Green Canyon Project if it had not been financially distressed!

Claimant Coalitions

Financial distress can create incentives to form stakeholder coalitions and "gang up" on one another. For example, suppose liquidation would produce the largest possible total value for a financially distressed firm. Despite this, claimants are likely to favor or oppose liquidation solely on the basis of how it would affect them. Managers, for example, may preempt liquidation by contracting with a bank for a loan to continue operations and a chance to save their jobs. Stockholders may favor or oppose such a loan, depending on whether continuing would hurt or help them. Stockholder benefit could come at a cost to the debtholders if the stockholders would get little from liquidation but a lot if the firm recovers.

The so-called S&L bailout in the 1980s became necessary because S&L managers acted in response to the extreme incentives created by financial distress. Dramatic increases in incentives and shifts in coalitions due to financial distress occur because of the options inherent in the situation. The S&Ls and their managers had little to lose and a lot to gain, a combination that created powerful incentives to take risks and engage in protracted legal battles.

Information

A financial contract is complex because it involves imperfect information. Although it would be nice if the meaning of all actions were absolutely clear, this is not the case. Interpretation can be complex and difficult. This represents a significant and ongoing asymmetric information problem.

Design of Debt Contracts

Because of the potential problems, bond indentures require the following of the borrower:

- Have its financial results prepared in accordance with generally accepted accounting principles and audited annually
- Furnish quarterly statements and evidence of bond covenant compliance

- Immediately notify lenders (or the trustee) if the firm violates any of the bond covenants, because a covenant violation is typically an event of default unless it is cured within a specified period of time

- Is specifically restricted from engaging in particular actions that might lead to asset substitution, underinvestment, and claim dilution[5]

The debtholders may also attempt legal action with respect to an existing contract, as in the case of Placid Oil's Green Canyon project. However, despite all attempts at restriction, some possibility remains that stockholders will expropriate wealth from the debtholders. The essential question is how much risk of that there is. The greater the risk is, the higher the required return. Such an increase is part of the firm's agency costs. Also, restrictions may limit more than just the targeted activities. Therefore, another agency cost is the reduction in decision-making flexibility, which could prevent the firm from making a positive-NPV decision.

Bond Covenants and Monitoring

The bond indenture affects the incentives by detailing responsibilities, constraints, punishments, and required monitoring. Covenants are designed to protect bondholder interests and are of two types: a *negative covenant*, which prohibits or limits certain actions, such as incurring more debt or paying dividends, and a *positive covenant*, which requires certain actions, such as making tax payments and providing periodic financial statements.

Bond covenants are monitoring devices that can provide an early warning of trouble. They are efficient because of the higher cost of more complete monitoring. Furthermore, even with a violation, corrective action is often possible before the problem becomes severe.

Covenant Modifications

Because bond covenants restrict flexibility and can eliminate positive-NPV investment opportunities, they can eliminate valuable options for the firm. It is possible to solicit bondholder consent to alter a restrictive covenant, but the process is cumbersome, time-consuming, and often expensive. And typically consent requires compensation—either immediate cash or an increase in the coupon rate. Finally, even if the firm gets a covenant altered, the lost time adds to the opportunity cost of that covenant. Understandably, there is a trade-off between the benefits and costs of bond covenants.

Real World Example: Seven-Up Removes a Restrictive Covenant
A few years ago, the owner of the Seven-Up Company offered a group of its bondholders the following financial incentives in return for changes in the bond indenture: (1) an immediate one-time payment of $25 per $1,000 bond, (2) an increase in the coupon rate from 12⅛ percent to 12⅜ percent for the next two and a half years, and (3) a further increase in the coupon rate to 12⅝ percent for the remaining five years of the bonds' life. At the same time, the Dr. Pepper Company offered a similar financial incentive to a group of its bondholders. The offers were in exchange for a consent to allow an LBO of each firm to form a single merged firm. The cost of the cash payment if all bondholders consented (a majority was required in each case) was $9.3 million. The increase in coupon rate, which would benefit every bondholder as long as a majority consented, amounted to $934,000 per year for the first increase and a further $934,000 per year for the second.

This is a particularly interesting example of managing *implicit* stakeholder claims. Both solicitation statements pointed out that the bondholder consents were not legally required for the planned LBO. Did this mean that the firm was paying something and getting nothing? No. The firm offered a financial incentive in exchange for explicit consent to preempt potential legal action from the bondholders. This was important because even if all protesting bondholders lost, they could have caused a costly, or even disastrous, delay.

Conversion Feature

One alternative to a particular group of restrictive bond covenants is to issue a convertible bond. The option in a convertible bond is a simple way to align stockholder and bondholder incentives. In effect, convertible bondholders are already shareholders because they will share in the upside if the firm is very successful. Smaller, younger firms often issue convertible bonds for this reason.

Monitoring

A bond indenture is a complex monitoring device because it involves imperfect information. There are a number of other potentially cost-effective monitoring devices.

New External Financing

A firm that seeks external financing gets special scrutiny, which is a form of monitoring. The firm must reveal new information. If the information is public, investors can look more closely at the firm. Even if the information is not made public, the new investors provide a form of monitoring and reassurance to existing investors by their willingness to invest their own money.

This reassurance concept is quite broad. Suppose a firm has a valuable new idea that would be damaged if it were made public, because competitors would copy it (the so-called free-rider problem). In such cases, the firm may be able to issue new securities through investment bankers that underwrite the issue.

Here is how it works. The firm explains the idea to the investment bankers now but does not make the idea public until it is marketed. With an underwritten issue, the investment bankers actually purchase the securities before reselling them to the public. Taking ownership, even for a short time, is much riskier than simply marketing the securities for a commission. Presumably investment bankers would not take this risk if they thought it was large. The investment bankers' purchase signals the market about the value of the new idea. As reputable middlemen, they can profit from their role as third-party monitor.

Other Monitoring Devices

Many elements of the financial environment serve as monitoring devices. People openly offer and seek information in the normal course of business. They also signal information through their actions. Even a firm's structure can convey information. There are other devices as well:

- *Financial statements.* Audited financial statements provide information.

- *Cash dividends.* Cash dividends provide monitoring in at least two ways. First, the failure to declare a cash dividend in the expected amount provides a warning. It may or may not be negative, but investors must determine the meaning of the deviation. Second, paying cash dividends may force the firm to seek external financing more frequently, the benefits of which we just noted.

- *Bond ratings.* Bond ratings provide monitoring at issuance and, to a lesser extent, over the bond's life.

- *Government regulation.* Numerous federal agencies, such as the IRS, SEC, and Food and Drug Administration, monitor firms for various legal and regulatory violations.

- *The entire legal system.* The legal system provides monitoring for many forms of illegal actions.

• *Reputation.* There are significant incentives to build or maintain a good reputation by providing accurate information, which facilitates monitoring.

Optimal Debt Contracts

An optimal contract balances the various agency costs against one another to minimize the total cost. Unfortunately, a contract cannot cover every possible contingency; there is no way to conceive of everything that might go wrong. In any case, dealing with every possible situation would involve tremendous time and expense. Each party must take reasonable precautions but must ultimately rely on the other parties to behave ethically and responsibly in situations not explicitly covered by the agreement. If either party behaves unethically, the contractual provisions may not prove very effective anyway.

Research on Corporate Debt Provisions

Research documents the importance of financial contracting in general and the relevance of debt provisions in particular. Among other things, empirical evidence finds significant differential wealth effects between alternative covenant packages in place at the time of a potential recapitalization and between the use of public versus private debt.

Covenants

Research documents the significant role of debt covenants across LBOs and leveraged restructurings.[6] Existing debtholders suffered an average wealth loss of 2.8 percent among forty-seven completed LBOs.[7] However, for debt with strong covenant protection, holders *gained* an average of 2.6 percent, whereas for debt with little or no covenant protection, holders lost an average of 5.2 percent. And bonds with strong covenant protection were more frequently retired, *defeased* (see chapter 13), secured, or renegotiated. Finally, the retired debt realized an average 5.8 percent excess gain, whereas debt that remained outstanding realized an average 5.9 percent excess loss. In another sample of LBO candidates, debtholders suffered an average wealth loss of 6.5 percent when the debt contained neither a dividend restriction nor a leverage restriction.[8] Holders of bonds that were downgraded to speculative-grade as a result of leveraged restructurings also suffered significant average losses: 7.77 percent during the six-month period preceding the event and 11.83 percent from issue to the event.[9]

In late 1988, many debt issues began to include *super poison put* covenants,[10] which allow debtholders to sell their debt back to the issuer at par value if any one of certain specified events occurs—for example, an LBO or a credit-rating downgrade to the speculative-grade range. Covenant structures also changed in apparent response to other events. During a period of high interest rates, many utility companies began exploiting the maintenance and replacement (M&R) fund provision as a means of refunding otherwise noncallable debt.[11] After several instances, a restriction on this tactic became common to prevent bondholder loss from an unexpected redemption at a below-market price.[12]

The M&R fund redemption is also interesting because many investors were apparently unaware of the possibility.[13] The idea of the M&R fund covenant was to protect bondholders by maintaining the value of the collateral securing their bonds. But the covenant was imperfectly crafted. Such cases emphasize the practical significance and difficulties of financial contracting, as well as the dynamic and sometimes evolving nature of the process.

In other cases, covenants have inadvertently hurt the firm.[14] The Burlington Northern Railroad Company had two issues of mortgage bonds that were secured by railroad, mineral, and timber properties; were noncallable; had no sinking fund; had no way to amend the indenture; and required proceeds from the sale of properties to be used either to redeem bonds (up to $500,000 per year) or to extend or maintain the railroad properties. The unintended consequence was that revenues from the sale of mineral or timber properties could not be used to purchase additional mineral deposits or timberland. The firm finally got a release of certain mineral and timber properties from the collateral pool in 1987 by paying bondholders $35.5 million (about 30 percent of the principal). The announcement of the settlement produced an excess return to the firm's stock of 9.5 percent—an aggregate market value increase of $475 million.[15]

Covenants can significantly affect a new debt issue's credit rating.[16] Stronger restrictions result in a higher credit rating and lower borrowing costs. But stronger restrictions can also reduce flexibility and impose opportunity costs. Not surprisingly, empirical evidence shows the trade-off between (1) lower direct borrowing costs and positive agency costs and (2) the opportunity costs and negative agency costs connected with a covenant package.

Debt Maturity

Several factors affect a firm's choice of debt maturity structure. Three hypotheses offer contributing explanations for the maturity structure of corporate debt: the costly-contracting hypothesis, the signaling hypothesis, and the tax hypothesis. These hypotheses are not mutually exclusive, and there is empirical evidence supporting the first two.[17]

The Costly-Contracting Hypothesis

Existing bondholders benefit from a profitable investment if it increases the chances of full payment, which can create an underinvestment problem. This problem can be controlled by borrowing less, including restrictive covenants in the firm's bond indenture, or using shorter-maturity debt. For example, the underinvestment problem disappears if the debt matures before the option to invest must be exercised. This implies that firms with more growth opportunities should employ shorter-maturity debt.[18] Other factors also affect the debt maturity choice.

Issuance costs for public debt involve economies of scale. Small firms, unable to take advantage of such economies, typically opt for private placements, which have lower fixed costs.[19] Larger, less risky firms are more likely to issue debt publicly.[20] Privately placed debt (including bank loans) has a shorter average maturity than public debt.[21] Together these results imply that smaller firms have shorter-maturity debt than large firms.

Regulated firms have less discretion over future investment decisions than unregulated firms do. Assuming reduced discretion helps control the underinvestment problem, regulated firms will issue longer-maturity debt than unregulated firms will.[22]

Riskier firms may benefit proportionately more from restrictive covenants.[23] Of course, covenants create enforcement and monitoring costs.[24] However, private lenders appear to have a comparative advantage in monitoring, and so the riskiest debt will be privately placed. Therefore, since bank loans and privately placed debt have shorter maturities than public debt, riskier firms will have shorter-maturity debt.

Another tool for controlling the underinvestment problem is to issue secured debt and other fixed claims with high priority.[25] However, even if short-term and long-term debt have the same security and legal priority, short-term debt has a higher effective priority because it is paid first.[26] Thus, short-term debt offers the same sort of benefits as secured debt.

The Signaling Hypothesis

The value of long-term debt is more sensitive than the value of short-term debt to changes in firm value. Consequently, if bond investors cannot distinguish between high-quality and low-quality firms, higher-quality firms will prefer to issue the less underpriced, short-term debt, whereas lower-quality firms will prefer to issue the more overpriced, long-term debt.[27] Bond investors will take these incentives into account when pricing risky corporate debt. In equilibrium, higher-quality firms will issue more short-term debt and lower-quality firms will issue more long-term debt.

Firms with favorable private information about their future prospects will prefer to issue short-term debt.[28] However, short-term debt exposes the firm to the risk of liquidation because lenders may be reluctant to refinance the debt if bad news arrives. This creates a trade-off between (1) the possible benefits from a future improvement in the firm's credit rating and (2) the possible loss from an inability to obtain refinancing. The highest-quality firms issue short-term debt because they are confident they will be able to refinance. Medium-quality firms issue long-term debt. Low-quality firms issue medium-term debt because they are unable to borrow on a long-term basis but want to limit their refinancing risk.

The Tax Hypothesis

If a firm can default on its debt contract, then whenever the term structure of interest rates is upward sloping, the expected value of the firm's tax liabilities is larger for long-term debt.[29] Also, when the tax structure includes a capital-gains tax-timing option, firms will prefer a longer maturity for their debt, even if there is no other tax advantage to debt financing.[30] Taken together, these factors suggest that tax considerations generally bias a firm toward longer-maturity debt, all else equal.

Realized Debt Maturity

The realized maturity of a debt instrument can differ from its stated maturity for many reasons, contractual and otherwise. Contractual possibilities include the exercise of a call option, sinking-fund payments, open-market repurchases, and tender offers. Noncontractual reasons include reorganization, default, or liquidation. Because of such possibilities, measures such as *duration* or some form of average maturity are used. For example, the possibility of default shortens a bond's expected maturity. This means that between two otherwise identical bonds (including identical stated maturity), the riskier bond has a shorter effective maturity and will therefore be less sensitive to interest rate changes.[31]

Debt payments are like a series of options with implicitly extendable maturities because assets are rarely turned over to the debtholders in any simple manner. Instead, reorganization, which provides an extension of maturity, is the norm. Therefore, a model with extendable and retractable maturities may offer insights into the choice of debt maturity, including the interaction of the sinking fund whereby default on a sinking-fund payment can, in effect, *retract* the maturity of the entire debt issue.[32]

Controlling Agency Costs

Bond issuers apparently use debt provisions to control agency costs arising from asymmetric information.[33] In particular, in a relatively more (less) symmetrically informed market, firms are likely to issue longer-maturity (comparatively shorter-maturity) debt.[34] In addition, average debt maturity is positively related to firm size, financial leverage, liquidity, and expenditures on research and development and negatively related to advertising expenditures.

Recent Evidence

Recent evidence finds that large, investment-grade (BBB or better) firms issued only 45 percent medium-term (five to twenty-nine years) and relatively more short-term (39 percent, four years or less) and long-term (16 percent, thirty years or more) debt. In contrast, 97 percent of the issues by speculative-grade firms were medium-term debt.[35] This is consistent with the signaling hypothesis.[36]

Figure 5.2 shows the average term to maturity of corporate debt issues between 1982 and 1993, with and without medium-term notes and Euronotes. Average maturity decreased during this period as short-term public debt issues replaced bank borrowings.[37]

Table 5.2 provides the distribution of new debt issues by issue type across bond ratings. Secured bonds are mostly investment-grade. Equity-linked debt is issued largely by speculative-grade firms, consistent with their greater agency costs. Medium-term notes are mostly investment-grade, reflecting investment-grade issuers' substitution of short-term public debt issues for bank borrowings. Finally, Eurobonds and Euronotes are issued predominantly by investment-grade firms, which are higher quality and well known to foreign investors. There have been periods when higher-quality firms have been able to borrow more cheaply in the Eurodollar market than in the domestic market because of clientele effects.[38]

Figure 5.2 Mean Term to Maturity for Corporate Debt Issues, 1982–1993

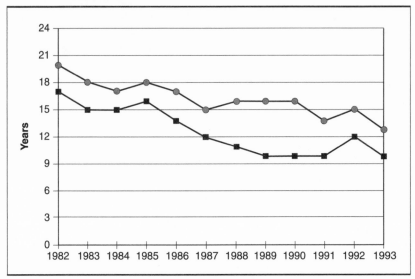

Source: Jose Guedes and Tim Opler, "The Determinants of the Maturity of Corporate Debt Issues," *Journal of Finance* 51 (December 1996), p. 1818.

Sinking Funds

A sinking fund shortens the debt's maturity and may play a role in controlling the agency costs of debt. Firms facing more severe agency problems with their debt (firms with greater growth rates, leverage ratios, dividend payout ratios, debt maturities, and smaller profit ratios and asset lives) are more likely to include a sinking fund.[39] Firms financing in a relatively more symmetrically informed market are more likely to use longer-maturity debt but include a sinking fund, whereas firms financing in a relatively less symmetrically informed market are more likely to use shorter-maturity (medium-term) debt with or without a sinking fund.[40]

Differences in Sinking-Fund Provisions

Beyond its inclusion, there can be significant differences among sinking-fund provisions. For example, the market charges a slightly higher rate for the added flexibility of the *funnel* versus the more common *specific* sinking-fund provision.[41] Also, an *indexed sinking-fund debenture* can help with managing differences in asset and liability interest rate sensitivity, especially in connection with mortgages, because the sinking-fund payments vary with interest rates.[42]

Table 5.2 Distribution of New Debt Issues by Issue Type Across Bond Ratings, 1982–1993

Issue Type	AAA	AA	A	BBB	BB	B	CCC	Unrated	Mean Term to Maturity (Years)
Straight debt	98	386	890	531	153	362	18	49	15
Secured bonds[a]	39	284	446	220	14	17	0	7	
Equity linked[b]	6	17	68	91	140	298	23	136	
Medium-term notes	40	313	964	477	23	1	0	26	4
Euronotes/bonds[c]	83	202	157	21	7	2	0	9	

Source: Jose Guedes and Tim Opler, "The Determinants of the Maturity of Corporate Debt Issues," *Journal of Finance* 51 (December 1996), p. 1820.

[a]Includes mortgage bonds and equipment trust certificates.

[b]Includes convertible bonds, liquid yield option notes (zero-coupon convertible bonds), and bonds issued with warrants.

[c]Includes foreign notes and bonds.

Reduction in Agency Costs

A sinking fund can be viewed as an additional monitoring device. Changes in debt-service obligations and dividends can convey useful information about the firm.[43] The sinking fund precommits additional cash flows—well beyond the interest—so the firm must take visible actions if it is not doing sufficiently well. Furthermore, the sinking-fund payments could have supported substantially more debt if they were instead used to pay interest. So the firm is borrowing less money than it could based on its cash flow.

Designing a Long-Term Debt Issue: Some Practical Considerations

A potential issuer first chooses the type of debt. Then it must decide on the features.

Choosing Debt Maturity

A firm should choose a debt maturity that aligns its total debt service stream (for all its debt) with its projected total operating cash flow stream (for all its assets). A repayment schedule that bunches obligations involves greater risk of trouble making the required payments. However, the matching does not have to be exact. For example, a rapidly growing or improving firm may issue some short-maturity debt so it naturally reconfigures its debt after the growth or improvement.

Including a Sinking Fund

A sinking fund provides monitoring and reduces the effective maturity. Therefore, *average life* is a better measure of the time the debt will be outstanding than stated maturity:

$$\text{Average life} = \sum_{t=1}^{N} t \times A_t \Big/ \sum_{t=1}^{N} A_t$$

A_t is the sinking-fund payment due t periods from issue. N is the stated maturity. A_t is positive when a sinking-fund payment is due and zero otherwise. Average life is the weighted average time of the principal payments (with $A_t/\Sigma A_t$ as the weights).

For example, a debt issue that matures in ten years requires five equal sinking-fund payments at the end of years 6 through 10. Its average life is eight years:

Average life = 6(0.2) + 7(0.2) + 8(0.2) + 9(0.2) + 10 (0.2) = 8 years

Duration

Market professionals often adjust this calculation. They calculate the present value of all payments, interest as well as principal, and use these present values as the weights. The resulting measure, *duration*, is often preferred to average life and stated maturity:

$$\text{Duration} = \frac{1}{P} \sum_{t=1}^{N} t\, CF(t)/(1+y)^t$$

where P is the bond price, $CF(t)$ is the interest plus principal cash flow from the bond at t, and y is the bond's yield to maturity (YTM) expressed per period (e.g., with semiannual interest payments, y is YTM/2). Duration is the present-value-weighted-average time of all the payments.

For example, a ten-year $100 million bond issue pays a 10 percent coupon rate semiannually and requires sinking-fund payments of $20 million each at the end of years 6 through 10. The yield to maturity is 9 percent, and its price is $106.504 million.

To determine the bond's duration, first calculate the cash flows. There are twenty interest periods. For the first eleven periods, the bond pays interest only, so $CF(1) = CF(2) =, \ldots, = CF(11) = \$5$ million. The bond pays principal at the end of period 12, so $CF(12) = \$25$ million. $CF(13) = \$4$ million, $CF(14) = \$24$ million, and so forth. Using the equation, duration equals 5.67 years:

$$\text{Duration} = \frac{1}{106.504} \sum_{t=1}^{20} \frac{t\, CF(t)}{(1.045)^t}$$

$$= \frac{1}{106.504} \left[\frac{1(5)}{1.045} + \frac{2(5)}{(1.045)^2} + \ldots + \frac{11(5)}{(1.045)^{11}} + \frac{12(25)}{(1.045)^{12}} \right.$$

$$+ \frac{13(4)}{(1.045)^{13}} + \frac{14(24)}{(1.045)^{14}} + \frac{15(3)}{(1.045)^{15}} + \frac{16(23)}{(1.045)^{16}}$$

$$\left. + \frac{17(2)}{(1.045)^{17}} + \frac{18(22)}{(1.045)^{18}} + \frac{19(1)}{(1.045)^{19}} + \frac{20(21)}{(1.045)^{20}} \right]$$

$$= 11.34 \text{ periods} = 5.67 \text{ years}$$

Duration gives a better measure of the average timing of the bond's total cash flows.

Pricing a New Debt Issue

To determine the coupon rate required for a bond with a sinking fund, investment bankers use average life or duration rather than its maturity. Graphs like figure 5.1 are based on average life or duration.

Maximum Maturity

Generally a finite maturity is required for interest to be tax deductible. However, within the past decade, there have been forty-, fifty-, and even hundred-year bond maturities, such as Coca-Cola's 1993 hundred-year debentures. Such debt with very long maturity can be used to increase the average life of a firm's total debt portfolio and improve the alignment of its debt and operating cash flows.

Setting the Coupon Rate

Most issuers of debt select a coupon rate that will make the bonds worth par. However, at times asymmetric taxes or asymmetric information can make it advantageous either to use a lower coupon rate or let the rate float according to some specified formula.

The yield curve for debt with a particular rating indicates the appropriate rate for a bond with that credit risk and any particular average life. Refer back to figure 5.1, which shows required yields on nonredeemable single-A-rated industrial bonds with maturities between three months and thirty years. To issue new single-A-rated industrial bonds with an average life of ten years as of June 30, 2000, would have required a 7.78 percent yield to maturity.

Deep-Discount Bonds

In 1981 and 1982, interest rates were very high by historical standards. Many firms issued deep-discount bonds, which had very low yields and sold at prices well below par. For example, DuPont sold $600 million principal amount of 6 percent debentures due 2001 at price 46.852 percent ($468.52 per $1,000 bond) on November 19, 1981. Zero-coupon bonds have the deepest possible discount. Beatrice Foods sold $250 million principal amount of zero-coupon notes due February 9, 1992, at a price of 25.50 percent on February 2, 1982.

Some investors find deep-discount bonds and zero-coupon bonds particularly attractive. The discount reduces the lender's reinvestment risk because the "income" each period is effectively reinvested at the yield to maturity, regardless of what interest rates are at that time. In addition, many issues were effectively noncallable, which further protected the investor's total return from interest rate movements between the dates of issuance and maturity. They also help investors, such as pension funds, to match their investment income with future liabilities better.

Issuers also found the deep-discount bonds and zero-coupon bonds particularly attractive because of a tax asymmetry. Until May 1982, issuers were permitted to deduct an equal portion of the discount (the difference between par value and the issue price) each period. Thus, interest could be deducted at a faster rate than it accrued, which substantially reduced the effective after-tax cost of the debt. Because most purchasers of zero-coupon bonds were tax exempt, the manner of amortizing the discount did not affect them.

Fixing the Coupon Rate or Letting It Float

Firms such as banks and financial firms, whose return on assets fluctuates with interest rate movements, often find it best to issue floating-rate long-term debt. Most other firms choose to fix the interest rate on long-term debt issues. They adjust their overall mix of fixed- and floating-rate debt by altering the mix of floating-rate short-term debt and fixed-rate longer-term debt. Before deciding whether to issue floating-rate long-term debt, a firm should at least compare the prospective terms for such an issue to the alternatives of (1) issuing a sequence of shorter-term issues, whose successive maturities match the successive interest-rate-adjustment dates, or (2) issuing fixed-rate debt because of maturity-matching considerations.

In the first case, the sequence of shorter-term issues will involve roughly the same degree of interest rate risk as the longer-term floating-rate issue. The sequence of shorter-term issues will involve greater issuance expenses than the longer-term floating-rate issue. But the issuer can benefit by refinancing at a lower interest rate if its credit situation improves. In the second case, the fixed-rate issue does not expose the issuer to the risk that interest rates will change. Therefore, it is not surprising that industrial firms generally borrow long term on a fixed-rate basis to fund investments in fixed assets. By contrast, when the issuer's revenues are sensitive to movements in interest rates, borrowing on a floating-rate basis may actually reduce the firm's financial risk by aligning the fluctuations in revenues and interest expense.

For example, Bankers Trust issued $500 million face amount of Global Floating Rate Notes due 2003 on May 11, 1998.[44] The notes pay interest quarterly on February 11, May 11, August 11, and November 11, at a rate equal to the 3-month LIBOR, plus a spread of 0.10 percent.

The issuer is a bank holding company whose principal subsidiary is Bankers Trust, a major money center bank the bulk of whose assets are interest rate sensitive. Thus, issuing floating-rate notes was consistent with good asset-liability management.

Conclusion

A bond is a contract between the borrower and the lenders. The bond contract specifies the maturity, interest rate, redemption features, any call or put options, and all the other terms of the debt issue. Research documents the importance of financial contracting considerations. As we shall see in later chapters, the design of the debt issue determines the pattern of cash flows required to service and retire the debt. The design determines the issue's expected cost and whether the realized cost will be higher or lower than the cost expected at the time of issue. Therefore, an issuer should design a new debt issue carefully because it may have to live with any mistakes for a long time, or worse, they could turn out to be exorbitantly expensive.

Chapter **6**

Institutional
Considerations

The purchase or sale of a debt security can give rise to important tax consequences that can be complex, especially when the debt security changes hands at a large premium or discount. The accounting can also be complex, especially when the debt instrument is a derivative. The accounting rules that apply to debt securities and derivatives have undergone significant revisions in recent years, and they could change further in the future.

Bond refundings are potentially even more complex because issuing new bonds and retiring old bonds each has unique tax and accounting effects. Moreover, the tax and accounting effects depend on the refunding structure.

Issuers and investors carefully consider the tax and accounting consequences of the available alternatives and base their decisions on the after-tax cost of debt and the after-tax yield, respectively, rather than on the pretax values. Therefore, a refunding analysis expresses the cash flows and discount rates on an after-tax basis. We will explain how to do this and in the process note that the Internal Revenue Code favors high-coupon bond refunding.

Issuers also consider the accounting consequences of a refunding. However, the reported gain or loss is simply the difference between the old and new bonds' book values adjusted for any related tax effects. This accounting "gain" or "loss" does not measure the value of a bond refunding; in many cases, the refunding creates a positive NPV and simultaneously reduces reported net income.

This chapter provides an overview of the tax and accounting consequences of issuing new debt and refunding outstanding debt. It

117

discusses the most important provisions and highlights some of the ways in which the design of new issues or refunding structure can affect the tax and accounting treatments and points out the significant impact of taxes and accounting considerations on these decisions. Debt decisions, like other corporate decisions, should promote shareholder wealth maximization. Accordingly, the impact on the amount and timing of tax payments is usually very important, whereas the impact on accounting statements is not normally so important. Nevertheless, in practice, many public companies seem to allow the window dressing considerations of accounting statements to influence managerial decisions.

Taxation of Debt Instruments

Interest is taxed as ordinary income to the recipient and deducted from ordinary income by the payer. During the past thirty years, the Internal Revenue Code has undergone a series of changes designed to measure interest income more accurately and thereby bring the taxation of interest into line with what is called the *pure accretion tax model*.[1] A major focus of this effort has been the tax treatment of discount bonds and loans: taxing not only the coupon rate of interest but also the accrual of interest that is implicit in the discount.

Original Issue Discount and Market Discount

The value of debt is less than its face amount if interest payments are less than the required return (the market yield on comparable risk and maturity bonds). Bonds may be issued with a below-market coupon, which gives rise to *original issue discount* (OID). Purchasing for less than face amount a bond that was originally issued at par gives rise to *market discount*.[2] An investor who buys a bond at a discount will realize the OID or market discount over the life of the bond. However, the taxation of OID differs from the taxation of market discount.

Tax rules require investors to include in each year's taxable income the implied interest from an OID bond based on its annualized yield to maturity, called the *constant-yield method*. In effect, it is as though the bond paid interest at the yield to maturity, with the noncash portion of each year's interest automatically reinvested. This amortization of the OID increases the investor's taxable income.

Bonds that are issued at par, or at prices near par, do not give rise to OID at issue. In general, to avoid OID, the discount must be no greater than one-quarter of 1 percent multiplied by the number of years to maturity. For example, for a twenty-year bond, only a discount greater than 5 percent must be amortized.

The tax code does not require the accrual of market discount. At maturity, there is a gain equal to the amount of the discount at purchase, which is treated as ordinary income when the bonds are sold or redeemed.[3]

Premium Bonds

Tax law also allows a mirror image amortization of the premium on *premium bonds*, whose coupon rate exceeds their required return. Amortization of the premium reduces the investor's taxable income. Investors can elect to amortize the premium over the remaining life of the bond, whether it was purchased at issue or in the secondary market. Amortization must be calculated using the constant-yield method as for discount bonds.

The constant-yield method is intuitively appealing. During each interest period, taxable interest income from the combination of cash payment and implied interest accrual of discount (or minus accrual of premium) equals the true interest income. Under reasonable assumptions, the method is in perfect accord with the so-called pure accretion tax model.[4]

Illustration of Original Issue Discount

Consider a new ten-year 8 percent coupon bond with a face amount of $1,000 and a yield to maturity of 10.00 percent, so its issue price is $877.11.[5] The OID accrual formula is

$$AA = YTM \times TB - C \qquad (6.1)$$

where AA is the accrual amount, YTM is the yield to maturity, TB is the tax basis at the beginning of the year (which accretes over the life of the bond), and C is the coupon rate. The formula assumes annual OID accruals.[6]

Each year the accrued amount adds to income, is taxed, and is "reinvested," so the value (tax basis) grows by the "reinvested" amount and interest grows in the following year by a corresponding amount.[7] Notice that the interest accrual process has allocated the entire OID: $122.89 ($1,000 − $877.11). At the end of year 10, the tax basis has risen to equal the face amount exactly, which is also the redemption amount (before interest) (see table 6.1).

Table 6.1 Illustration of Accrual of OID Under the Constant-Yield Method (10-year bond; issued at $877.11; annual coupon is $80.00; face amount is $1,000.00; and yield to maturity is 10.00%)

Year	Beginning-of-Year Tax Basis	Interest Earned	Interest Payment	Amount Accrued	End-of-Year Tax Basis
1	$877.11	$87.81	$80.00	$ 7.71	$ 884.82
2	884.82	88.48	80.00	8.48	893.30
3	893.30	89.33	80.00	9.33	902.63
4	902.63	90.27	80.00	10.27	912.90
5	912.90	91.29	80.00	11.29	924.19
6	924.19	92.42	80.00	12.42	936.61
7	936.61	93.66	80.00	13.66	950.27
8	950.27	95.02	80.00	15.02	965.29
9	965.29	96.53	80.00	16.53	981.82
10	981.82	98.18	80.00	18.18	1,000.00

Subsequent Transactions

Complexity arises when an investor purchases a bond with OID in the secondary market at a price that differs from the bond's tax basis. There are three separate cases to consider:

- If the purchase price exceeds the face amount, the OID does not have to be accrued. In the preceding example, this situation would occur if the required return fell below 8 percent.

- If the purchase price is less than the bond's face amount but exceeds the bond's tax basis,[8] the future OID accrual decreases. The new OID accruals are calculated as in table 6.1, treating the bond as though it had just been issued at the purchase price. Suppose the bond in table 6.1 is sold for $975 at the end of year 5. The original purchaser's gain is $50.81 ($975.00 − $924.19), which is taxed as a capital gain. The purchaser accrues OID as though he or she had bought a five-year 8 percent bond for $975. The new OID accruals are related to the old OID accruals approximately in the proportion:

$$\frac{\text{Face amount} - \text{Purchase price}}{\text{Face amount} - \text{Tax basis at purchase}} \qquad (6.2)$$

In the example, the OID accruals in years 6 through 10 are a fraction of the amounts shown in table 6.1: ($1,000.00 − $975.00) / ($1,000.00 − $924.19) = 0.3298.[9]

- If the purchase price is below the bond's tax basis, the OID accruals do not change, and the difference is treated as market discount, which is taxed at the time of sale or redemption in the manner described below.

Market Discount

If a bond is issued at a premium or at par and is subsequently purchased at a discount, the bond becomes a *market discount bond*. The tax code does not require the investor to amortize market discount, but when the bond is sold or redeemed, it treats an allocated portion of market discount as ordinary income rather than capital gain. If the bond is sold prior to maturity, the portion of the discount that would have accrued under the constant-yield method must be included in ordinary income.

Suppose the bond in table 6.1 was a fifteen-year bond originally issued at par but fell in price and was purchased for $877.11 with ten years remaining to maturity. Suppose the investor subsequently sells the bond for $950 at the end of year 5. The amount of accrued discount for years 1 through 5 is $47.08 ($7.71 + $8.48 + $9.33 + $10.27 + $11.29). The investor's gain is $72.89 ($950.00 − $877.11), of which $47.08 is taxed as ordinary income and $25.81 ($72.89 − $47.08) is taxed as capital gain.

Market Discount with OID Bonds

When an investor buys an OID bond at a price that is less than the bond's tax basis, the difference is again market discount. As with non-OID bonds, market discount can cause some of the gain on sale or redemption to be treated as ordinary income rather than capital gain. Calculating the taxable gain and the allocation between ordinary income and capital gain is more complicated for OID bonds than for non-OID bonds, but the tax principle is the same: Market discount is amortized over the bond's remaining life, and upon sale or redemption any gain must be allocated first to the amortized portion of market discount and included in ordinary income.

Suppose the bond in table 6.1 was purchased after five years for $900. Thus, there is $24.19 ($924.19 − $900.00) of market discount, which must be amortized over the last five years. Treat $924.19, the OID tax basis of the bond, as the face amount, and use $900.00 as the

Table 6.2 Accrual of Market Discount Under the Constant-Yield
Method (5 years until maturity; coupon is 8%; redemption
value is $924.19; annual interest is $73.9352; purchase price
is $900.00; and yield to maturity is 8.667%)

Year	Amount Accrued	Total Accrual to Date
1	$4.07	$4.07
2	4.42	8.49
3	4.80	13.29
4	5.22	18.51
5	5.68	24.19

purchase price. The constant yield implied by the purchase price is
8.667 percent. Table 6.2 shows the market discount accrual based on
this yield. Suppose the investor sells the bond two years later for
$975.00. The OID tax basis of the bond at that time is $950.27 (see table
6.1) because the investor has had to report the OID accruals based on
the original schedule as income for the two years the bond was
owned.[10] The gain on sale is $24.73 ($975.00 − $950.27). Table 6.2 indi-
cates that during the two-year holding period, $8.49 of market discount
accrued. Thus, $8.49 of the investor's gain is ordinary income, and the
remaining $16.24 ($24.73 − $8.49) is capital gain.

Premium Bonds

The bondholder can elect to amortize the premium (new issue, or
market) over the remaining life of the bond. A taxable investor would
normally find this advantageous because the amortization amount
reduces taxable income. The amortization method is the same constant-
yield method that applies to OID. Table 6.3 illustrates the parallel treatment of the amortization of original issue premium.

The bond in table 6.3, like the bond in table 6.1, matures in ten
years and yields 10 percent, but its coupon is 12 percent and its price is
$1,122.89. The amortization formula is

$$PA = C - YTM \times TB \qquad (6.3)$$

where PA is the accrual amount and C, YTM, and TB are the same as in
equation 6.1. The total premium, $122.89, is allocated to years 1
through 10, and the tax basis of the bond at maturity equals the
redemption value, $1,000.

Table 6.3 Amortization of a Bond Premium Under the Constant-Yield Method (10-year bond; issued at $1,122.89, annual coupon is $120.00; face amount is $1,000; and yield to maturity is 10.00%)

Year	Beginning-of-Year Tax Basis	Interest Earned	Interest Payment	Amount Amortized	End-of-Year Tax Basis
1	$1,122.89	$112.29	$120.00	$ 7.71	$1,115.18
2	1,115.18	111.52	120.00	8.48	1,106.70
3	1,106.70	110.67	120.00	9.33	1,097.37
4	1,097.37	109.73	120.00	10.27	1,087.10
5	1,087.10	108.71	120.00	11.29	1,075.81
6	1,075.81	107.58	120.00	12.42	1,063.39
7	1,063.39	106.34	120.00	13.66	1,049.73
8	1,049.73	104.98	120.00	15.02	1,034.71
9	1,034.71	103.47	120.00	16.53	1,018.18
10	1,018.18	101.82	120.00	18.18	1,000.00

Tax-Trading Strategies

Interest is not taxed according to the pure accretion tax model, and investors have flexibility in timing the recognition of capital gains and losses—so-called tax-timing options that give rise to potentially profitable tax-trading strategies. One study has found that the value of the tax-timing options represented between 3.05 percent and 11.55 percent of the prices of bonds issued at close to par, between 1.42 percent and 4.93 percent of the prices of bonds issued at a moderate discount, and between 4.23 percent and 13.45 percent of the prices of zero-coupon bonds, depending on the investor's tax situation.[11] The tax-trading benefits for deep-discount bonds are due principally to the OID rules; the OID rules make deeper-discount bonds more valuable because of the tax-timing options and related trading strategies to which they give rise. This suggests that the OID rule revisions have not eliminated the tax bias in favor of discount bonds.

Tax trading is more beneficial for long maturities because their greater volatility makes the tax-timing options more valuable. Therefore, tax trading tends to skew the yield curve in favor of longer maturities.

Debt Maturity and the Tax Deductibility of Interest

The Internal Revenue Code requires that a bond either have a stated maturity date or else give bondholders the right to force redemption (i.e., a put option) on a stated date in order for the issuer to deduct the interest payments for tax purposes. Some foreign jurisdictions allow tax deductibility even for perpetual bonds. In 1995, after U.S. firms began issuing fifty-year and hundred-year bonds, the Treasury Department proposed eliminating the tax deduction for interest on greater-than-forty-year bonds, but it did not become law. As a result, very long-dated bonds still generate tax deductions, but the law is subject to change. If it does change, issuers will undoubtedly adjust the maturity of their new issues to preserve the tax deductibility of interest.[12]

Taxation of Debt with Contingent Payments

Debt instruments with contingent payments challenge a tax system that is designed to tax income on an annual basis if the contingency is not resolved before the end of the tax year. Suppose that a ten-year note pays interest at a stated rate every six months and in addition makes a single payment at maturity based on any appreciation in the Standard & Poor's 500 Index since the note was issued. Each year the holder receives an interest payment, but the actual return, and the issuer's cost of debt, cannot be determined accurately until the notes mature and the value of the contingent payment can be determined. Nevertheless, the tax law must provide rules for determining the investor's annual interest income and the issuer's annual interest expense. A commonsense approach would be to tax interest as it accrues and to tax the contingent payment at maturity. The IRS tried four times to issue tax regulations governing contingent debt before finally settling on some very complex regulations.[13]

The IRS adopted the most recent regulations governing contingent-payment debt in July 1996. They require the accrual of interest on the entire issue price of a contingent-payment debt instrument, using market information to determine a "reasonable" interest rate for accruing interest taking into account the contingent payment. In effect, the market information suggests a reasonable expectation concerning the amount of the contingent payment.

Computations occur at three stages:

1. At issuance, a hypothetical debt instrument is constructed with a yield equal to a comparable non-contingent debt instrument of the issuer. If the contingent payment can be tied to the forward price of a market-traded instrument,[14] then the forward price should be

used to "fix" the contingent payment for the purpose of specifying the hypothetical debt payment schedule. If the contingent payment cannot be tied to any forward price, the projected payments on the hypothetical instrument must be based on expected values. In either case, the payments may need to be adjusted to provide the required yield. If the projected contingent-payment amounts plus the scheduled redemption payments exceed the purchase price, then the debt instrument involves OID. The OID allocation rules are complex in this case because each contingent payment may give rise to OID. The payment schedule that shows all the fixed payments of principal and interest and all contingent-payment amounts is used throughout the life of the investment to calculate interest deductions and interest income.

2. When a contingent payment turns out to be more (less) than the projected amount, the holder's interest income and the issuer's interest expense are increased (decreased). If the decrease exceeds the current year's interest income or expense, the additional amount is an ordinary loss for the holder and ordinary income for the issuer. Buying a contingent-payment debt instrument at a different price from the OID tax basis means dealing with tax rules for OID, market discount, and contingent payments. The tax complexity can be a significant disincentive for investing in such instruments.

3. Any gain from sale or redemption of the instrument is interest income, not capital gain, and this holds even if the gain is due to favorable changes in interest rates or the issuer's credit rating. This is to prevent a holder from converting interest income into capital gain when the contingent payment is much larger than originally expected by selling the instrument just before the payment becomes fixed. Any loss is an ordinary loss until the entire interest income is eliminated; any loss beyond that is a capital loss.

The contingent-payment tax regulations do not apply to either traditional convertible securities or what the IRS terms *variable debt*. To qualify as variable debt, an instrument must provide for stated interest, payable or compounded at least annually, based on one of the following rates:

- *Qualified floating rate.* Changes in the value of the interest rate must reasonably be expected to track market interest rates in the debt's denominated currency. Caps or floors are permitted.

- *Objective rate.* The interest rate must use a single formula that incorporates qualified floating rates, yield or price changes in a traded security, or changes in a qualified index or economic variable.

- *Qualified inverse floating rate.* Changes in the value of the interest rate must reasonably be expected to track market interest rates in the debt's denominated currency but the interest rate rises (falls) when the market rates fall (rise).

The IRS regulations permit variable debt to have a limited amount of contingent principal and still qualify.

Generally it is better to avoid the complexity of the contingent-payment-debt rules by using convertibility or a floating rate to qualify for simpler tax rules.

Taxation of Dividends

Seventy percent of the dividends (on common or preferred stock) a corporation receives from an unaffiliated corporation are not taxed. As a result, the receiving corporation's tax rate on dividend income is effectively 10.5 percent (30 percent of the 35 percent statutory federal corporate tax rate). This tax rule is usually an important consideration in designing preferred stock instruments because the return on preferred stock comes primarily from its dividends.

In chapter 14 we describe a sequence of innovations designed to create a preferred stock substitute for high-grade debt. Such substitutes exploit a tax arbitrage that arises when a non-tax-paying corporation sells preferred stock to tax-paying unaffiliated corporations that claim the dividends-received deduction. Both sides can benefit. The dividend rate can be lower than the pre-tax interest rate on similar debt to benefit the issuer, while investors realize a higher after-tax return.

General Tax Consequences of a Bond Refunding

Taxes affect the profitability of refunding high-coupon and low-coupon debt. Current tax law generally favors refunding high-coupon debt by allowing the issuer to deduct the call premium and disfavors refunding low-coupon debt because it taxes the "gain."

All of the expenses connected with a refunding can be deducted either in the year of the refunding or over the life of the new issue. The basic rule is that expenses connected with retiring the old issue may be deducted in the year of the refunding and the expenses connected with the new issue must be amortized over its remaining life.

The High-Coupon Case

The following expenses are deductible in the year of a high-coupon refunding:

- The call premium.

- The old debt's unamortized balance of issuance expenses plus original issue discount (or minus original issue premium).

- Legal fees, printing costs, and fees paid to the trustee for canceling the old bonds.

- Overlapping interest when the new bonds are sold before the old bonds are retired. This represents the difference between the investment return from, and the interest cost of, having both issues outstanding in the time after issuing the new bonds and before retiring the old bonds. If the investment return exceeds the interest cost, the surplus is taxable.

The expenses of new issues, including any discount or premium, must be amortized over the life of the new issue. If a discount or premium is an OID or new issue premium, its amortization is as described previously in this chapter.

The Low-Coupon Case

Nearly all tax effects are the same in both low-coupon and high-coupon refundings. The major difference is that there is no call premium to consider in the low-coupon case, because the low-coupon debt is repurchased at a discount.

Under Section 108 of the Internal Revenue Code, when a corporation repurchases its own debt at a discount, the gain is considered for tax purposes a *discharge of indebtedness*, which is taxable as ordinary income. This tax liability is often so substantial that it makes low-coupon refunding unprofitable. Section 108 states, however, that if the corporation had originally incurred or assumed the old debt in connection with property used in its business, it may elect, in accordance with Section 1017, to exclude the gain from its taxable income provided that it reduces the cost or other taxable basis of its depreciable property. In effect, this provision allows the gain to be deferred but not eliminated. However, this election is essentially limited to firms that are either bankrupt or insolvent.

The deferral is advantageous because it reduces the present value of the tax liability. The longer the deferral is, the lower is the present value. To minimize the tax liability, the corporation should apply the gain to those eligible assets with the longest depreciable lives.[15]

Accounting Considerations

Under Accounting Principles Board Opinion No. 21 (APB 21), a bond's balance sheet liability is its present-value cost when issued.[16] Any discount or premium is amortized over the bond's life. Changes over time in the bond's market price are ignored. Thus, at times, the market price and balance sheet liability of a bond may be substantially different. For example, if current market rates are higher than when the bonds were issued, the market value of the bonds will be lower than their book value.

Accounting for Investments in Fixed-Income Securities

Financial Accounting Standard No. 115 (FAS 115) governs the financial reporting of investments in debt and other securities.[17] Prior to FAS 115, financial institutions reported their debt investments predominantly at amortized cost, not market value. Technically amortized cost could be used only for investments the investor intended to hold to maturity, but this hold-to-maturity requirement was unevenly enforced.[18] FAS 115 introduced strict enforcement provisions intended to allow amortized-cost reporting for only those securities really intended to be held to maturity. All other securities investments must be reported at fair market value.[19]

FAS 115 applies to all debt security assets but not to unsecuritized residential mortgage loans and partnership interests.[20] Nor does it apply to liabilities. Debt securities must be classified in one of three ways:

- *Held to maturity (HTM).* All debt securities classified as HTM must be owned with both the intent and the ability to hold them to maturity. A security cannot be classified as HTM if the holder might want to sell it for traditional portfolio management reasons, such as asset-liability management or total return management. FAS 115 permits the investor to sell HTM securities in unusual circumstances provided they could not have been reasonably anticipated, as, for example, when a customer defaults unexpectedly and the investor must find another source of cash to pay its own obligations on short notice. HTM securities can be reported at amortized cost, which means that their book value does not change with their market value.

- *Trading securities.* Trading securities are intended for quick resale. They are reported at their fair market value, with increases and decreases included as gains and losses in net income.

- *Available for sale (AFS).* AFS securities are all securities not included in the other two categories. They are reported at fair market value, but changes in their value are not included in net income until the securities are sold except in instances where there is an other-than-temporary impairment. In the meantime, unrecorded gains or losses are shown in a separate component of shareholders' equity.

AFS or trading securities can be freely sold. AFS securities can be transferred to the HTM category virtually without restriction. However, transfers or sales from the HTM category should be rare and must be justified. Sales or transfers out of the HTM category, except in rare circumstances, will most likely disqualify a firm from classifying any of its securities as HTM.[21]

Accounting for Fixed-Income Liabilities

The Financial Accounting Standards Board's (FASB) Financial Instruments Project was created to develop a consistent, conceptual framework for reporting securities assets and liabilities on a market-value, as opposed to historical-cost, basis. As part of that project, the FASB issued FAS 107, which requires issuers of securities to report the fair market value of these instruments in the footnotes to their financial statements.[22] FASB has also issued a Discussion Memorandum and continues to discuss the presentation of all financial instruments at fair value.

Accounting for Derivatives

FASB Statement No. 133 (FAS 133) establishes a new model for accounting for derivatives and hedging activities and standardizes the accounting treatment of derivatives.[23] The accounting framework of FAS 133 is based on four principles:

1. Derivative instruments represent assets or liabilities.

2. Derivatives should be reported at their fair market value.

3. Derivative gains or losses are neither assets nor liabilities and therefore should not be reported as deferred items on the balance sheet.

4. Hedge accounting applies only to qualifying items, where changes in the hedging instrument's market value (cash flows) are expected

to be highly effective at offsetting changes in the hedged item's market value (cash flows).

FAS 133 requires fair value recognition of all asset and liability derivatives positions on the balance sheet. Gains or losses will be reported in net income or other comprehensive income in the current period if the derivative is both designated by the firm and qualifies under strict criteria as a hedging instrument under FAS 133. Gains or losses recorded in other comprehensive income shall be reclassified into earnings in the same period or periods during which the hedged forecasted transaction occurs.

Impact of the New Accounting Standards

These new accounting standards are intended to make financial statements more informative. The changes do not achieve true perfect mark-to-market reporting for all assets and liabilities. Nevertheless, we think they are much better than traditional historical-cost rules.

These new standards will increase the need for valuation models to value the full range of fixed-income securities and derivatives. They will also create opportunities for people who are skilled in the development and use of fixed-income valuation models.

Accounting for Bond Refundings

According to APB 26, the difference between an extinguished debt's reacquisition price and its net carrying amount shall be recognized in income as a gain or loss in the period of the extinguishment.[24] The difference may not be amortized. Accordingly, reacquiring high-coupon (premium) debt or low-coupon (discounted) debt results in a loss or gain, respectively, for financial reporting purposes. Following FAS 4, if the extinguished bond has more than a year remaining to maturity, the gain or loss shall be reported as an extraordinary item.[25] In addition, FAS 140 allows a debtor to remove a liability from its balance sheet if it has been extinguished either by paying the creditor in full or obtaining a legal release from being the primary obligor. EITF 96-19 recognizes that a substantial modification of the terms of a debt instrument is financially equivalent to extinguishing and replacing the old debt with new debt.

The problem is that the reported gain or loss on reacquisition is not the true economic gain or loss. The accounting simply reflects the difference between market value and adjusted historical cost, and has no relation to the present value of the change in after-tax debt service requirements that result from a refunding.

The following examples illustrate the difference between a refunding's accounting impact and its true profitability. Chapters 10 and 12 provide the details of such calculations. Here, we ignore historical and current transaction costs to simplify the illustration.

Suppose an issuer repurchases a high-coupon bond for $1,018.00 and uses the freed-up after-tax cash flow (debt service) to support a newly issued bond for $1,028.63. The repurchase price is the face amount of $1,000.00 plus a $30.00 call premium minus a $12.00 tax savings, because the call premium is tax deductible at a tax rate of 40 percent ($12.00 = [$30.00]0.40). The issuer's profit, called the *net advantage of refunding,* is $10.63 ($1,028.63 – $1,018.00).

In a second example, an issuer repurchases a low-coupon bond for $955.75 and uses the freed-up after-tax debt service to support a newly issued bond for $972.17. The gain of $44.25 ($1,000.00 – $955.75) creates an ordinary income tax liability of $17.70 ([$44.25]0.40). The net advantage is –$1.28 ($972.17 – $955.75 – $17.70).

The book value of each old bond is $1,000 (the issue price). The accounting impact is:

	High-coupon	Low-coupon
Repurchase cost	($1,030.00)	($955.75)
Book value	1,000.00	1,000.00
Tax effect	12.00	(17.70)
Gain (loss)	(18.00)	26.55

Note the perversity. The low-coupon refunding leads to an *accounting gain* of $26.55, but its net advantage is –$1.28 (a loss). Conversely, the high-coupon refunding results in an accounting loss of $18.00, but its net advantage is $10.63 (a gain).

The provisions of APB 26 are somewhat controversial. Critics claim that the opinion is misleading and can create opportunities for misuse and abuse. Financial managers eager to report a gain may undertake a refunding that is not consistent with maximizing shareholder wealth, while managers who want to avoid reporting a loss may shun a profitable refunding.

One possible remedy would be to amortize the gain or loss over the life of the new issue, or what would have been the remaining life of the old issue, thereby reducing the one-time accounting impact.[26] Alternatively, APB 21 could be amended to allow recording debt at its market value, which would eliminate any significant difference between a bond's reacquisition price and its carrying amount.[27]

Fixed-Rate Capital Securities: Tax Deductible Equity?

Fixed-rate capital securities allow the issuer both to deduct the periodic payments (like conventional debt) and augment nondebt capital (like preferred stock). Fixed-rate capital securities combine features of debt and preferred stock. They provide regular monthly or quarterly income at a stated rate (a percentage of liquidation value), the liquidity of a publicly traded instrument, and an investment-grade credit quality. Like corporate debt securities, they generally rank senior to common and preferred stock in the issuer's capital structure, have a stated maturity, and the interim payments qualify as interest for income tax purposes.

Unlike preferred stock, fixed-rate capital securities do not qualify for the corporate 70 percent dividends-received deduction. They also carry certain risks, including the risks of optional redemption, deferred payments, and extension, in addition to the normal risks of investing in fixed-income securities.

How Fixed-Rate Capital Securities Work

A firm usually sets up a special-purpose entity (a trust or a partnership) that issues the fixed-rate capital securities and invests the proceeds in an issue of the parent firm's junior subordinated debentures. Both the fixed-rate capital securities and the junior subordinated debentures have a five-year interest-deferral feature.[28]

In most cases, the capital is recorded as minority interest, a nondebt liability, on the issuer's balance sheet. An offering of fixed-rate capital securities does not affect the parent firm's balance sheet to the same extent as an issue of conventional debt. Rating agencies seem to view fixed-rate capital securities as similar to preferred equity because they provide long-term capital that permits the issuer to defer payments in case of financial distress.

Three Basic Structures

There are three basic types of fixed-rate capital securities, depending on whether the parent company issues the securities directly or through a special-purpose financing vehicle. Table 6.4 summarizes the alternative structures, and figure 6.1 shows how these securities are structured when they involve a special-purpose vehicle, the most common structure.

Table 6.4 Summary of Alternative Fixed-Rate Capital Securities

	Partnership Preferred	Trust Preferred	Junior Subordinated Debentures
Issuer	Limited partnership (LP) or limited liability company (LLC) organized by parent company	Grantor trust established by parent company	Parent company
Use of proceeds	To purchase junior subordinated debentures of parent company. Parent company uses proceeds for general corporate purposes.	To purchase junior subordinated debentures of parent company. Parent company uses proceeds for general corporate purposes.	General corporate purposes
Names of security[a]	MIPS, QUIPS	Trust Preferred Securities QUIPS, SKIS TOPrS, TruPS	MIDS QUICS QUIDS
Payment frequency	Monthly or quarterly	Quarterly or semiannually	Quarterly (QUICS, QUIDS) Monthly (MIDS)
Listing	NYSE	NYSE or none	NYSE or none
Denominations	$25	$25 or $1,000	$25 or $1,400

(continued)

Table 6.4 (continued)

	Partnership Preferred	Trust Preferred	Junior Subordinated Debentures
Maturity	No, but must redeem when under-lying debentures are redeemed, generally 20–49 years after issuance.	No, but must redeem when under-lying debentures are redeemed, generally 20–49 years after issuance.	Yes, 20–49 years.
Maturity exten-sion feature	Yes, on most but not all deals, though generally not beyond 49 years.	Yes, on most but not all deals, though generally not beyond 49 years.	No
Interest-deferral feature	Yes, generally maximum of 5 years.	Yes, generally maximum of 5 years.	Yes, generally maximum of 5 years.

Source: Fixed-Rate Capital Securities (New York: Bond Market Trade Association, 1997), pp. 16–17.

[a]The various forms of fixed-rate capital securities are known by the following names and acronyms:

MIDS	(Monthly Income Debt Securities)	SKIS	(Subordinated Capital Income Securities)
MIPS	(Monthly Income Preferred Shares)	TOPrS	(Trust Originated Preferred Securities)
QUICS	(Quarterly Income Capital Securities)	TruPS	(Capital Trust Pass-through Securities)
QUIDS	(Quarterly Income Debt Securities)		Trust Preferred Securities
QUIPS	(Quarterly Income Preferred Securities)		

Figure 6.1 Structure of Fixed-Rate Capital Securities

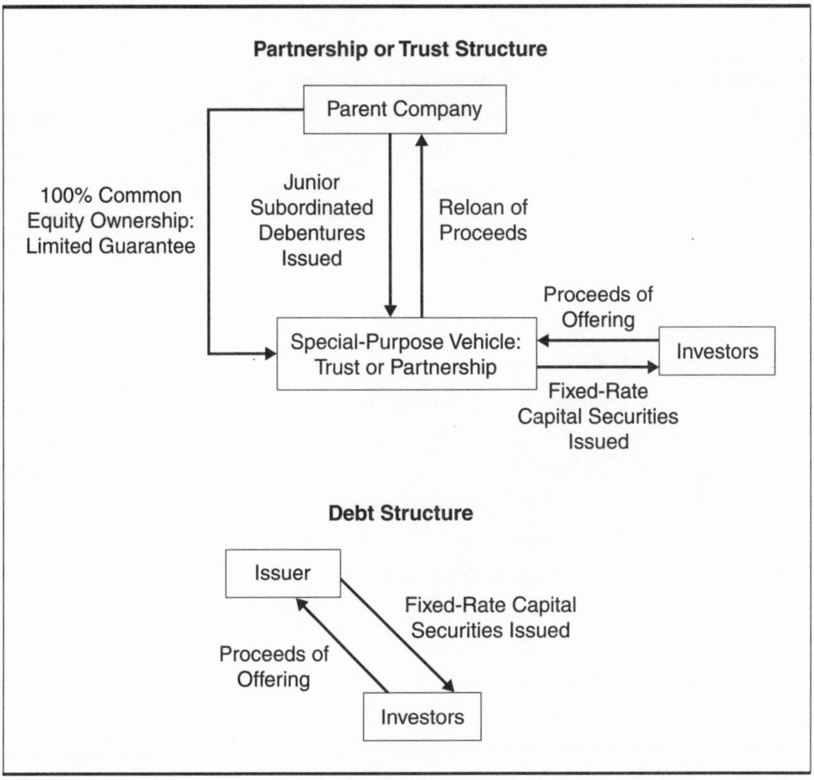

Source: Fixed-Rate Capital Securities (New York: Bond Market Trade Association, 1997), p. 5.

Distributions

Although monthly or quarterly payments are tax deductible, unlike conventional bonds, most fixed-rate capital securities allow deferral of distributions for up to five years.[29] Like regular preferred stock, deferral requires suspension of all dividends (common and preferred).

Maturity and Redemption

Most fixed-rate capital securities have an initial maturity between twenty and forty-nine years. Some non-U.S. firms have issued perpetual fixed-rate capital securities. Most also have a call feature. As with any other bonds, the issuer would most likely call the securities if interest rates fall sufficiently to lower its cost of capital. In most cases, however, the issuer cannot call the fixed-rate capital securities for at least the first five or ten years.

Because fixed-rate capital securities were created to provide tax-deductible payments, they also include a *special event redemption option.* This allows the issuer to redeem the securities at their liquidation value if a change in tax law disallows the tax deductibility.[30]

In some cases, the issuer also has the option to extend the maturity of the securities, although it cannot be used if payments are being deferred. Neither can the payment-deferral option be used to extend the maturity. If the issuer defers payments, the deferred income continues to accrue for tax purposes, although the investor receives no cash payments.

Is It Debt or Is It Equity?

The rating agencies treat fixed-rate capital securities as a hybrid, much like preferred stock, which we discuss in chapter 14. We mention them here because they reflect a common theme in securities innovation: Investment bankers frequently try to craft securities that qualify as debt for income tax purposes but have equity-like features.

The distinction between debt and equity is more subtle in practice than it is in theory. There is a fuzzy line between the two. In the case of fixed-rate capital securities, we come down on the side of debt!

Conclusion

This chapter described the tax and accounting treatments of debt instruments and the significance of tax and accounting factors in a refunding.

A bond refunding analysis should be based on after-tax cash flows, which are discounted at the after-tax cost of the new issue. Accounting considerations should play little role in a decision whether to refund; the decision should be based on the transaction's effect on shareholder wealth. The discounted-cash-flow calculation, rather than the accounting earnings impact, should determine whether to refund an outstanding debt issue.

Although further changes in corporate income tax rates are likely, the basic analytical frameworks described and illustrated in this book will remain fundamentally correct. The net advantage of any particular refunding, however, will be sensitive to the tax code. Thus, verifying the tax treatment is an important preliminary step in any bond refunding analysis.

Chapter 7

Fixed-Income Derivatives

Since the 1970s, a rich variety of new financial instruments, called derivatives, have been developed to help manage interest rate risk. A *derivative* is a financial instrument whose value depends on (i.e., derives from) the value of some other financial asset price, reference rate, or index. Derivatives help market participants manage interest rate and other risks more cost-effectively. This chapter focuses on interest rate derivatives and shows how firms and investors can use them to manage interest rate risk.

Some derivatives are new, but others have been around for years. Futures contracts on commodities have been traded on organized exchanges since the 1860s, and forward contracts are even older. The Chicago Board of Trade (CBOT) introduced commodity forwards in 1842 and commodity futures in 1865. Financial futures are newer. The International Monetary Market of the Chicago Mercantile Exchange (CME) introduced foreign-currency futures in 1972 and interest rate futures in 1975.

The development of organized markets for options and financial futures were two of the most significant financial developments of the 1970s, and the development of the swap markets was one of the most significant developments of the 1980s. These new financial instruments increased the ability to manage interest rate risk. As a result, interest rate risk can be reallocated more efficiently, and investors are better able to invest in their preferred return distributions.

Basic Building Blocks

The four basic types of derivatives—forward contracts, futures contracts, options, and swaps—function as the basic derivative building

137

blocks. They can be combined with conventional debt instruments to build more complex derivatives. For example, a structured note combines a derivative and a conventional fixed-rate or floating-rate note. An understanding of how the basic building blocks work is the foundation for analyzing more complex securities.[1]

Forward Contracts

A *forward contract* obligates the holder to buy a specified amount of a particular asset at a stated price on a particular future date. All are fixed at the time the contract is entered into. The specified future price is the *exercise price*. Most forward contracts are for commodities or currencies. Banks write forward contracts on interest rates called *forward-rate agreements.*

At origination, the NPV of a forward contract is zero because the exercise price is set equal to the expected future price. No cash changes hands. Buyer and seller settle up at maturity. Neither buyer nor seller realizes a profit if the asset's market price equals the exercise price at maturity. However, beyond that, it is a zero-sum game with a symmetric payoff distribution. The buyer—that is, the long position—profits (loses) if the market price is higher (lower) than the exercise price at maturity. The reverse holds for the seller—that is, the short position. Long and short positions have an unlimited potential for profits or losses.

Features of Forward Contracts

A forward contract has default risk: The seller might fail to deliver the asset, and the buyer might fail to pay for it.[2] Credit risk is important in determining who is able to transact in the forward market. Access is usually limited to large corporations, governments, and other creditworthy parties.

Futures Contracts

A *futures contract*, which is very similar to a forward contract, obligates the holder to buy a specified quantity of a particular asset at a specified exercise price on a specified future date. There are futures contracts for interest-bearing securities, including Treasury bills, Treasury notes, Treasury bonds, and Eurodollar deposits, as well as for agricultural commodities, precious metals, industrial commodities, currencies, and stock market indexes.

Futures contracts are standardized, exchange-traded instruments. They have greater liquidity than forward contracts, which are customized and traded over the counter. Unlike forward contracts, which realize gains or losses only on the settlement date, futures contracts realize gains or losses daily. A futures contract has little default risk because it is marked to market and settled at the end of every business day; there are margin requirements, which serve as a performance bond; and there is a clearinghouse, which guarantees each party's performance.

Options

An *option* is a contingent claim that gives the owner the right (without the obligation) to purchase or sell the underlying asset at a specified price during a specified time period. A *call option* is the right to buy, and a *put option* is the right to sell. The specified price is the *strike price*. A call (put) option provides an advantage over a market buy (sell) whenever the underlying asset is worth more (less) than the strike price.

Unlike forwards and futures, options have asymmetric payoff distributions. A call option holder benefits from increases in underlying asset value above the strike price and has unlimited profit potential, but loss is limited to the price paid for the option. A lottery ticket is a particular type of call option, and insurance is a particular type of put option. A put option protects its owner against decreases in underlying asset value below the strike price.

Call options on bonds benefit the holder when interest rates drop and bond prices rise; put options on bonds benefit the holder in the opposite situation. Interest rate call options are attractive to market participants who believe interest rates will fall. Interest rate put options are attractive to market participants who believe interest rates will rise and those who want to hedge a fixed-income investment against the effect of a rise in interest rates.

Interest Rate Swaps

Often a firm prefers fixed-rate debt to floating-rate debt, or vice versa. Banks use interest rate swaps to convert one into the other. In a plain vanilla *swap*, two borrowers exchange interest-payment obligations, with one paying a fixed rate and the other a floating rate based on a stated *notional principal* amount. By convention, the fixed-rate payer (and floating-rate receiver) is said to be *long* the swap; the counterparty is *short* the swap. A firm can convert an existing debt without having to pay the cost of replacing it. For this reason, and because of their usefulness in managing risk, the swap market has grown rapidly since swaps were introduced in 1981.

Features of Swaps

A swap contract obligates two parties to exchange specified series of cash flows at specified intervals. In an *interest rate swap*, the cash flows are determined by two different interest rates.[3] Each cash flow is either fixed or determined by multiplying a notional principal amount by the specified interest rate, price, or index value.

How an Interest Rate Swap Works

Suppose one party pays at an 8 percent fixed rate and the other pays a floating rate based on six-month LIBOR. Alternatively, the two might be different floating rates. Payments are conditional; if one party defaults, the other is released from its obligation.

Figure 7.1 illustrates an interest rate swap. In its simplest form, a *fixed-rate/floating-rate swap*, one interest rate is fixed and the other is floating. One party pays out a series of cash flows determined by the fixed interest rate R_{fixed}. It receives a series of cash flows determined by the floating interest rate $R_{floating}$. The floating-rate payment varies over time as market interest rates change. The floating rate is usually three-month or six-month LIBOR. The cash flows for the swap counterparty are the mirror image of those in figure 7.1.

A swap has less default risk than a loan because no principal changes hands and the payments are netted. The party with the greater obligation pays the other the difference.

Figure 7.1 An Interest Rate Swap

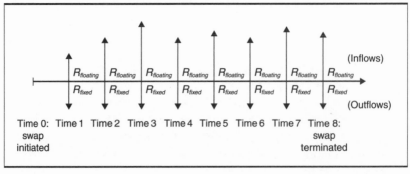

Suppose McDonald's Corporation enters a fixed-rate/floating-rate swap, agreeing to pay six-month LIBOR and receive 8 percent, based on $100 million notional principal amount. Net payments will be made semiannually. The amount of the first payment is determined on the swap date. LIBOR is 6 percent. Six months later, McDonald's receives a check for $1,000,000 ($100,000,000[0.08 − 0.06]/2). In the meantime, LIBOR has risen to 9 percent. Six months later, McDonald's writes a check for $500,000 ($100,000,000[0.09 − 0.08]/2).

Hedging

Derivatives are used to hedge. A *hedge* is a guard against changes in such things as an interest rate, the price of a commodity, or a foreign exchange rate. Therefore, derivatives are very useful for managing certain types of risk.

How a Hedge Works

Figure 7.2 describes the rationale for hedging using interest rate risk as the example. In figure 7.2A, the firm's value decreases as interest rates increase. Perhaps interest rates are increasing on the firm's floating-rate debt, or there is a rise in rates just as the firm is about to issue fixed-rate debt.

If the firm can take a position in a derivative whose value will increase as interest rates increase, it can neutralize the impact of the interest rate increase. In figure 7.2B, the value of the hedge position follows the dashed line. The position is carefully selected so that changes in its value offset changes in the value of the hedged asset. Figure 7.2B illustrates a perfect hedge: The value changes offset precisely so the value of the firm is unaffected. Although perfect hedges are rare, proper hedging can substantially reduce the firm's exposure to interest rate or other risks.

Hedging with Forwards and Futures

Figure 7.3 illustrates the use of forward contracts and futures contracts to hedge interest rate risk. When interest rates rise, both the values of the firm and an interest rate forward contract decrease. A short position in an interest rate forward contract moves exactly opposite to the contract and therefore opposite to firm value. Therefore, going short an interest rate forward contract (or interest rate futures contract) provides a hedge against changes in firm value.

Figure 7.2 Rationale for Hedging

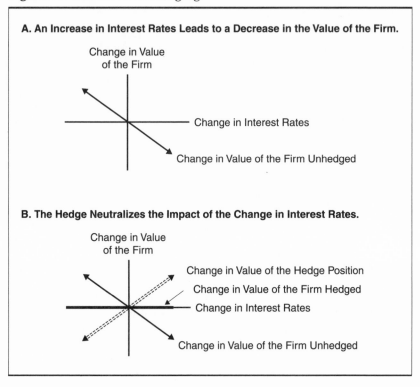

A. An Increase in Interest Rates Leads to a Decrease in the Value of the Firm.

Change in Value of the Firm

Change in Interest Rates

Change in Value of the Firm Unhedged

B. The Hedge Neutralizes the Impact of the Change in Interest Rates.

Change in Value of the Firm

Change in Value of the Hedge Position

Change in Value of the Firm Hedged

Change in Interest Rates

Change in Value of the Firm Unhedged

The example that follows is based on futures, but forwards and futures have basically identical structures. The critical factor in futures hedging is determining the hedge ratio. The *hedge ratio* is defined by

$$\text{Hedge ratio} = \frac{\text{Change in price of bond to be hedged}}{\text{Change in price of hedging instrument}} \qquad (7.1)$$

New Age Foods plans to issue $50 million of bonds. But it needs a month to prepare the documentation and is concerned that interest rates could rise by a percentage point. It can sell Treasury bond futures to hedge this risk. Right now, it could sell thirty-year 10 percent notes. If the required return increases to 11 percent, it would get 8.7249 percent less in proceeds (100.00 − 91.2751):

$$PV = \sum_{t=1}^{60} \frac{5}{(1.055)^t} + \frac{100}{(1.055)^{60}} = 91.2751$$

Figure 7.3 Using Forwards and Futures to Hedge

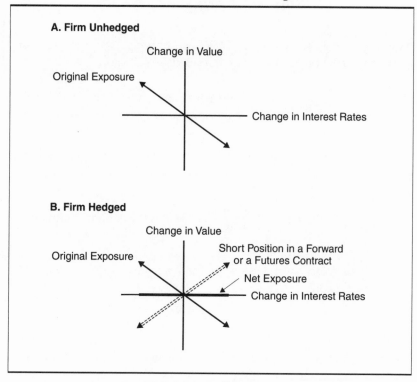

New Age estimates that the yield on an 8 percent, twenty-year Treasury bond would also increase by 1 percent, from 9 percent currently to 10 percent. At a 9 percent yield, a $100 par 8 percent Treasury bond is worth $90.7992:

$$PV = \sum_{t=1}^{40} \frac{4}{(1.045)^t} + \frac{100}{(1.045)^{40}} = 90.7992$$

At a 10 percent yield, it is worth $82.8409:

$$PV = \sum_{t=1}^{40} \frac{4}{(1.05)^t} + \frac{100}{(1.05)^{40}} = 82.8409$$

The change in value is 7.9583 (90.7992 − 82.8409). The hedge ratio is 1.0963:

$$\text{Hedge ratio} = \frac{8.7249}{7.9583} = 1.0963$$

New Age needs to sell short 1.0963 underlying 8 percent Treasury bonds for each bond to be hedged. It needs to sell short:

$$\frac{\text{Number of}}{\text{contracts}} = \text{Hedge ratio} \left[\frac{\text{Principal amount to be hedged}}{\text{Par value of hedging instrument}} \right] \quad (7.2)$$

Treasury bond futures contracts are $100,000 principal. So according to equation 7.2,

$$\frac{\text{Number of}}{\text{contracts}} = 1.0963 \left[\frac{50,000,000}{100,000} \right] = 548 \text{ Treasury bond contracts}$$

To verify, suppose interest rates rise by 1 percent. The loss to New Age will be $4,362,450:

$$\$50,000,000(0.087249) = \$4,362,450$$

But 99.97 percent of that is offset by a profit on the futures of $4,361,148:

$$548(\$100,000)0.079583 = \$4,361,148$$

Hedging with Options

Options provide a way to guard against a bad outcome and still have a chance at a good outcome. For example, life insurance companies sell products that promise a minimum rate of return. If rates fall and the firm does not earn the minimum, it will have a loss. It can hedge its risk by buying call options on interest rate futures. Firms that would be hurt by rising interest rates can hedge their exposure by buying put options.

As an example, let us say that Professional Asset Management (PAM) purchased $10 million principal amount of thirty-year 8 percent Treasury bonds. Interest rates are up 100 basis points (1 percent) since it bought the bonds a year ago. PAM would like to hedge the risk of even higher interest rates and a further decline in the value of its Treasury bonds over the next six months.

PAM can buy a six-month put option. With a 9.00 percent yield, the bonds' price is:

Fixed-Income Derivatives 145

$$PV = \sum_{t=1}^{58} \frac{4}{(1.045)^t} + \frac{100}{(1.045)^{58}} = 89.7539$$

If the yield does not change, the bonds' price will increase in the next six months to

$$PV = \sum_{t=1}^{57} \frac{4}{(1.045)^t} + \frac{100}{(1.045)^{57}} = 89.7928$$

If PAM buys a put option on $10 million principal amount of the bonds with a strike price of 89.7928, it will be fully hedged against a rise in yield above 9.00 percent. Table 7.1 illustrates the possible outcomes. Suppose interest rates rise to 10 percent over the next six months. Then PAM loses $851,440 on its bonds but makes $855,330 on its put option, for a net increase of $3,890 (before taking into account the cost of the put option). Note that if the bonds' yield had remained at 9.00 percent, PAM would also have made $3,890.

Hedging with Interest Rate Swaps

Figure 7.4 illustrates how a floating-rate borrower can use a swap to hedge against interest rate changes. A BBB-rated firm takes on a

Table 7.1 Possible Outcomes on the Option Hedge

Yield on the Treasury Bonds	Price of the Treasury Bonds	Gain (Loss) on Cash Position[a]	Value of the Put Option[b]	Net Gain (or Loss)[c]
7.00%	112.2752%	$2,252,130	—	$2,252,130
7.50	105.8490	1,609,510	—	1,609,510
8.00	100.0000	1,024,610	—	1,024,610
8.50	94.6662	491,230	—	491,230
9.00	89.7928	3,890	—	3,890
9.50	85.3315	(442,240)	$ 446,130	3,890
10.00	81.2395	(851,440)	855,330	3,890
10.50	77.4790	(1,227,490)	1,231,380	3,890
11.00	74.0165	(1,573,740)	1,577,630	3,890

[a]Calculated as the difference between the price of the Treasury bonds and 89.7539 multiplied by the principal amount ($10 million) and divided by 100.
[b]The greater of (1) the difference between 89.7928 and the price of the Treasury bonds multiplied by the principal amount ($10 million) and divided by 100, and (2) zero. Note that the value of the put option is zero if the price of the underlying bond has increased since the put option was purchased.
[c]Equals the sum of (1) gain (loss) on cash position and (2) value of the put option.

Figure 7.4 Using a Swap to Convert a Floating-Rate Loan to a Fixed-Rate Loan

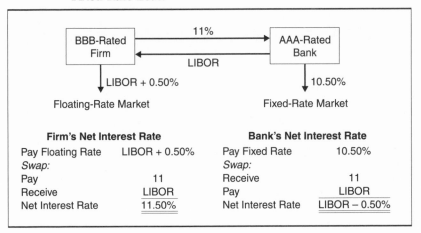

Firm's Net Interest Rate		Bank's Net Interest Rate	
Pay Floating Rate	LIBOR + 0.50%	Pay Fixed Rate	10.50%
Swap:		*Swap:*	
Pay	11	Receive	11
Receive	LIBOR	Pay	LIBOR
Net Interest Rate	11.50%	Net Interest Rate	LIBOR − 0.50%

floating-rate bank loan. It then enters into a swap, which essentially converts the actual floating-rate loan into a *synthetic* fixed-rate loan, changing the firm's interest cost from LIBOR plus 0.50 percent floating to 11.50 percent fixed.

A Complex Risk Management Example

A manufacturing firm knows in August that it will soon have to borrow because seasonal sales variations will require a buildup of inventory and receivables in anticipation of next spring's season. The firm will require a $10 million revolving line of credit to be drawn down around mid-November (in three months) and repaid three months after that. It has been quoted an interest rate of three-month LIBOR plus 1.00 percent. The yield curve is currently upward sloping, and the expected three-month LIBOR three months forward is 5 percent, so the loan's expected interest rate is 6 percent. The firm has four alternatives to reduce its interest rate risk exposure:

1. Do nothing. However, a 10-basis-point increase in LIBOR will increase the six-month interest expense by $5,000 ($10,000,000[.001]/2).

2. Sell the December 01 three-month Eurodollar futures contract short, currently quoted at 94.90, implying a forward rate of 5.10 percent. The principal amount of the Eurodollar futures contract is $1 million. Substituting into equations 7.1 and 7.2, the firm would have to sell approximately twenty contracts:

$$\text{Number of contracts} = \frac{6 \text{ months}}{3 \text{ months}} \times \frac{\$10,000,000}{\$1,000,000} = 20$$

The firm would cover its short position in mid-November when it draws down on the credit line. Closing out the futures position before the contracts expire would leave the firm exposed to a small degree of basis risk.

3. Buy a put option on the Eurodollar futures. This would also pro- vide protection against rising interest rates (falling prices), but unlike the futures hedge, it would allow the firm to benefit from falling rates (rising prices). The cost of this interest rate risk protec- tion is the up-front option premium. Suppose December puts with an exercise price of 95.00 are currently trading at $400. Thus, the firm can cap its LIBOR rates at 5 percent by purchasing twenty con- tracts for $8,000 (20 contracts × $400).

4. Make a forward-rate agreement (FRA) for $10 million notional with the bank, which is quoting a three-month FRA on three-month LIBOR at 5.10 percent. Suppose three-month LIBOR is 6.00 percent when the firm draws the loan. The bank pays it $22,500 ($10,000,000 × [.06 − .051]/4), reducing its interest cost to 6.10 percent (6.00 − 0.90 + 1.00). If LIBOR is less than 5.10 percent, the firm pays the bank the difference, and its interest cost is still 6.10 percent.

Relationships Among the Basic Building Blocks

There are usually multiple combinations of the basic derivative building blocks that will produce the same position because the build- ing blocks can be recharacterized in terms of each other. Probably best known is *put-call parity*, wherein every situation that can be described in terms of a call option has a parallel description in terms of a put option.

A Futures Contract as a Series of Forward Contracts

Recall that futures contracts are marked to market daily. In effect, a futures contract is a series of forward contracts. Each day, yesterday's contract is settled, and a new one is written.

An Interest Rate Swap as a Series of Forward Contracts

A swap can be viewed as a series of interest rate forward con- tracts—one for each swap settlement date. Paying a fixed rate on a swap and receiving LIBOR is agreeing to pay the fixed rate (the forward price) in exchange for LIBOR (the underlying asset).

Interest Rate Swaps and Back-to-Back Loans

The fixed-rate payer has a long position and the fixed-rate receiver a short position. Two financial structures are equivalent only if the cash flows are identical period by period and all other terms and conditions are the same, including covenants, default-risk exposure, and tax treatment. A long position in a par value swap is equivalent to a long position in an unrestricted floating-rate note (FRN) and a short position in a fixed-rate note:

$$
\begin{array}{ccc}
\text{Long} & \text{Long} & \text{Short} \\
\text{interest rate swap} = \text{unrestricted FRN} + \text{fixed-rate note}
\end{array} \quad (7.3)
$$

In a par value swap, neither party pays the other any cash at the inception of the swap because the present values of the long and short positions are equal.

An unrestricted FRN has no constraint on the rate other than a lower bound of zero. As indicated by equation 7.3, the fixed-rate payer will realize the same future cash flows as if it had purchased an unrestricted FRN (at LIBOR flat) and sold a fixed-rate note to the counterparty (with a coupon rate equal to the swap's fixed-rate). Equation 7.3 can be rewritten as

$$
\begin{array}{ccc}
\text{Short} & \text{Short} & \text{Long} \\
\text{interest rate swap} = \text{unrestricted FRN} + \text{fixed-rate note}
\end{array} \quad (7.4)
$$

A short position in a par value swap—paying floating rate and receiving fixed—is equivalent to issuing an unrestricted FRN and buying a fixed-rate note with the proceeds.

A Forward Contract as a Pair of Options

A long position in a call option coupled with a short position in a put option is equivalent to a long position in a forward (or futures) contract:

$$
\begin{array}{ccc}
\text{Long} & \text{Long} & \text{Short} \\
\text{forward contract} = \text{call option} + \text{put option}
\end{array} \quad (7.5)
$$

An Option as a Dynamic Portfolio

A call option can be replicated by continuously adjusting a portfolio that contains Treasury bills and forward, futures, or swap contracts.[4]

The critical element is that as the price of the underlying asset (the forward price, the futures price, or the value of the swap) rises (falls), the portfolio proportion invested in Treasury bills declines (increases), and the proportion invested in the underlying asset increases (decreases) correspondingly. Similarly, a put option can be created synthetically using a dynamic replication strategy.

Swaptions

A *swaption* (also called a *swap option*) is an option on an interest rate swap. It gives the holder the right (without the obligation) to enter into a specified interest rate swap at a certain time in the future. For example, suppose a firm knows that it will draw down a ten-year floating-rate bank term loan in six months and that it will want to enter into an interest rate swap to convert the loan into a fixed-rate loan. It can buy a six-month swaption giving it the right to enter into a fixed-for-floating interest rate swap to pay, say 8 percent fixed, and receive LIBOR on the agreed notional amount for ten years. If the swap rate exceeds 8 percent in six months, the firm exercises the swaption. Otherwise it lets the swaption expire and arranges a swap at the lower fixed rate currently available. This call swaption guarantees that the swap's fixed rate will not exceed 8 percent.

There are alternatives to swaptions. One is a *forward swap* (also called a *deferred swap*). Forward swaps, like forward contracts generally, have no up-front cost but are not options. They obligate the holder to enter into the swap on the specified future date.

We explain in chapter 11 how a firm can use a swaption to create a synthetic bond call option and describe how these are used in debt management.

Interest Rate Caps, Floors, and Collars

Three interest rate derivative instruments—interest rate caps, floors, and collars—can be developed directly from the basic building blocks.

Caps

An *interest rate cap* hedges the contract holder against a rise in rates. It is analogous to a put option on a debt security. For example, a cap on LIBOR can be interpreted as a series of put options on a Eurodollar time deposit. The holder of a cap has the right, but not the obligation, on each settlement date to sell the writer of the cap a time deposit having a coupon rate equal to the cap rate. In return for an up-front fee, the cap buyer can exercise this option if LIBOR exceeds the cap rate, effectively selling the low-coupon deposit to the cap writer at par. For example, the buyer of a 10 percent cap on LIBOR will receive any excess of LIBOR over 10 percent. The payment, if any, on each settlement date equals the difference between LIBOR and 10 percent, adjusted for the fraction of a year elapsed, multiplied by the contract's notional principal amount. If LIBOR is less than the cap rate, the option is out of the money, and no payment is made.

A cap can also be viewed as a call option on LIBOR.[5] It is in the money when LIBOR is above the cap rate. Figure 7.5 illustrates this view.

Figure 7.5 Interpreting a Cap as a Call on Interest Rates

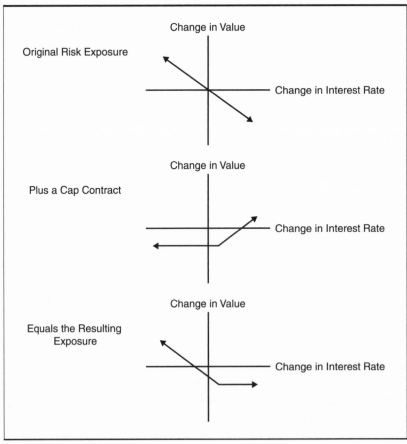

Floors

An *interest rate floor* hedges the contract holder against a drop in interest rates. It is analogous to a call option on debt. For example, analogous to a cap, a floor on LIBOR can be viewed as a series of call options on a Eurodollar time deposit. The buyer receives any excess of the floor rate over LIBOR. The settlement date payment calculation is similar for caps and floors. No payment is made if LIBOR is above the floor rate. For example, an investor in floating-rate notes that pay three-month LIBOR plus 1 percent who purchases a 4 percent floor contract can never receive less than 5 percent interest in any period.

A floor can also be viewed as a put option—in this case, a put option on three-month LIBOR with a strike price of 4 percent.[6] Figure 7.6 illustrates this situation.

Figure 7.6 Interpreting a Floor as a Put on Interest Rates

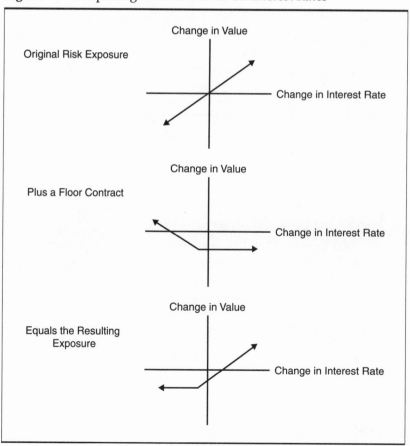

Collars

An *interest rate collar* is like simultaneously buying a cap and selling a floor. A collar always costs less than a cap at a given rate because the sale price of the floor offsets part of the cost of the cap. A collar hedges against the interest rate falling outside a particular range. For example, a long position in a 4 percent–8 percent collar can be described as:

$$\frac{\text{Long collar}}{\text{(4\% strike–8\% strike)}} = \frac{\text{Long cap}}{\text{(8\% strike)}} + \frac{\text{Short floor}}{\text{(4\% strike)}} \qquad (7.6)$$

When the strike rates are structured so that there is no net premium, it is called a *zero-cost collar*. However, the cap and floor rates are usually set to provide the seller with a net premium.

Caps, Floors, Collars, and Swaps

A collar with the cap and floor rate equal is equivalent to an interest rate swap. For example, buying a 6 percent cap and writing a 6 percent floor both on three-month LIBOR is equivalent to going long a swap to pay 6 percent fixed and receive three-month LIBOR:

$$\frac{\text{Long cap}}{\text{(6\% strike)}} + \frac{\text{Short floor}}{\text{(6\% strike)}} = \frac{\text{Long interest rate swap}}{\text{(pay 6\% fixed, receive LIBOR)}} \qquad (7.7)$$

If a par value swap has a 6 percent fixed rate, the 6 percent cap premium must equal the 6 percent floor premium.

More Complex Floating-Rate Notes

Financial engineers have combined plain vanilla FRNs with packages of derivatives to create a rich variety of complex FRNs. These instruments have been in demand because they exhibit interest rate sensitivities that satisfy market participants' risk-return preferences.

Collared FRNs

A variety of innovative financial instruments have been introduced in the floating-rate securities market. Many contain embedded interest rate options.

The coupon rate of a typical FRN resets each period at a reference rate, often LIBOR, plus a fixed margin. The coupon rate may be subject to a cap or a floor (or both). The margin reflects the default risk of the issuer as well as other characteristics of the security, including any call or put options. The margin is greater (smaller) (1) the greater (smaller) the default risk or (2) the lower (higher) the maximum (minimum) coupon rate. A call option requires a greater margin, a put option a smaller margin.

How a Collared FRN Works

A collared FRN has a cap and a floor. For example, purchasing an FRN with a coupon of LIBOR plus 0.50 percent, a 10 percent maximum coupon, and a 5 percent minimum coupon is equivalent to purchasing an unrestricted FRN at LIBOR flat, buying a 50-basis-point annuity and an interest rate floor, and selling a cap. The annuity equals the fixed margin, consisting of a series of level payments (if negative) or receipts (if positive):

$$
\begin{matrix}
\text{Long} \\
\text{collared FRN} \\
\text{(LIBOR + 0.50\%,} \\
\text{maximum 10\%,} \\
\text{minimum 5\%)}
\end{matrix}
=
\begin{matrix}
\text{Long} \\
\text{unrestricted FRN} \\
\text{(LIBOR)}
\end{matrix}
+
\begin{matrix}
\text{Long} \\
\text{annuity} \\
\text{(0.50\%)}
\end{matrix}
+
\begin{matrix}
\text{Long} \\
\text{floor} \\
\text{(4.50\%} \\
\text{strike)}
\end{matrix}
+
\begin{matrix}
\text{Short} \\
\text{cap} \\
\text{(9.50\%} \\
\text{strike)}
\end{matrix}
$$

(7.8)

A long position in the collared FRN in equation 7.8 offers the same promised future cash receipts as buying (1) an unrestricted FRN paying LIBOR, (2) an annuity paying 0.50 percent, and (3) a floor on LIBOR at a 4.50 percent strike rate,[7] and selling (4) a cap on LIBOR at a 9.50 percent strike rate.

Synthetic Collared FRNs

The unrestricted FRN can be reexpressed as a combination of long positions in the collared FRN and the cap and short positions in the annuity and the floor:

$$
\begin{matrix}
\text{Long} \\
\text{unrestricted FRN} \\
\text{(LIBOR)}
\end{matrix}
=
\begin{matrix}
\text{Long} \\
\text{collared FRN} \\
\text{(LIBOR + 0.50\%,} \\
\text{maximum 10\%,} \\
\text{minimum 5\%)}
\end{matrix}
+
\begin{matrix}
\text{Long} \\
\text{cap} \\
\text{(9.50\%} \\
\text{strike)}
\end{matrix}
+
\begin{matrix}
\text{Short} \\
\text{annuity} \\
\text{(0.50\%)}
\end{matrix}
+
\begin{matrix}
\text{Short} \\
\text{floor} \\
\text{(4.50\%} \\
\text{strike)}
\end{matrix}
$$

(7.9)

That portfolio can be substituted into equation 7.3 to obtain:

$$
\begin{array}{ccc}
\begin{array}{c} \text{Long} \\ \text{interest rate swap} \\ \text{(pay SFR,} \\ \text{receive LIBOR)} \end{array} =
& \begin{array}{c} \text{Long} \\ \text{collared FRN} \\ \text{(LIBOR} + 0.50\%, \\ \text{maximum 10\%,} \\ \text{minimum 5\%)} \end{array} +
& \begin{array}{c} \text{Short} \\ \text{annuity} \\ (0.50\%) \end{array}
\end{array} \qquad (7.10)
$$

$$
+ \begin{array}{c} \text{Short} \\ \text{floor} \\ (4.50\% \text{ strike}) \end{array} +
\begin{array}{c} \text{Long cap} \\ (9.50\% \text{ strike}) \end{array} +
\begin{array}{c} \text{Short} \\ \text{fixed-rate note} \\ (\text{SFR}) \end{array}
$$

where SFR denotes the fixed rate in the swap. Now rearrange terms in equation 7.10 and combine the annuity and the fixed-rate note to obtain:

$$
\begin{array}{ccccc}
\begin{array}{c} \text{Long} \\ \text{fixed-rate note} \\ (\text{SFR} + 0.50\%) \end{array} =
& \begin{array}{c} \text{Long} \\ \text{collared FRN} \\ (\text{LIBOR} + 0.50\%, \\ \text{maximum 10\%,} \\ \text{minimum 5\%)} \end{array} +
& \begin{array}{c} \text{Short} \\ \text{interest rate} \\ \text{swap} \\ (\text{pay LIBOR,} \\ \text{receive SFR)} \end{array} +
& \begin{array}{c} \text{Short} \\ \text{floor} \\ (4.50\% \\ \text{strike}) \end{array} +
& \begin{array}{c} \text{Long} \\ \text{cap} \\ (9.50\% \\ \text{strike}) \end{array}
\end{array}
$$

$$(7.11)$$

A fixed-rate loan paying the swap fixed rate plus 0.50 percent is equivalent to long positions in (1) a collared FRN and (2) a 9.50 percent cap, plus short positions in (3) an interest rate swap and (4) a 4.50 percent floor.[8] Equation 7.11 can be rewritten to express a collared FRN as:[9]

$$
\begin{array}{ccccc}
\begin{array}{c} \text{Long} \\ \text{collared FRN} \\ (\text{LIBOR} + 0.50\%, \\ \text{maximum 10\%,} \\ \text{minimum 5\%)} \end{array} =
& \begin{array}{c} \text{Long interest} \\ \text{rate swap} \\ (\text{pay SFR,} \\ \text{receive LIBOR)} \end{array} +
& \begin{array}{c} \text{Long} \\ \text{fixed-rate note} \\ (\text{SFR} + 0.50\%) \end{array} +
& \begin{array}{c} \text{Long} \\ \text{floor} \\ (4.50\% \\ \text{strike}) \end{array} +
& \begin{array}{c} \text{Short} \\ \text{cap} \\ (9.50\% \\ \text{strike}) \end{array}
\end{array}
$$

$$(7.12)$$

Equations 7.8 and 7.12 are alternative synthetic collared FRNs. In equation 7.12, paying a fixed rate in the swap cancels out all but 50 basis points of the coupon on the fixed-rate note. The cap and floor constrain the coupon to the range permitted by the FRN's collar.

We interpreted equation 7.11 from the investor's side of the transaction. Reversing the signs flips the interpretation to the issuer's side. The issuer is short the note. Issuing a fixed-rate note like that in equation 7.11 is equivalent to (1) issuing a collared FRN, (2) selling a 9.50 percent cap, and buying (3) an interest rate swap and (4) a 4.50 percent floor.

The Comparative Advantage Argument

It has been argued that comparative advantage was responsible for the rapid growth of interest rate swaps. Although this argument is appealing, it ignores arbitrage. With no barriers to capital flows, arbitrage would eventually eliminate any comparative advantage. Over time, the swap market would shrink, not grow.

Equation 7.3 provides a framework within which we can examine the comparative advantage argument. Rewrite the equation as

$$\begin{matrix} \text{Short} & \text{Short} & \text{Long} \\ \text{fixed-rate note} & = & \text{unrestricted FRN} & + & \text{interest rate swap} \end{matrix} \quad (7.13)$$

Selling an unrestricted FRN and buying a swap (to pay fixed and receive floating) is equivalent to issuing a synthetic fixed-rate note.

The comparative advantage argument holds that many firms—for example, an electric utility whose assets are very long term and not very sensitive to interest rate changes—have a natural preference for fixed-rate funding. Suppose an electric utility issues floating-rate debt and then buys an interest rate swap (to pay fixed and receive floating), creating synthetic fixed-rate debt. It benefits if the synthetic fixed-rate debt has a lower cost than conventional fixed-rate debt. The other side of the swap can be examined by reversing equation 7.13. Firms with a natural preference for variable-rate debt, such as a money center bank, issue fixed-rate debt and sell an interest rate swap to create synthetic floating-rate debt. If the net costs of the synthetic instruments are lower than those for their conventional alternatives, the swap benefits both firms.

The conventional explanation for this comparative advantage is that the floating-rate market accepts a smaller differential default-risk premium than the fixed-rate market. The weaker credit (the electric utility) has a comparative advantage in the floating-rate market, and the stronger credit (the bank) has a comparative advantage in the fixed-rate market. However, the evidence supporting this explanation is suspect because of several problems in measuring the arbitrage gains. It is essential that the alternatives be truly comparable. A common mistake is to neglect the value of the call option often included in medium- to long-term corporate bonds. Including a call option requires a higher yield than an otherwise identical noncallable bond. The size of this yield premium depends on the length of the call grace period (before the issuer can exercise the option), the specified schedule of call prices, and the volatility of interest rates.

As an example, look again at figure 7.4. The firm issued floating-rate debt and swapped into 11.50 percent fixed-rate debt. Suppose a conventional fixed-rate debt issue would cost it 11.75 percent. The swap structure appears to deliver a 25-basis-point cost saving. But suppose the 11.75 percent fixed-rate bond is callable and the call option is worth 25 basis points, whereas both the FRN and the swap are non-callable. The comparison is misleading because the arbitrage gain is illusory. The lower cost of funds merely represents the fair value of the call option.

Default Risk

One must also account for the default risk connected with the interest rate swap. If either party defaults, the counterparty must replace the swap. Consider the fixed-rate payer. If the floating-rate payer defaults and interest rates have risen, the fixed-rate payer will have to pay more for a replacement swap. Any cost saving must be measured net of default risk. Clearly a simple comparison of interest rates can be misleading.

Information asymmetries and transaction costs can explain much of the growth in interest rate swaps. Suppose a firm has information not available to the market that leads it to believe that its credit quality will improve. Refunding short-term debt is generally cheaper and easier than refunding long-term debt. Issuing short-term floating-rate debt and swapping into fixed rate will enable the firm to exploit the information asymmetry.

Stripping the Caps

Until the mid-1980s, FRNs typically had embedded floors but not caps. The introduction of FRNs containing an embedded interest rate cap is noteworthy because it gave rise to an arbitrage opportunity. Derivatives dealers "stripped" the cap and sold it at a profit. The framework just developed can be used to illustrate how this was done.

First, note that buying a collared FRN is equivalent to buying an FRN with a floor but no cap and selling a cap contract. To illustrate, suppose a collared FRN pays interest at the rate of LIBOR plus 0.50 percent subject to a floor of 5 percent and a cap of 10 percent. Then:

$$\begin{matrix} \text{Long} \\ \text{collared FRN} \\ \text{(LIBOR} + 0.50\%, \text{maxi-} \\ \text{mum } 10\%, \text{minimum } 5\%) \end{matrix} = \begin{matrix} \text{Long FRN} \\ \text{(LIBOR} + 0.50\%, \\ \text{minimum } 5\%) \end{matrix} + \begin{matrix} \text{Short cap} \\ \text{(9.50\% strike)} \end{matrix} \quad (7.14)$$

Reversing equation 7.14 and rearranging terms shows that issuing the collared FRN and selling the cap agreement is equivalent to issuing the FRN with a floor constraint:

$$
\begin{array}{c}
\text{Short} \\
\text{collared FRN} \\
\text{(LIBOR} + 0.50\%, \text{maxi-} \\
\text{mum 10\%, minimum 5\%)}
\end{array}
+
\begin{array}{c}
\text{Short cap} \\
\text{(9.50\% strike)}
\end{array}
=
\begin{array}{c}
\text{Short FRN} \\
\text{(LIBOR} + 0.50\%, \\
\text{minimum 5\%)}
\end{array}
\quad (7.15)
$$

Suppose that the firm could issue the FRN (with a floor) at par assuming the coupon reset is LIBOR plus 0.5 percent and its minimum coupon rate is 5.0 percent. Also suppose that the collared FRN could be sold at a price of 98.0 percent of par value to reflect the cap constraint. Then if the issuer can write a cap agreement and sell it for more than 2 points (i.e., more than 2 percent of the notional principal, which equals the face value of the FRN), there is a pure arbitrage profit. The issuer obtains the same variable-rate funding in either case but at a lower cost in the case of the collared FRN because its net proceeds are greater. A number of investment and commercial banks have exploited such an arbitrage opportunity beginning in 1985.

Inverse FRNs

Inverse floaters, also known as *reverse floaters, bull floaters,* and *yield curve notes,* were introduced in 1986.[10] The traditional FRN coupon adjusts each period in direct relation to changes in market interest rates. In fact, the market price returns to par value after each reset unless the margin no longer sufficiently compensates fully for the default or other risks. Therefore, price changes are very limited as compared to fixed-rate bonds of the same maturity.

How an Inverse FRN Works

Inverse FRNs have a coupon-reset formula in which LIBOR is subtracted from a fixed percentage rate. As LIBOR increases (decreases), the coupon payment on an inverse FRN decreases (increases). By design, this type of security is attractive to investors who expect interest rates to fall and are therefore bullish on bond prices. The inverse FRN is attractive because its price volatility is greater than (typically about double) that of a fixed-rate note of the same maturity. To compensate for its greater riskiness, the initial coupon rate is typically higher than on a traditional FRN. Investors thus realize a higher yield if interest rates remain steady or fall, but risk larger price declines if interest rates rise.

Inverse FRNs can hedge an exposure to floating interest rates. For instance, a thrift institution that is exposed to higher deposit rates could issue an inverse FRN to smooth out its cost of funds. The coupon payments on the inverse FRN offset those on the traditional FRN.[11]

Synthetic Inverse FRNs

A synthetic inverse FRN can be created in multiple ways. Suppose the coupon-reset formula is 14 percent – LIBOR. Issuing an inverse FRN is equivalent to issuing two fixed-rate notes paying interest at 7 percent, buying an unrestricted FRN paying LIBOR flat, and selling a 14 percent cap on LIBOR:

$$
\begin{array}{c}
\text{Short} \\
\text{inverse FRN} \\
(14\% - \text{LIBOR})
\end{array}
=
\begin{array}{c}
\text{Short} \\
2 \text{ fixed-rate notes} \\
(7\%)
\end{array}
+
\begin{array}{c}
\text{Long} \\
\text{unrestricted} \\
\text{FRN} \\
(\text{LIBOR})
\end{array}
+
\begin{array}{c}
\text{Short cap} \\
(14\% \text{ strike})
\end{array}
\quad (7.16)
$$

Without the cap, the synthetic inverse FRN would pay a negative coupon rate when LIBOR rises above 14 percent. Rewriting equation 7.13, a long position in an unrestricted FRN paying LIBOR is equivalent to a long position in a fixed-rate note with interest at the SFR plus a long position in an interest rate swap. Substituting this into equation 7.16 gives:

$$
\begin{array}{c}
\text{Short} \\
\text{inverse FRN} \\
(14\% - \text{LIBOR})
\end{array}
=
\begin{array}{c}
\text{Short} \\
2 \text{ fixed-rate} \\
\text{notes} \\
(7\%)
\end{array}
+
\begin{array}{c}
\text{Long} \\
\text{fixed-rate} \\
\text{note} \\
(\text{SFR})
\end{array}
+
\begin{array}{c}
\text{Long} \\
\text{interest} \\
\text{rate swap} \\
(\text{pay SFR,} \\
\text{receive LIBOR})
\end{array}
+
\begin{array}{c}
\text{Short cap} \\
(14\% \\
\text{strike})
\end{array}
$$
$$(7.17)$$

Next, combine the fixed-rate notes and rearrange terms. The inverse FRN is equivalent to a synthetic fixed-rate note, an interest rate swap, and a cap:

$$
\begin{array}{c}
\text{Short} \\
\text{inverse FRN} \\
(14\% - \text{LIBOR})
\end{array}
=
\begin{array}{c}
\text{Short} \\
\text{fixed-rate note} \\
(14\% - \text{SFR})
\end{array}
+
\begin{array}{c}
\text{Long} \\
\text{interest rate swap} \\
(\text{pay SFR, receive} \\
\text{LIBOR})
\end{array}
+
\begin{array}{c}
\text{Short cap} \\
(14\% \text{ strike})
\end{array}
$$
$$(7.18)$$

The inverse FRN is equivalent to issuing a synthetic fixed-rate note paying 14 percent – SFR, paying SFR on an interest rate swap and receiving LIBOR, and selling a 14 percent cap on LIBOR.

Why Issue Inverse FRNs?

Equation 7.18 can be rewritten as:

$$
\begin{array}{l}
\text{Short} \\
\text{fixed-rate note} \\
(14\% - \text{SFR})
\end{array}
=
\begin{array}{l}
\text{Short} \\
\text{inverse FRN} \\
(14\% - \text{LIBOR})
\end{array}
+
\begin{array}{l}
\text{Short} \\
\text{interest rate swap} \\
(\text{receive SFR,} \\
\text{pay LIBOR})
\end{array}
+
\begin{array}{l}
\text{Long cap} \\
(14\% \text{ strike})
\end{array}
$$

$$(7.19)$$

If issuing the inverse FRN, going short an interest rate swap (to receive fixed rate and pay LIBOR), and buying a 14 percent cap on LIBOR is less costly than a conventional fixed-rate note, then issuing the inverse FRN is cheaper.[12] However, as with any other derivatives structure, it is important to assess any difference in default risk before concluding there is an arbitrage gain.

Structured Products

Interest rate swaps, fixed-rate notes, and floating-rate notes can be structured to conform to a specific view on future movements of interest rates (or a currency or commodity price). This is usually done by including one or more interest rate options, as we illustrate later in the chapter. These instruments are known as *structured products*.[13] Generally they are designed around an interest rate swap and called *structured swaps*, or they are designed around a fixed-rate or floating-rate note and called *structured notes*. Prior to a recent change in the accounting for derivatives, structured swaps were often preferred because it was easier to keep them off the balance sheet.[14]

What Structured Products Are Designed to Achieve

Market participants almost always have a view on interest rates. Often their view is based on a forecast. Such forecasts are important in market participant decisions. But even when there is no explicit forecast and no intended bet on the course of interest rates, there is an implicit view in each investment and new issue decision taken or postponed. Even a simple decision to invest in back-to-back three-month Treasury bills rather than buying six-month Treasury bills has an implicit view— in this case, that the three-month T-bill rate on the rollover date is likely to be above the rate that the forward curve now predicts.

Structured products are distinguished by the specificity of the view. The view can be tailored in any number of ways, such as a specific interest rate staying within a particular interest rate band, or the difference between specified short-term and long-term interest rates changing in a particular way. One can bet on the direction of interest rates, changes in the shape of the yield curve, shifts in interest rate volatilities, and so on.

Taking a View on the Direction of Interest Rates

We have already discussed one structure that facilitates a bet on the direction of short-term interest rates: the inverse FRN. This first-generation product was subsequently modified to enhance its price sensitivity to interest rate changes.

Leveraged Inverse FRNs

Let us examine the investor's motive for purchasing inverse FRNs. Reverse equation 7.18 to obtain the investor's perspective:

$$
\begin{array}{c}
\text{Long} \\
\text{inverse FRN} \\
(14\% - \text{LIBOR})
\end{array}
=
\begin{array}{c}
\text{Long} \\
\text{fixed-rate note} \\
(14\% - \text{SFR})
\end{array}
+
\begin{array}{c}
\text{Short} \\
\text{interest rate swap} \\
(\text{pay LIBOR,} \\
\text{receive SFR})
\end{array}
+
\begin{array}{c}
\text{Long cap} \\
(14\% \text{ strike})
\end{array}
$$

$$(7.20)$$

An inverse FRN, barring default, is equivalent to purchasing a fixed-rate note, going short a swap (to pay floating and receive fixed), and buying an interest rate cap. Figure 7.7 shows how layering additional short swaps on top of a long position in an FRN creates different synthetic fixed-rate and floating-rate debt instruments. In figure 7.7A, an investor purchases FRNs. In figure 7.7B, the investor then sells a swap (to receive 7 percent fixed and pay LIBOR). The swap's notional amount equals the principal amount of the FRNs. Combining the long position in the FRNs and the short position in the swap produces a synthetic fixed-rate note paying 7.50 percent.

In figure 7.7C, selling a second swap that is identical to the first (or doubling the notional amount of the first swap) transforms the synthetic fixed-rate note into a synthetic inverse FRN paying 14.50 percent – LIBOR. This synthetic instrument combines a long position in FRNs and two identical swaps to receive 7 percent and pay LIBOR.

In figure 7.7D, selling a third identical swap converts the synthetic inverse FRN into a synthetic *leveraged inverse FRN*. The term *leveraged* refers to the multiple applied to LIBOR—in this case, 2. The coupon

Figure 7.7 Creating Synthetic Inverse Floaters

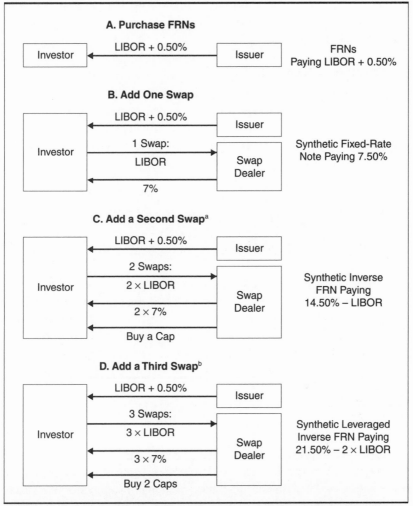

[a]This result can also be achieved by doubling the notional amount of the first swap.
[b]This result can also be achieved by tripling the notional amount of the first swap.

rate of the leveraged inverse FRN in figure 7.7 declines twice as fast as the coupon of the inverse FRN as LIBOR rises. The leveraged inverse FRN pays interest at the rate of 21.50 percent − 2 × LIBOR. Investors buy inverse FRNs rather than create synthetics because the inverse FRN is simpler and has less credit risk. Issuers of inverse FRNs usually have strong credit, often AAA-rated. The synthetic involves bearing credit risk on the underlying FRN, the two swaps, and the cap. Also, some potential investors might be prohibited, by policy or regulation, from buying derivative contracts. Embedding the derivatives in a structured note, such as an inverse FRN, can provide a way around such restrictions.

Duration of Inverse FRNs

Next consider the duration of inverse FRNs and leveraged inverse FRNs. The duration of a portfolio equals the market-value-weighted average of the durations of the instruments that compose the portfolio. Reverse equation 7.16 to express an investment in a synthetic inverse FRN:

$$
\begin{array}{c}
\text{Long} \\
\text{inverse FRN} \\
(14\% - \text{LIBOR})
\end{array}
=
\begin{array}{c}
\text{Long} \\
\text{2 fixed-rate} \\
\text{notes} \\
(7\%)
\end{array}
+
\begin{array}{c}
\text{Short} \\
\text{unrestricted} \\
\text{FRN} \\
(\text{LIBOR})
\end{array}
+
\begin{array}{c}
\text{Long cap} \\
(14\% \text{ strike})
\end{array}
\qquad (7.21)
$$

The duration of a traditional FRN is relatively low; it can be approximated by the time to the next reset date. Since the durations of the FRN and the cap partially offset each other, the duration of the inverse FRN is roughly twice the duration of a fixed-rate note that is worth par and matures on the same date. Similarly, a leveraged inverse FRN has an even longer duration, which can be adjusted by altering the leverage (i.e., the multiple of LIBOR).

Conclusion

Firms have responded to the volatility of financial markets by seeking better ways to hedge their risk exposure, and financial engineers have responded by developing new hedging instruments. Financial engineering designs financial structures that provide superior, previously unavailable risk-return combinations, often by combining new interest rate–derivative products, such as interest rate swaps, caps, floors, and collars, with traditional fixed- and floating-rate notes.

The key to developing better interest rate risk management vehicles is to design instruments that provide the desired future cash flow profile. The basic derivative building blocks are combined with traditional fixed-income instruments to meet the risk-management objective. There are usually multiple ways available. The challenge is to determine which of the equivalent ways is most cost-effective. But in analyzing the alternatives, care must be taken because structures that include interest rate swaps and long positions in caps and floors always have some default risk. Although credit enhancements can be added to offset the default risk, they add to the cost.

Designing new instruments to solve problems requires a thorough understanding of the basic derivative building blocks and how they can be used to alter the interest rate sensitivity of a fixed-income instrument. With this knowledge, a skilled financial engineer can tailor positions for market participants to be where they want on the risk-return spectrum for interest rates.

Chapter *8*

Debt Innovations

*F*inancial engineering involves crafting innovative financial instruments to solve financial problems.[1] A new financial instrument is truly innovative only if it enables market participants to accomplish something they could not achieve with existing securities. The goal may be a higher after-tax return or lower after-tax cost for a given level of risk, greater liquidity, or perhaps just a more desirable pattern of cash flows. Often the objective is more cost-effective hedging vehicles. A new instrument can combine simple instruments, such as a fixed- or floating-rate note, with options, swaps, and other basic building blocks, into a package that solves a particular problem or meets a special need. The challenge is to determine if the new security is truly beneficial—or if it is intended only to enrich those who designed and sold it.

The rapid pace of securities innovation has brought about revolutionary changes in the array of fixed-income instruments. A variety of factors stimulate securities innovation. Among them are interest rate volatility, tax and regulatory changes, deregulation of the financial services industry, and increased competition within the investment banking industry.[2]

Significant securities innovations help the capital markets operate more efficiently or make them less incomplete.[3] Greater efficiency can come from reducing transaction costs. A new security that provides contingent after-tax returns that cannot be replicated by any combination of existing securities makes the capital markets less incomplete.

Innovations endure if they provide a new way of meeting fundamental economic demands. For example, financial futures have enjoyed ever-expanding growth since their inception in the early 1970s. Other innovations, such as zero-coupon bonds, were issued in large volume for a time but have since been issued less frequently because changes in tax law eliminated their advantages or more recent innovations superseded them. Extendable notes, medium-term notes, and collaterized mortgage obligations have had a more lasting impact. And some innovations disappear quickly, sometimes after just one issue.

This chapter describes a variety of innovative fixed-income securities and identifies the sources of their value added. The value added explains the staying power for securities that have endured and the lack of innovation in those that have failed.

Sources of Value Added

Securities innovation can add value in the following ways:

- Reallocating some form of risk from issuers or investors to other market participants who are either less risk averse or else willing to bear them at a lower cost

- Increasing liquidity

- Reducing agency costs arising from conflicts of interest among the firm's stakeholders

- Reducing issuers' underwriting fees and other transaction costs

- Reducing the combined taxes of issuer and investors

- Circumventing regulatory restrictions or other constraints on investors or issuers

Risk Reallocation

Most debt innovations (see table 8.1) involve some form of risk reallocation as compared to conventional debt instruments. Risk reallocation adds value by transferring risks to others better able to bear them. It may also be beneficial to design a security that better suits the risk-return preferences of a particular class of investors. Investors with a comparative advantage in bearing certain risks will pay more—or, alternatively, have a lower required return—for innovative securities that allow them to specialize in bearing such risks.

Suppose an oil producer issued "oil-indexed" debt with interest payments that rise and fall with oil prices. It might have a lower required return for two reasons: (1) the firm's after-interest cash flows will be more stable than if it issued straight, fixed-rate debt, thereby reducing default risk, and (2) some investors may be seeking a "play" on oil prices—an opportunity to bet on the direction of oil prices—not otherwise available in the financial markets.

Table 8.1 Selected Debt Innovations

Security □ Distinguishing Characteristics ● Enhanced Liquidity ○ Reduction in Transaction Costs	Year First Issued □ Risk Reallocation ● Reduction in Agency Costs ○ Tax and Other Benefits	Number of Issues	Aggregate Proceeds ($billions)
■ **Adjustable-Rate Notes and Floating-Rate Notes**	■ 12/22/70	■ 14,403	■ 1,731.8
□ Coupon rate floats with some index, such as the 91-day Treasury bill rate.	□ Issuer exposed to floating-interest-rate risk but initial rate is lower than for fixed-rate issue.		
● Price remains closer to par than price of fixed-rate note of same maturity.			
■ **Bonds Linked to Commodity Price or Commodity Price Index**	■ 04/10/80	■ 54	■ 3.6
□ Interest and/or principal linked to a specified commodity price or commodity price index.	□ Issuer assumes commodity price risk in return for lower (minimum) coupon. Serves as a hedge if the issuer produces the commodity.		
	○ Attractive to investors who would like to speculate in commodity options but cannot, for regulatory reasons, purchase them directly.		
■ **Catastrophe Bonds**	■ N/A	■ N/A	■ N/A
□ The interest payments or the principal payment, or both, are reduced according to a specified formula if the insurance company issuer suffers insurance losses from certain specified natural disasters, such as a hurricane or an earthquake.	□ Investors bear a portion of the risk of loss from the specified natural disasters. The bonds securitize reinsurance. Because natural catastrophic risk has very low correlations with financial risks, catastrophe bonds are potentially attractive for diversification purposes.		
● More liquid than traditional reinsurance contracts.	● Reinsurance involves significant adverse selection and moral hazard risks for investors.		
■ **Collateralized Debt Obligations**	■ 03/24/83	■ 943	■ 67.4
□ A portfolio of junk bonds or bank loans, or some of each, is placed in a trust or special-purpose entity, which issues multiple classes of debt obligations that are prioritized with respect to their right to receive payments from the debt pool.	□ The senior classes are investment-grade. Credit risk can be reallocated among investors in a cost-efficient manner.		
● The CDOs are usually more liquid than the underlying debt instruments.			

(continued)

Table 8.1 (continued)

■ Security □ Distinguishing Characteristics ● Enhanced Liquidity ○ Reduction in Transaction Costs	■ Year First Issued □ Risk Reallocation ● Reduction in Agency Costs ○ Tax and Other Benefits	■ Number of Issues	■ Aggregate Proceeds ($billions)
■ **Collateralized Mortgage Obligations (CMOs) and Real Estate Mortgage Investment Conduits (REMICs)**	■ 04/23/81	■ 9,826	■ 2,815.6
□ Mortgage payment stream is divided into several classes, which are prioritized in terms of their right to receive principal payments. ● More liquid than individual mortgages.	□ Reduction in prepayment risk to classes with prepayment priority. Appeals to different classes of investors; sum of parts can exceed whole.		
■ **Commercial Real Estate–Backed Bonds**	■ 03/14/84	■ 1,985	■ 237.1
□ Nonrecourse bonds backed by specified piece (or portfolio) of real estate. ● More liquid than individual mortgages.	□ Reduced yield due to greater liquidity. ○ Appeals to investors who like to lend against real estate properties.		
■ **Credit Card Receivable–Backed Securities**	■ 01/16/87	■ 1,167	■ 403.7
□ Investor buys an undivided interest in a pool of credit card receivables. ● More liquid than individual receivables. ○ Investors could not achieve the same diversification as cheaply on their own.	□ Supplemental credit support in the form of a letter of credit, surety bond, limited guarantee, overcollateralization, or senior-subordinated structure.		
■ **Credit-Sensitive Notes**	■ 05/19/88	■ 14	■ 3.6
□ Coupon rate increases (decreases) if the issuer's credit rating falls (improves). Alternatively, another structure provides that the coupon of an investment-grade note would step up by 200 basis points if the note is downgraded to junk status.	□ Protects the investor against deterioration in the issuer's credit quality because coupon increases when rating declines.		
■ **Deferrable Interest Debentures**	■ 01/06/95	■ 25	■ 4.2
□ Junior subordinated debentures that pay interest monthly or quarterly and that permit the issuer to defer interest payments for up to five years without triggering a default. Interest compounds during the deferral period.	□ Investors bear more credit risk than a conventional junior subordinated debt issue would involve but the issuer gets some "equity" credit from the rating agencies.		

Instrument			
Deferred-Interest Debentures □ Debentures that accrue—and do not pay in cash—interest for a period. □ Reduces bankruptcy risk during the interest deferral period.	09/17/82	32	9.1
Direct-Issue Demand Notes □ Notes, which are issued directly to investors, that pay interest at a variable money market rate and are repayable on demand by the holder. ○ By eliminating the intermediary, the issuer can borrow more cheaply than issuing commercial paper while paying investors a higher interest rate than money market funds.	N/A	N/A	N/A
Dollar BILS □ Floating-rate zero-coupon note with effective interest rate determined retrospectively based on the value of a specified corporate bond index. □ Issuer assumes reinvestment risk. Useful for hedging and immunization purposes because dollar BILS have a zero duration when duration is measured with respect to the specified index.	08/22/88	1	0.1
Dual Coupon Bond/Fixed-Floating-Rate Bonds □ Interest is calculated on a fixed-rate basis during the early life of the bond and on an inverse-floating-rate basis for the bond's remaining life. □ Issuer exposed to the risk that interest rates may decrease during the inverse-floating-rate period because the coupon will increase if the specified market benchmark interest rate decreases. ○ Useful for hedging and immunization purposes because of the very long duration.	11/25/85	527	31.7
Dual Currency Bonds □ Interest payable in U.S. dollars but principal payable in a currency other than U.S. dollars. □ Issuer has foreign currency risk with respect to principal repayment obligation. Currency swap can hedge this risk and lead in some cases to yield reduction. ○ Euroyen-dollar dual currency bonds popular with Japanese investors subject to regulatory restrictions and desiring income in dollars without principal risk.	01/21/83	864	84.2
Euronotes and Euro-Commercial Paper □ Euro-commercial paper is similar to U.S. commercial paper. □ Elimination of intermediary brings savings lender and borrower can share. ○ Corporations invest in each other's paper directly rather than through an intermediary.	N/A	N/A	N/A

(continued)

Table 8.1 (continued)

■ Security □ Distinguishing Characteristics ● Enhanced Liquidity ○ Reduction in Transaction Costs	■ Year First Issued □ Risk Reallocation ● Reduction in Agency Costs ○ Tax and Other Benefits	■ Number of Issues	■ Aggregate Proceeds ($billions)
■ **Extendable Notes** □ Interest rate adjusts every two or three years to a new interest rate the issuer establishes, at which time the note holder also has the option to put the notes back to the issuer. ○ Lower transaction costs than issuing two- or three-year notes and rolling them over.	■ 03/09/82 □ Coupon based on two- to three-year put date, not on final maturity. ● Investor has a put option, which provides protection against deterioration in credit quality or below-market coupon rate.	■ 239	■ 34.5
■ **Fixed-Rate Capital Securities** □ Long-term subordinated debt is issued to a trust or a special-purpose company wholly owned by the parent. This entity issues cash-matching preferred stock. The parent can defer interest payments for up to five years without triggering a default, but interest compounds during the deferral period.	■ 10/27/93 □ Investors bear more credit risk than on a conventional subordinated debt issue, and the issuer gets some "equity" credit from the rating agencies. ○ Parent company can deduct the interest payments on the underlying subordinated debt.	■ 155	■ 33.1
■ **Floating-Rate, Rating-Sensitive Notes** □ Coupon rate resets quarterly based on a spread over LIBOR. Spread increases if the issuer's debt rating declines. ● Price remains closer to par than the price of a fixed-rate note of the same maturity.	■ 06/28/88 □ Issuer exposed to floating-interest-rate risk, but the initial rate is lower than for fixed-rate issue. ● Investor protected against deterioration in the issuer's credit quality because of increase in coupon rate when rating declines.	■ 9	■ 1.6
■ **Global Bonds** □ Debt issue structured so as to qualify for simultaneous issuance and subsequent trading in U.S., European, and Japanese bond markets. ● Structure facilitates a relatively large issue. Simultaneous trading in the United States, Europe, and Japan coupled with large size enhances liquidity.	■ 06/14/89	■ 1,906	■ 942.1

Increasing-Rate Notes
- 01/21/88 ■ 61 ■ 13.7
- □ Coupon rate increases by specified amounts at specified intervals.
- □ Defers portion of interest expense to later years, which increases duration.
- ● When issued with bridge financing, step-up in coupon rate compensates investors for the issuer's failure to redeem the notes on schedule.

Indexed-Currency-Option Notes/Currency-Linked Notes
- 10/24/85 ■ 22 ■ 0.6
- □ Issuer pays reduced principal at maturity if specified foreign currency appreciates sufficiently relative to the U.S. dollar.
- □ Investor assumes foreign currency risk by effectively selling the issuer a call option denominated in the foreign currency.
- ○ For investors who would like to speculate in foreign currencies but cannot purchase currency options directly.

Indexed Sinking-Fund Debentures
- 07/12/88 ■ 6 ■ 3.7
- □ The amount of each sinking-fund payment is indexed to a specified interest rate index (typically the ten-year constant maturity Treasury yield).
- □ The security's duration and convexity are closer to those of a fixed-rate mortgage than a conventional fixed-rate bond so it is useful to financial institutions that invest in mortgages for duration-matching purposes.

Interest-Rate-Reset Notes
- 06/01/83 ■ 78 ■ 13.2
- □ Interest rate is reset three years after issuance to the greater of (1) the initial rate and (2) a rate sufficient to give the notes a market value equal to 101% of their face amount.
- ● Reduces the (initial) yield due to the reduction in agency costs.
- ○ Investor is compensated for a deterioration in the issuer's credit standing within three years of issuance.

Loan-Backed Certificates
- 05/15/85 ■ 2,053 ■ 485.2
- □ Investor buys an undivided interest in a pool of automobile, manufactured housing, residential second lien, or other consumer loans.
- □ Supplemental credit support in the form of letter of credit, limited guarantee, surety bond, overcollateralization, or senior-subordinated structure. Provider of credit support bears residual default risk. Reduced yield due to the benefit to the investor of credit support, diversification, and greater liquidity.
- ● More liquid than individual loans.
- ○ Investors could not achieve the same diversification as cheaply on their own. Can be structured as a sale of assets to remove loans from balance sheet.

Medium-Term Notes
- 04/17/73 ■ 37,421 ■ 3,426.1
- □ Notes are sold in varying amounts and in varying maturities on an agency basis.
- □ Issuer bears market price risk during the marketing process.
- ○ Agents' commissions are lower than underwriting spreads.

(continued)

Table 8.1 (continued)

Security □ Distinguishing Characteristics ● Enhanced Liquidity ○ Reduction in Transaction Costs	■ Year First Issued □ Risk Reallocation ● Reduction in Agency Costs ○ Tax and Other Benefits	■ Number of Issues	■ Aggregate Proceeds (\$billions)
Mortgage-Backed Bonds □ Bonds issued by financial institutions (or other borrowers) that are collateralized by a specified pool of mortgages.	12/16/70	1,003	111.2
	□ Collateral provides added security to the investors, making possible a lower interest rate than an unsecured issue of like maturity.		
Mortgage Pass-Through Certificates □ Investor buys an undivided interest in a pool of mortgages. ● More liquid than individual mortgages. ○ Investors could not achieve the same diversification as cheaply on their own.	09/21/77	7,021	872.2
	□ Supplemental credit support in the form of a letter of credit, surety bond, limited guarantee, senior-subordinated structure, insurance, or a reserve fund. Provider of credit support bears residual default risk. Reduced yield due to the benefit to the investor of credit support, diversification, and greater liquidity. ○ Can be structured as a sale of assets to remove loans from the balance sheet.		
Negotiable Certificates of Deposit □ Certificates of deposit are registered and sold to the public on an agency basis. ● More liquid than nonnegotiable CDs. ○ Agents' commissions are lower than underwriting spreads.	07/10/79	10,613	689.8
	□ Issuer bears market price risk during the marketing process.		
Notes with Indexed Optional Redemption Prices □ The call price is equal to the greater of (1) par value and (2) the present value of the remaining debt service payments discounted at a specified (small) spread to the applicable Treasury yield.	11/01/91	1,202	342.8
	□ Investors face less call risk than a conventional bond redemption schedule involves, but the issuer has correspondingly less refunding flexibility.		
Pay-in-Kind Debentures/Variable Duration Notes □ Debentures on which the interest payments can be made in cash or additional debentures, at the option of the issuer. Variable duration notes give the issuer this option throughout the life of the security.	09/18/87	5	1.4
	□ Defers the risk that the issuer will not be able to make timely debt service payments. Reduces bankruptcy risk during the pay-in-kind period.		

Principal-Exchange-Rate-Linked Securities
- 03/12/87
- 26
- 1.6
  - Principal repayment is linked to a specified foreign exchange rate. Amount of repayment in U.S. dollars increases (decreases) as the specified foreign currency appreciates (depreciates) relative to the dollar.
  - Investor has effectively purchased a call option on the specified foreign currency and sold a put option on the same currency.
    - Attractive to investors who would like to speculate in foreign currencies but cannot purchase currency options directly.

Puttable Bonds
- 08/16/73
- 3,253
- 518.8
  - Bond redeemable at holder's option, or in the case of "poison put" bonds, if a certain specified "event" occurs.
  - Option to redeem benefits holders if interest rates rise.
    - Put option provides protection against deterioration in the issuer's credit standing.

Real Yield Securities/Inflation-Indexed Bonds
- 01/20/88
- 3
- 0.4
  - Coupon rate resets quarterly to the greater of (1) change in consumer price index plus the "real yield spread" (3.0% in the first such issue) and (2) the real yield spread, in each case on a semiannual-equivalent basis.
  - Issuer exposed to inflation risk, which may be hedged in the CPI futures market. Real yield securities have a longer duration than alternative inflation-hedging instruments.
    - Real yield securities could become more liquid than CPI futures, which tended to trade in significant volume only around the monthly CPI announcement date.
    - Investors obtain a long-dated inflation-hedging instrument that they could not create as cheaply on their own.

Remarketed Reset Notes
- 12/15/87
- 20
- 4.2
  - Interest rate resets at the end of each interest period to a rate the remarketing agent determines will make the notes worth par. If issuer and remarketing agent cannot agree on rate, then the coupon rate is determined by formula, which dictates a higher rate the lower the issuer's credit standing.
  - Coupon based on length of interest period, not on final maturity.
    - Investors have a put option, which protects against issuer and remarketing agent agreeing to set a below-market coupon rate; flexible interest rate formula protects investors against deterioration in issuer's credit standing.
    - Designed to trade closer to par value than a floating-rate note with a fixed-interest-rate formula.
    - Intended to have lower transaction costs than auction rate notes and debentures, which require periodic Dutch auctions.

(continued)

Table 8.1 (continued)

■ Security □ Distinguishing Characteristics • Enhanced Liquidity ○ Reduction in Transaction Costs	■ Year First Issued □ Risk Reallocation • Reduction in Agency Costs ○ Tax and Other Benefits	■ Number of Issues	■ Aggregate Proceeds ($billions)
■ **Reverse Principal-Exchange-Rate-Linked Securities** □ Principal repayment is linked to a specified foreign exchange rate. Amount of repayment in U.S. dollars increases (decreases) as the dollar appreciates (depreciates) relative to the specified foreign currency.	10/03/88 □ Issuer has effectively purchased a call option on the specified foreign currency and sold a put option on the same currency. ○ For investors who would like to speculate in foreign currencies but cannot purchase currency options directly.	■ 6	■ 0.5
■ **Spread-Adjusted Notes** □ The interest rate spread off a specified Treasury benchmark yield is reset on each interest payment date through a Dutch auction.	05/08/91 □ Investor protected against credit risk but, unlike conventional auction rate debt, is still exposed to interest rate risk. • Interest rate spread off Treasury benchmark yield will increase if issuer's credit standing deteriorates, whether or not issuer's credit rating changes.	■ 1	■ 0.2
■ **Spread-Protected Debt Securities** □ The notes can be redeemed on a specified date (in one case, two years after issuance) prior to maturity, at the option of the holders, at a price equal to the present value of the remaining debt service stream calculated on the exercise date by discounting the future debt service payments at a rate equal to a specified Treasury benchmark yield plus a fixed spread.	01/15/87 □ Investor protected against credit risk up to the put date but is not protected against interest rate risk. • Investor has a put option, which provides protection against deterioration in the issuer's credit standing prior to the put date.	■ 1	■ 0.1
■ **Standard & Poor's 500 Index Notes (SPINs)/Stock Index Growth Notes (SIGNs)/Equity-Indexed Notes** □ Zero-coupon note, principal payment on which is linked to appreciation in value of specified share price index above a specified threshold.	11/21/85 □ Equivalent to a package consisting of a zero-coupon bond and a long-dated call option on a specified share price index. ○ Cheaper than buying a combination of a zero-coupon note and rolling over a series of shorter-term options.	■ 506	■ 22.6

Step-Down Floating-Rate Notes

□ Floating-rate notes on which the interest margin over the specified benchmark (e.g., thirty-day high-grade commercial paper rate) steps down to a smaller margin on a specified date during the life of the instrument.

- 07/11/88
- 27
- 4.0

□ Designed to reduce interest rate margin to reflect direct dependence of required margin on remaining maturity of notes.

Step-Up Callable Bonds

□ Long-term bonds with an interest rate that steps up if the issue is not called on a specified date, in one case ten years after issue. Thereafter, the interest rate floats.

- 07/26/89
- 1,951
- 140.3

● Step-up in interest rate at least partially compensates investors if the issuer's credit standing declines and the issuer fails to redeem the bonds.

Stripped Mortgage-Backed Securities

□ Mortgage payment stream subdivided into two classes: one with below-market coupon and the other with above-market coupon, or one receiving interest only and the other receiving principal only, from a pool of mortgages.

- 07/08/86
- 96
- 24.7

□ Securities have unique option characteristics that make them useful for hedging purposes. Designed to appeal to different classes of investors; sum of the parts can exceed the whole.

Super Premium Notes

□ Intermediate-term U.S. agency debt instrument (typically maturing in one to three years) that carries a coupon rate well above current market rates (and therefore sells at significant premium to its face amount).

- 11/18/88
- 5
- 0.9

○ Attractive to government bond funds that would like to report very high-coupon debt in their portfolios and do not have to amortize the premium over the life of the instrument (or in some cases, money market mutual funds that do not have to show a capital loss even at redemption). As a result, Super Premium Notes provide a lower cost of funds than conventional U.S. agency notes of like maturity.

Tobacco Asset Securitization Bonds

□ Political jurisdictions, such as New York City, that are entitled to share in the proceeds of the master settlement agreement (MSA) entered into by four cigarette manufacturers, forty-six states, and six other jurisdictions to settle certain smoking-related litigation have issued bonds to securitize their right to receive initial and annual payments under the MSA.

- 11/05/99
- 12
- 2.0

□ Investors are exposed to settlement-related credit risk, although the senior-subordinated structure and reserve accounts provide strong protection to senior bondholders.

● The issuer can monetize its right to receive future settlement payments in order to use the proceeds to fund capital expenditures or meet its other funding needs currently.

(continued)

Table 8.1 (continued)

Security □ Distinguishing Characteristics ● Enhanced Liquidity ○ Reduction in Transaction Costs	Year First Issued □ Risk Reallocation ● Reduction in Agency Costs ○ Tax and Other Benefits	Number of Issues	Aggregate Proceeds ($billions)
Variable-Coupon Renewable Notes □ Coupon rate varies weekly and equals a fixed spread over the ninety-one-day T-bill rate. Each ninety-one days the maturity extends another ninety-one days. If put option exercised, spread is reduced. ○ Lower transaction costs than issuing one-year note and rolling it over.	02/02/88 □ Coupon based on one-year termination date, not on final maturity. ○ Designed to appeal to money market mutual funds, which face tight investment restrictions, and to discourage put to issuer.	8	2.2
Variable-Rate Renewable Notes □ Coupon rate varies monthly and equals a fixed spread over the one-month commercial paper rate. Each quarter the maturity automatically extends an additional quarter unless the investor elects to terminate the extension. ○ Lower transaction costs than issuing one-year note and rolling it over.	02/02/88 □ Coupon based on one-year termination date, not on final maturity. ○ Designed to appeal to money market mutual funds, which face tight investment restrictions.	24	5.0
Yield Curve Notes/Maximum-Rate Notes/Inverse-Floating-Rate Notes □ Interest rate equals a specified rate minus LIBOR.	11/18/85 □ Issuer exposed to the risk that interest rates may decrease, which would raise the coupon. Can reduce yield relative to conventional debt when coupled with an interest rate swap against LIBOR. ○ Useful for hedging and immunization purposes because of long duration.	66	5.5
Zero-Coupon Bonds (sometimes issued in series) □ Non-interest-bearing. Payment in one lump sum at maturity.	04/22/81 □ Issuer assumes reinvestment risk. Issues sold in Japan carried below-taxable-market yields reflecting tax advantage over conventional debt. ○ Straight-line amortization of original issue discount pre-TEFRA (Tax Equity and Fiscal Responsibility Act of 1982). Japanese investors realized significant tax savings.	1,797	168.2

Source: John D. Finnerty, "An Overview of Corporate Securities Innovation," *Journal of Applied Corporate Finance* 4 (Winter 1992), pp. 29–32; Thomson Financial Securities Data.

That certain investor clienteles are willing to pay more for scarce securities is clear. Financial intermediaries have earned considerable profits by simply buying existing securities, repackaging their cash flows into new securities, and selling the new securities.[4] The success of stripped U.S. Treasury securities (created by separating the coupon payments from the principal repayment obligation of bearer U.S. Treasury bonds) and stripped municipal securities illustrates that the sum of the value of the parts can exceed the whole.[5] In another example, investment banks purchased portfolios of mortgages from originating institutions, placed them in trusts or special-purpose corporations, and then used those new entities to issue new securities called *mortgage pass-through certificates.* The investment bank pockets the difference (with an important exception noted later) between the payments it receives and those it pays out. Issuers can capture these benefits for themselves by designing new issues of securities appropriately.

Like mortgage pass-through certificates, *credit card receivable–backed securities* and *automobile loan–backed certificates* are undivided ownership interests in portfolios of, respectively, credit card receivables and consumer automobile loans. Such securities allow the originator to transfer the loan's interest rate risk and default risk (or at least a portion of it) to others.[6] The required return on the securitized assets is lower because of the diversification from the pooling.

Managing Reinvestment Risk

Pension funds face reinvestment risk when they reinvest interest payments received on standard debt securities. Zero-coupon bonds were designed in part to appeal to such investors by eliminating the need to reinvest the interest payments. With zero-coupon bonds, interest is effectively reinvested and compounded over the bond's life at its yield to maturity when it was purchased. The yield to maturity on PepsiCo's first issue of zero-coupon bonds was almost four percentage points below the yield on U.S. Treasury securities of the same maturity.

Managing Prepayment Risk

Both *collateralized mortgage obligations* (CMOs) and *stripped mortgage-backed securities* address a somewhat different kind of reinvestment risk that investors in mortgage pass-through certificates found troublesome.[7] Most mortgages are prepayable at par at the option of the mortgagor. The fact that many mortgages will be paid off if interest rates decline creates a significant prepayment risk for lenders; if the principal is returned prematurely, they will be forced to reinvest at lower rates.

To address this "prepayment" risk, CMOs repackage the payment stream from a portfolio of mortgages into several series of debt instruments—sometimes more than five dozen—that are prioritized by their right to receive principal payments. In the simplest form of CMO, each series must be repaid in full before any principal payments can be made to the holders of the next series. Such a CMO effectively shifts most of the mortgage prepayment risk to the lower-priority classes, and away from the higher-priority classes, which benefit from a significant reduction in the uncertainty as to when the debt obligation will be fully repaid.

With the same motive, stripped mortgage-backed securities divide the payment stream into two separate instruments. In their most extreme form, such securities offer one set of claims on the interest payments exclusively (IOs) and another on just principal repayments (POs).[8]

Other New Vehicles for Managing Interest Rate Risk

Adjustable-rate notes and *floating-rate notes* are among the many other innovative securities. By adjusting interest payments to correspond to changes in market interest rates, such floating-rate securities reduce the lender's principal risk by transferring interest rate risk to the borrower. Of course, such a transfer exposes the issuer to floating-rate risk, but this can be of mutual benefit to issuers with assets whose values are directly correlated with interest rate changes. For this reason, banks and credit card companies are prominent among issuers of these securities.

Inverse Floaters

One mechanism for transferring interest rate risk goes by different names because it has different sponsoring securities firms. *Yield curve notes* and *maximum-rate notes,* known collectively as *inverse floaters,* carry an interest rate that decreases as interest rates rise (and vice versa). These instruments are described in chapter 7.

Managing Price and Exchange Rate Risks

Commodity-linked bonds were developed in response to rising and increasingly volatile prices.[9] The principal repayment and, in some cases, the coupon payments of a commodity-indexed bond are tied to the price of a particular commodity, such as the price of oil or silver, or a specified commodity price index. To the extent that interest or principal payments rise and fall with the firm's revenues, the new security reduces the volatility of the firm's (after-interest) cash flow by shifting the debt cost from times when the commodity producer is least able to pay to periods when it is most able to do so.

Dual currency bonds, indexed-currency-option notes, principal-exchange-rate-linked securities (PERLs), and reverse principal-exchange-rate-linked securities (reverse PERLs) illustrate different forms of currency risk reallocation. They allow institutions that want to deal in foreign currencies, but cannot for regulatory or other reasons, to purchase currency options.

Enhanced Liquidity

If a firm can securitize a loan so it becomes publicly traded, the liquidity lowers the required return, reflecting the ability to sell the security without lowering the price or incurring high transaction costs. Examples of such securitization are CMOs, credit card receivable–backed securities, stripped mortgage-backed securities, and loan-backed certificates. All are publicly registered securities with yields significantly lower than those on the underlying assets.[10]

Reductions in Agency Costs

A new security can add value by reducing agency costs arising out of conflicts of interest among managers, stockholders, and bondholders. For example, managers in some cases may increase shareholder value at the expense of bondholders by leveraging up the firm. *Interest-rate-reset notes* address this problem by providing bondholders with protection against a drop in the issuer's credit standing.[11] Similarly, *credit-sensitive notes* and *floating-rate, rating-sensitive notes* bear a coupon rate that varies inversely with the issuer's credit standing.[12]

Puttable bonds provide a series of put options that also protect bondholders against deterioration in the issuer's credit standing. Certain puttable bonds reduce agency costs by giving investors the right to put the bonds back to the issuer if there is a change in control of the corporation or if the corporation increases its leverage above a specified level through a recapitalization. Such *poison-put* options protect bondholders against *event risk.*

Increasing-rate notes, in connection with bridge financing, provide an incentive for the issuer to redeem the notes (using the proceeds of a more permanent financing) on schedule. Unfortunately, as many issuers have discovered, if the increasing-rate notes cannot be refinanced quickly enough, the increasing coupon rate acts like a ticking time bomb that threatens to damage the issuer's credit standing by continually eroding the issuer's interest coverage.[13]

Reductions in Transaction Costs

A number of innovative debt securities increase stockholder value by reducing the underwriting commissions and other transaction costs associated with raising capital. *Extendable notes, variable-coupon renewable notes, variable-rate renewable notes, puttable bonds,* and *remarketed reset notes* are all designed to do this by giving the issuer or investor the option to extend the maturity. For example, extendable notes typically provide for an interest rate adjustment every two or three years, and thus represent an alternative to rolling over two- or three-year note issues without additional issuance expenses. Refinements of the extendable note concept, such as certain puttable bonds and remarketed reset notes, give the issuer greater flexibility in resetting the terms of the security.

Euronotes and *Euro-commercial paper* represent the extension of commercial paper to the Euromarket. Commercial paper reduces transaction costs because corporations bypass a financial intermediary and invest directly in one another's securities.

Securities backed by a diversified portfolio of assets, such as mortgage pass-through certificates, can have a lower required return. The difference depends on how costly it is to obtain the diversification by other means.

Reductions in Taxes

Issuers can add value by designing securities that reduce the total amount of taxes that the firm and its investors pay. Such tax arbitrage occurs when a firm issues debt to investors with a marginal tax rate on interest income that is lower than the firm's marginal income tax rate. For example, as noted in chapter 5, prior to May 1982, zero-coupon bonds offered a tax arbitrage. The issuer could amortize the original issue discount (OID) on a straight-line basis for tax purposes rather than as the interest really compounds. Many zero-coupon bonds were issued before, but since the tax change, they have all but disappeared (except in convertible form).

Circumvention of Regulatory Restrictions or Other Constraints

Bank regulations for debt instruments to qualify as *primary capital* have changed several times in recent years. Banks have responded predictably with new debt securities designed primarily to meet such regulations. Examples include *equity-contract notes,* which obligate holders contractually to convert the notes into the common stock of the bank (or its holding company); *equity-commitment notes,* which the issuer (or its parent) commits to refinance by issuing securities that qualify as capital; and sinking-fund debentures, which pay sinking-fund amounts in common stock rather than cash.

Variable-coupon renewable notes are a refinement of the concept of extendable notes. The maturity of the notes automatically extends ninety-one days at the end of each quarter unless the holder elects to terminate the automatic extension, in which case the interest rate spread decreases. The reduction in spread can be avoided by selling the notes. These features were designed to meet investment regulations on money market mutual funds at the time.[14]

Commodity-linked bonds allow institutions to speculate in commodity options, or invest in them as an inflation hedge, when regulatory or other reasons disallow them from purchasing commodity options directly. Similarly, bonds with interest or principal payments tied to a foreign exchange rate or denominated in a foreign currency allow institutions to speculate in foreign currencies, or invest in them as a hedge, when they cannot make such investments directly. Many of the securities developed in the 1980s and since then contain embedded commodity options or currency options of various forms and were motivated by a desire to circumvent regulatory restrictions.

Value Added from Structuring Securities to Reduce or Reallocate Risk

An *asset-backed security* passes through to security holders the cash flows from a portfolio of financial assets, such as mortgage loans. Complexity arises because principal and interest are not always passed through pro rata; there may be two or more classes of asset-backed securities, which are prioritized by their right to receive cash from the portfolio. The number of classes may be large—sixty or more—and the complexity of the priority rules can challenge even the most sophisticated investors.

Securitized Assets

A representative, but by no means complete, list of securitized assets includes residential mortgage loans, multifamily mortgage loans, commercial mortgage loans, computer installment loans, automobile installment loans, boat installment loans, manufactured housing installment loans, agricultural equipment loans, truck installment loans, franchisee payment obligations, credit card receivables, equipment leases, home equity loans, oil distribution rights, time share loans, recreational vehicle installment loans, commercial bank loans, dealer floor plan loans (to finance an auto dealer's inventory of new cars), consumer loans, foreign sovereign debt, and music royalties.

The U.S. asset-backed securities market is maturing. More than 50 percent of all residential mortgage loans and credit card receivables have been securitized, as well as about 15 percent of automobile installment loans. In contrast, only a relatively small percentage of residential mortgage loans have been securitized in Europe, but such securitization is increasing in the United Kingdom and has also taken place in Australia, Canada, France, Germany, Italy, Japan, Spain, Sweden, and several other countries.

Risk Reallocation or Reduction

The development of the asset-backed securities market has enabled financial institutions to reduce or reallocate the four principal risks associated with the assets:

- *Prepayment risk.* Most U.S. residential mortgagors can, and often do, prepay some or all of the loan without prepayment penalty. CMOs prioritize the right to receive prepayments. Investors who have a preference for shorter-maturity investments can purchase the highest-priority class, and investors who prefer longer-maturity investments can buy the lowest-priority classes. Also, special securities classes can be tailored to suit a particular investor's preferences.

- *Default risk.* In the United States, Freddie Mac (FHLMC) and Fannie Mae (FNMA) provide payment guarantees for certain classes of residential mortgage loans.

- *Liquidity risk.* Mortgage-backed securities and other classes of asset-backed securities are easier and cheaper to trade than the underlying financial assets.

- *Interest rate risk.* An unanticipated increase in interest rates will reduce the value of a fixed-rate loan.[15] Securitization gets fixed-rate loans off a financial institution's books.

Evolution of the Asset-Backed Securities Market

The asset-backed securities market began in the United States in 1970 when Ginnie Mae (GNMA) issued the first mortgage pass-through securities.[16] Prior to its development, there was a secondary market for whole loans, that is, unsecuritized mortgages, but trading was cumbersome, and the market had little liquidity.

Mortgage Securitization

Mortgage pass-through securities also pass through mortgage pre-payment risk. Institutional investors, particularly life insurance companies and pension funds, limited their investments in mortgage pass-through securities because of their aversion to prepayment risk. In response, the CMO was developed in 1983. The earliest CMO, issued by Freddie Mac, had three classes that receive principal payments sequentially: Class A-1 gets all the principal payments from mortgages in the underlying portfolio until it is fully retired; then Class A-2 begins receiving principal payments and gets all the principal payments until it is retired; finally, Class A-3 gets all remaining principal payments. The mortgage-backed securities market has since seen a sequence of more complex structures.

Other Assets

Securities backed by financial assets other than residential mortgages were introduced in 1985 with the sale of computer-lease-backed notes by Sperry Lease Finance Corporation. Later that same year, General Motors Acceptance Corporation (GMAC) introduced securities backed by automobile installment sales contracts. It was a straight pass-through of principal and interest and was supported by a limited GMAC guarantee. In October 1986, First Boston created the first CMO-like issue of automobile loan–backed securities. It had the sequential-pay structure of the early CMOs and was supported by a limited GMAC guarantee, a letter of credit from Crédit Suisse, and the equity of the special-purpose issuer so as to insulate investors from default risk. The first credit card receivable–backed securities were issued in 1987. The development of the structures for other asset-backed securities has generally followed a pattern very similar to the development of the mortgage-backed securities market.

Foreign Securitizations

In 1985 the United Kingdom had the first securitization of assets outside the United States.[17] Securitization developed slowly in the U.K. The regulatory environment there is markedly different from that in the United States, and most residential mortgages there have floating-rate structures as well as other features that required modifications to the securitization techniques in use in the United States. But a market for sterling floating-rate mortgage-backed securities gradually developed. The first sterling CMO appeared in 1989, six years after CMOs first appeared in the United States. Mortgage-backed securities markets also developed in Canada and Australia during the latter half of the 1980s.[18]

Commercial mortgages, export-import bank loans, and leases have been securitized in the United Kingdom, and more recently automobile loans and credit card receivables have also been securitized.[19] Both markets are very small relative to the U.K. mortgage market, making issuance economies of scale difficult to achieve. U.K. stamp duty and consumer credit laws also inhibited automobile loan securitization. Lack of homogeneity in financial lending methods and U.K. title law, which is not conducive to transferring and bundling assets, inhibited the securitization of credit card receivables as well as automobile loans.[20]

Asset securitization could not take place in France until the requisite legal and regulatory framework was put into place with the enactment of La Loi Titrisation in December 1988.[21] The first French asset securitization occurred in December 1989. Its assets were loans extended by the Société des Bourses Françaises to stockbrokers. Business receivables and consumer loans have also been securitized in France.[22]

In addition to the countries noted, there have been occasional issues of securities backed by mortgages, automobile loans, or credit card receivables in Germany, Spain, and Japan, and asset securitization has increased dramatically in Italy. Both Belgium and Spain have worked hard to create a legal environment conducive to asset securitization. The first securitization of automobile receivables in Canada took place in 1991.

Structures for Reallocating Prepayment Risk

CMOs, which reallocate prepayment risk by prioritizing principal repayments among various classes, are designed to take advantage of the segmentation and incompleteness of the bond market. Prepaid mortgages are not a problem for money market mutual funds and other short-term investors, whereas pension funds and other long-term investors do not want mortgages prepaid. By carving up the payment stream, the CMO creates slow-pay (fast-pay) classes that appeal to long-term (short-term) investors. Other structures help to complete the capital market by providing previously unavailable risk-return combinations.[23]

Sequential-Pay Securities

The earliest CMOs were of the sequential-pay variety. An example is the Fannie Mae Guaranteed REMIC Pass-Through Certificates issued April 24, 1990 (Fannie Mae REMIC Trust 1990-55), which has seven classes. Principal prepayments are applied sequentially to classes: A, B, C, D, E, Z (for zero-coupon accrual class), and R (for residual class). No principal is paid on any class until all prior classes have been fully repaid. In addition, the Z class will accrue interest, with the cash used to make principal distributions to prior classes, until the class E certificates have been repaid in full. Holders of the class R certificates are entitled to any assets remaining in the trust after all others have been fully repaid.

Table 8.2 shows the impact of prepayment speed on weighted average life, by class and for the pool. Prepayment speed is a percentage of the PSA standard.[24] Note that pool prepayment risk is neither enhanced nor diminished; it is simply reallocated among the various classes. A CMO enhances value when the aggregate proceeds exceed the cost of the underlying mortgage portfolio, plus the cost of the Fannie Mae guarantees, plus transaction costs.

Planned/Targeted Amortization Classes and Companion Classes

Planned-amortization-class (PAC) bonds and *targeted-amortization-class* (TAC) bonds substantially reduce investors' prepayment risk.[25] PAC bonds repay principal according to a given schedule so long as pool prepayments remain within a specified range (e.g., 100 percent PSA to 300 percent PSA) and provide a predictable cash flow over a wide range of possible future interest rates. However, since prepayment risk is simply reallocated, some of the pool's other classes, called *companion classes*, act as prepayment shock absorbers and bear most of the pool's prepayment risk.

TAC bonds evolved from PAC bonds. They are targeted to a narrower range of prepayment rates.

Prepayment Guarantees or Insurance

PAC/TAC classes have substantially lower—but not zero—prepayment risk. Prepayment risk is sufficiently low for automobile and truck loans that financial institutions sometimes bear all of it. For example, Morgan Guaranty Trust Company of New York committed to a Minimum Principal Payment Agreement for the Asset Backed

Table 8.2 Impact of Different Prepayment Speeds on the Average Lives of the Classes of Fannie Mae REMIC Trust, 1990-55

Class	Weighted Average Life Based on Prepayment Speed (in years)						Range of Weighted Average Life
	0 Percent PSA	100 Percent PSA	185 Percent PSA	300 Percent PSA	500 Percent PSA		
A	6.7 years	1.9 years	1.4 years	1.1 years	0.8 years		5.9 years
B	14.7	5.5	3.6	2.6	1.9		12.8
C	18.3	8.5	5.6	3.9	2.7		15.6
D	20.2	10.9	7.4	5.2	3.5		16.7
E	22.6	14.8	11.0	8.0	5.4		17.2
Z	27.3	22.9	19.0	14.5	9.8		17.5
R	30.0	29.6	29.6	29.6	27.6		2.4
Pool	17.1	9.2	6.6	4.8	3.3		13.8

Source: Federal National Mortgage Association, REMIC Trust 1990-55, prospectus, April 24, 1990.

Securities Corporation's $1,410,840,000 of Asset Backed Obligations Series 4 issued in July 1987. The agreement obligated Morgan Guaranty to purchase automobile receivables from the issuer when prepayments are too slow or invest funds on behalf of the issuer when prepayments are too fast, to maintain the sinking-fund schedule specified in the prospectus.[26] The elimination of prepayment risk reduced the required yield by about one-third of a percentage point.

Interest Only/Principal Only Securities

Interest only (IO) and principal only (PO) CMO classes, called IO STRIPS and PO STRIPS, respectively, are created by dividing the cash flows from a pool of mortgages (or mortgage securities) into two (or in some cases more than two) securities. The IO STRIPS get all the interest, and the PO STRIPS get all the principal.[27]

IO STRIPS and PO STRIPS have different prepayment risk (as well as interest rate risk). When prepayments accelerate, PO STRIPS, which have large positive durations, increase in value because principal is received sooner. IO STRIPS, which have large negative durations, decrease in value because the faster repayment of mortgage principal means that the aggregate flow of interest payments is reduced. Understandably, both have high price volatility.[28]

IO/PO STRIPS are ideal for making a bet on prepayment rates (speculating) or transferring prepayment risk to others (hedging).[29] For example, a financial institution that is concerned that a slower prepayment rate (say, due to an increase in interest rates) will reduce the value of its mortgage portfolio can hedge that risk by buying IO STRIPS. A financial institution that wishes to protect a portfolio of high-coupon mortgages against rising prepayments (say, due to a decrease in interest rates) can purchase high-coupon PO STRIPS. If prepayments do accelerate, the increase in the value of the PO STRIPS will at least partially offset the loss on the mortgage portfolio. IO/PO STRIPS can also be combined with other types of mortgage-backed securities to alter the prepayment rate (and interest rate) sensitivities of mortgage portfolios.

Structures for Reducing or Reallocating Default Risk

Asset-backed securities reduce default risk through diversification. They have also been designed to reallocate the remaining default risk. There are two basic structures:

1. The issuer of the asset-backed security can purchase a guarantee, letter of credit, surety bond, or similar promise of payment from a creditworthy third party.

2. The issuer can assume a disproportionate share of the default risk by subordination to other investors, by pledging a cash collateral account to cover defaults, or by agreeing to provide replacements for defaulted contracts.

U.S. Agency Guarantees of Mortgage-Backed Securities Payments

The mortgage-backed securities issued by Freddie Mac, Fannie Mae, and Ginnie Mae carry payment guarantees that transfer much of the default risk to these agencies. Freddie Mac guarantees the timely payment of interest on its Participation Certificates (Freddie Mac PCs) and also guarantees the ultimate payment of principal on the underlying residential mortgage loans by no later than the stated final payment date. It guarantees the timely payment (rather than just ultimate payment) of principal and interest on what are called its *Gold PCs*. Fannie Mae guarantees the timely payment of interest and principal on its Guaranteed Mortgage-Backed Securities (Fannie Mae MBSs). The mortgages underlying the Ginnie Mae securities are either insured by the Federal Housing Administration (FHA) or guaranteed by the U.S. Department of Veterans Affairs (VA), and Ginnie Mae guarantees timely payment.

Guarantee/Insurance Security Structures

A mortgage, automobile, or credit card lender can retain the bulk of the default risk associated with a specific pool of assets by providing a limited corporate guarantee, overcollateralizing the asset-backed securities issue, or retaining a subordinated interest in the asset pool. Alternatively, the default risk can be transferred to creditworthy third parties by arranging a letter of credit, a pool insurance policy (often used in connection with mortgage pools), or a surety bond. The two basic structures that are used for this purpose are a pass-through structure and a pay-through structure. They must be modified to accommodate credit card receivables.

Pass-Through Structure

Figure 8.1 illustrates a typical *pass-through structure*. There are several variations that operate similarly. The seller-servicer provides a limited guarantee, establishes a reserve fund, arranges a letter of credit,

Figure 8.1 Pass-Through Installment Loan Securitization Structure

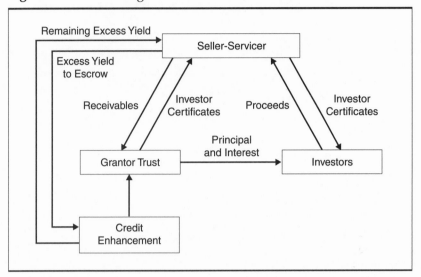

or purchases pool insurance or a surety bond. The loans are transferred to a grantor trust in exchange for pass-through certificates, which are proportional ownership claims on the trust that are sold to investors. To overcollateralize, a seller-servicer sells less than 100 percent of the claims.

All payments, interest, principal repayments, and prepayments, are collected in a segregated bank account that the trustee maintains and are passed through to investors on the specified payment dates. The trustee can draw on the credit enhancement mechanism as required to make up for defaults. Normally the seller-servicer must advance funds, or arrange for a credit line, to cover delinquencies that are expected to be recovered eventually.

The pass-through structure has been used to securitize residential mortgage loans, commercial mortgage loans, automobile installment loans, credit card receivables, recreational vehicle installment loans, equipment leases, boat installment loans, manufactured housing installment loans, and home equity loans.

Pay-Through Structure

Figure 8.2 illustrates a typical *pay-through structure*. The seller transfers assets to a special-purpose corporation (SPC), which issues notes collateralized by the assets. Any of the forms of credit enhancement used in the pass-through structure can also be used in the pay-through structure.

Figure 8.2 Pay-Through Installment Loan Securitization Structure

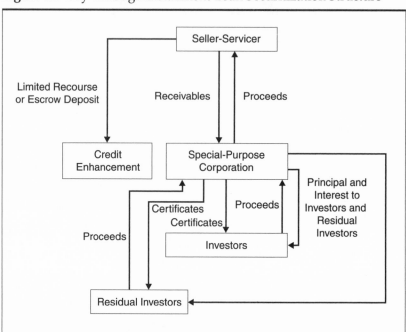

The pay-through structure permits the seller-servicer to modify the cash flows received on the underlying collateral. Such a structure has been used to provide automobile loan–backed and truck loan–backed securities with fixed sinking-fund schedules, which eliminate the certificate holder's exposure to prepayment risk. The restructuring of the cash flows is often used when nonmarket, incentive interest rate automobile loans are securitized.

The pay-through structure has been used to securitize automobile installment loans, truck installment loans, and consumer loans.

Credit Card Receivable–Backed Trust Structure

Credit card receivables have such relatively high monthly average payment rates that a credit card receivable–backed issue would mature within about a year if all the payments were passed through. In order to create an intermediate-term security, credit card receivable–backed certificates typically pay only interest for a specified period, normally twenty-four to sixty months. Principal payments received during this *revolving period* are reinvested in newly generated credit card receivables. Figure 8.3 illustrates how the credit card receivable–backed cer-

Figure 8.3 Amortization Structure of a Credit Card
Receivable–Backed Security

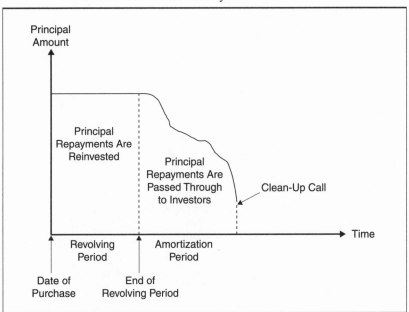

tificates amortize. When the pool balance falls below a specified level, typically either 5 or 10 percent of the original amount (at which point it becomes too expensive to administer the pool), the seller-servicer can redeem the outstanding certificates.

Figure 8.4 illustrates a typical credit card receivable–backed securitization structure. The seller-servicer normally sells more receivables to the trust than the aggregate value of the certificates sold to investors. The seller's interest in the trust is the difference. It typically starts at 15 to 30 percent of the total pool and declines due to cardholder attrition (cardholders' closing their accounts and either paying off or defaulting) unless new accounts are added to the pool. The seller-servicer is required to maintain a specified minimum interest, typically between 5 and 10 percent, to keep the pool balance from falling below the amount of outstanding certificates. The minimum seller interest is a buffer against default risk and prepayment risk.

Default risk is reallocated in three ways:

1. The seller-servicer arranges a letter of credit or surety bond for the benefit of the trust, or the seller subordinates the seller interest in the pool to the investor interest.

Figure 8.4 Basic Credit Card Receivable–Backed Securitization Structure

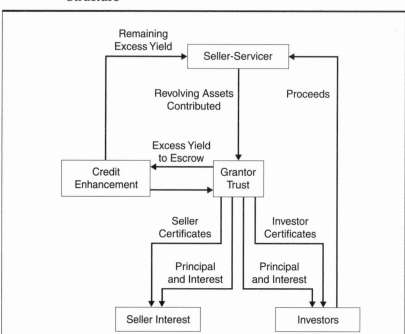

2. Any excess funds remaining after interest on the certificates, servicing fees, and credit enhancement fees have been paid are put in an escrow or reserve account that reimburses the letter of credit or surety bond issuer for any draws made under those facilities.

3. An early, accelerated amortization period begins if the level of loan losses exceeds a specified level, the base yield on the receivables portfolio falls below a specified level, insufficient new receivables are generated to maintain the minimum required seller interest, or certain other *pay-out events* occur.

Senior-Subordinated Asset-Backed Securities

Freddie Mac and Fannie Mae are restricted by law to purchasing mortgages with a balance no greater than a stated maximum, and there are legal restrictions on the size of mortgage the FHA can insure or the VA can guarantee. Mortgages that do not meet these tests are called *nonconforming loans*. The earliest mortgage pass-through securities backed by nonconforming loans relied on mortgage pool insurance or special hazard insurance for credit enhancement. Uncertainty regarding the availability of satisfactory mortgage pool insurance stimulated the development of a senior-subordinated structure.[30] This structure can also be used to reallocate default risk for automobile installment loans, credit card receivables, commercial mortgage loans, manufactured housing installment loans, home equity loans, time-share loans, or any other type of installment loan contract.

Basic Structure for Amortizing Loans

Figure 8.5 illustrates the *senior-subordinated structure* for loans that amortize, such as residential mortgage loans and automobile installment loans. The financing entity issues two (or in some cases more) classes of securities. In the typical case, one class, designated the *senior class,* represents a 90 to 95 percent interest in the trust and receives a prior claim on cash payments. The other class, designated the *subordinated class,* represents the residual interest, which provides credit support for the senior class. The financial institution that formed the trust normally retains the subordinated class, but some have sold the subordinated classes. The size of the subordinated class depends on the type of collateral, the extent of diversification of the collateral, and the experience and capabilities of the servicer.

Senior-subordinated mortgage-backed securities are generally structured in either of two ways: a *reserve-fund structure* or a *shifting-interest structure:*[31]

- *Reserve-fund structure.* Senior-subordinated automobile loan–backed securities are generally of this type. The sponsoring financial institution establishes a reserve fund of between 0.10 and 0.50 percent of the originating pool balance. The subordinated certificate holder gets no cash until the fund builds up to a prespecified level, typically 1 to 2 percent of a pool balance for mortgages and up to 4 to 5 percent for automobile loans. The senior certificate holders and subordinated certificate holders share pro rata in any payments of principal and interest once the reserve fund reaches the specified level. The reserve fund is tapped to the extent that cash flow due to subordinated certificate holders is inadequate to cover senior certificate payment shortfalls.

- *Shifting-interest structure.* The senior certificate holders have first claim on the trust's cash receipts. Any payment shortfall is covered by deducting an equal amount from the subordinated certificate ownership percentage and adding it to the senior certificate ownership percentage.

Figure 8.5 Senior-Subordinated Structure for Amortizing Loans

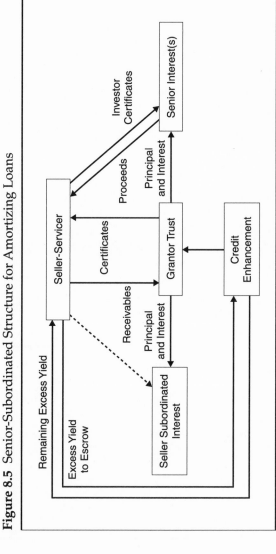

The two structures involve a critical difference: The reserve-fund structure is designed to compensate senior certificate holders immediately for any cash shortfalls that would otherwise occur, whereas the shifting-interest structure compensates senior certificate holders on a deferred basis by increasing the proportion of future cash flows they will receive. In a perfect capital market, the two alternatives would be perfect substitutes. In practice, investors prefer the reserve-fund structure, which has consequently accounted for the majority of the senior-subordinated mortgage-backed securities issues sold in recent years.

Basic Structure for Revolving Loans

Senior-subordinated structures are also commonly used to securitize revolving loans, such as credit card receivables. Figure 8.6 illustrates this structure. There is a revolving period and other features that are typically found in credit card receivable–backed guarantee-insurance security structures. The principal difference is that the seller's interest is expressly subordinated to the investor interest. This subordination replaces the insurance, letter of credit, limited corporate guarantee, or surety bond in the guarantee-insurance structure. The same basic structure has also been used to securitize automobile dealer revolving floor plan financing.

Figure 8.6 Senior-Subordinated Structure for Revolving Loans

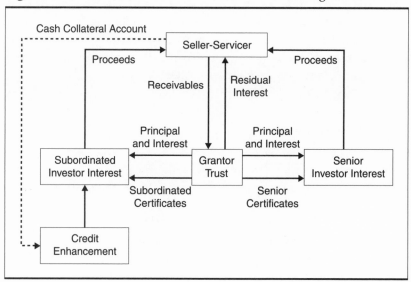

Reduced Liquidity Risk

Asset securitization reduces liquidity risk:

• The asset-backed security is less costly to transfer than the underlying assets because the loan files remain with the pool servicer.

• Credit enhancement, such as a government agency guarantee (e.g., from Fannie Mae or Freddie Mac), reduces default risk.

• The asset-backed securities are either registered for public sale or issued by government agencies that are exempt from securities registration requirements, making the asset-backed securities freely tradable.

• The packagers of asset-backed securities make markets in them.

• Asset-backed securities are designed to avoid temporary payment delinquencies on the underlying loans. For example, mortgage-backed securities usually require the servicer to advance funds as required to make scheduled payments. Senior-subordinated structures typically solve the problem through subordination. Other asset-backed securities use a reserve fund or letter-of-credit facility.

The tobacco asset securitizations are a good example. In November 1998, four cigarette manufacturers reached a historic settlement of smoking-related litigation with forty-six states and six other political jurisdictions. The settlement obligates the manufacturers to pay more than $200 billion over about twenty-five years. New York City sold $709 million of Tobacco Flexible Amortization Bonds in November 1999 to monetize part of its share in the settlement and obtain funds for its capital program. It used a senior-subordinated structure and reserve accounts to obtain a single-A rating for the senior bonds.

Conclusion

Securities innovation can improve capital market efficiency by offering cost-effective means of transferring risks, increasing liquidity, and reducing transaction and agency costs. One of the most important innovations, asset securitization, redirects cash flows through an intermediary and offers new risk-return alternatives. Asset securitization has not only led to new products but also attracted new classes of investors to the mortgage and consumer receivables markets. The reallocation of various types of risk, principally prepayment risk, default risk, liquidity risk, and interest rate risk, is one of the main benefits of securitization.

Asset securitization is part of the natural evolution of an increasingly sophisticated global capital market. And the pace has accelerated during the past two decades. Yet legal and regulatory restrictions, tax laws, and institutional impediments have tended to segment the separate domestic markets for asset-backed securities—and slowed the process of securitization. Globalization is likely to take the form of cross-border financings, perhaps one day even backed by multinational asset pools, and involve the development of new structures to reallocate currency, political, and other types of risk to achieve greater overall economic efficiency.

Securities innovation is a profit-driven response to changes in the economic, tax, and regulatory environments. You may wonder whether securities innovation has reached the point of diminishing returns. If the tax regime remains static, interest rates stabilize, and the regulatory landscape solidifies, diminishing returns to securities innovation are bound to set in. But to the extent that securities innovation occurs in response to unexpected changes, a steady stream of abrupt shifts can keep the process of securities innovation going indefinitely. And together with a continuously changing economic and regulatory climate, further consolidation within the financial services industry will intensify competition, driving market participants to seek better securities designs and more efficient ways of conducting securities transactions.

For a corporate treasurer or chief financial officer, the opportunity to issue a new security can be tempting. Firms that innovate successfully can increase shareholder wealth (along with the treasurer's and the chief financial officer's reputational capital). But the process is not costless (nor riskless), as the highly publicized failed experiment several years ago with something called *unbundled stock units* so clearly demonstrates. Four firms announced their plan to issue the new security and embarked on a lengthy national marketing blitz organized by the securities dealer who invented it. Despite several weeks of aggressive marketing, the new security failed to catch on. The SEC gave everyone involved the opportunity to save face when it objected to the accounting treatment (which five of the leading accounting firms had already blessed), and the offering plans were canceled.

A firm should issue a new security only after it has determined that there is a market for it and that issuing it will increase shareholder wealth.

Chapter 9

Valuing Bonds and Bank Loans

Valuation has a critical role in debt management. The value of each debt feature is needed to be able to choose the best design for a new issue. Accurate values for outstanding bonds and potential new issues are required to make refunding decisions.

The best measure of bond value is the most recently traded price in a liquid market. Unfortunately, this measure is not always available. Unlike many stocks, bonds are generally not exchange listed and not traded in liquid markets. In such situations, we must infer a value from either comparable bonds trading in liquid markets or benchmark yields.

This chapter begins with the basic discounted-cash-flow (DCF) approach to valuing bonds. DCF analysis assumes the yield curve is flat and remains stationary over the bond's life and also that there is no interest rate uncertainty. But the yield curve is seldom flat and rarely stationary, and future interest rates are uncertain. Therefore, a more robust valuation method is needed when accuracy is critical. The binomial model, which explicitly incorporates interest rate uncertainty and can value a broad range of debt securities, can be very useful in making decisions on the design of new issues and refunding.

Discounted-Cash-Flow Analysis

In DCF analysis, the bond's value equals the present value of its payment stream.

Interest Rate Conventions

Interest rates are quoted as annual percentage rates (APRs), which are nominal rates. A 12 percent corporate bond paying interest semiannually

199

actually pays 6 percent per semiannual period. Similarly, a 12 percent mortgage paying monthly interest pays 1 percent per month. When using time-value-of-money formulas, the APR (12 percent in our example) must be given as the rate per period (6 percent for the corporate bond and 1 percent for the mortgage), and time must be given as the number of periods (two or twelve times the number of years).

Present Value of a Bond

The value of any financial instrument can be expressed as the present value of its expected cash flows. A bond can be valued in three steps:

1. Estimate the expected cash flows.
2. Estimate the required return.
3. Calculate the present value of the expected cash flows.

The expected cash flows for some bonds are easy to compute; for others, the task is more difficult. The bond indenture spells out the terms of the bond that determine the expected cash flows when there is little or no risk of default. The cash flows for a noncallable bond consist of regular interest payments at the stated coupon rate plus repayment of principal. The required yield reflects the yield that investors can realize on bond investments with comparable risks. Estimating it requires identifying comparable bonds and calculating their yields.

The value of a bond when there is no sinking fund is

$$P = \sum_{n=1}^{N} \frac{C}{(1 + r)^n} + \frac{M}{(1 + r)^N} \tag{9.1}$$

where

P = value of the bond (in dollars),
N = number of semiannual interest periods (number of years to maturity times 2),
C = semiannual coupon payment (in dollars),
r = discount rate (required APR divided by 2), and
M = principal amount repayable at maturity.

Equation 9.1 can be used for any frequency of coupon payments, but N, C, and r must be in consistent time units (e.g., monthly or quarterly).

Note that a zero-coupon bond can be valued using equation 9.1. Simply set $C = 0$.

Relationship Between Price and Yield

A bond's value and its yield (required return) are inversely related. The higher the yield, the lower is the present value. Figure 9.1 illustrates the relationship for a noncallable bond. It is convex. When the yield is below (above) the coupon rate, bond value is above (below) par value.

Next Coupon Payment Due in Less than Six Months

When the next coupon payment is due in less than six months, the first interest payment will be received within a fraction f of the normal six-month interest period. The accepted method for computing the value of the bond is:

$$P = \sum_{n=1}^{N} \frac{C}{(1 + r)^f(1 + r)^{n-1}} + \frac{M}{(1 + r)^f(1 + r)^{N-1}} \tag{9.2}$$

$$f = \frac{\text{Days between settlement and next coupon payment}}{\text{Number of days in the six-month interest period}} \tag{9.3}$$

Figure 9.1 Price Sensitivity of a Fifteen-Year 10 Percent Bond

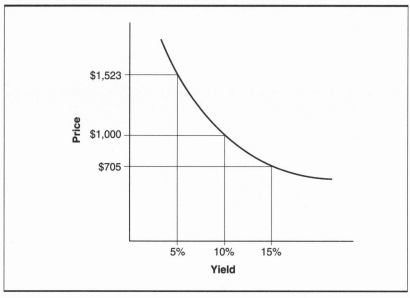

and N is the number of coupon payments remaining in the life of the bond.

Consider a fifteen-year 10 percent bond with a required return of 11 percent, thirty semiannual coupon payments remaining, and the next payment is two months away.

First apply equation 9.3: $f = 2/6 = 1/3$.[1] Next apply equation 9.2:

$$P = \sum_{n=1}^{30} \frac{50}{(1.055)^{1/3}(1.055)^{n-1}} + \frac{1,000}{(1.055)^{1/3}(1.055)^{29}} = \$961.03$$

Sinking-Fund Bonds

When a bond issue contains a sinking fund, the present-value formula is:

$$P = \sum_{n=1}^{N} \frac{CF_n}{(1 + r)^n} \tag{9.4}$$

where

CF_n = cash flow in period n, including repayment of principal,
P = price of the bond, and
N = number of periods in the remaining life of the bond.

Note that equation 9.4 can be modified to calculate the price of a sinking-fund bond between coupon payment dates.

Measuring Bond Yield

The yield on any bond is the discount rate that satisfies equation 9.4 for a given price P.

Converting Yields to a Different Basis

Most U.S. bonds pay interest semiannually, but others pay interest at different intervals. For example, Eurobonds usually pay interest annually. Comparing the yields on bonds that pay interest at different intervals requires converting the yields to a common basis.

To calculate the *effective annual yield* (also called the annual percentage yield, APY):

$$eay = (1 + r/m)^m - 1 \tag{9.5}$$

where *eay* is the effective annual yield, *r* is the APR, *m* is the number of interest payments per year, and r/m is the interest rate per period.

Suppose the semiannual interest rate per period is 4 percent. Then

$$eay = (1.04)^2 - 1 = 0.0816, \text{ or } 8.16 \text{ percent}$$

This process can also be reversed to calculate the interest rate per period from the *eay*:

$$r/m = (1 + eay)^{1/m} - 1 \tag{9.6}$$

Conventional Yield Measures

Four yield measures are common in the bond market: current yield, yield to maturity, yield to call, and yield to worst.

Current Yield

The *current yield* is:

$$\text{Current yield} = \frac{\text{Annual dollar coupon interest}}{\text{Bond price}} \tag{9.7}$$

The current yield ignores the time value of money and the capital gain (or loss) when a bond is purchased at a discount (or premium) and held to maturity. Therefore, it is not very useful.

Yield to Maturity

The *yield to maturity* is the APR for the yield from equation 9.4.

Consider a twelve-year 8 percent bond with a par value of $1,000 selling for $800. The cash flow stream is twenty-four coupon payments of $40 every six months and $1,000 twenty-four six-month periods from now. The current yield is $80/800 = 10.00$ percent. The yield to maturity (indicated by the symbol *y*) solves

$$800 = \sum_{n=1}^{24} \frac{40}{(1 + y)^n} + \frac{1,000}{(1 + y)^{24}} \quad y = .05524$$

per period, or 11.05 percent (2×5.524) per year.

Yield to maturity is clearly superior to current yield because it takes into account the time value of money and any capital gain or loss. However, yield to maturity assumes the investor will hold the bond until maturity and can reinvest the coupon payments at the same yield. If the bond is called, the investor may not realize the yield to maturity.

Yield to Call

Investors calculate the *yield to call* for callable bonds, which assumes the bonds will be redeemed on a particular call date. The yield to call is calculated using equation 9.4, where N is the number of interest periods until the call date, and the final payment CF_N equals the optional redemption (or call) price plus interest up to the call date.

Suppose a twenty-year 7 percent bond with a par value of $1,000 is selling for $1,050. The first call date is ten years from now, and the call price is $1,035. If the bond is called in ten years, its cash flows are $P = 1050$, $N = 20$, $CF_1 = CF_2 = ... = CF_{19} = 35$, and $CF_{20} = 1070$. The yield to call is $y = .0328$, or 6.56 percent per year.

Yield to Worst

Risk-averse bond investors compute the yield to call for various call dates and the yield to maturity for a callable bond selling at a premium. The lowest of these is the *yield to worst*. Their interest in this number is understandable. The issuer will exercise the call option when it is most advantageous to itself—and least advantageous to the investors.

Valuing Floating-Rate Bonds and Bank Loans

The cash flows of a *floating-rate bond* or bank loan (or more simply a *floater*) depend on the future values of the reference rate used to adjust the coupon rate. The coupon rate equals the specified *reference rate* plus some *spread* (or *margin*). For example, the floater's coupon rate might be given as three-month LIBOR (the reference rate) plus 50 basis points (the spread).

The price of a floater depends on two factors: the spread over the reference rate and any restrictions on the coupon rate. For example, a floater can have a maximum coupon rate (a cap) or a minimum coupon rate (a floor). A floater will trade close to its par value on the coupon reset dates as long as the spread agrees with what the market requires (i.e., the issuer's credit quality does not change) and neither the cap nor the floor is reached.[2] If the market requires a larger (smaller) spread, the floater will trade below (above) par. If the cap (floor) is reached (and even somewhat before reaching either threshold), the floater will trade below (above) par.

Effective Margin

Because future interest rates are not known precisely, it is impossible to calculate a yield to maturity for a floater. Instead, we calculate an *effective margin*, which measures the expected average margin over the reference rate that is implicit in the floater's current price. To calculate the value of a floater that is not market traded, the effective margin for comparable loans is added to the reference rate to determine the discount rate to use. The procedure for calculating the effective margin has four steps:

1. Calculate the cash flows assuming the reference rate never changes.

2. Plug the cash flows calculated in step 1 into equation 9.1.

3. Solve for r using the current market price of the bond.

4. Calculate the difference between r obtained in step 3 and the current value of the reference rate to get the effective margin.

Say that a three-year floating-rate loan is selling for 99.7506. It pays a coupon based on six-month LIBOR plus 100 basis points that adjusts every six months. Current six-month LIBOR is 10 percent. Table 9.1 illustrates how to determine the effective margin. At an assumed margin of 110 basis points (55 semiannually), the present value equals the loan price (99.7506).[3]

This procedure assumes the reference rate will not change over the life of the security, and there is no cap or floor. The LIBOR or Treasury bill futures markets can be used to obtain predictions for these reference rates. Each cash flow can be discounted back one period at a time using the reference rate for that period plus the assumed margin. For example, if the first period's reference rate in table 9.1 is 9 percent, the first period's cash flow is $5.0 million ([.09 + .01] × 100/2). With an assumed margin of 110 basis points, the period 1 discount rate is 5.05 percent ([.09 + .011]/2). Each of the cash flows for periods 2 through 6 is discounted back to the end of period 1 using the same 5.55 percent per period rate used in table 9.1 and then discounted to time zero at 5.05 percent. Second, a cap or floor can be taken into account in calculating the cash flows. Uncertainty concerning the future reference rates can be incorporated using a binomial model discussed later in the chapter.

Table 9.1 Calculation of the Effective Margin for a Bank Loan or a Floating-Rate Note

Maturity: three years (six periods)
Coupon rate: reference rate + 100 basis points (resets every six months)

Period	Six-Month LIBOR	Cash Flow[a]	Present Value of Cash Flow at Assumed Margin (in basis points)					
			100	105	110	115	120	
1	10%	5.5	5.2133	5.2120	5.2108	5.2096	5.2083	
2	10	5.5	4.9415	4.9392	4.9368	4.9345	4.9321	
3	10	5.5	4.6839	4.6805	4.6772	4.6739	4.6706	
4	10	5.5	4.4397	4.4355	4.4313	4.4271	4.4229	
5	10	5.5	4.2082	4.2033	4.1983	4.1933	4.1884	
6	10	105.5	76.5134	76.4047	76.2962	76.1879	76.0797	
	Present value =		100.0000	99.8752	99.7506	99.6263	99.5020	

[a]For periods 1 through 5, cash flow = 100(reference rate + assumed margin)(0.5); for period 6, cash flow = 100(reference rate + assumed margin)(0.5) + 100.

Drawbacks to Traditional Yield Spread Analysis

Traditional yield spread analysis for valuing a corporate bond involves calculating the bond's yield to maturity (or yield to call) and subtracting the yield to maturity of a Treasury bond with a maturity (or duration) equal to that of the corporate bond. For example, consider two 9 percent coupon twenty-five-year bonds:

Issue	Price	Yield to Maturity (%)
Treasury	$97.5792	9.25
Corporate	88.8069	10.25

The yield spread is 100 basis points (10.25 percent – 9.25 percent). It measures the yield premium that investors require as compensation for the corporate bond's default risk. There are two main drawbacks to this convention, however.

First, the yield calculation for both bonds fails to account for what is called the *term structure of interest rates.* Second, in the case of a callable or puttable corporate bond, interest rate volatility may alter the bond's cash flows. The yield calculation is a cumbersome way of accounting for this possibility. There is a separate yield calculation for each assumed cash flow stream.

Next we discuss how to take interest rate volatility directly into account when valuing a callable or puttable bond and suggest an alternative to the traditional yield spread calculation.

Bonds with Embedded Options

A bond may give the issuer a call option or the bondholder a put option, which alters the expected cash flows. Although we use corporate bonds as our discussion example here, the same valuation techniques can be applied to agency and municipal bonds.

Investment Characteristics of a Callable Bond

A *callable bondholder* has effectively sold the issuer a call option to redeem the issue prior to maturity. This call option exposes the bondholder to reinvestment risk. It also limits bond price appreciation potential: If bond value goes up too much because interest rates fall, the issuer will redeem the bonds at the call price. This phenomenon is called *price compression.*

Because of these disadvantages, why would anyone invest in a callable bond? The answer, of course, is only if they get a sufficiently large yield premium.

Price-Yield Relationship for a Callable Bond

Figure 9.2 compares the price-yield relationship for callable and noncallable bonds. The convex curve ABC is the price-yield relationship for the noncallable bond. The line ABD is the price-yield relationship for the callable bond. It bends "backward" between B and D. When the yield is above the coupon rate, y_1, a call is unlikely. The bond has the same convex price-yield relationship as a noncallable bond shown in figure 9.1.

As market yields drop, the likelihood increases that the issuer will call the bond. At yields below y_1, the price-yield relationships separate. Consider a bond that is immediately callable at 105. Suppose the market yield would price a comparable noncallable bond at 110. Rational investors would not pay 110 for the callable bond. If they did and the bond were called, they would get only 105 (the call price) for a bond they had just bought for 110.

Figure 9.2 Price-Yield Relationship for Callable and Noncallable Bonds

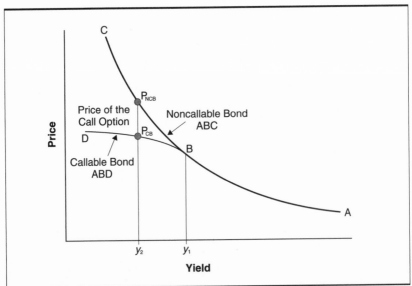

Price compression exists below y_1. The BD portion of the callable bond curve exhibits *negative convexity,* meaning that the price appreciation will be less than the price depreciation for a given change in yield.

A bond can still trade above its call price even if it is highly likely to be called sometime. Consider a twenty-year 10 percent coupon bond that is callable in one year for 105. Suppose yields on twenty-year and one-year bonds of the same credit quality are 7 percent and 6 percent, respectively. Investors will expect the bond to be called in one year and will value it as a one-year bond for $108.54 ($5.00/1.03 + 110/(1.03)^2$). Although this exceeds the call price, it must be the bond's value to give a purchaser the going rate of return (6 percent) on the one-year investment.

Bond Value and Option Value

We can decompose the value of a callable bond into the values of its constituent parts.

Decomposition

A callable bond effectively involves two separate transactions: buying a noncallable bond and selling a call option. The value of the callable bond is the difference:

$$\text{Price of callable bond} = \text{Price of noncallable bond} - \text{Price of call option} \tag{9.8}$$

The value of the call option is subtracted because the bondholder sells the call option to the issuer. This is shown in figure 9.2 where P_{NCB} is the price of the noncallable bond, P_{CB} is the price of the callable bond, and $P_{NCB} - P_{CB}$ is the price of the call option.

Puttable Bonds

Similar logic applies to *puttable bonds*. The bondholder has purchased the right to sell the bond to the issuer at a designated price and time. The investor buys a noncallable bond and buys the put option. The value of a puttable bond is the sum:

$$\text{Price of puttable bond} = \text{Price of nonputtable bond} + \text{Price of put option} \tag{9.9}$$

The Binomial Valuation Model: Preliminary Concepts

The *binomial model* for valuing bonds with embedded options has two advantages over the traditional yield approach. First, it incorporates the term structure of interest rates and uses a separate discount rate for each cash flow. Second, it takes into account explicitly the volatility of interest rates.

Treasury Yield Curve

The binomial model calculates spot and forward rates from the Treasury yield curve. In this way, the model is calibrated so as to price accurately the on-the-run Treasury securities. We develop the binomial model using a very simple four-period example to help keep the mathematics manageable.

Using a single yield from the traditionally constructed Treasury yield curve as the sole discount rate is not the most accurate method of valuing a coupon-paying bond. Bonds with the same maturity may actually have different yields because of coupon rate differences. It is better to calculate zero-coupon yields to avoid the coupon effect on yield to maturity.

Constructing the Spot Rate Curve

In general, we can view any bond as a package of zero-coupon instruments and calculate its total value by summing the component values. To determine the value of each zero-coupon component, first find the yield on a zero-coupon Treasury of like maturity. This is called the *spot rate*. The spot rates from the yields of actively traded full-coupon Treasury debt securities make up the spot rate curve, which is called the *term structure of interest rates*.[4] We illustrate the process using the hypothetical Treasury yield curve in table 9.2 and a $100 par value.

The six-month Treasury security is effectively a zero-coupon security because it makes no interim payments of interest. Its annualized yield of 8.00 percent is the six-month spot rate, or 4.0 percent per period. We use this spot rate to calculate the 1.0-year spot rate.[5] The one-year coupon rate (and yield) for a par value Treasury of 8.50 percent is 4.25 percent per period, so it will pay $4.25 interest in six months and $104.25 interest and principal in one year. The price of the 1.0-year Treasury is the present value of its two payments when each is discounted at the appropriate spot rate:

Table 9.2 Treasury Yield Curve and Corresponding Spot Rate Curve

Period	Term to Maturity (years)	Coupon	Market Value	Yield to Maturity	Spot Rate	Implied Six-Month Forward Rate
1	0.5	8.00%	100%[a]	8.00%	8.0000%	8.0000%
2	1.0	8.50	100[a]	8.50	8.5107	9.0227
3	1.5	9.00	100	9.00	9.0305	10.0739
4	2.0	9.50	100	9.50	9.5613	11.1618

[a]Sometimes the six-month and one-year issues are zero-coupon instruments. In that case, their market prices will be at a discount to their face amount and their yields are the six-month and one-year spot rates, respectively.

$$100 = \frac{4.25}{1.04} + \frac{104.25}{(1 + z_2)^2}$$

Solving for the 1.0-year spot rate, z_2, gives $z_2 = 0.0425535$ per period, or 8.5107 percent per year.

Using the six-month and 1.0-year spot rates, we can extend the process to compute the 1.5-year spot rate. The 1.5-year Treasury rate of 9.00 percent is 4.50 percent per period, so it will pay $4.50 in six months, $4.50 in 1.0 year, and $104.50 in 1.5 years:

$$100 = \frac{4.50}{1.04} + \frac{4.50}{(1.0425535)^2} + \frac{104.50}{(1 + z_3)^3}$$

Solving for the 1.5-year spot rate, z_3, gives $z_3 = 0.0451525$ per period, or 9.0305 percent per year.

Finally, the two-year spot rate is $z_4 = 0.0478065$, or 9.5613 percent per year. This process of calculating each next spot rate from the previously determined rates is called *bootstrapping*.

Spot Rates, the Base Interest Rate, and the Risk Premium

A corporate bond's value is the present value of its payments when each is discounted at the appropriate risk-adjusted rate. The risk-adjusted rate for each payment is a base rate, the Treasury spot rate for that maturity, plus a risk premium. The risk premiums are estimated by fitting the binomial interest rate tree to the (par value) yield curve for corporate bonds with the same bond rating. The steps in the procedure are outlined below.

Forward Rates

We can extrapolate from the yield curve the market's consensus forecast of future interest rates. Consider the following two investment alternatives:

Alternative 1: Buy a one-year zero-coupon bond.

Alternative 2: Buy a six-month zero-coupon bond, and when it matures in six months, roll over the investment by buying another six-month zero-coupon bond.

These two alternatives are equivalent if they produce the same total dollar return over the one-year investment horizon. Given the one-year spot rate, there is some rate on a six-month zero-coupon bond issued six months from now that will achieve this result. Denote this rate by f.

Investing \$1 in the one-year instrument at the two-period spot rate, z_2, will generate $FV_2 = \$1(1 + z_2)^2$ at the end of two periods (one year). Investing \$1 at the six-month spot rate, z_1, will generate $FV_1 = \$1(1 + z_1)$ at the end of six months. Then, reinvesting FV_1 at the subsequent six-month rate f, called the *forward rate*, the total at the end of one year will be $FV_{1,1} = \$1(1 + z_1)(1 + f)$.

The two alternatives are equivalent if FV_2 and $FV_{1,1}$ are equal, which requires

$$f = \frac{(1 + z_2)^2}{1 + z_1} - 1$$

For example, using table 9.2, the six-month forward rate, six months from now, is

$$f = \frac{(1.0425535)^2}{1.04} - 1 = 0.0451133$$

per period, or 9.0227 percent per year.

More generally, given the spot rates for two consecutive periods, z_t and z_{t-1}, the one-period forward rate for time $t-1$ (period t in table 9.2), f_{t-1} is

$$f_{t-1} = \frac{(1 + z_t)^t}{(1 + z_{t-1})^{t-1}} - 1 \tag{9.10}$$

Relationship Between Six-Month Forward Rates and Spot Rates

The t-period spot rate is calculated by compounding the current six-month spot and six-month forward rates:

$$z_t = [(1 + z_1)(1 + f_1)(1 + f_2)(1 + f_3) \ldots (1 + f_{t-1})]^{1/t} - 1 \tag{9.11}$$

Let us say that we have calculated the spot rates $z_2 = 8.5107$ percent and $z_3 = 9.0305$ percent. Substituting into equation 9.10 gives the forward rate f_2:

$$f_2 = \frac{(1.0451525)^3}{(1.0425535)^2} - 1 = 0.0503697$$

per period, or 10.0739 percent per year.

The values for f_1 through f_3 are shown in table 9.2. (Note that today's forward rate is $f_0 = z_1 = 8.0000$ percent.) Then, using equation 9.11,

$$z_4 = [(1.04)(1.0451133)(1.0503695)(1.0558090)]^{1/4} - 1 = 0.0478065$$

or 9.5613 percent per year.

Equivalence of Using Spot Rates and Forward Rates to Value a Bond

Consider a 10 percent option-free bond with a two-year remaining maturity. This bond's value can be calculated by discounting the payments at the spot rates in table 9.2:

$$\frac{\$5.00}{1.04} + \frac{\$5.00}{(1.0425535)^2} + \frac{\$5.00}{(1.0451525)^3} + \frac{\$100 + \$5.00}{(1.0478065)^4} = \$100.8966$$

Alternatively, get the same value by discounting the payments at the six-month forward rates:

$$\frac{\$5.00}{1.04} + \frac{\$5.00}{(1.04)(1.0451133)} + \frac{\$5.00}{(1.04)(1.0451133)(1.0503697)}$$

$$+ \frac{\$100 + \$5.00}{(1.04)(1.0451133)(1.0503697)(1.0558090)} = \$100.8966$$

We will use forward rates in the binomial model. But note that discounting the bond's cash flows at the forward rates period by period gives the same bond value as first calculating the spot rates and then using them to discount the cash flows.

Constructing the Binomial Interest Rate Tree

The binomial model derives its name from assuming that given today's rate, there are only two possible interest rates one period later. Somewhat surprisingly, this very simple structure can value bonds with complex embedded options.

Interest Rate Tree

The binomial model treats interest rate movements along a *binomial interest rate tree*, which is a graphical depiction of the one-period forward rates over the life of the bond.

Figure 9.3 Three-Period Binomial Interest Rate Tree

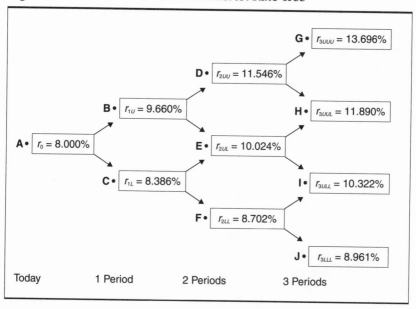

Figure 9.3 contains a three-period binomial interest rate tree. Each node (bold circle) is labeled with a letter before it and an interest rate after it. The subscripts of interest rate r indicate the time period and the path that the one-period forward rates took to get to that node. U represents the upper branch and L the lower branch.

Forward Rates in Period 1

Look at node A with r_0, the current one-period rate. The binomial model assumes there are only two possible values for the next period's rate (the one-period forward rate), and those outcomes are equally likely; each has probability 0.5. The arrows point to the possible outcomes:

r_{1L}, the lower possible forward rate in the first period (at time 1), the lower branch

r_{1U}, the higher possible forward rate in the first period (at time 1), the upper branch

At each node there are only two possible values for the next period's rate. If the forward rate at time 1 turns out to be the higher outcome, r_{1U}, the forward rate at time 2 can then only be r_{2UU} or r_{2UL}. If the forward rate at time 1 turns out to be the lower, r_{1L}, the forward rate at time 2 must be r_{2UL} or r_{2LL}. Note that the order of steps does not matter, so r_{2LU} (which is not shown) equals r_{2UL}. Similarly, in the third period, $r_{3LUU} = r_{3ULU} = r_{3UUL}$, and $r_{3LLU} = r_{3LUL} = r_{3ULL}$. This simplification makes it irrelevant which path was followed to get to the current node.[6]

Volatility

The standard deviation, σ, describes the volatility of the one-period forward rate. The relationship between the two possible interest rates at any given node is

$$r_U = r_L e^{2\sigma\sqrt{\Delta t}} \tag{9.12}$$

where Δt is the length of the time period measured in years, and e is the natural logarithm base, approximately 2.7183.

Suppose each period is one year, r_{1L} is 4 percent, and σ is 10 percent per year. Then

$$r_{1U} = 4.0000 \ (e^{2 \times 0.10}) = 4.8856 \text{ percent}$$

In the binomial model, volatility is proportional to the current level of interest rates. For example, if σ is 10 percent and the one-year rate (r_0) is 4 percent, then the standard deviation of the one-year forward rate is 0.4 percent ($4\% \times 10\%$).

The standard deviation can be estimated from historical Treasury rate data. Table 9.3 gives an example. Using historical data is fine if interest rate volatility is stable. Alternatively, the *implied volatility* can be obtained from the current market prices of interest rate options.[7]

Determining the Value at a Node

The bond's value at a node is the present value of the bond's expected value in the next period. The appropriate discount rate is the one-period forward rate at that node. There are two possible future values: one if the one-period rate is the higher rate and the other if it is the lower rate. Because these outcomes are equally likely, the bond's expected future value is simply the average of the two. Therefore, the bond's value at the node is

$$V = \text{bond value} = \frac{\frac{1}{2}(V_U + V_L) + C}{1 + r} \tag{9.13}$$

Table 9.3 Calculation of Interest Rate Volatility σ Using Weekly Data

Week	r_t	r_{t-1}	$\log(r_t/r_{t-1})$	Week	r_t	r_{t-1}	$\log(r_t/r_{t-1})$
1	10.52%	10.25%	.01129	11	9.75%	9.95%	−.00882
2	10.36	10.52	−.00666	12	9.63	9.75	−.00538
3	10.05	10.36	−.01319	13	9.25	9.63	−.01748
4	10.53	10.05	.02026	14	9.85	9.25	.02729
5	10.75	10.53	.00898	15	9.50	9.85	−.01571
6	11.00	10.75	.00998	16	9.43	9.50	−.00321
7	10.80	11.00	−.00797	17	9.27	9.43	−.00743
8	10.35	10.80	−.01848	18	9.65	9.27	.01745
9	10.75	10.35	.01647	19	9.78	9.65	.00581
10	9.95	10.75	−.03359	20	10.35	9.78	.02460

Average $(r_t) = \mu = \dfrac{1}{20} \sum_{t=1}^{20} r_t = \dfrac{1}{20}(.00421) = 0.00021.$

Variance $(r_t) = \sigma^2 = \dfrac{1}{19} \sum_{t=1}^{20} (r_t - \mu)^2 = \dfrac{1}{19}(.00515) = 0.00027.$

Standard deviation $= \sigma = \sqrt{0.00027} = 0.01647$, or 1.647 percent per week

Annualized standard deviation

= Standard deviation per week$\sqrt{\text{Number of weeks per year}}$

$= 0.01647\sqrt{52} = 0.11877$, or 11.877 percent per year

where

V_U = the bond's value on the upper branch,
V_L = the bond's value on the lower branch,
C = coupon payment on the bond, and
r = one-period forward rate at the node where the bond's value is being calculated.

Constructing the Tree

This section illustrates how to construct a binomial interest rate tree using the on-the-run Treasury yields in table 9.2. Volatility σ is 10 percent. Figure 9.3 shows the initial interest rate tree.

Initializing

At each node, the two possible forward interest rates must satisfy equation 9.12 and average the implied forward rate calculated from the spot rates (see table 9.2). Initializing with σ = 0.10 and Δt = 0.5 (six-month time periods),

$$r_U = r_L e^{2\sigma\sqrt{\Delta t}} = r_L e^{2(0.10)\sqrt{0.5}} = 1.151910 r_L$$

Start at node A. The forward rates for the upper branch are denoted f_B at node B and f_C at node C. Therefore:

$$f_B = 1.151910 f_C$$

Second, the average of these rates must equal the period 2 implied forward rate in table 9.2:

$$0.5 f_B + 0.5 f_C = 9.0227$$

Solving for the two rates, we get $f_B = 9.660$ percent and $f_C = 8.386$ percent.

Similarly, the forward rates at time 3 must satisfy the conditions: $f_E = 1.151910 f_F$, $f_D = 1.151910 f_E = (1.151910)^2 f_F$, and their average must equal the period 3 implied forward rate in table 9.2:

$$0.25 f_D + 0.50 f_E + 0.25 f_F = 10.0739 \text{ percent}$$

Solving for the three rates, we get $f_F = 8.702$ percent, $f_E = 10.024$ percent, and $f_D = 11.546$ percent.

Proceeding along the same lines, the forward rates at time 4 are $f_J = 8.961$ percent, $f_I = 10.322$ percent, $f_H = 11.890$ percent, and $f_G = 13.696$ percent.

Calibrating

Next, we calibrate the interest rate tree using a trial-and-error method to adjust the forward rates.

It is important to understand that equating the expected forward rate each period to the implied forward rate, as we just did, is not the same as equating the expected price of the bond to the observed market price. Recall from figures 9.1 and 9.2 that the price-yield relationship is not linear, so the model will not price the on-the-run Treasuries exactly without some adjustment.

The initial rate does not require any adjustment. It *is* the forward one-period rate as of time 0. Consider period 2, time 0.5. The two possible short-term rates, which may need to be adjusted, are 8.386 percent and 9.660 percent. To determine any needed adjustment, we calculate the possible values of a one-year Treasury security six months from now; from table 9.2, that security yields 8.50 percent, to be valued today at par:

1. The bond's value one year from now (at maturity) is $104.25 ($100.00 + 4.25).

2. The initial discount rate estimate along the upper branch is 4.83 percent (9.660%/2) per period, so the bond's value at time 1 is $V_U = \$99.4467$ ($104.25/1.04830).

3. For the lower branch, the discount rate is 4.193 percent, and $V_L = \$100.0547$.

4. The bond's coupon is $4.25, and the time 0 six-month forward rate is 4.00 percent per period (8.00%/2). From equation 9.13, the bond's value at node A is $100.0007:

$$V = \text{bond value} = \frac{\frac{1}{2}(V_U + V_L) + C}{1 + r} = \frac{\frac{1}{2}(99.4467 + 100.0547) + 4.25}{1 + .04}$$

$$= \$100.0007$$

5. Compare the step 4 value to the bond's market value. If the two agree, no adjustment is needed. If this value is greater (less) than the market value, increase (decrease) the estimate of r_{1L}, use equation 9.12 to recalculate r_{1U}, and repeat the calculations. Continue to adjust the estimate until, using trial and error, you find the correct rate.

Using trial and error will verify that the correct value is $r_{1L} = 8.388$ percent, so the correct value for the upper one-year forward rate is 9.662 percent (8.388% × 1.151910). The binomial tree for this calculation is shown in Figure 9.4.

Unfortunately, we're not done. Now we must "grow" this tree for one more year by calibrating it to the 1.5-year and 2-year Treasury securities. Use the 1.5-year 9.00 percent on-the-run Treasury issue to adjust the one-year forward rates by finding the value for r_{2LL} that produces an average present value at node A equal to the price of the 1.5-year Treasury bond. The correct value of r_{2LL} is 8.708 percent. Similarly, the correct value of r_{3LLL} is 8.974 percent. Figure 9.5 shows the fully calibrated binomial interest rate tree, which can be used to value any option-free bond or any bond with embedded options.

The calibrated interest rate tree is arbitrage free because it produces fair prices for all the on-the-run Treasury issues.

Figure 9.4 Six-Month Forward Rates at the End of the First Period Using the One-Year 8.50 Percent On-the-Run Issue

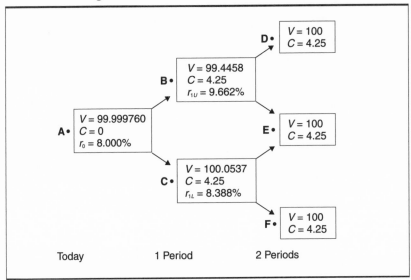

Valuing Bonds

Next we use the binomial model to value bonds.

Valuing an Option-Free Bond

Consider a 10 percent option-free, default-free bond with two years remaining to maturity. Suppose the issuer's on-the-run yield curve is the one given in table 9.2, and the appropriate binomial interest rate tree is the one in figure 9.5. Figure 9.6 shows the valuation process, which produces a bond value of $100.897.

To calculate bond value, we work backward from its known terminal value at maturity. For example, the value of the bond is 100 at nodes K and L because it matures at time 4. The coupon is 5. The forward rate is 6.858 percent per period (13.716%/2). Then, using equation 9.13:

$$\text{Value at node G} = \frac{\frac{1}{2}(V_U + V_L) + C}{1 + r} = \frac{\frac{1}{2}(100.00 + 100.00) + 5.00}{1 + .06858} = \$98.261$$

The values at each of the other nodes are similarly calculated and shown in figure 9.6.[8]

Figure 9.5 Calibrated Binomial Interest Rate Tree

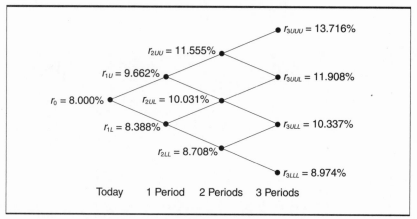

$r_{3UUU} = 13.716\%$

$r_{2UU} = 11.555\%$

$r_{1U} = 9.662\%$

$r_{3UUL} = 11.908\%$

$r_0 = 8.000\%$ $r_{2UL} = 10.031\%$

$r_{1L} = 8.388\%$

$r_{3ULL} = 10.337\%$

$r_{2LL} = 8.708\%$

$r_{3LLL} = 8.974\%$

Today   1 Period   2 Periods   3 Periods

Valuing a Callable Default-Free Bond

Bonds with embedded options can be valued using the same process but with one critical exception: When a bond is callable, its value at a node equals the lesser of its value if it is not called and the call price. This is because the issuer will call when it is most advantageous to the issuer—and, by implication, when it is least advantageous to the bondholders.[9]

Suppose a bond is identical to the one in figure 9.6, except that it is callable at $100 beginning in one year. Figure 9.7 shows the values at each node of the interest rate tree. The discounting process is identical to that shown in figure 9.6, except that at nodes F and J, the call price replaces the higher formula-calculated values ($100.778 at F and $100.491 at J).

The lower value at node J affects the values for nodes F, C, and A, but does not affect the values for other nodes. Working backward from node J, recalculate the value at node F:

$$\text{Value at node F} = \frac{\frac{1}{2}(V_U + V_L) + C}{1 + r} = \frac{\frac{1}{2}(99.840 + 100.00) + 5.00}{1 + .04354} = \$100.542$$

This recalculated value is also above the $100 call price. Thus, in figure 9.7, 100 (rather than 100.542) replaces the 100.778 value calculated for node F in figure 9.6.

The bond cannot be called before period 2. Therefore, the value at node C is recalculated on the basis of a value of 100 for node F. Finally,

Figure 9.6 Valuing a Two-Year Option-Free Default-Free Bond

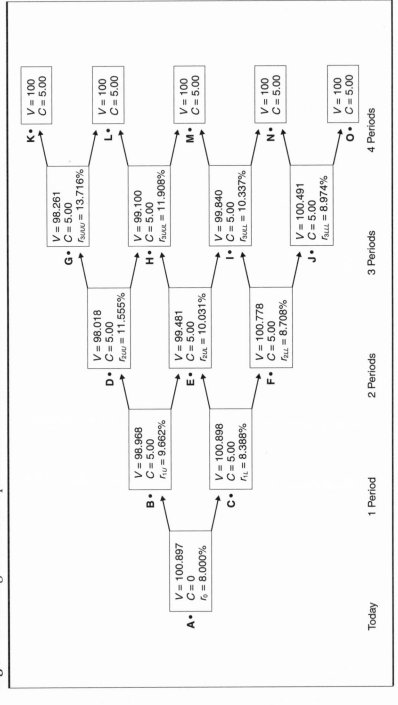

Figure 9.7 Valuing a Callable Default-Free Bond with Two Years to Maturity

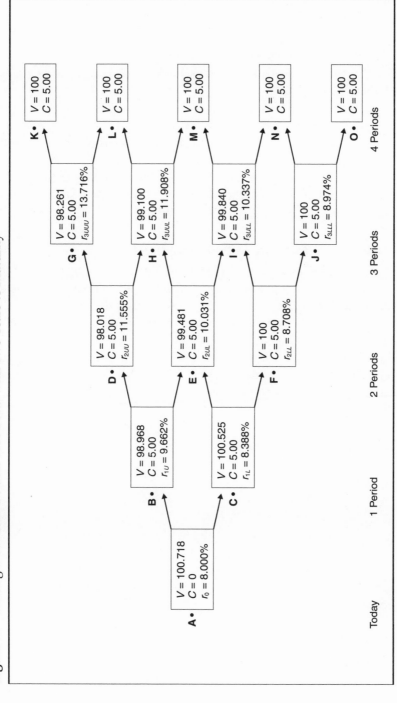

the recalculated value for node C is used to recalculate the value for node A, which is the bond's value of $100.718.

Determining the Value of a Call Option

The value of the call option can be obtained by rearranging equation 9.8:

$$\begin{array}{c} \text{Price of} \\ \text{call option} \end{array} = \begin{array}{c} \text{Price of} \\ \text{noncallable bond} \end{array} - \begin{array}{c} \text{Price of} \\ \text{callable bond} \end{array} \qquad (9.14)$$

In the previous example, the value of the noncallable bond is $100.897, and the value of the callable bond is $100.718, so the value of the call option is $0.179.

Valuing a Puttable Default-Free Bond

The binomial model can be used to analyze other embedded options, such as put options and caps and floors on floating-rate notes. Once again, consider a bond that is identical to the one in figure 9.6, except this one is puttable at $100 in exactly one year but at no other time. The interest rate tree is again given in figure 9.5. Figure 9.8 shows the values at each node of the interest rate tree with the put price replacing the node D and E values because it exceeds the calculated bond values at these two nodes. The value of the puttable bond is $101.590.

Determining the Value of a Put Option

The value of a puttable bond can be obtained by rearranging equation 9.9:

$$\begin{array}{c} \text{Price of} \\ \text{put option} \end{array} = \begin{array}{c} \text{Price of} \\ \text{puttable bond} \end{array} - \begin{array}{c} \text{Price of} \\ \text{nonputtable bond} \end{array} \qquad (9.15)$$

As an example, the value of the puttable bond is $101.590, and the value of the nonputtable bond is $100.897, so the value of the put option is $0.693.

Multiple Options

The binomial model can handle multiple options. The bond value at each node is altered according to whichever option would be exercised.

Figure 9.8 Valuing a Puttable Default-Free Bond with Two Years to Maturity

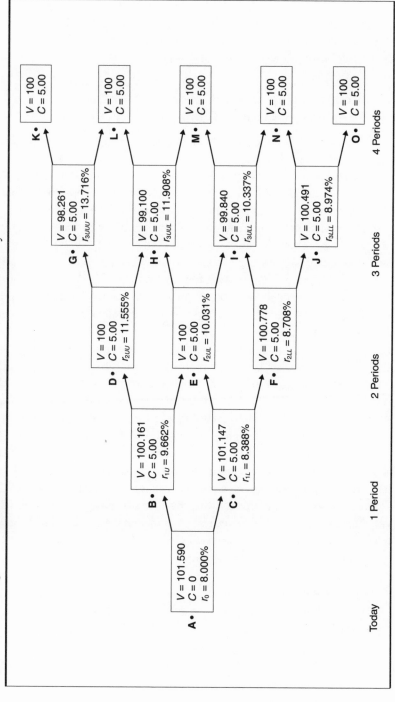

Sensitivity to the Volatility Assumption

Higher volatility increases option value. For a callable bond, higher (lower) volatility lowers (raises) its value. For a puttable bond, higher (lower) volatility raises (lowers) its value.

Incorporating Default Risk: The Option-Adjusted Spread

Thus far, we have examined default-free bonds. However, corporate and other bonds involve default risk. One approach to incorporating this risk is to calibrate a binomial interest rate tree that specifically accounts for the bond's default risk, as follows. First, use credit analysis to determine the target bond's credit rating. Then select a set of actively traded nonredeemable corporate bonds with the same credit rating and use them to calibrate a binomial interest rate tree using the method already illustrated in this chapter. This approach incorporates a default risk premium into each forward rate.

Another approach uses the Treasury (i.e., default-risk-free) binomial interest rate tree. Use this tree and an accurately priced bond with the same credit rating and duration as the target bond to determine a constant *credit spread*. For reasons that will become clear shortly, this credit spread is called the *option-adjusted spread* (OAS). (The reason the bond durations must match is that default risk increases with the bond's duration.) The OAS is added to each forward rate in the Treasury binomial interest rate tree and used to value the target bond.

These two approaches generally produce the same bond value. The first procedure is better for valuing a large number of bonds with the same credit rating but varying maturities. Fit one binomial interest rate tree for that credit rating category and use it to value all the bonds. The second procedure is better for valuing a small number of bonds with varying credit ratings. In some cases, you may even be able to get a credit spread from a securities dealer rather than having to estimate it using the Treasury interest rate tree.

Calibrating the Model

Suppose we want the credit spread (OAS) for two-year A-rated corporate bonds, based on an actively traded 10 percent coupon nonredeemable two-year A-rated corporate bond with a market price of 98.75. We will use the calibrated risk-free (Treasury) interest rate tree in figure 9.5.

The OAS is the amount that when added to each forward rate produces a bond value of 98.75, the bond's market value. OAS must be determined by trial and error. Using a spreadsheet model, force the calculated bond price to equal the market price by varying OAS.

Figure 9.9 shows the bond value calculation. The OAS is 121 basis points. Note that the interest rate at each node in figure 9.9 is 1.21 percent higher than the corresponding value in figure 9.5. The OAS can then be used to value any two-year A-rated corporate bond (or other bond with the same duration), because it measures the market default-risk premium on such bonds.

Valuing a Callable Bond

Now consider another two-year A-rated 10 percent corporate bond; this one is callable for 99 1.5 years from today but at no other time. Having determined that the OAS is 121 basis points for such bonds, we can use the forward rates in figure 9.9 to value this callable bond.

Since the values at nodes I and J would otherwise exceed 99, the bond would be called and the investor would get 99 at these nodes. Nodes N and O disappear because the bond will be retired prematurely. Figure 9.9 shows the revised tree. This callable bond is worth $98.571.

Calculating the OAS of a Callable Bond

In the preceding example, we used the OAS to value a callable bond. Alternatively, suppose we are given the price of a callable bond and asked to calculate its OAS.

Continuing the example, suppose the bond's market price was 99. In that case, the forward rates must be lower than those in figure 9.9 to give a price of 99 > 98.571. Because the risk-free forward rates do not change and an OAS of 121 gave a value of 98.571, the OAS implied by a price of 99 must be smaller than 121 basis points. But how much lower?

The OAS must again be found by trial and error, with the valuation procedure taking into account the call option. Using a spreadsheet model that takes into account the bond's call feature, the OAS that produces a calculated bond price of 99 is 93 basis points. That produces forward rates that are 28 (121 − 93) basis points lower than the ones in figure 9.9 at each node.

Figure 9.9 Valuing a Redeemable Two-Year A-Rated Corporate Bond

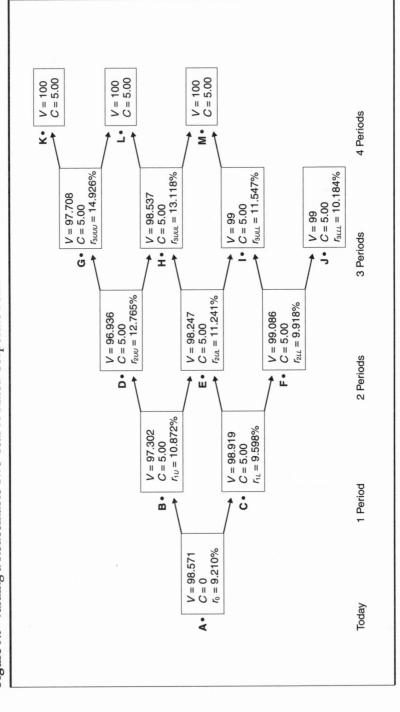

Interpreting OAS

The credit spread of 93 basis points is called the bond's *option-adjusted spread* because the OAS calculation takes into account the impact of any embedded options on the bond's cash flows. The calculation assumes that options are exercised whenever it is profitable to do so. OAS is superior to the various other yield measures because it incorporates the term structure of interest rates and takes into account future interest rate volatility.

Conclusion

Bond valuation plays a critical role in debt management. Each debt feature must be valued in order to identify the cost-minimizing design. Also, if callable bonds have been issued, accurate valuation is needed to be able to decide whether and when to refund them.

This chapter presented a variety of discounted-cash-flow techniques for valuing bonds and explained the binomial model for valuing bonds. It is a versatile analytical tool that is specifically designed to value bonds with one or more embedded options. It can also value bonds that are subject to default risk, and it is useful in designing bonds.

We also introduced the concept of option-adjusted spread. Practitioners use it to compare the returns on bonds that contain embedded options and are also subject to default risk. OAS has replaced the traditional yield spread measure because it explicitly takes into account the bond's option characteristics and their impact on the value of the bond.

Chapter *10*

Bond Refunding: Measuring the Net Advantage

*F*irms pay extra when a bond includes an optional redemption feature. Such call options are valuable because when interest rates drop, the firm may be able to refund its debt profitably with lower-cost debt, just as homeowners refinance their mortgages at a lower interest rate.

Well-managed firms actively manage their liabilities by refunding existing above-par bonds with lower-cost debt, repurchasing existing below-par bonds, or exchanging new lower-cost securities for existing bonds. Volatile interest rates create profitable bond refunding opportunities. Between 1977 and 1981, for example, a sharp increase in interest rates (see figure 10.1) drove the prices of debt issued before 1977 well below par, offering firms the opportunity to repurchase their bonds at significant discounts.

To improve their cash flows and strengthen their balance sheets, many firms used *equity-for-debt exchanges*, swapping newly issued shares of stock for existing below-par bonds and retiring the bonds. More than $7 billion worth of equity-for-debt exchanges were made in 1981 and 1982. In 1981, interest rates on long-maturity U.S. Treasuries reached a postwar high in excess of 15 percent. By 1986, when long Treasuries had fallen back to below 7.5 percent, the refunding protection on many issues sold in 1981 had just expired, and in 1986 and 1987, many corporations refunded above-par bonds. Similarly, when interest rates fell between 1990 and 1993 and again between 1994 and 1998, billions of dollars of corporate, agency, and municipal bonds were refunded.

Figure 10.1 Average Yield on AA-Rated Long-Term Corporate Bonds, 1970 to 2000

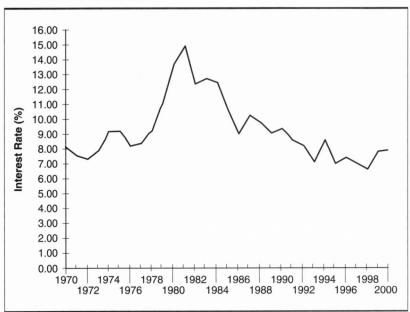

Source: Moody's Bond Record.

Overview of Bond Refunding

First, some definitions are necessary to ground this discussion. Replacing an outstanding bond with a new bond is referred to as a *refunding*. The issuer can *retire* outstanding debt in any of three ways: (1) if contractually permitted, it can *call* and *redeem* the bonds by paying bondholders the cash call (strike) price; (2) it can repurchase bonds, either in the market or using a tender offer; or (3) if bondholders agree, it can exchange new securities for the bonds.

A firm should undertake a refunding only if it will increase shareholder wealth, a decision that rests on the answers to two basic questions. First, will the refunding be profitable? Second, if an immediate refunding would be profitable, would it be better to postpone it? We focus on the profitability question in this chapter and the timing issue in chapter 11.

Financial experts long disagreed over how to analyze a refunding. The development of the *debt service parity* (DSP) approach established the linkage of tax effects, capital structure side effects, the choice of discount rate, and shareholder wealth. The DSP approach led to analytical models that measure correctly the impact of bond refundings on share-holder wealth.[1]

Why Refund?

There are three main reasons to refund: reduce borrowing cost, eliminate restrictive bond covenants, or change debt maturity.

The first reason accounts for most refundings, but our analytical framework also applies to the other two. For example, suppose a refunding is intended to replace restrictive bond covenants with more favorable covenants. If the NPV of refunding is negative, it is a cost to be weighed against the benefit of eliminating the old covenants.

A bond refunding may be either a *high-coupon* or *low-coupon* refunding. In the first case, interest rates have fallen and the bonds are premium bonds, selling above par value. So the existing (old) bonds' coupon is *higher* than the coupon on new bonds of the same risk class and duration. In the second case, interest rates have risen and the bonds are discount bonds, selling below par. So the existing bonds' coupon is *lower* than the coupon on new bonds of the same risk class and duration.

Callable bonds can be redeemed (usually after a grace period) at a prespecified call price. Table 5.1 shows a typical bond redemption price schedule for a thirty-year bond. The profitability of a high-coupon refunding comes mainly from the option to call the high-coupon bond at a price below its market value. That profitability is increased by the tax deductibility of the call premium.

Refunding Expenses

Refunding expenses are very similar for high- and low-coupon refundings. Both have flotation costs, overlapping interest expense,[2] trustee fees for canceling the old bonds, legal fees, and printing costs. A high-coupon refunding also involves a call premium. Refunding expenses are tax deductible and therefore are included on an after-tax basis.

Discounted-Cash-Flow Analysis

If the NPV of a discounted-cash-flow analysis of a refunding is positive when the costs are financed with the new issue, the refunding is advantageous. In a high-coupon refunding, the savings derive from lower interest cost.

Until the development of the DSP approach, financial experts disagreed over how to measure the NPV of a refunding correctly. The issues in dispute were the effects of capital structure changes; whether to discount pretax or after-tax cash flows; and whether the discount rate should be the pretax cost of new debt, the after-tax cost of new debt, or the cost of capital.[3] This controversy arose largely because early methods were not rooted in security valuation, and they lacked a consistent analytical framework to measure a refunding's effect on shareholder wealth. Financial experts now agree that a refunding analysis must neutralize any capital structure side effects and measure all cash flows after taxes.[4] The DSP approach is the only analytical framework that meets those criteria.

Debt Service Parity

A refunding can change a firm's capital structure. The DSP approach avoids this problem and potential side effects by explicitly holding the firm's total after-tax debt service constant across the refunding for analytical purposes. The assumption is that the primary determinant of a firm's capital structure is the amount of after-tax cash flow it has committed to service debt.[5]

The DSP approach is fundamentally simple in concept: Determine how much hypothetical new debt can be issued today, in exchange for promising to pay the existing (old, or refunded) debt's remaining after-tax period-by-period debt service obligations instead to new replacement debtholders (the refunding issue). If the proceeds of this hypothetical new debt would be more than enough to repurchase the old issue and pay any transaction costs, then the refunding generates a cash surplus that can be distributed immediately to shareholders, and refunding would be profitable. On the other hand, if the proceeds of the new issue would not be enough to repurchase the outstanding issue and pay all transaction costs, then refunding would decrease shareholder wealth and should not be undertaken.

The DSP principle extends beyond cash flows. Parity also requires that all rights and obligations be maintained for analytical purposes. The covenants of the hypothetical new issue, for instance, must conform to those of the old issue.

A high-coupon refunding analysis must also take into account that the one-time call option has been exercised. If the hypothetical new issue were callable, the call option effectively would be restored to the same value it had when the old bonds were issued. As a result, the new issue's coupon would be "too large," and the analysis would be biased against refunding. However, refunding can create an opportunity cost by giving up any remaining option value. Therefore, some adjustment may be needed in either case. Our analysis is based on a noncallable hypothetical new issue and adjusted for any lost option value.[6]

Choice of Discount Rate

The refunding decision affects only the liability side of the firm's balance sheet and is conceptually connected directly to a particular means of financing: the new debt. The opportunity cost of a refunding is the cost of this new debt. Since the cost would be tax deductible, the correct discount rate for a refunding is the *after-tax* rate on the new debt.

A Single-Period Example

We provide three different ways to view the net advantage of refunding, *NA*.

Net Gain from Replacement

First, it is the net gain from replacing existing debt with a hypothetical new debt issue that would *exactly* maintain debt service parity. *NA* equals the net proceeds, *NI*, from the hypothetical new debt minus the after-tax cost of repurchasing the old debt (*RP*) and the various after-tax expenses of the refunding (*E*):

$$NA = NI - RP - E \qquad (10.1)$$

NI is the present value of the old debt's after-tax debt service cash flows, discounted at the new debt's after-tax rate. Let r' be the coupon rate that would make the new issue sell for par value, and *T* be the firm's marginal ordinary income tax rate. Then the after-tax rate on the new debt is $(1 - T)r'$. If *NA* is positive, refunding will increase shareholder wealth; if *NA* is negative, refunding will decrease shareholder wealth.

Suppose a firm has an existing bond with a one-period remaining maturity and a coupon rate *r*. At maturity the bondholder will get $1,000 principal plus interest, or $1,000(1 + r)$. Therefore, the firm's after-tax debt service for the old bond is $1,000(1 + r[1 - T])$. The present value of this amount, discounted at the after-tax rate on the new bond, is *NI*, the proceeds from the hypothetical new issue:

$$NI = \$1,000 \, \frac{[1 + (1 - T)r]}{[1 + (1 - T)r']} \qquad (10.2)$$

In other words, *NI* is what a new bond with a coupon rate r' could be sold for today.

Suppose $r = 13$ percent and $r' = 8$ percent. Suppose also that the firm has the option to call the outstanding bond for $1,025 (a 2.5 percent call premium) and that flotation costs for the new issue are $10. Finally, the firm's tax rate is 40 percent.

Using equation 10.2, the new issue proceeds, *NI*, equal $1,028.63. The after-tax repurchase price, *RP*, equals $1,015.00 ($1,000 + $25[1 – 0.40]), because the $25 call premium is tax deductible. The difference, $13.63, minus the after-tax flotation cost of $6.00 ($10[1 – 0.40]), results in a net advantage of refunding, *NA*, of $7.63. Refunding would be profitable.

Intrinsic Value of the Call Option

A second way to view the net advantage of refunding is to say that *NA* is the intrinsic value of the firm's call option minus expenses. The intrinsic value is the net amount the firm would get if it exercises its option. This amount equals the value of the asset without a call option minus the strike price and minus expenses. Therefore, the intrinsic value of this option is the market value of the old bond if it were non-callable minus the after-tax cost of calling the bond and minus the after-tax flotation costs. If the firm did not have a call option, the market value of the old bond would be the present value of its after-tax debt service cash flows, discounted at the current market rate for such debt. Because the current market rate on such debt is r' (the rate on a new issue), this present value equals *NI* in equation 10.2, which is $1,028.63. Subtracting the $1,015.00 after-tax cost of calling the old bond and the $6.00 after-tax flotation cost gives the same *NA* of $7.63 we calculated previously.

In chapter 9, we measured the value of the call option from the bondholders' perspective. The value to the issuer may differ from the value to investors, and often does, because of differences in their marginal tax rates and differences in how gains or losses are taxed. As discussed later here and in chapter 12, tax factors can be important to refunding profitability.

Net-Present-Value Savings

The third way to view *NA* is as the NPV of refunding. Refunding would reduce the one remaining after-tax debt service obligation by $30.00 ($1,078.00 – 1,048.00). The present value of this $30.00 at the new issue's after-tax rate is $28.63 ($30.00/[1 + 0.08(1 − 0.40)]). The NPV equals this positive present value minus the costs, which are the $15.00 after-tax call premium ([1 − 0.40]25) and after-tax flotation costs ($6.00). Thus, once again, $NA = \$7.63$.

Substituting equation 10.2 into equation 10.1, and algebraically rearranging, we can express NA in terms of this third view, as the NPV of refunding:

$$NA = \frac{(1 - T)(r - r')D}{[1 + (1 - T)r']} - (1 - T')(P - D) - E \qquad (10.3)$$

where D is the par value of the old debt ($1,000 in the example); P is the cost of retiring the old debt ($1,025 in the example); T' is the tax rate that applies to the gain or loss on retiring the old debt;[7] E is the refunding's after-tax transaction costs; and r, r', and T are as defined previously. P is the call price in a high-coupon refunding, but it is the old bond's market price in a low-coupon refunding.

General Analytical Framework

To recap, refunding high-coupon debt will increase shareholder wealth if the firm can issue new debt that has the same after-tax debt service requirements period by period as the old debt and, after paying all costs associated with the refunding, still have something left over to distribute to its shareholders. This surplus, the net advantage of refunding, will result when the present value of the future after-tax interest savings exceeds the immediate cost of undertaking the refunding.

We now extend our model of one-period debt to longer-maturity debt. Two important complications arise in this more general case. First, it may be better to refund only part of an issue when it has a sinking fund. Second, for an issue that can be refunded profitably now, it may be even more advantageous to wait and refund it later. We postpone dealing with these complications until later chapters.

In the multiperiod case, we will also be more explicit about the cost of the refunding. The cost of refunding high-coupon debt has six components:

1. *Retiring the old bonds, the largest cost.* Virtually all corporate bonds are callable for some period prior to maturity. A call option can benefit both sides when the firm's marginal rate is higher than bondholders' because the call option is worth more to the issuer

than its after-tax cost.[8] The cost of the option is a higher interest rate plus any call premium. Both components are tax deductible expenses.

2. *An underwriting commission and various other costs for issuing bonds, such as lawyers' and accountants' fees and printing costs.* On the positive side, any issuance expense not yet claimed on the old bonds becomes immediately tax deductible.

3. *Expenses of calling the old debt.* These include the cost of printing the redemption notice in newspapers and paying the bond trustee's fees for canceling the old bonds.

4. *Overlapping interest.* Generally issuers sell the new debt before calling the old debt, both to get the funds to pay off the old debt and lock in the new debt's interest cost. Overlapping interest is the difference between the interest earned on the extra funds invested during the overlap and the interest cost of those funds. It is a cost (unless the return exceeds the cost, in which case it is a saving).

5. *Accrued interest at redemption.* If the old debt is redeemed on other than an interest payment date, the issuer must pay the partial period's accrued interest at redemption. This accelerates the payment of the accrued interest from the next scheduled interest payment date to the redemption date.

6. *Any remaining time premium.* The (unexpired) call option may have some remaining time premium. It is generally better to sell rather than exercise an American call option because exercising gives up any remaining time premium. This also holds for a firm that calls its debt. Say that the firm's outstanding bonds are selling in the capital market for $1,035, but the call price is $1,050. The $15 difference measures the time premium of the (unexpired) call option (discussed in note 6), which is a real opportunity cost but not a tax deductible expense. It accounts for the fact that the old bonds are callable, whereas the hypothetical new bonds are noncallable. Of course, actual new bonds that the firm decides to issue may well be callable, but that is a decision that must be made separately to measure the net advantage of refunding correctly.

The cash outlays required to meet these costs are offset partly by tax savings, as discussed in chapter 6. The basic rule is that expenses connected with retiring the old debt are tax deductible in the year of the refunding, and expenses connected with the new debt must be amortized over its life. In particular, the call premium and any unamortized balance of issuance expenses plus original issue discount (or less original issue premium) are tax deductible in the refunding year. Any tax credits or liabilities due to annual expense amortization are combined with the annual savings from refunding.

Discounted-Cash-Flow Model

Equation 10.3 is easily extended to the more general case of longer-remaining-maturity debt:

$$NA = \sum_{n=1}^{N} \frac{(1-T)(r-r')D}{[1+(1-T)r']^n} - (1-T')(P-D) - E \qquad (10.4)$$

where

N = number of periods until the old debt was scheduled to mature,

T = issuer's ordinary income tax rate,

T' = the tax rate that applies to the gain or loss on retiring the old debt,

r = old issue coupon rate (per period),

D = principal amount of the old debt,

r' = new issue coupon rate (per period),

P = cost of reacquiring the old debt before tax effects, and

E = present value of the after-tax expense associated with the refunding.

The net after-tax expense, E, is expressed on a present-value basis:

$$E = C + (1-T)F - T(U) - \sum_{n=1}^{N} \frac{T[(C-U)/N]}{[1+(1-T)r']^n} + (P-B) + OI \quad (10.5)$$

where U is the unamortized balance of issuance expenses plus original issue discount (or less original issue premium) on the old issue, which is tax deductible in the year of refunding.

Equation 10.5 states that the net after-tax expense equals:

- C, the out-of-pocket costs for the new issue that must be amortized,

- plus $(1-T)F$, any tax deductible out-of-pocket cost for the new issue,

- minus $T(U)$, the tax credit engendered by U,

- minus the present value of the increase in future expense tax credits, $T[(C − U)/N]$ per period, assuming amortization on a straight-line basis, as it is currently,

- plus $(P − B)$, the call option's time premium, where B is the old bonds' market price (excluding accrued interest),

- plus OI, any overlapping interest expense net of interest earnings.[9]

A Simplified Case

If we set $E = 0$ in equation 10.4, we get a useful back-of-the-envelope calculation:

$$NA = \sum_{n=1}^{N} \frac{(1 − T)(r − r')D}{[1 + (1 − T)r']^n} − (1 − T')(P − D) \qquad (10.6)$$

Finally, if there were no taxes, we can simplify even further:

$$NA = \sum_{n=1}^{N} \frac{rD}{(1 + r')^n} + \frac{D}{(1 + r')^N} − P \qquad (10.7)$$

This equation says that the net advantage is the price of the bond if it were noncallable minus the redemption price; this difference equals the intrinsic value of the call option.

Some Important Clarifications

The DSP calculation requires debt service parity, including par value callable new debt that is of the same amount and maturity as the old debt. However, maintaining debt service parity in the *actual* refunding is not important. DSP is simply an analytical tool to isolate and measure correctly the net advantage of refunding, without confusing the refunding decision with other decisions. It is very important to understand that once the firm has decided to refund its debt, it can then decide to make actual transactions different from the hypothetical DSP prescriptions.

For example, it is only for analytical purposes that the new debt's maturity must match that of the old debt. If the firm is going to incur the transaction costs of refunding, it very well may decide to take the opportunity to increase (or decrease) its debt maturity because the incremental transaction costs to do so are zero. In other words, whereas the benefit from changing debt maturity may be positive but insufficient to justify the cost, the refunding offers an opportunity to get that benefit without the additional cost. Similarly, among other possibilities, the actual new debt may (1) be callable, (2) be an amount larger or smaller than the old debt, (3) have a different indenture, and (4) have a coupon rate that is different from r' because of other considerations, such as taxes.[10]

The discount rate in equations 10.4 and 10.6 is the after-tax cost of debt, not the pretax cost. The net advantage of refunding can also be calculated by discounting at the pretax cost *if* the respective numerators are modified to reflect the value to shareholders of having the capacity to service additional debt as a result of the refunding.[11] That is, either the numerator or the denominator in equations 10.4 and 10.6 can be adjusted to reflect the financial structure side effects, but only one such adjustment is required. Adjusting the discount rate is simpler.

An Example of a Bond Refunding

On January 6, 1986, Southern Bell Telephone Company called its 12.875 percent debentures due 2020 for 110.61, or $1,106.10 per bond. There were 300,000 bonds, or $300 million in principal. In anticipation, a month earlier Southern Bell had issued $300 million principal amount of 10.75 percent debentures due 2025. Table 10.1 shows the net advantage of the refunding.

At the time, a thirty-five-year Southern Bell issue required roughly the same coupon as a forty-year issue. The refunding issue, however, was callable after five years, as was customary for telephone utility debt issues. Thus, the 10.75 percent coupon overstates the interest rate that a noncallable issue would have required by about 30 basis points.[12] Subtracting this amount from 10.75 percent implies a 10.45 percent coupon for a noncallable issue.

This refunding cost about $25,848,000 after taxes, but it saved Southern Bell $4,819,626 per year in after-tax interest expense. The present value of this $2,409,813 semiannual savings, discounted at the after-tax cost of the refunding issue (3.514 percent per six months), was about $62,464,619, providing a $36,616,619 net advantage of refunding. As long as the new issue rate for noncallable (callable) debt was below 12.16 percent (12.46 percent), the net advantage was positive.

Table 10.1 Net Advantage of Refunding Southern Bell Telephone's High-Coupon Bonds

Assumptions	Old Issue	New Issue
Amount	$300,000,000	$300,000,000
Coupon	12.875%	10.45%
Remaining life	35 years	35 years
Original proceeds	98.625%	98.175%
Current tax basis[a]	98.797%	98.175%
Issuer's tax rate	34%	34%
Cost of Repurchase (% of par)		
Price per bond		110.610%
Current tax basis		98.797
Tax deduction[b]		11.813
Tax benefit		4.016
After-tax price		106.593
Debt repurchase expense		.300
After-tax repurchase expense		.198
Total after-tax cost[c]		106.791%
Cost in dollars		$320,373,000
Net proceeds of new issue		294,525,000
After-tax cash outflow		$ 25,848,000
Benefits of Refunding		
Semiannual cost of old issue		
Interest expense		$ 19,312,500
After-tax interest		12,746,250
Amortization tax benefit		17,529
		$ 12,728,720
Semiannual cost of new issue		
Interest expense		15,675,000
After-tax interest		10,345,500
Amortization tax benefit		26,593
		$ 10,318,907
Semiannual interest savings		$ 2,409,813
Present value of savings[d]		$ 62,464,619
After-tax cash outflow		25,848,000
Net advantage of refunding		$ 36,616,619

[a] Original proceeds plus amortization, to the date of redemption, of the discount and expenses for the new issue.
[b] The tax deduction resulting from the redemption premium plus the tax deduction resulting from writing off the unamortized balance of issuance expenses plus original issue discount (or less original issue premium) can be calculated by subtracting the issuer's tax basis in the old issue from the redemption price for the old issue and multiplying this difference by the issuer's marginal tax rate (34 percent).
[c] Calculated as the after-tax price plus after-tax repurchase expense. In addition to the stated redemption price, the issuer must pay interest accrued to the date of redemption. Southern Bell paid 2.897 percent pretax per bond of accrued interest on the 12.875 percent debentures, so that its total redemption cost was 107.777 percent.
[d] Discounted at the after-tax cost of the new issue (3.514 percent per semiannual period).

A More Exact Debt Service Parity Model

Strictly speaking, the DSP approach involves determining exactly how much new debt the firm can issue while preserving debt service parity. Equation 10.4 assumes all new debt has the same rate, which makes it somewhat inaccurate when the yield curve is not flat. However, in practice, the error is usually inconsequential.

We can illustrate this concept by redoing the Southern Bell example. In addition to the information in table 10.1, assume that up to $65,000,000 in thirty-five-year semiannual installment debt would cost Southern Bell 10.30 percent, with only negligible additional transaction costs.

Southern Bell's after-tax debt service on its old bonds is $12,728,720 every six months. The principal amount of $300,000,000 of new 10.45 percent bonds would require an after-tax debt service of $10,318,907 every six months. The difference between these two amounts is $2,409,813. Figure 10.2 shows the schedule of after-tax cash flows for the new bonds overlaid on those for the old bonds.

Suppose Southern Bell issued $300,000,000 in new thirty-five-year bonds. That would leave $2,409,813 in after-tax savings every six months for thirty-five years, which would support extra debt, but how much extra? The savings are identical each period, with no final large payment. This is different from the other debt, which requires a large principal repayment at maturity. The difference in patterns means that the extra debt must be *installment debt* to maintain debt service parity.

Figure 10.2 After-Tax Cash Flows for the New Bonds Overlaid on the After-Tax Cash Flows for the Old Bonds

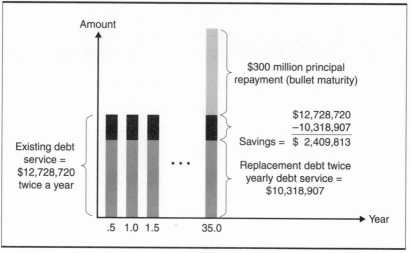

The extra (installment) debt for which the after-tax savings can be exchanged is the present value of the series of extra after-tax savings. However, the discount rate is the after-tax new issue rate on installment debt, which is 3.399 percent ([1 − 0.34] 10.30/2). Therefore, the extra new debt amounts to

$$\sum_{n=1}^{70} \frac{2,409,813}{(1.03399)^n} = \$64,066,639$$

Table 10.2 shows the more exact refunding calculation, which is based on a hypothetical $64,066,639 worth of extra new debt. Note that the combined after-tax debt service on the two new issues exactly equals the after-tax debt service on the old debt, as the DSP approach requires. The more exact net advantage of refunding is $38,218,639. This is $1,602,020, or about 4 percent, larger than the value calculated in table 10.1. The increase is due to the lower interest cost of the installment debt. Of course, if the installment debt's cost had instead been higher, the more exact net advantage of refunding would instead be smaller than calculated in table 10.1.

Firms seldom issue such a large amount of installment debt, so estimating the new issue rate on installment debt can be difficult. Still, if it can be estimated accurately and if it differs by more than a few basis points from the conventional debt new issue rate, we recommend calculating the more exact net advantage of refunding.

The actual new debt does not have to be identical to what the DSP calculation assumes and, as a practical matter, usually is not. For example, firms often raise just enough funds to retire the old debt rather than issue all the new debt in the exact DSP refunding calculation.

Table 10.2 A More Exact Refunding Calculation

	After-Tax Debt Service per Period	Savings/Cost
New Issues:		
Conventional (5.225% semiannual)	$10,318,907	$300,000,000
Installment (5.15% semiannual)	2,409,813	64,066,639
Total	$12,728,720	$364,066,639
Old Issue (6.4375% semiannual)	$12,728,720	300,000,000
Present-value savings (PVS)		$ 64,066,639
Total after-tax transaction costs (TC)		25,848,000
Net advantage of refunding (NA)		$ 38,218,639

Premium Debt Swaps

Since 1998, several firms have undertaken par-for-par debt exchanges for bonds selling at a substantial premium.[13] These so-called *premium debt swaps* can be favorable in terms of both taxes and accounting. They are particularly interesting because, as we note in chapter 6, refundings with favorable tax consequences (such as high-coupon refunding) often have undesirable accounting consequences, and, vice versa, refundings with favorable accounting consequences (such as low-coupon refunding) often have undesirable tax consequences. These new premium debt swaps (debt-for-debt exchanges) achieve the tax deductibility of the repurchase premium without triggering an accounting loss in the firm's income statement.

UPS Premium Debt Swap

In January 1998, UPS had 8.375 percent bonds outstanding that matured in 2020.[14] The bonds were trading at 123.76.[15] UPS offered to exchange for them new bonds maturing in 2030, which would pay the same 8.375 percent coupon through 2020 but a 7.62 percent coupon for the remaining ten years. This extension coupon was selected to make the new bonds worth 124.77 to bondholders, a little more than the old bonds (about 1 point), giving bondholders an incentive to exchange. The exchange was designed to be tax free to investors, so the exchange incentive applied equally to all bondholders. Note also that the new debt matches the cash flows of the old debt through 2020.

The swap is more complicated from the issuer's viewpoint. The $24.77 per bond premium became immediately tax deductible and, based on a 40 percent tax rate, provided a tax credit of $9.91 per bond. In addition, there was no accounting loss because the exchange involved equal principal amounts.

Benefits of the Swap

UPS's new bonds had an original issue premium (OIP) (see chapter 6). OIP can be amortized over the life of the new issue under the constant-yield method and is taxable income to the issuer.

The swap benefited UPS because it got to deduct the repurchase premium immediately. UPS effectively reissued the premium in the form of OIP, which it amortizes over the life of the new issue. If the new and old debt prices are identical, the aggregated OIP income equals the repurchase premium expense, and the aggregated tax liabilities from OIP equal the tax credit from the repurchase premium. However, UPS gets the repurchase tax credit immediately, but the tax liability from OIP income is spread over thirty-two years. The swap created a net tax benefit because of the time value of money. The benefit equals the NPV of the tax items, which is the tax credit minus the present value of all the tax liabilities. The favorable accounting treatment avoided the financial reporting disincentive that usually accompanies high-coupon refunding. Finally, UPS extended the maturity of its debt.

UPS's after-tax new debt service cost was 123.76. With a 9.91 tax credit per bond, UPS's net cost was 113.85. The after-tax cost of servicing the old bonds was 117.2.[16] Therefore, UPS's net advantage of refunding was about 3.35 percent of the debt's par value (117.2 – 113.85).

Impact of a Sinking Fund

Long-term corporate bond issues typically contain a sinking fund that retires a significant portion of the issue at annual intervals before maturity. As described in chapter 5, the sinking-fund provision specifies a sequence of scheduled redemptions. For sinking-fund purposes, bonds are typically redeemed at par value. In contrast, a call option usually includes a premium over par value that declines over time and becomes zero only in the last few years before maturity.

When refunding is attractive but the call price exceeds the sinking-fund price, it may be better to call and redeem only a portion of the issue and wait to redeem the balance at the lower sinking-fund price. We can adapt the procedure developed earlier in this chapter to determine how much of the issue to call now and how much to postpone.[17]

Suppose a firm with a 40 percent tax rate has $20 million in par value of 14 percent annual debt outstanding, with a sinking fund that requires $10 million installments after one and two years. The call price is 102, and the new issue rate for both one- and two-year issues is 12 percent. We will ignore issuance expenses to focus on the central issue.

Calculate the net advantage of refunding an amount equal to each sinking-fund payment by treating it as a separate debt issue and applying equation 10.6. For the first one, we get:

$$NA = \frac{\$0.60(0.02)10,000,000}{1.072} - 0.60(0.02)10,000,000 = -\$8,060$$

The net advantage of refunding the second $10 million sinking-fund payment is:

$$NA = \frac{\$0.60(0.02)10,000,000}{1.072} + \frac{0.60(0.02)10,000,000}{1.072^2}$$

$$- \; 0.60(0.02)10,000,000 = \$96,362$$

The net advantage of refunding the entire issue is the sum of these amounts, $88,302. But it is not profitable to refund the first sinking-fund amount. The firm's shareholders are better off if it calls only $10 million for immediate redemption and waits one year to redeem the balance at par through the sinking fund. This strategy produces a net advantage of $96,362.

General Approach

The correct procedure for evaluating the net advantage of refunding a high-coupon sinking-fund debt issue is to separate the issue into a serial debt obligation with each series maturing on one of the sinking-fund payment dates.[18] Bond indentures typically include a *designation option* to credit bonds that it previously reacquired (but has not yet credited) against any future sinking-fund obligation and the flexibility to call less than the entire issue.

For example, a firm is considering calling its 12 percent bonds that have a remaining life of ten years and require ten annual sinking-fund payments of $5 million each. The call price is 106. The unamortized balance of issuance expenses is $250,000. The firm's marginal tax rate is 34 percent. The yield curve is flat, and the new issue rate for one- to ten-year debt is 10 percent. Issuance expenses in each case amount to 1 percent of an issue's proceeds. How much of the issue should be called?

Table 10.3 summarizes the net advantage of refunding calculations. Calling the most distant six sinking-fund amounts now, $30 million in principal, produces a net advantage of $833,902. Calling less distant sinking-fund amounts is not profitable.

Understandably, the number of sinking-fund amounts that can be called profitably on any particular date is greater the lower the new issue rate and the smaller the call premium. Chapter 12 discusses the implications of these factors for sinking-fund management.

Exchanging Debt for Other Securities

Corporations exchange one issue of securities for another for two main reasons: to change their capital structure or to refund an outstanding issue of debt or preferred stock. Exchanging debt for stock

Table 10.3 Net Advantage of Refunding High-Coupon Sinking-Fund Debt

Years to Sinking-Fund Payment	After-Tax Interest Savings		Increase (Decrease) in Amortization Tax Shields		After-Tax Cost (Savings)				Net Advantage of Refunding
	Amount	Semiannual Amount	Net Present Value	Semiannual Amount[a]	Net Present Value	Redemption Premium	Other Costs[b]	Write-Off of Unamortized Balance	
1	$5,000,000	$33,000	$ 62,871	$4,250	$8,097	$198,000	$59,900	$(8,500)	$(178,432)
2	5,000,000	33,000	121,789	2,125	7,842	198,000	59,900	(8,500)	(119,769)
3	5,000,000	33,000	177,003	1,417	7,600	198,000	59,900	(8,500)	(64,797)
4	5,000,000	33,000	228,746	1,063	7,368	198,000	59,900	(8,500)	(13,286)
5	5,000,000	33,000	277,236	850	7,141	198,000	59,900	(8,500)	34,977
6	5,000,000	33,000	322,677	708	6,923	198,000	59,900	(8,500)	80,200
7	5,000,000	33,000	365,261	607	6,719	198,000	59,900	(8,500)	122,580
8	5,000,000	33,000	405,167	531	6,520	198,000	59,900	(8,500)	162,287
9	5,000,000	33,000	442,565	472	6,330	198,000	59,900	(8,500)	199,495
10	5,000,000	33,000	477,612	425	6,151	198,000	59,900	(8,500)	234,363

[a]Assumes that the unamortized balance is allocated pro rata over the ten sinking-fund payments.
[b]Assumed to be tax deductible cost of $3.00 per bond plus 1 percent of issuance proceeds ($50,000).

(preferred or common) or preferred stock for common stock increases the firm's leverage. Exchanging stock for debt or common stock for preferred stock has the opposite effect. The stock market generally reacts positively (negatively) to the announcement of exchange offers that would increase (decrease) the firm's leverage.[19]

Conclusion

This chapter developed an analytical framework for evaluating the net advantage of refunding bonds regardless of their maturity and the presence or absence of a sinking fund. When the issue contains a sinking fund, the debt issue is treated as a serial issue, with each sinking-fund payment treated as a separate issue with a bullet maturity.

For many years, financial experts disagreed over how to analyze a refunding. They now generally agree that a refunding analysis must neutralize any side effects to the refunding decision, thereby isolating and measuring only the effect of refunding. The DSP approach provides an appropriate analytical framework for evaluating the net advantage of refunding debt by calculating the NPV of refunding. This NPV equals the present value of the after-tax debt service savings (discounted at the after-tax cost of the new debt), minus the after-tax transaction costs, and adjusted for any tax effects from retiring the old debt. High-coupon (premium) old debt engenders a tax savings from the premium paid to retire it. Low-coupon (discount) old debt can engender a tax liability on the gain realized in retiring it.

Chapter 11

Bond Refunding:
The Timing Decision

The issuer of callable bonds is continually facing a refund-or-wait decision. If new bonds would require a lower interest rate than the old bonds, the issuer must decide whether it is profitable to exercise the call option now or continue to wait. We discuss this timing decision in this chapter. Alternatively, if the new bonds would require a higher interest rate than the old bonds, the bonds will be trading at a discount, and calling them will not be profitable. But prepurchasing them, for example, in anticipation of future sinking-fund obligations, may be profitable. We discuss sinking-fund complications in chapter 12.

Just because a firm finds it profitable to refund bonds immediately does not mean that refunding them immediately is in its shareholders' best interest. They might realize a greater net advantage if the firm postpones the refunding and interest rates decrease sufficiently. When a firm exercises its call option, it captures the intrinsic value of the option and at the same time forgoes the option's remaining time premium. In order to decide whether to refund immediately, the issuer needs to assess the likelihood that interest rates might fall further and weigh the benefit of an immediate refunding against the cost of postponing. The risk is that interest rates might rise and thereby reduce, or possibly even eliminate, the current net advantage of refunding. In general, a firm should refund now only if the call option's remaining time premium is zero.

The refund-or-wait decision would be much simpler in a frictionless market, which has no taxes, no transaction costs, no restrictions on short sales, and so on. In such a market, nonconvertible bonds should be redeemed when, and only when, the market price of the bonds reaches the effective call price, which is the stated call price plus accrued interest through the redemption date.[1] If the market price is below the effective call price, calling would transfer wealth from the shareholders to the bondholders. If the market price is above the effective call price, the issuer will have waited too long to refund and paid too much interest to the bondholders. Waiting so long to call the bonds would transfer wealth from the bondholders to the shareholders.

The simple perfect-market rule is incorrect in practice. Market imperfections make it necessary to consider explicitly the call option's remaining time premium.

Recall the Southern Bell refunding discussed in chapter 10. Suppose the new issue rate required one year later on a noncallable thirty-four-year Southern Bell issue is 9 percent. Assume the same debt retirement and new issue expenses as in table 10.1. If we substitute the 9 percent new issue rate for 10.45 percent, the 10.26 percent redemption premium one year later for 10.61 percent, and thirty-four years for thirty-five and then reduce the unamortized balance of issuance expenses on the outstanding issue to reflect an additional year's amortization, the net advantage of refunding the Southern Bell 12.875s on January 6, 1987, would be $85,769,325. Assuming the rate for a one-year Southern bell issue on January 6, 1986, is approximately 8 percent, the present value of the net advantage of refunding one year later at a 9 percent new issue rate would be $81,413,927—far more than the $36,616,619 net advantage of immediate refunding calculated in table 10.1.

If Southern Bell's new issue rate decreases to 9 percent next year, it is better to wait to refund. But if interest rates increase next year, it is better to refund now. Southern Bell officials had to weigh the relative likelihood of future interest rate changes to decide whether to postpone a refunding that currently had a positive net advantage.

Break-Even Analysis

Break-even analysis provides a useful initial approach to the timing problem. If the net advantage of refunding now is X, what must future new issue rates be to produce the same net advantage on a present-value basis?

Continuing the Southern Bell example, the current 10.45 percent pretax rate offers a net advantage of refunding of $36,616,619, but suppose Southern Bell believes interest rates are likely to decrease over the next five years. How much would interest rates have to fall to make refunding in five years better than refunding now? If Southern Bell's five-year new issue rate for noncallable debt is 10 percent (3.3 percent after-tax per six months), this question can be rephrased as follows: What new issue rate is required in five years to provide a net advantage at that time of $50,661,898 ($36,616,619[1.033]^{10})? The call price five years hence is 108.84 percent. Solving for the new issue cost that results in a net advantage at that time of $50,661,898 gives 10.19 percent (for a thirty-year noncallable issue). Thus, interest rates would have to fall 26 basis points, from 10.45 percent to 10.19 percent, over the next five years for Southern Bell to be better off waiting and refunding in five years.

Although break-even analysis is a good starting point, it is a very blunt tool because it compares only two alternatives at a time. Comparing the current net advantage of refunding to the net advantage at each of many future dates can be cumbersome and can lead to the wrong decision if the best future refunding date is not included in the analysis. A comprehensive analytical approach avoids this error.

Refunding Efficiency

In a perfect market, the issuer should wait until the call option's remaining time premium is zero. That is the optimal stopping point (i.e., to stop waiting) to refund the old bonds. In practice, because of market imperfections, issuers tend to call bonds somewhat early, exercising the call option when they can lock in about 85 to 90 percent of the maximum expected net advantage.[2] The fraction of the value of the call option they actually realize is the *efficiency* of the refunding. The efficiency of a high-coupon bond refunding is

$$\text{Efficiency} = \frac{\text{Net advantage of refunding}}{\text{Value of the call option}} \qquad (11.1)$$

The net advantage of refunding is the intrinsic value of the call option, that is, the value of exercising it. The total value of the call option equals the intrinsic value plus the remaining time premium. When the time premium is zero, the option's entire value is the net advantage, and refunding would be 100 percent efficient. There would be no benefit to waiting because the option's time premium is zero.

The risk aversion of decision-makers may also affect the timing decision. A risk-neutral decision-maker would never settle for less than 100 percent efficiency, at least not in a perfect market. But in practice, financial decision-makers are generally willing to sacrifice the

Figure 11.1 Efficiency of Refunding a 10 Percent Thirty-Year Bond

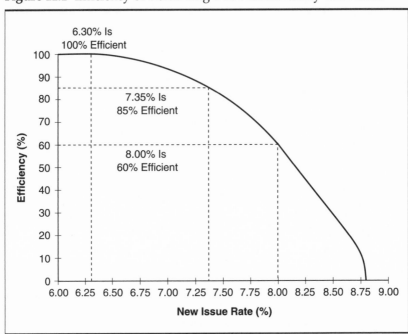

incremental 10 to 15 percent of the potential net advantage to lock in the currently available 85 to 90 percent and eliminate the risk that delaying would reduce the net advantage.

Figure 11.1 illustrates refunding efficiency. A 10 percent thirty-year bond becomes callable in year 5. The net advantage of refunding is positive whenever the new issue rate is below 8.80 percent. However, refunding at 8.80 percent would be 0 percent efficient. Refunding at 8.00 percent is 60 percent efficient, 7.35 percent is 85 percent efficient, and 6.30 percent is 100 percent efficient.

The shape of the refunding efficiency curve depends on the volatility of interest rates because volatility drives the option's remaining time premium. Figure 11.2 shows how the remaining time premium and refunding efficiency depend on interest rate volatility. Later we explain how to draw this curve.

Dynamic Programming

A more reliable approach to the timing problem uses dynamic programming, which allows a comparison of the profitability of each refunding opportunity with all possible future refunding opportuni-

Figure 11.2 The Refunding Efficiency Curve Depends
on Interest Rate Volatility

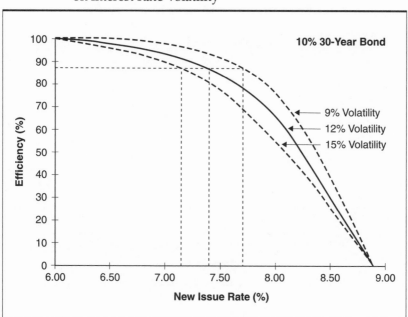

ties.[3] The analysis produces a *stopping curve*, which indicates for each point in time the refunding rate at which the firm is indifferent between refunding now and waiting. Figure 11.3 provides the stopping curve for the example of the forty-year Southern Bell bonds. The issue bears interest at a 12.875 percent rate and is noncallable for five years. The stopping curve covers the call option's entire thirty-five years. At new issue rates above (below) the curve, Southern Bell should wait to (call and) refund the issue, because the net advantage is less than (exceeds) the expected savings from waiting.

Constructing the Stopping Curve

A stopping curve is constructed by working backward in time from the maturity date. At each time, the value of waiting is compared to the value of calling and refunding. But the value of waiting depends on what happens in the future. By working backward, we can use the two alternative values from the previous step in the binomial model (i.e., one period later in time) to calculate the alternative values for the current step. Each calculation thus reflects what might happen in all future periods up to maturity.

Figure 11.3 Stopping Curve for Timing the Refunding of the 12.875s of 2020

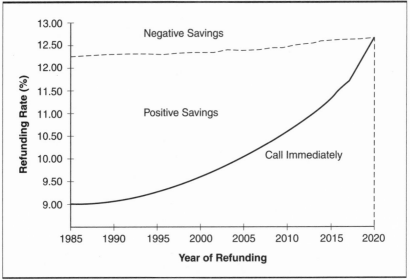

Dynamic programming transforms the overall problem into a sequence of one-period decisions. Stepping ahead each time period, the current new issue rate is compared to the stopping curve to determine whether to refund now or wait one period.

We illustrate the construction of a stopping curve using the Southern Bell refunding example. To simplify, we use equation 10.6, the stripped-down net advantage calculation, which ignores issuance and other expenses. Also, assume the issue can be called at only two times: 2010 or 2015. Another simplification is to discount the interest savings in the net advantage calculation at 10 percent (6.6 percent after-tax) rather than r'.

In table 11.1, the present-value savings (PVS) are the greater of (1) the net advantage from refunding and (2) the net advantage of waiting. Working backward, first consider 2015, the last chance to refund. At 2015, the PVS equals 2.772 $(12.875 - r')$ if r' is less than 12.875 percent and zero otherwise because if it is not refunded then, the issue will never be refunded.

Next consider what might happen in 2010. If the issue is refunded now, $NA = 60.32 - 4.776r'$. The break-even refunding rate in 2010, where $NA = 0$, is 12.62 percent. Calculating the value of waiting is more

Table 11.1 Example Computation for the Stopping Points Five and Ten Years Before Maturity

---

Refunding Decision in 2015 (Final Opportunity)

Because the call price is par, the issuer will refund if and only if the refunding rate (r') is below the coupon rate (12.875 percent). Therefore:[a]

$$PVS = 0 \qquad\qquad \text{if } r' \geq 12.875$$

and

$$PVS = (0.66)\frac{(12.875 - r')}{2}(8.401)$$

$$= 2.772\,(12.875 - r') \qquad\qquad \text{if } r' < 12.875$$

Refunding Decision in 2010

If the bond is refunded in 2010 at refunding rate r', then:[b]

$$PVS = (0.66)\frac{(12.875 - r')}{2}(14.473) - (1.769)(0.66)$$

$$= 60.32 - 4.776r'$$

The break-even refunding rate (BERR) is the value of r' for which PVS = 0:

$$BERR = 12.62 \text{ percent}$$

However, if the issuer waits and refunds in 2015 (if it is profitable at that time), the expected savings are:[c]

$$EPVS = [(0.5)(0) + (0.5)(2.722)(12.875 - (r' - 0.268r'))] \times 0.723$$

$$= 12.669 - 0.720r'$$

Therefore, the issuer should refund only if PVS exceed EPVS:

$$60.32 - 4.776r' > 12.669 - 0.720r'$$

or

$$r' < 11.75 \text{ percent}$$

---

[a] The stream of interest savings is discounted at a 10 percent (6.6 percent after-tax) rate back to 2015:

$$8.401 = \sum_{i=1}^{10}(1 + (0.66)(0.10/2))^{-i}$$

Fixing the discount rate at 10 percent does not substantially alter the results but simplifies the problem by making PVS a linear function of r'.

[b] The stream of interest savings is discounted at a 10 percent (6.6 percent after-tax) rate back to 2010:

$$14.473 = \sum_{i=1}^{20}(1 + (0.66)(0.10/2))^{-i}$$

The call premium in 2010 is 1.769.

[c] The present-value savings as of 2015 are discounted back to 2010 at a 10 percent (6.6 percent after-tax) rate:

$$0.723 = (1 + (0.66)(0.10/2))^{-10}$$

complex than for 2015 because of the option to refund in 2015. But this decision depends on how interest rates might change between 2010 and 2015.

Suppose that based on historical interest rate movements for similarly rated long-term telephone bonds, the standard deviation of the new issue rate at the end of a five-year period equals 0.268 of the rate at the start of the five-year period. To incorporate interest rate changes, assume the interest rate in the following period is equally likely to be either plus or minus one standard deviation from the interest rate in the current period. For example, if the interest rate in 2010 is r' percent, the interest rate in 2015 is either $r' + (0.268)r'$ or $r' - (0.268)r'$, each with probability 0.5. Assume that in 2015, *NA* is negative at the higher possible rate and the firm will not refund, but positive at the lower possible rate, in which case the firm will refund. The expected value of waiting (EVPS) in 2010 is the present value of the probability-weighted outcome for 2015, which is $[12.669 - (0.720)r']$, as calculated in table 11.1.

The decision rule is: Refund in 2010 only if PVS is more than EPVS—that is, only if the PVS that can be locked in immediately exceed the expected PVS for waiting. In this example, at interest rates lower than 11.75 percent, the optimum strategy is to call and refund now. At interest rates between 11.75 percent and 12.62 percent (the break-even rate), refunding would be profitable, but waiting is better. At interest rates higher than 12.62 percent, refunding would reduce shareholder wealth. Applying the procedure just illustrated to monthly intervals between 1985 and 2020 would produce the stopping curve in figure 11.3.

Interpreting the Stopping Curve

From a timing standpoint, if the new issue rate is on the stopping curve in figure 11.3, the refunding would be 100 percent efficient. In that case, the call option on the old debt would have zero remaining time premium and the hypothetical new debt would be noncallable with a coupon rate of r'.

If the new issue rate is below the stopping curve, the remaining time premium is still zero, but the issuer has waited too long to redeem the bonds. If the new issue rate is above the stopping curve, the option's positive time premium is an opportunity cost to be weighed against the net advantage of refunding, and waiting may be better. As noted earlier, in practice, timing efficiencies of 85 to 90 percent are common.

A Binomial Model for the Call-or-Wait Decision

We can adapt the binomial model developed in chapter 9 to analyze the call-or-wait decision. We limit the discussion to bonds with a bullet maturity (i.e., no sinking fund) in this chapter and deal with high-coupon sinking-fund bonds in chapter 12.

Calibrating the Interest Rate Tree

First, use a set of noncallable par value bonds in the same default risk class as the target bonds to calibrate the interest rate tree as illustrated in chapter 9. This provides an arbitrage free evolution path of one-period-forward interest rates. We do not model bond defaults explicitly but simply make whatever default adjustment is implicit in the new issue interest rates used in the calibration.

We will use the calibrated tree in figure 9.5. For simplicity, assume the marginal bond investor is tax-exempt, so that we can value bonds just as we did in chapter 9 without additional explicit adjustment for taxes.[4] You could adjust explicitly for income taxes at the marginal investor's income tax rate—if you can determine that tax rate—but typically the additional complexity is not worthwhile. As long as investors value bonds on an after-tax basis, market interest rates reflect the effect of the marginal investor's income tax rate on bond value.

Corporate Income Taxes

Multiplying each forward rate by $1 - T$, where T is the firm's marginal income tax rate, incorporates the effect of corporate taxes. As noted in chapter 10, a bond refunding is evaluated on an after-tax basis.

Calculating the Value of a Bond to the Issuer at Each Node

V_{ij} (wait) is the value of the bond to the issuer at node (i,j), assuming the issuer decides to wait until a future period to retire it, where i identifies the time period and j identifies the interest rate outcome at that node, as in chapter 9. Note that the issuer's debt management objective is to minimize the bond's value, V_{ij}. The bond's value to investors at node (i,j) is P_{ij}.

In the binomial model, the one-period interest rate can move to only one of two possible future states from node (i,j): up (denoted U) or down (L). Again assume these movements are equally likely (each has probability $1/2$). Let r_{ij} be the one-period forward rate at node (i,j).

The value of the bond to the issuer at node (i,j) is the after-tax present value of the expected future value:

$$V_{ij}\,(\text{wait}) = \frac{(1-T)C + \frac{1}{2}(V_{i+1,U} + V_{i+1,L})}{1 + (1-T)r_{ij}} \tag{11.2}$$

where $V_{i+1,U}$ and $V_{i+1,L}$ are the values of the bond at nodes $(i+1, U)$ and $(i+1, L)$, respectively, and C is the coupon rate to be paid at time $(i+1)$. (See figure 9.3 and the associated discussion in chapter 9.) These bond values in turn depend on whether the bond is retired at either of these nodes. The bond's principal amount is 100.

The firm will call the bond at node (i,j) to minimize bond value if

$$V_{ij}\,(\text{wait}) > 100 + (1-T)\text{Pr}(i) + E \tag{11.3}$$

where $(1-T)\text{Pr}(i)$ is the after-tax cost of the call premium in period i, and E is the refunding's after-tax expense. In practice, E is usually small enough that it can be set to zero without significantly affecting the timing decision.

If equation 11.3 holds and the bond is called, the bond's value to the issuer at node (i,j), V_{ij}, is

$$V_{ij} = 100 + (1-T)\text{Pr}(i) + E$$

On the other hand, if P_{ij} is less than 100, calling is not profitable. However, under certain circumstances, *repurchasing* the bond could be profitable. If the bond is a non-sinking-fund bond, these circumstances are limited, as we discuss in chapter 12. For now, it is sufficient simply to recognize the possibility. Repurchasing the bond at price P_{ij} less than 100 gives rise to "forgiveness-of-indebtedness" income of $100 - P_{ij}$, which is taxable as ordinary income.[5] The after-tax cost of repurchasing the bond is $P_{ij} + T(100 - P_{ij})$. The firm will repurchase the bond at node (i,j) if

$$V_{ij}(\text{wait}) > P_{ij} + T(100 - P_{ij}) \tag{11.4}$$

in which case,

$$V_{ij} = P_{ij} + T(100 - P_{ij})$$

Finally, if the bond is trading at more than its face value but is not yet callable, the firm might nevertheless still benefit from repurchasing it because any premium is tax deductible.[6] The firm would pay $P_{ij} > 100$ and immediately deduct $P_{ij} - 100$ from its taxable income. The after-tax price is again $P_{ij} - T(P_{ij} - 100) = P_{ij} + T(100 - P_{ij})$. In that case, the decision criterion is again equation 11.4.[7]

Combining equations 11.2, 11.3, and 11.4, the value of the bond at node (i,j) is

$$V_{ij} = \min\{V_{ij}(\text{wait}); 100 + [1 - T]\text{Pr}(i) + E; P_{ij} + T(100 - P_{ij})\} \quad (11.5)$$

The Issuer's Decision

Applying equation 11.5, the bond's value at time 0 is:

$$V_0 = \min\{V_0(\text{wait}); 100 + [1 - T]\text{Pr}(0) + E; P_0 + T(100 - P_0)\} \quad (11.6)$$

Depending on which quantity in equation 11.6 provides the minimum, the firm should (1) wait and reconsider refunding next period, (2) call and refund the bonds now, or (3) repurchase the bonds (either in the market or using a tender offer) and refund now.

Timing Decision Examples

Consider a callable 12 percent two-year single-A-rated corporate bond paying semiannual interest. Figure 9.9 in chapter 9 provides the calibrated interest rate tree for two-year A-rated corporate bonds.[8] The bond's call prices are given in table 11.2. Figure 11.4 values the bond assuming investors are tax-exempt. It reports both B, the value of an equivalent noncallable bond, and the actual price P, which takes into account the call option.

As illustrated in figure 11.4, if the bond is noncallable, it is worth 102.294 to (tax-exempt) investors. Under the conservative (from the investors' perspective) assumption that the issuer will call the bond if its market price exceeds the call price, the bond is worth only 102.000 to investors. The value of the noncallable bond exceeds the call price at nodes A, C, F, and J. The current price is

$$P = \min\{102, [6 + (100.045 + 101.500)/2] \div 1.04605\} = 102$$

Is waiting or refunding now better?

Table 11.2 uses the bond values in figure 11.4, a 35 percent tax rate, and the given schedule of call prices to analyze the timing decision. For example, the after-tax call price in period 3 is 100.325 (100 + [1 − 0.35][0.50]) and the after-tax repurchase price at node C is 100.975 (101.500 + 0.35 [100 − 101.500]).

Table 11.2 Bond Refunding Timing Decision

Node	Period	V_{ij} (wait)	$Pr(i)$	Pretax Call Price	After-Tax Call Price[a]	After-Tax Repurchase Price[a]	Decision	V_{ij}
G	3	99.093	0.500	100.50	100.325	99.115	Wait	99.093
H	3	99.652	0.500	100.50	100.325	99.659	Wait	99.652
I	3	100.142	0.500	100.50	100.325	100.139	Repurchase	100.139
J	3	100.571	0.500	100.50	100.325	100.325	Call	100.325
D	2	99.159	1.000	101.00	100.650	99.190	Wait	99.159
E	2	100.137	1.000	101.00	100.650	100.138	Wait	100.137
F	2	100.880	1.000	101.00	100.650	100.650	Call	100.650
B	1	100.014	1.500	101.50	100.975	100.029	Wait	100.014
C	1	101.139	1.500	101.50	100.975	100.975	Call	100.975
A	0	101.361	2.000	102.00	101.300	101.300	Call	101.300

[a]Assumes a 35 percent marginal income tax rate and zero transaction costs.

Figure 11.4 Value of the Two-Year A-Rated Corporate Bond

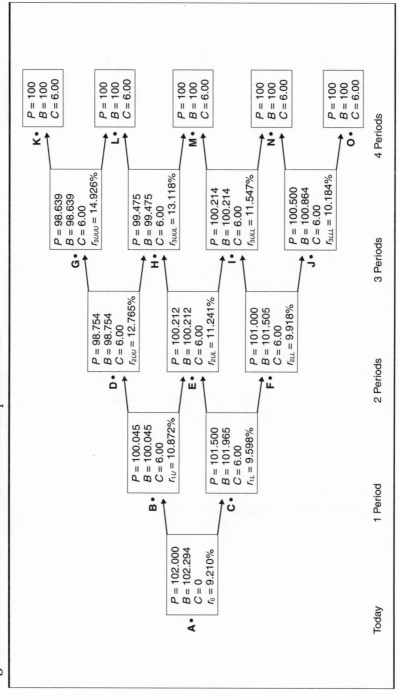

The value of waiting is calculated for each node. For example, using equation 11.2, the value of waiting at node G is

$$V(\text{wait}) = \frac{(1 - 0.35)6.00 + (\frac{1}{2})(100 + 100)}{1 + (1 - 0.35)0.14926/2} = 99.093$$

The value of waiting at node E is

$$V(\text{wait}) = \frac{(1 - 0.35)6.00 + (\frac{1}{2})(99.652 + 100.142)}{1 + (1 - 0.35)0.11241/2} = 100.138$$

And the value of waiting at node C is

$$V(\text{wait}) = \frac{(1 - 0.35)6.00 + (\frac{1}{2})(100.138 + 100.650)}{1 + (1 - 0.35)0.09598/2} = 101.139$$

Waiting is better than calling at nodes G, H, I, D, E, and B, but calling is better at the other nodes. Therefore, the bonds should be called and refunded now.

We found in chapter 9 that the new issue rate for two-year A-rated corporate bonds is 10.71 percent, which consists of the default-free rate of 9.50 percent plus an OAS of 121 basis points. Using equation 10.6, the net advantage of refunding now per $100 bond is

$$NA = \sum_{t=1}^{4} \frac{(1 - 0.35)(0.12 - 0.1071)100/2}{1 + (1 - 0.35)0.1071/2} - (1 - 0.35)2 = 0.241$$

disregarding refunding expenses other than the after-tax call premium.

To illustrate further, suppose the period 1 call price in table 11.2 is 101.00 instead of 101.50. Table 11.3 recalculates the values at nodes A, B, and C under this alternative assumption.

The bond would be called at 101.00 at node C, so its market price is 101.00. As a result, the market price of the bond at node A is

$$[6.00 + (\frac{1}{2})(100.045 + 101.000)]/1.04605 = 101.833$$

The after-tax call price at node A is again 101.300, but the bond's after-tax value for waiting is

$$V(\text{wait}) = \frac{(1 - 0.35)6.00 + (\frac{1}{2})(100.015 + 100.650)}{1 + (1 - 0.35)0.09210/2} = 101.203$$

Table 11.3 Bond Refunding Timing Decision When the Call Price Is 101.00 in Period 1

Node	Period	Market Price	V_{ij} (wait)	$Pr(i)$	After-Tax Call Price[a]	After-Tax Repurchase Price[a]	Decision	V_{ij}
B	1	100.044	100.014	1.00	100.650	100.029	Wait	100.014
C	1	101.000	101.139	1.00	100.650	100.650	Call	100.650
A	0	101.833	101.203	2.00	101.300	101.191	Repurchase	101.191

[a]Assumes a 35 percent marginal income tax rate and zero transaction costs.

It is better to wait. However, because the repurchase premium is tax deductible (the price minus the assumed par value tax basis), as many of the bonds as possible should be repurchased in the market for an after-tax cost below 101.203.[9]

Finally, figure 11.5 identifies the nodes in the binomial interest rate tree at which the bonds should be called, given the call price schedule in table 11.2. These call dates are consistent with the bond pricing in figure 11.4, so our analysis of the bond timing decision is internally consistent.

Measuring Refunding Efficiency

Equation 11.1 expresses the efficiency of a refunding as the ratio of the intrinsic value of the call option to its total value. It can be rewritten as:

$$\text{Efficiency} = \frac{V_{NC} - [100 + (1 - T)\text{Pr}(0)]}{V_{NC} - V_0} \tag{11.7}$$

where V_{NC} is the value of the bond to the issuer without the call option, V_0 is the actual value of the (callable) bond to the issuer, and $100 + (1 - T)\text{Pr}(0)$ is the after-tax call price. If a bond can be called immediately, V^0 cannot exceed the after-tax call price, $100 + (1 - T)\text{Pr}(0)$. Recall that when V_0 is less than that amount, a call would be less than 100 percent efficient and would transfer the difference between V_0 and the after-tax call price from the stockholders to the bondholders. If the new issue rate falls to where V_0 equals the after-tax call price, a call would be 100 percent efficient. At even lower interest rates, the call is still 100 percent efficient, but the issuer will have waited too long to refund.

V_{NC} is measured by ignoring the call options when working backward through the interest rate tree. Consider again the two-year A-rated corporate bond in figure 11.4. If the bond is noncallable, its value to the issuer at each node is equal to the minimum of V_{ij} (wait) and the after-tax repurchase price. The calculation, shown in table 11.4, indicates $V_{NC} = 101.491$. Applying equation 11.7, the efficiency of the refunding is

$$\text{Efficiency} = \frac{101.491 - 101.300}{101.491 - 101.300} = 1.00, \text{ or } 100 \text{ percent}$$

Next consider the two-year A-rated corporate bond in table 11.3. The efficiency of refunding this bond is

Figure 11.5 Conditions Under Which the Bonds Would Be Called

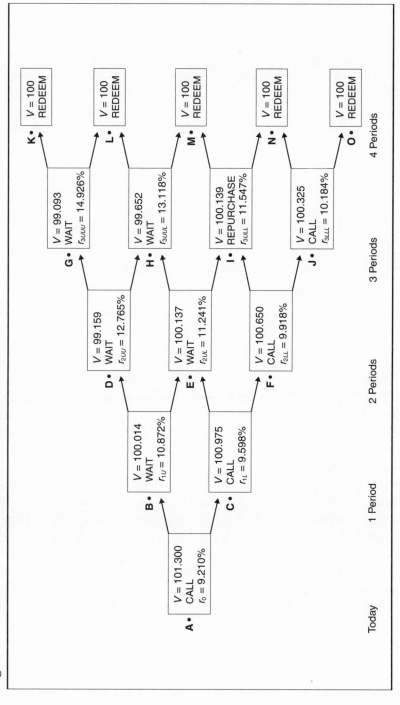

Table 11.4 Value of the Noncallable Bond

Node	Period	V_{ij} (wait)	After-Tax Repurchase Price[a]	Decision	V_{ij}
G	3	99.093	99.115	Wait	99.093
H	3	99.652	99.659	Wait	99.652
I	3	100.142	100.139	Repurchase	100.139
J	3	100.571	100.562	Repurchase	100.562
D	2	99.159	99.190	Wait	99.159
E	2	100.137	100.138	Wait	100.137
F	2	100.995	100.978	Repurchase	100.978
B	1	100.014	100.029	Wait	100.014
C	1	101.298	101.277	Repurchase	101.277
A	0	101.507	101.491	Repurchase	101.491

[a]Assumes a 35 percent marginal income tax rate and zero transaction costs.

$$\text{Efficiency} = \frac{101.491 - 101.300}{101.491 - 101.191} = 0.637, \text{ or } 63.7 \text{ percent}$$

This confirms our earlier conclusion that waiting is better even though the net advantage of refunding is positive. Even the most relaxed criterion in practice favors waiting.

Figure 11.5 provides the information for graphing the stopping curve and the refunding efficiency curve. The figure shows that calling now is 100 percent efficient because calling is more valuable than waiting. Shifting the yield curve underlying figures 11.4 and 11.5 upward and parallel to its current path so that the value of calling equals the value of waiting identifies the highest new issue rate at which 100 percent efficiency would be achieved. Refunding at still higher new issue rates is, of course, less than 100 percent efficient.

The stopping curve is the set of future new issue rates, one for each period in figure 11.5, for which the value of calling would equal the value of waiting. For example, in period 1, the point on the stopping curve is between the 1.5-year new issue rates that correspond to r_{1U} = 10.872 percent and r_{1L} = 9.598 percent. By shifting the yield curve up or down (by trial and error) until the values of calling and waiting are the same, we can obtain the 1.5-year new issue stopping rate.[10] A programmed spreadsheet can make this calculation easily.

Synthetic Bond Call Options

In chapter 7 we showed that an interest rate swap is equivalent to exchanging a fixed-rate bond for a floating-rate bond (see equation 7.3) and introduced the term *swaption*, which is an option on an interest rate swap. A call swaption is equivalent to having an option to buy a fixed-rate bond (for the swap's notional amount) because the floating-rate bond is worth par at the start of the swap. Therefore, a call swaption is also like owning a call option on a bond, such as the call option embedded in a callable bond. As a result, if a firm sells a call swaption that matches the terms on its callable bond, it is as if the firm is selling the bond's call option but keeping the rest of the bond. That is, the firm will be effectively transforming its callable bond into a noncallable bond. A properly crafted call swaption, then, is a synthetic bond call option.

Why would a firm want to sell a synthetic bond call option and transform its callable bond into a noncallable bond? Recall that one of the bond refunding costs is the opportunity cost created by exercising the call option and thereby giving up the option's time premium. If a firm sells an equivalent synthetic bond call option instead of exercising its bond call option, it captures the entire call option value, including the option's time premium.

In a similar way, suppose a firm decided that it should have included a call option on noncallable bonds that it issued some time ago. The firm can "fix its mistake." It can buy a call swaption as a synthetic bond call option to transform its noncallable bonds into callable bonds.

Consider an issuer of an 8 percent ten-year callable bond that would like to capture the value of (in effect, sell) its call without redeeming the bond. The par value of the bonds callable at 105 is $100 million, and refinancing would cost $1 million in out-of-pocket expenses. The issuer's tax rate is 40 percent. It can borrow fixed rate at 7 percent or floating rate at LIBOR plus 25 basis points (bp). The after-tax cost of calling the 8 percent bonds is $103.6 million.[11] The firm can sell a ten-year call swaption with a notional amount of $103.6 million, a fixed rate of 7.722 percent ($8 million divided by $103.6 million), and a floating rate of LIBOR plus 25 bp to mirror the bonds' call option. If the purchaser exercises, the firm pays $8 million interest annually, which it can offset by calling its bonds, and it would get LIBOR plus 25 bp on $103.6 million, which it can offset by borrowing the same amount at the same rate from its bank to pay the cost of redeeming its bonds.

Tender Offers and Open Market Purchases

Some long-term bonds are noncallable, and even callable bonds typically include an initial grace period when they cannot be called. Other bonds have restrictions, such as they cannot be replaced by a new issue that costs less and ranks on a parity with or senior to them. Nevertheless, a firm can purchase such protected bonds in the market or by tender offer. And even if it is not able to retire the entire issue, shareholders can benefit if part of the issue is refunded profitably.

Issuer Versus Investor Motivations

Repurchasing high-coupon debt may be more profitable to the issuer than purchases by investors for the following main reasons:

- The issuer can deduct the premium for tax purposes in the year of repurchase, whereas an investor must amortize it over the life of the issue.

- The issuer can deduct the unamortized balance of expenses plus original issue discount in the year of repurchase.

- The issuer is not subject to the risk that the bonds will be called for redemption unexpectedly.

Repurchasing high-coupon debt generally is most profitable when the yield curve is upward sloping and investors think a call is likely as soon as the period of call protection expires.

Analyzing Open Market Purchases and Tender Offers

With three adjustments, the method of analysis illustrated in table 10.1 applies also to repurchase and tender offer refundings. First, the price equals or exceeds (with a tender offer) the market price rather than being a fixed call price. Second, holders are free to accept or reject the issuer's offer. Consequently, both the amount of debt refunded and the effective redemption premium are uncertain. In practice, these amounts can only be estimated. Third, there are added transaction costs associated with a repurchase program or a tender offer. In a repurchase program, the issuer typically repurchases bonds through securities firms, which add the bid-ask spread (i.e., their "profit margin") to their cost of acquiring the bonds. This premium can simply be included in the purchase price the issuer pays. In a tender offer, the issuer normally engages securities firms to acquire as many bonds as possible at the tender price. In such cases, the issuer must pay a *soliciting dealer fee*, typically between $2.50 and $7.50 per bond, depending on market conditions and other factors.

On March 21, 1986, Mountain States Telephone & Telegraph Company tendered at a price of 114.5 percent for its $250 million principal amount of 11.625 percent debentures due June 8, 2023. At the time of the tender, the firm could have issued new 9 percent thirty-seven-year conventional debt.

As table 11.5 shows, $190 million principal worth of the bonds were tendered. This created $1,628,689 of semiannual after-tax interest and expense amortization savings with a present value of $48,000,710. The cost was $19,167,200 after taxes, and the refunding produced a net advantage of about $28,833,510.

The choice of tender premium depends on such factors as investors' taxes and interest rate expectations, the composition of the bondholder group, and alternative investment yields. The Mountain States tender premium was determined by calculating the tender price that would provide a yield to first call comparable to the yield from investing in U.S. government agency issues over the same time horizon. For example, just before the tender offer, the market value of Mountain States bonds was about 110, implying a yield to first call of 7.49 percent. (Once a tender is announced, the market value increases to the tender price.) By tendering and then reinvesting the proceeds in a government agency issue, a bondholder could have earned the same 7.49 percent but with less credit risk. This is why the proportion of bonds tendered was high (76 percent).

Which Method Is Cheaper?

Repurchasing is generally cheaper than tendering when that bond's market is liquid enough that the repurchase program does not exert much upward pressure on price. Bonds can be repurchased from different holders at varying prices, depending on what each one is willing to accept. For larger programs, however, firms often prefer the fairness of a tender offer, with all bondholders offered the same price.

Timing the Tender Offer

Timing is another critical factor in tender offers. The analysis is the same as that for timing other redemptions: Is it better to wait or refund now? Refunding locks in the currently available savings, but waiting may offer greater savings later, after the bonds become callable at a lower call price.

Table 11.5 Tendering and Refunding Versus Waiting

Assumptions (prices as % of par)		
Amount refunded		$190,000,000
Tender date		6/8/86[a]
First call date		6/8/88
First call price		107.50%
Tender price		114.50%
Refunding transaction costs		0.30%
Maturity (new and old issues)		6/8/2023
Coupon: Old issue		11⅝%
New issue		9%
Original proceeds: Old issue		96.25%
New issue		98.50%
Tax rate		34%

Cost of Refunding	Tender	Call
Price per bond (% of par)	114.500%	107.500%
Tax basis (6/8/86)	96.531	96.719
Tax deduction	17.969	10.781
Tax benefit	6.109	3.666
After-tax price	108.390	103.834
Transaction costs	0.300	0.300
After-tax transaction costs	0.198	0.198
Total after-tax cost	108.588%	104.032%
Cost in dollars	$206,317,200	$197,660,800
Proceeds of new issue	187,150,000	187,150,00
Cash outflow on refunding	$ 19,167,200	$ 10,510,800
NPV on 6/8/86[a]	$ 19,167,200	$ 9,332,583

Benefits of Refunding (after taxes)		
Benefits begin	6/8/86	6/8/88
Semiannual interest savings	$ 1,645,875	$ 1,645,875
Increase (decrease) in semi- annual amortization deduction	(17,186)	(16,438)
Semiannual savings	$ 1,628,689	$ 1,629,437
NPV on 6/8/86[b]	$ 48,000,710	$ 41,968,425
Net advantage of refunding	$ 28,833,510	$ 32,635,842
Net advantage (% of par)	15.18%	17.18%

[a] To simplify the analysis, the net advantage of refunding is calculated as if the tender offer took place on the next interest payment date, June 8, 1986.
[b] Discounted at the after-tax cost of the refunding issue (3.0169 percent per semiannual period).

For the Mountain States tender, the first call price was 107.5. As shown in table 11.5, waiting to call would have saved $70 per bond ($1,145 – $1,075), for a total of $8,788,000 after taxes (at a 34 percent rate). However, delaying would have sacrificed the interest savings between then and the first possible call date, and risked having a higher new issue rate.

The benefit of waiting can be analyzed using the approach illustrated in figures 11.4 and 11.5 and table 11.2.

Conclusion

Prior to the advent of embedded option valuation and the notion of refunding efficiency, refunding decisions were usually based only on the net advantage of refunding and a "gut feel" about future interest rates. Dynamic programming provides a superior decision tool because it considers all possible refund-or-wait scenarios.

An analysis of a possible bond refunding should include the alternative of waiting. A very useful but simple rule is to wait to refund until the call option's remaining time premium is approximately zero.

The chapter described two approaches to deciding when it is most advantageous to refund a high-coupon debt issue. Break-even analysis is a good starting point for tackling the timing decision. Dynamic programming is more useful but also more complex. Still, a thorough refunding analysis is critical to achieving acceptable refunding efficiency.

The chapter also discussed market repurchases and tender offers. Both methods can be used to reacquire high-coupon debt when refunding is profitable but the bonds are not currently callable. With only slight modifications, the basic approaches for calculating the net advantage of a refunding (developed in chapter 10) and deciding when to refund the old debt (developed in this chapter) work equally well for market repurchases and tender offers.

Chapter 12

Sinking-Fund Management

A sinking fund is a very common bond feature, with a name that is somewhat of a misnomer. In almost every case, it is not really a fund. Rather, as we discussed in chapter 5, the sinking fund specifies the pattern of bond redemptions when principal will be repaid in some way other than a single lump sum at maturity. Typically sinking-fund redemptions can be achieved either by repurchasing bonds in the market or calling bonds and paying par value for them. Active management of a sinking fund creates opportunities to reduce the overall cost of debt.

This chapter provides a general framework for managing sinking funds, in particular, for deciding how best to retire sinking-fund bonds. Sinking-fund management is approached on a marginal, not an average, basis. At a given price, doubling the amount of bonds refunded may not double the net advantage. Recall from chapter 10 that the most profitable refunding strategy for a high-coupon sinking-fund issue may entail only a partial call, with the rest of the bonds retired through the sinking fund. The marginal approach, as we shall see, shows that acquired low-coupon bonds should be applied to the earliest sinking-fund obligations, while high-coupon bonds should be applied to the most distant obligations.

Types of Sinking Funds

The typical corporate bond sinking fund calls for annual *sinking-fund payments*. These payments may vary from period to period, and bank loans often require quarterly or semiannual, rather than annual, payments. The amount retired at maturity is called the *balloon*. It may be much larger than other payments, sometimes even more than all the other payments combined.

The issuer usually has a choice in satisfying the sinking-fund requirement: It can pay for bonds with a cash payment to the trustee or purchase bonds in the market and deliver bond certificates. In the first case, the trustee determines, usually by lottery, the specific bonds to be retired and notifies the holders. This is a European call option, and payment is almost always par value. Combinations of amounts are possible, and amounts can be designated in advance for specific payments. These designation and delivery options are valuable.

Acceleration Provision

The *acceleration provision* allows the retirement at par of some specified multiple of the mandatory amount. It is a sequence of noncumulative European call options. For example, the *double-up option* allows the issuer to call twice the mandatory amount. The multiplication factor is usually between 1.5 and 3.0. The acceleration provision (like the sinking fund itself) becomes valuable when a decline in interest rates makes the bonds worth more than par because it allows more of the bonds to be purchased for par. The acceleration provision is noncumulative; if it is not fully used in a given year, the unused portion cannot be carried forward to a future year.

Private Placements

Although this chapter focuses on the typical sinking-fund structure for a U.S. corporate public debt issue, the basic concepts are equally valid for alternative sinking-fund structures. Private placements, however, must be analyzed differently. Private placements normally do not allow the issuer to deliver certificates in lieu of cash. Thus, the bonds that the issuer purchases cannot be designated toward a specific sinking-fund payment. Moreover, the issue must be redeemed on a pro rata basis. For example, an investor who holds 20 percent of the issue will provide exactly 20 percent of the bonds being retired. In some private placements, any bonds retired by call option must be applied to the tail end of the sinking fund.

Other Sinking-Fund Structures

Many Canadian debt securities involve a *purchase fund*. It operates like a regular sinking fund, but only when the bonds are selling at a discount. When the bonds are trading at a premium, the issuer is not allowed to call at par.

Some electric utilities have a *funnel* sinking fund, which requires the issuer to retire each year a specified percentage of the aggregate outstanding amount of a set of debt issues. For example, suppose there are twelve issues totaling $1.5 billion, and each year 1 percent of the total ($15 million) must be retired. The funnel sinking fund should be managed as a portfolio, where it may be possible to call high-coupon bonds at par or repurchase low-coupon bonds at a discount. Because of the many alternatives and the interdependence of the sinking-fund and call provisions, the analysis of a funnel sinking fund is often extremely complicated.

Other sinking-fund provisions require retirement by market purchases of the necessary amounts. In some cases, the issuer must repurchase its own bonds; in others, the issuer may purchase bonds of other specified issuers. The latter case applies to several Canadian crown corporations. The bonds purchased during the life of the issue provide for the repayment of principal at maturity. This particular, and now very unusual, provision comes closest to the antiquated notion of an actual "fund," wherein it is like the issuer's depositing money in a sinking fund to pay off the debt.

Overview of Sinking-Fund Management

Consider how to meet an upcoming sinking-fund payment. If the bonds are selling at a discount, repurchasing is cheaper than paying par. Such repurchases usually must be made at least one month ahead but can be made even earlier. We will explain when it makes sense to buy ahead in anticipation of sinking-fund obligations. If the bonds are selling at a premium, it is normally better to pay par to the trustee. Nevertheless, buying ahead can be a profitable strategy even for premium bonds in the right circumstances.

Basic Analytical Approach

Sinking-fund management also relies on the debt service parity (DSP) approach. As noted in chapter 10, each sinking-fund payment is treated as an individual "bullet" bond with its own maturity and call price schedule. The original issue is viewed as a serial bond issue, with each series of bonds corresponding to a different sinking-fund date. At any time, each "series" of bonds has the same call price. It is possible to determine a separate refunding efficiency curve and a separate stopping curve for each series of bonds.

If the current interest rate is much higher than the coupon rate and rates are expected to remain unchanged, the issuer would like to keep this low-coupon debt outstanding as long as possible. In contrast, investors would like to have such bonds redeemed as soon as possible. The issuer can minimize its cost of debt by maximizing the debt's average life. It should designate repurchased bonds to the first sinking-fund payment.

If instead the current interest rate is much lower than the coupon rate, the issuer has relatively expensive debt. It can minimize its cost of debt by minimizing the debt's average life. It should designate repurchased bonds to the balloon payment. As table 10.3 illustrates, the most distant sinking-fund payments are the most profitable to extinguish.

Public debt issuers have great flexibility in designating bonds to meet specific sinking-fund obligations. This flexibility is valuable in deciding whether to purchase bonds at the current market price. As a general rule, discounted bonds are designated to the first unsatisfied payment obligation, and premium bonds are designated to the last sinking-fund payment.

Call and Sinking Fund Interaction

Corporate sinking-fund issues normally also have a call provision. Recall from chapter 10 that the most profitable strategy for a high-coupon issue may be to call only part of it at a premium and sink the rest at par. The call and sinking-fund provisions are interdependent; once a bond is called and retired, it cannot be sunk at par at a later time.

The Timing Decision

The timing decision is analyzed in the manner described in chapter 11 for a bullet issue. The break-even and optimal refunding rates are computed for each sinking-fund payment. Figure 12.1 shows the break-even and optimal rates at the end of year 10 (1990) for each future sinking-fund payment for a thirty-year 15 percent issue. For example, the year 2000 sinking-fund payment could be refunded profitably if the new issue rate in 1990 is less than about 13.75 percent. However, it is better to wait unless the new issue rate at that time is less than about 11.5 percent, to capture the call option's remaining time premium.[1]

Two additional factors should be considered. First, the costs of calling individual payments are not independent of each other, because

Figure 12.1 Break-Even and Optimal Refunding Rates by Sinking-Fund Payment Date Computed at the First Call Date in 1990

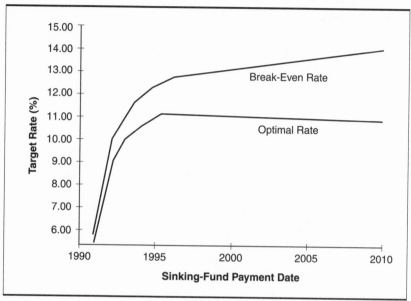

certain fixed expenses can be shared. Thus, it may make sense to call more than if such joint expenses did not exist. Second, by calling a sinking-fund bond, the issuer sacrifices the option to call it later if rates decline or to purchase it below par if rates dramatically increase. This consideration applies only to the sinking-fund payments, not to the balloon portion.

Acceleration Provision

The analysis is easily extended to bonds that include an acceleration provision. Such a provision is most valuable to the issuer when interest rates drop following issuance and the sinking fund commences before call protection expires, because it represents a call at par for a larger portion of the issue.

Refunding Discounted Debt

Prepurchasing low-coupon bonds in anticipation of future sinking-fund needs should be analyzed as a refunding of discounted (low-coupon) debt. Perhaps the most controversial issue in bond refunding is whether discounted debt can be profitably refunded. The correct treatment of tax-related factors, using the appropriate discount rate, and the impact of the refunding on the firm's debt capacity are crucial to this analysis.

The analytical approach is essentially the same as the one developed for high-coupon debt in chapter 10. When debt service parity is maintained, the net advantage of refunding discounted debt is the NPV of the change in after-tax debt service payments discounted at the after-tax cost of the new debt minus the after-tax refunding expenses.

When Refunding Discounted Debt Is Profitable

Refunding discounted debt can be profitable if it increases the proportion of the debt service stream that is tax deductible *and* if these savings are not outweighed by income tax on the saving from retiring debt for less than par.[2] Such refunding is a form of tax arbitrage that can benefit a firm when its marginal income tax rate is higher than that of the bondholders. In that case, refunding discounted debt reduces the firm's and its bondholders' combined tax liability. In practice, most corporate bonds are owned by either pension funds, which are tax-exempt, or by life insurance companies, whose tax rate is lower than the full corporate tax rate. Thus, tax arbitrage is possible in practice.

In general, refunding discounted debt increases the present value of the pretax debt service payments more than it decreases the principal repayment.[3] However, it also increases the proportion of debt service payments that is tax deductible, which can make refunding discounted debt profitable. Therefore, refunding discounted debt increases shareholder wealth only if the value of the resulting tax shields exceeds the sum of (1) the present value of the increase in pretax debt service requirements, (2) transaction costs, and (3) any tax incurred on the gain. In general, refunding discounted debt will not be profitable for a non-tax-paying firm.[4]

The tax treatment on the gain is crucial.[5] If a firm must pay tax on the gain at ordinary income tax rates, even on a deferred basis, refunding discounted debt is rarely profitable.

As an illustration, let's redo the single-period example in chapter 10, but with the coupon and new issue rates reversed. In this case interest rates have risen from 8 percent to 13 percent (i.e., $r = 0.08$ and $r' = 0.13$). The old $1,000.00 8 percent bond matures in one year. It can be repurchased for $955.75 ($1,080/1.13). Using equation 10.2, a new $1,000.00 13 percent one-year bond can be sold for $972.17 ($1,000[1 + 0.08(1 − 0.40)]/

[1 + 0.13(1 – 0.40)]). The difference is $16.42 and comes from the tax arbitrage. Only $80.00 (7.41 percent) of the $1,080.00 of the old bond's pretax debt service is tax deductible, whereas $126.05 (11.5 percent) of the $1,095.66 of the new bond's pretax debt service is tax deductible. Thus, the new debt provides a $50.42 tax credit ($126.05[0.40]), whereas the old debt provides only a $32.00 tax credit ($80[0.40]).

With a $6.00 after-tax flotation cost, it looks good so far, but we are not done. The gain from extinguishing discounted debt (i.e., the difference between the outstanding bond's tax basis and its repurchase price) is generally taxable as ordinary income in the United States. Unless the firm can avoid this tax or defer it for a considerable time, it typically makes refunding discounted debt unprofitable.[6]

Using equation 10.3 and assuming the gain is taxed at the ordinary tax rate ($T' = 40$ percent), refunding will be an unprofitable –$7.28:

$$NA = \frac{(1 - 0.40)(0.08 - 0.13)1{,}000}{[1 + (1 - 0.40)0.13]} - (1 - 0.40)(955.75 - 1{,}000) = -\$7.28$$

General Analytical Framework

We developed equations 10.3 and 10.4 to be applicable also to refunding discounted debt. Therefore, the net advantage of refunding is[7]

$$NA = \sum_{n=1}^{N} \frac{(1 - T)(r - r')D}{[1 + (1 - T)r']^n} - (1 - T')(P - D) - E \qquad (10.4)$$

where the variables are as defined in chapter 10. We can now see that, more precisely, T' is the effective present-value tax rate on the gain, $D - P$. Often at least a portion of the tax on the gain can be deferred. T' is determined by the present value of any tax liability on the gain, calculated by discounting each tax payment at the after-tax yield that would be required on a zero-coupon note maturing on the date the tax payment comes due. The present value of the after-tax expense associated with the refunding, E, is given by equation 10.5, with $P = B$.[8] The issuer can profitably refund the discounted debt only if NA is positive, but as with high-coupon debt, there remains the important issue of whether the firm should refund it now or wait.

Recall that equation 10.6 offers a simplified calculation, assuming $E = 0$, and equation 10.7 simplifies even further by assuming no taxes:

$$NA = \sum_{n=1}^{N} \frac{rD}{(1 + r')^n} + \frac{D}{(1 + r')^N} - P \qquad (10.7)$$

In a discounted debt refunding, the value NA in equation 10.7 equals the value of the out-of-the-money call option. When the old debt is trading at a large discount, the call option is essentially worthless, and consequently, the net advantage of refunding is zero. In the absence of taxes, refunding discounted debt would not be profitable and is in fact negative because of transaction costs.

Finally, note once again that debt service parity is required only for analytical purposes. As with a high-coupon refunding, a firm can use a discounted debt refunding as an opportunity to make other profitable decisions simultaneously.

Here is an example. A firm is considering refunding its 10 percent $50 million bond issue that matures in ten years. The bonds have a market price of 77.705 ($777.05 per bond), and a yield to maturity of 14.25 percent. The firm can reacquire the discounted debt in such a way that it will not incur any tax liability on the gain. The old bonds' remaining unamortized balance of issuance and other expenses is $400,000. The firm's new issue rate for noncallable ten-year debt is 15 percent, 75 basis points higher than the yield to maturity on its existing bonds because of tax and transaction cost considerations.

As shown in table 12.1, the net advantage of refunding is $475,191 (assuming the gain is tax free). Suppose instead that the firm is able to defer the tax on the gain for only ten years and must then pay tax at a 34 percent rate. The effective tax rate, expressed on a present-value basis, is 0.1279 $(0.34[1.05012]^{-20})$. The firm incurs a present-value tax obligation of $1,425,765 (0.1279[$50,000,000 − $38,852,500]). This tax liability makes the net advantage of refunding negative, −$950,574 ($475,191 − $1,425,765). Of course, if the gain was immediately taxed as ordinary income, the tax liability would be $3,790,150 (0.34[$50,000,000 − $38,852,500]), and refunding would be even more unprofitable.

Timing

The timing of refunding discounted debt can also be analyzed like that of a high-coupon refunding. Two methods were discussed in chapter 11. First, consider break-even analysis of waiting one year to refund. Assume the one-year after-tax discount rate is 6.778 percent (a pretax yield of 10.27 percent). What must the new issue rate be one year from now for the firm to have the same net advantage of refunding (a present value of $475,191)? This rate is determined by trial and error using

Table 12.1 Net Advantage of Refunding Discounted Debt

Assumptions	Old Issue	New Issue
Principal amount	$50,000,000	$38,852,500
Coupon rate	10.00%	15.00%
Remaining life	10 years	10 years
Issuance expenses plus original issue discount (less original issue premium)	$ 400,000[a]	$ 380,000
Debt retirement expenses[b]	$ 150,000	
Issuer's tax rate	34%	34%

Benefits of Refunding	**Pretax**	**After-Tax**
Semiannual expense amortization:		
New issue	$ 19,000	$ 6,460
Old issue	20,000	6,800
Savings (cost)	$ (1,000)	$ (340)
Present value of semiannual savings (cost)[c]		$ (4,225)
Present value of decrease in principal repayment obligation[c]		4,241,590
Total benefits		$ 4,237,335

Costs of Refunding	**Pretax**	**After-Tax**
Semiannual interest expense:		
Old issue	$ 2,913,938	$ 1,923,199
New issue	2,500,000	1,650,000
Semiannual increase	$ 413,938	$ 273,199
Present value of increase in semiannual interest expense[c]		$ 3,419,144
Tax on the gain	—	—
New issue expense	380,000	380,000
Debt retirement expenses	150,000	99,000
Less write-off of unamortized balance of issuance expenses on refunded issue	(400,000)	(136,000)
Total costs		$ 3,762,144
Net advantage of refunding		$ 475,191

[a] Unamortized balance.
[b] Calculated as $3.00 per bond.
[c] Discounted at the semiannual after-tax new issue rate (4.95 percent per semiannual period).

a spreadsheet calculation. This rate makes the present value (discounted back two periods at 6.778 percent) of the net advantage of refunding (as in table 12.1 but with eighteen time periods) equal to $475,191. The rate that does this is a yield to maturity on the old bonds of 14.11 percent, producing a bond price of 79.40 (versus 77.705 today). Assuming the new issue rate is again 75 basis points above the yield to maturity on the old bonds implies a break-even new issue rate of 14.86 percent. Consequently, if the firm believes there is a strong likelihood that interest rates will not decrease more than 14 basis points (the difference between 15.00 percent and 14.86 percent), it may prefer to postpone the refunding.

Advance Purchases of Low-Coupon Bonds

Now we turn to discounted sinking-fund bonds. The maturity of the sinking-fund slot to which a repurchased bond will be designated is the maturity to use to determine the new issue rate for calculating the net advantage of refunding. Once again, actual transactions often do not maintain DSP, and advance purchases of small blocks are usually funded with cash.

Net Advantage of Refunding

Equation 10.4 assumes the debt will be redeemed for par value, D; however, discounted debt is repurchased for less than par, so equation 10.4 must be modified for sinking-fund purchases. Assume a sinking-fund payment D is due at time N and the market price of the bonds is $P_N < D$ at that time. It costs P_N to retire the bonds plus a tax liability of $T'(D - P_N)$. Modifying equation 10.4, the net advantage of refunding is

$$NA = \sum_{n=1}^{N} \frac{(1 - T)rD}{[1 + (1 - T)r']^n} + \frac{P_N + T'(D - P_N)}{[1 + (1 - T)r']^N} - P - T'(D - P) \quad (12.1)$$

The net advantage of an immediate advance purchase decreases as P_N decreases. The lower the bond's expected future price, the lower the net advantage of refunding now. Therefore, using equation 10.4 rather than equation 12.1 biases the decision toward immediate advance purchase and leads to excessive advance purchases.

Although equation 12.1 leads to better decisions, estimating P_N is problematic. The binomial model developed later in the chapter avoids this problem by considering a reasonable range of future bond prices (eliminating the need to forecast a single value for P_N).

Break-Even Analysis

Suppose the only current purchase alternative is to buy bonds for price P at the sinking-fund date. The net advantage of refunding can be computed using equation 12.1. Obviously the higher the future price

P_N, the greater the savings are from advance purchase, but what is the price below which the firm should not make the purchase, that is, what is the break-even price?

Consider a possible advance purchase of a 7 percent bond with fifteen years left to maturity, assuming no taxes. The purpose would be to meet a sinking-fund payment due six years from now. The bond's market price is currently 77.375, and the six-year new issue rate is 9.5 percent. The advance purchase would save both the next six interest payments and purchasing the bond in six years. For the firm to be indifferent between purchasing now and waiting for six years, the present value of those savings must equal today's purchase price. So the break-even price is 80.125, because the present value at 4.75 percent (9.5/2) of the combined $3.50 ($7.00/2) per six months and $80.125 at the end is 77.375.

The break-even calculation treats the advance purchase as a single-period problem, considering only the alternatives of purchasing now or waiting six years. Of course, the decision is more complex. If not made today, such a prepurchase could be made at any time within the next six years. Dynamic programming can provide the solution to the multiperiod case, as we discuss later in the chapter.

Impact of Accumulation

As we have seen, the advantage of an advance purchase depends on the future bond price. Unfortunately, it is impossible to know future prices. Even predicting a reasonable range of future prices is difficult. Unlike a bullet issue (with a lump-sum maturity), the price of a sinking-fund issue depends on the ownership distribution of the issue as well as on future interest rates. Like issuers, investors follow a marginal approach in making their buy and sell decisions.

Suppose a single investor owns the remaining $5 million of what was originally a $100 million noncallable sinking-fund issue, which now has a ten-year remaining maturity. The next sinking-fund payment of $5 million would have been due in three years, but the previously acquired $95 million has already satisfied all remaining required sinking-fund payments. As a result, the investor can value the $5 million block as a bullet bond maturing in ten years.

Now consider another extreme. Assume the same basic scenario, except that the entire issue is still outstanding. A single investor owns $95 million of the $100 million issue, has been offered the remaining $5 million, and realizes that purchasing it would provide 100 percent issue ownership. With 100 percent ownership, the investor can force the issuer to call sinking-fund payments for par. Therefore, the investor can value the $5 million block as if it were a small bullet issue maturing in three years.

Guaranteed Par Value Date

In the example, year 3 is the investor's *guaranteed par value date* (GPVD), because on that date the investor is certain to receive par for any bond currently purchased.[9] The GPVD depends on the proportion of the issue already owned by the investor. As long as no investor owns more than a small proportion, the GPVD of each bond is the issue's maturity. Such widely held issues tend to be relatively cheap for the issuer to repurchase. If, on the other hand, a single investor, called an *accumulator* (or *collector*), acquires most of the bonds, the price may drastically increase.

Accumulators are important participants in the bond market, because any accumulator's gain comes at the issuer's expense. Therefore, bond issuers must consider the potential for accumulation in both their design decisions for new issues about whether to include a sinking fund and their refunding decisions about advance purchases to meet sinking-fund payments.

Discouraging Accumulation

Many firms prepurchase bonds well in advance of their sinking-fund needs.[10] The *designation option* is valuable when interest rates are high (and bond prices are discounted). If accumulators have bought most of the issue, the remaining bonds may be hard to find, and the firm may be forced to buy bonds from accumulators at prices well above their comparable market value (or else call them for par). But if the issuer has bonds in the treasury, it can designate them for the next sinking-fund payment. Having bonds in its treasury could deter potential accumulators from hoarding its bonds in the first place.[11] Another way to discourage accumulation is to structure the issue with a large balloon payment, because the accumulator must buy more than the balloon before it can affect the GPVD.

A sinking-fund issue's GPVD, the designation option, and the related problem of valuing collected issues can be handled within the dynamic programming framework, to which we turn next.

A Binomial Model for Sinking-Fund Management

Dynamic programming is especially useful in sinking-fund management because of the complexity of the timing problem when there is a sinking fund.

Designation

As before, the first step in the sinking-fund analysis is calibration, which is performed in the same way as for a non-sinking-fund bond, using par value noncallable bullet maturity bonds of the same default risk class. This is appropriate because most bond indentures allow the sinking-fund bond issue to be treated as a serial obligation—a series of bullet maturity issues that can be analyzed separately—for both optional and mandatory redemption purposes.

Next, bonds are designated to satisfy specific sinking-fund obligations. However, unless the bond indenture requires designation when bonds are purchased, these designations are only for analytical purposes. Postponing formal designation as long as possible preserves flexibility, which maximizes the value of the designation option because the issuer can change its designations (prior to notifying the trustee) if interest rates change.[12]

Bonds already designated (formally or for analytical purposes) to meet specific sinking-fund obligations are excluded from the analysis. For a sinking-fund payment S_J due at time J, the cost is the present value of the after-tax debt service payments,

$$C_J = \sum_{n=1}^{J} \frac{(1-T)rS_J}{[1+(1-T)r']^n} + \frac{S_J}{[1+(1-T)r']^J} \tag{12.2}$$

where r is the coupon rate on the old debt, r' is the cost of the new debt, and T is the firm's income tax rate. The firm should designate bonds (including any already prepurchased but not yet designated) to the most expensive obligation first, any remaining bonds to the next most expensive obligation, and so on.[13]

If designations have not covered the current sinking-fund obligation entirely, then it must be addressed first. This obligation can be met by first making market purchases of any bonds that can be purchased for less than the sinking fund's mandatory redemption price and then by redeeming whatever additional bonds are needed by having the bond trustee call them.

An alternative is to use the calibrated interest rate tree to calculate the present-value cost of each sinking-fund obligation and determine the cost-minimizing designations. The example presented later in the chapter illustrates this technique.

Pricing the Sinking-Fund Bonds

After designations meet the current needs, the remaining sinking-fund payments form a serial bond issue, any portion of which is eligible for advance purchase or optional redemption. These sinking-fund amounts are $F_1, F_2, \ldots, F_N$; $F_j = 0$ for a fully designated obligation.[14] This serial debt obligation has an aggregate principal amount F, and the F_j must sum to F.

As in chapter 11, we assume the marginal bond investors are tax-exempt. The serial debt obligation can be valued by working backward through the calibrated interest rate tree. (Use the tree before any adjustment for corporate income taxes.) The value of the bonds is the present value of the interest payments and sinking-fund payments.

B_{ij} is the aggregate market value of the bonds to investors at node (i,j), where i is the time period, j is the interest rate outcome, and r_{ij} is the one-period forward rate. The aggregate market value of the bonds at node (i,j) is the present value of the expected future cash flows:

$$\text{Initial } B_{ij} = \frac{\frac{1}{2}(B_{i+1,U} + S_{i+1,U} + B_{i+1,L} + S_{i+1,L}) + C_{i+1}}{1 + r_{ij}} \qquad (12.3)$$

where C_{i+1} is the aggregate coupon paid at time $i + 1$; $B_{i+1,U}$ and $B_{i+1,L}$ are the aggregate market values of the bonds at nodes $(i + 1, U)$ and $(i + 1, L)$, respectively, immediately after the interest and sinking-fund payments due at time $i + 1$ are paid; and $S_{i+1,U}$ and $S_{i+1,L}$ are the values of the sinking-fund payment obligation at time $i + 1$ conditional on the interest rate at that time. (See figure 12.2.) These bond values in turn depend on whether the firm decides to retire any of the bonds at either of these nodes.

If the issuer does not plan to call any bonds at time i, the price of the bonds at node (i,j) is equal to the aggregate market value of the bonds, B_{ij}, divided by the face amount of bonds that remain outstanding after the issuer has made the sinking-fund payment at time i, $\sum_{t=i+1}^{N} F_t$:

$$B_{ij} \bigg/ \sum_{t=i+1}^{N} F_t \qquad (12.4)$$

The issuer will call the bonds if this value exceeds the call price. Thus, the market price of the bonds at node (i,j), P_{ij}, is the lesser of equation 12.4 and the call price:

$$P_{ij} = \min\{B_{ij} / \sum_{t=i+1}^{N} F_t, \, 100 + \Pr(i)\} \qquad (12.5)$$

where $\Pr(i)$ is the call premium at time i and the par value is 100.

Figure 12.2 Calculating the Price of a Bond at a Node

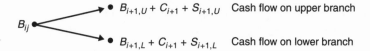

$$B_{ij} = \frac{\frac{1}{2}(B_{i+1,U} + S_{i+1,U} + B_{i+1,L} + S_{i+1,L}) + C_{i+1}}{1 + r_{ij}}$$

$B_{i+1,U} + C_{i+1} + S_{i+1,U}$ Cash flow on upper branch

B_{ij}

$B_{i+1,L} + C_{i+1} + S_{i+1,L}$ Cash flow on lower branch

r is the one-period discount rate

$B_{i+1,U}$	=	The outstanding bonds' aggregate value on the upper branch net of the sinking-fund payment
$B_{i+1,L}$	=	The outstanding bonds' aggregate value on the lower branch net of the sinking-fund payment
C_{i+1}	=	Coupon payment on the bonds at time $i + 1$
$S_{i+1,U}$	=	Value of the sinking-fund payment obligation at time $i + 1$ on the upper branch (possibly zero)
$S_{i+1,L}$	=	Value of the sinking-fund payment obligation at time $i + 1$ on the lower branch (possibly zero)
r_{ij}	=	One-period forward rate at the node where the bond's value is being calculated

Finally, if the bonds are called, then $P_{ij} = 100 + \text{Pr}(i)$, and the value of the bonds is equal to their aggregate call price. In that case, replace B_{ij}:

$$[100 + \text{Pr}(i)] \sum_{t=i+1}^{N} F_t = \text{Final } B_{ij} \qquad (12.6)$$

Impact of Call or Repurchase

The firm will either call bonds or repurchase them in the open market to meet its immediate sinking-fund obligation. If the bonds are trading at a discount, the issuer will repurchase bonds. In that case, set

$$S_{ij} = F_i \times P_{ij}/100 \qquad (12.7)$$

Otherwise the issuer will call bonds for the sinking fund at par. In that case, set

$$S_{ij} = F_i \qquad (12.8)$$

When the values of B_{ij}, S_{ij}, and P_{ij} have been determined for all the nodes corresponding to time i, you can move to time $i - 1$ and repeat the process.

Current Market Price

Work backward through the interest rate tree. The aggregate market value of the bonds at time zero, after making the sinking-fund payment due at that time, is the lesser of B_0, the expected present value of the future cash flows, and the aggregate call price $[100 + \text{Pr}(0)] \times \sum_{t=1}^{N} F_t$. Thus, the market price of the bonds at time zero, P_0, is

$$P_0 = \min\{B_0 / \sum_{t=1}^{N} F_t, 100 + \text{Pr}(0)\} \tag{12.9}$$

which is just like equation 12.5.

Equation 12.9 assumes that the price of the bonds at time zero is based on the post–time 0 debt service payments. If this price is less than par, the market price before taking into account the time 0 sinking-fund obligations may differ from P_0, depending on how the issuer plans to meet these obligations and what expectations bond investors have about the issuer's behavior. This price is mainly affected by accumulation.

Impact of Accumulation

As noted, accumulators can drive up the price of the bonds. When interest rates are high and the bonds should trade at a discount to the sinking-fund price, accumulators can force the issuer to pay an above-market price by cornering the bonds and leaving the issuer with no alternative but to buy from them.[15]

We can incorporate the impact of accumulation in the bond pricing model by setting the value of the sinking-fund payment equal to the price at which the bonds could be repurchased from accumulators for those dates when this is the only alternative available to the firm. For those dates, we recommend using equation 12.8, $S_{ij} = F_i$, rather than equation 12.7.

Impact of Advance Purchases

As noted, the value to investors falls as advance purchases increase. This is because each advance purchase eliminates the sinking-fund payments that are the most expensive to the issuer—and thus the most valuable to investors. Due to the interaction among advance purchases and redemptions, accumulation, and the bonds' market price at each date, the bonds should be repriced and the sinking-fund-management analysis updated after each repurchase or redemption.

Market Price Tree

The process of pricing the bonds results in a set of market prices, one for each node in the interest rate tree, as in figure 12.3. Associated with each node are a bond price P_{ij}, the cost of meeting this obligation S_{ij}, the aggregate market value of the remaining bonds B_{ij}, and the forward rate r_{ij}, plus the sinking-fund amount F_i and the aggregate coupon rate on the bonds C_i for that period.

Corporate Income Taxes

The interest rates in figure 12.3 are those in figure 9.9, adjusted to reflect the firm's marginal income tax rate T by multiplying each forward rate by $1 - T$.

Managing the Sinking Fund

The sinking-fund issue should be treated as a serial debt obligation. Each sinking-fund payment is treated as a separate bullet maturity issue. Each "issue" should be evaluated separately using the calibrated interest rate tree as adjusted for corporate income taxes. The value of each "issue" to the issuer is the present value of the after-tax cash flows required to service the sinking-fund amount until the firm retires it. The firm's objective in actively managing its sinking-fund obligations is to minimize the overall cost of its debt. There is an interdependency among these sinking-fund obligations because any advance purchase will affect the prices P_{ij}, and thus the profitability of later advance purchases.

To take into account these interdependencies, each sinking-fund payment should be analyzed for call or advance purchase. Reacquire the most expensive sinking-fund amount (assuming it is profitable to call or purchase at least one amount). Then set the appropriate F_j to zero and recalculate the price tree. Next, reevaluate the sinking-fund amounts for redemption or repurchase. Stop the process when none of the remaining amounts can be called or repurchased profitably.

Figure 12.3 Valuing a Two-Year Option-Free, Default-Free Sinking-Fund Bond

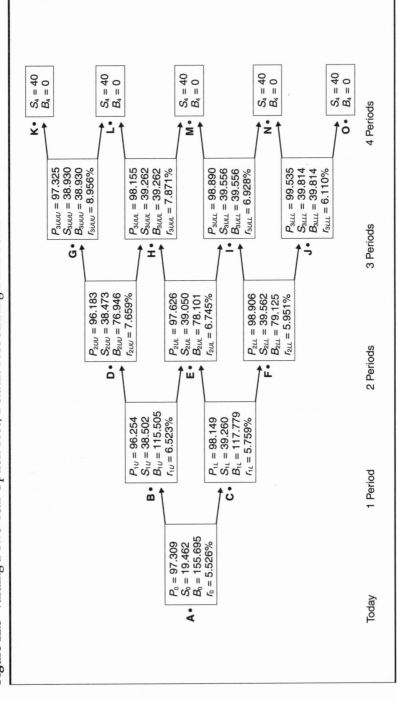

Today   1 Period   2 Periods   3 Periods   4 Periods

Calculating the Value to the Issuer of the Bonds in a Sinking-Fund Payment

Use the procedure explained in chapter 11 to analyze each bullet-maturity sinking-fund "issue":

1. Calculate the present value of the bond to the issuer at node (i,j), using equation 11.2.

2. Evaluate the profitability of a call at each node, using equation 11.3.

3. Evaluate the profitability of an advance purchase at each node using the market prices in the bond price tree, using equation 11.4.

4. Value the bonds at each node, using equation 11.5.

This process results in a set of recommended decisions, one for each sinking-fund amount: (1) call the bonds for optional redemption, (2) repurchase the bonds in the open market, or (3) wait one period to reconsider the decision. It would be very unusual for this analysis to indicate that some sinking-fund amounts should be called while others should be repurchased in the open market. It is almost always one or the other.

If the issuer can profitably call two or more sinking-fund amounts, it should select the bonds in order of their value of V_0 (wait), starting with the highest value. Recall that redeeming or repurchasing bonds affects the future prices P_{ij}. The issuer should delete these bonds from the sinking-fund schedule, repeat the analysis, and test whether it is profitable to call any additional sinking-fund amounts. Our experience is that when the initial analysis indicates that two or more sinking-fund amounts should be called, the more detailed sequential analysis (selecting one amount at each step) will usually identify the same set of bonds for optional redemption. Nevertheless, using the more detailed approach provides more assurance.

If the issuer can instead profitably make advance purchases of two or more sinking-fund amounts, the rule is the same: Select the bonds in descending order of V_0 (wait). Our experience is that with advance purchases, the interdependency of the distribution of bond ownership, the amount of bonds in the firm's treasury, and the market price of the bonds make it necessary to recalculate the market prices of the bonds and repeat the analysis after identifying each additional sinking-fund amount for advance purchase.

An Example of a Sinking-Fund Analysis

A firm has $200 million face amount of 8 percent low-coupon sinking-fund bonds, $20 million of which are in its treasury and undesignated. The issue requires an immediate sinking-fund payment of $40 million and additional future payments of $40 million, each at six-month intervals. The bonds are A-rated, and the calibrated interest rate tree is the same set of after-corporate-tax rates from figure 9.9 used in figure 12.3. The firm's income tax rate is 40 percent. Consider the following three questions:

1. To which sinking-fund payment should the $20 million of treasury bonds be designated?
2. How should the immediate sinking-fund obligation be met?
3. Should any bonds be redeemed or repurchased beyond those needed for the immediate use?

Designation

Consider each sinking-fund obligation separately. The cost of the immediate obligation, assuming redemption at par, is 100 per bond. The present-value cost of each sinking-fund obligation is calculated by backward induction, as in chapters 9 and 11. For example, the third sinking-fund obligation requires 100 of principal and 2.40 of after-tax interest two periods from now. The present-value costs as of the two nodes in period 1 are

$$\frac{102.4}{1 + 0.06523/2} = 99.166 \qquad \frac{102.4}{1 + 0.05759/2} = 99.534$$

The present-value cost as of period 0 is

$$\frac{\frac{1}{2}(99.166 + 99.534) + 2.4}{1 + 0.05526/2} = 99.014$$

Applying this to each obligation, the after-tax costs of the five obligations decrease as the obligation becomes more distant: 100, 99.647, 99.014, 98.113, and 96.957. Therefore, the firm should designate its treasury bonds to its immediate sinking-fund obligation.

Pricing the Sinking-Fund Bonds

The future sinking-fund obligations are $F_1 = F_2 = F_3 = F_4 = 40$. We consider the remaining immediate sinking-fund obligation $F_0 = 40 - 20$

= 20 separately. The calculation of the bond prices is given in figure 12.3. These bonds are callable, at call premiums of 0.5 in period 3, 1.0 in period 2, 1.5 in period 1, and 2.0 today.

Start at node H. The bonds are fully redeemed the following period, and so after the sinking-fund payment, $B_{4uuuu} = B_{4uuuL} = 0$. The sinking-fund obligation is $S_{4uuuu} = S_{4uuuL} = F_4 = 40$ million. $C_2 = 40 \times 0.08/2 = 1.6$ million. Thus, by equation 12.3,

$$\text{Initial } B_{3uuu} = \frac{\frac{1}{2}(0 + 40 + 0 + 40) + 1.6}{1 + 0.13716/2} = 38.930$$

The price is less than par, so the firm should buy, rather than redeem, bonds for the sinking fund:

$$S_{3uuu} = 38.930$$

Also, it is not profitable to call bonds for optional redemption. Thus, by equation 12.5,

$$P_{3uuu} = 38.930/40 = 0.97325, \text{ or } 97.325 \text{ percent}$$

and

$$\text{Final } B_{3uuu} = 38.930$$

Similar calculations at nodes I, J, and K show that it is not profitable to repurchase, redeem at par, or call the bonds for the sinking fund in each case.

Move backward (in time) to node D. Applying equation 12.3 with $C_3 = 3.2(80 \times 0.08/2)$ gives

$$\text{Initial } B_{2uu} = \frac{\frac{1}{2}(38.930 + 38.930 + 39.262 + 39.262) + 3.2}{1 + 0.11555/2} = 76.946$$

Since 76.946 is less than 80.00, the issuer would buy bonds rather than redeem them. Thus, by equations 12.5 and 12.7,

$$P_{2uu} = 76.946/80 = 0.96183, \text{ or } 96.183 \text{ percent}$$

$$S_{2uu} = 40 \times 96.183/100 = 38.473$$

and

$$\text{Final } B_{2uu} = 76.946$$

Calculations for nodes E and F show that it would be profitable to repurchase bonds for the sinking fund in each case, but neither redemption at par nor calling would be profitable.

Move backward (in time) to node B. Again apply equation 12.3:

$$\text{Initial } B_{1u} = \frac{\frac{1}{2}(76.946 + 38.473 + 78.101 + 39.050) + 4.8}{1 + 0.09662/2} = 115.505$$

Since 115.505 is less than 120, the issuer would again buy bonds rather than redeem them. Thus, by equations 12.5 and 12.7,

$$P_{1u} = 115.505/120 = 0.96254, \text{ or } 96.254 \text{ percent}$$

$$S_{1u} = 40 \times 96.254/100 = 38.502$$

and

$$\text{Final } B_{1u} = 115.505$$

A similar calculation at node C indicates Final $B_{1L} = 117.779$, and $S_{1L} = 39.260$, and that a bond redemption would not be profitable. Finally,

$$B_0 = \frac{\frac{1}{2}(115.505 + 38.502 + 117.779 + 39.260) + 6.4}{1 + 0.08/2} = 155.695$$

Thus, by equation 12.9,

$$P_0 = 155.695/160 = 0.97309, \text{ or } 97.309 \text{ percent}$$

Meeting the Immediate Sinking-Fund Obligation

Since the bonds are trading below the sinking-fund price (par), it is best to buy the additional $20 million of bonds needed for the sinking fund. If the firm could buy the entire amount at the current market price, its cost would be $19,461,800 ($20,000,000 × 0.97309). Of course, if buying drives the price above par, it should stop buying bonds and redeem the balance of the sinking-fund amount at the par mandatory redemption price.

Profitability of Advance Purchases

With the discount bonds, calling does not make sense. However, advance purchases in anticipation of future sinking-fund requirements might be profitable. Treat the debt issue as a serial debt obligation. Start with the next scheduled sinking-fund obligation because in the low-coupon case, the nearest obligation is usually the most profitable (or least costly) to refund.

Table 11.2 provides a useful template. Table 12.2 presents the profitability analysis. The market price of the bonds next period will be either 96.254 or 98.149. As a result, the issuer would be better off at that time buying the bonds rather than redeeming them at par. The after-tax repurchase price will be either 97.752 (96.254 + 0.4[100 – 96.254]) or 98.889 (98.149 + 0.4[100 – 98.149]). The after-tax coupon rate per bond is 2.4 (8[1 – 0.4]/2). Applying equation 11.2,

$$V_0 \text{ (wait)} = \frac{2.4 + \frac{1}{2}(97.752 + 98.889)}{1 + (1 - 0.4)0.0921/2} = 98.012$$

The call premium is 2.0, making an after-tax call price of 101.200 (100 + [1 – 0.4]2.0). The after-tax repurchase price at time zero is 98.385 (97.309 + 0.4[100 – 97.309]). Applying equation 11.6,

$$V_0 = \min\{98.012, 101.200, 98.385\} = 98.012$$

Therefore, the issuer should neither redeem nor repurchase the next sinking-fund amount.

Applying the same analysis to the other three sinking-fund obligations leads to the same result: a negative net advantage to advance purchase. Table 12.3 summarizes the results. Note that the more distant the sinking-fund obligation is, the more negative the net advantage is. In any case, the firm should neither redeem nor repurchase any future sinking-fund amounts at this time, buying just enough to meet the current obligation.[16]

Case Study: Sinking-Fund Management at the World Bank

In May 1991, the World Bank was considering whether to double up the sinking-fund payment due July 1, 1991, on its outstanding 8.85s

Table 12.2 Profitability of Advance Purchasing One Period Ahead

Node	Period	V_{ij} (wait)	Pr(i)	After-Tax Call Price[a]	Market Price	After-Tax Repurchase Price[b]	Decision	V_{ij}
B	1	—	—	100.000	96.254	97.752	Repurchase	97.752
C	1	—	—	100.000	98.149	98.889	Repurchase	98.889
A	0	98.012	2.000	101.200	97.309	98.385	Wait	98.012

[a]Sinking-fund redemption price.
[b]Assumes a 40 percent marginal income tax rate and zero transaction costs.

Table 12.3 Summary of Advance Purchase Analysis

Sinking-Fund Obligation	1	2	3	4
V_0 (wait)	98.012	97.647	97.274	96.958
After-tax repurchase price	98.385	98.385	98.385	98.385
Net advantage of advance purchase	−0.373	−0.738	−1.111	−1.427

due 2001.[17] The size of the payment was $20 million, of which the World Bank had a little less than half in its treasury. At the time, the World Bank had among its liabilities twelve U.S. dollar–denominated sinking-fund bonds with an aggregate face amount of approximately $1.8 billion. The World Bank's bond indenture allowed it to hold in its treasury any bonds it had purchased in the open market until it designated them for a specific sinking-fund payment.[18] Bonds acquired through a conventional call can be designated toward any future payment, but they have to be designated at the time of the call. Bonds obtained through acceleration have to be applied against the longest remaining sinking-fund obligation.

Efficiency and Sinking-Fund Management

The notion of refunding efficiency embodied in equation 11.1 can be extended to high-coupon sinking-fund bonds. Because of the presence of multiple interrelated options, the option value the issuer forfeits when it exercises a conventional call option or an acceleration option should account for the total optionality forfeited when the option is exercised:[19]

$$\text{Efficiency} = \frac{\text{Present-value savings}}{\text{Value of the options forfeited}}$$

(12.10)

$$= \frac{\text{PV of contractual flows before} - \text{PV of contractual flows after}}{\text{Total option value before} - \text{Total option value after}}$$

The Refunding Opportunity

In mid-May 1991, the World Bank 8.85s due 2001 were quoted at 100.844 bid and 101.344 asked. The bonds were callable at par for the sinking fund and at 102.75 for optional redemption purposes. The double-up provision allowed the World Bank to call an additional $20 million face amount of bonds at par. The investment banks the World Bank consulted recommended that it exercise the acceleration option and buy at par bonds that the market was valuing at about 101, to realize NPV savings estimated at about $624,000.

Table 12.4 analyzes the refunding opportunity. The final payment on the 8.85s due 2001 also amounted to $20 million. A provision in the World Bank's bond indenture would require it to designate bonds acquired through acceleration against this final payment, shortening the issue's maturity by one year, to 2000. But this maturity shortening would reduce the value of the World Bank's delivery options on the balance of the issue, as well as reduce the value of its conventional call option on the final sinking-fund payment. It was estimated that the total option value forfeited would amount to about $1,379,000.[20] Applying equation 12.10, the refunding efficiency is only:

Efficiency = 624,000/1,379,000 = 0.45, or 45 percent

On the basis of this analysis, the World Bank decided not to double up.

Subsequent Performance

One year later, when interest rates were sharply lower, the World Bank retired $40 million of the 8.85s at par through the sinking fund and the double-up provision. It also called the remaining $160 million face amount at 101.375, retiring the entire debt issue with a refunding efficiency of 100 percent.

Conclusion

Sinking-fund bonds, which combine elements of option strategy and game theory, are among the most interesting and complicated debt securities. Sinking-fund management is challenging because such bonds contain five types of interrelated options:

- A series of conventional American call options with a sequence of declining call prices

- A series of European call options with call prices of par and exercisable on the sinking-fund dates

- Delivery options that come into play when interest rates are high

- Acceleration options that apply when the bonds contain an acceleration provision and interest rates are low

Table 12.4 Profitability of Doubling Up the 8.85s Due 2001 on July 1, 1991

Face Amount Outstanding[a]	Theoretical Flat Price per Bond	Theoretical Option Value per Bond	NPV of Contractual Cash Flows per Bond	NPV of Contractual Cash Flows	NPV Savings	Theoretical Option Value	Forfeited Option Value
$200,000,000	100.281	3.219	103.499	$206,998,000		$6,437,000	
$180,000,000	100.731	2.810	103.541	206,374,000[b]	$624,000	5,058,000	$1,379,000

Source: A. J. Kalotay, F. M. Saldanha, and G. O. Williams, "The Management of Sinking Funds: The World Bank Experience," *Journal of Fixed Income* 3 (1993), p. 37.

Note: The first line summarizes the valuation results under the assumption that the sinking-fund payment is not doubled up. The second line assumes that the payment is doubled up. The net present value of the contractual flows after doubling up includes the cost of purchasing (and financing) the $20 million balloon portion.

[a]After making the scheduled sinking-fund payment on July 1, 1991.
[b]Includes $20,000,000 cost of exercising the double-up option.

- Designation options when the issuer has the flexibility to purchase bonds ahead of its sinking-fund obligations and apply them to payment obligations of its choosing

The interplay of these options and market factors can create profitable opportunities for issuers to reduce their cost of debt through active sinking-fund management.

From the issuer's perspective, the sinking-fund provision represents an obligation when interest rates are high and a call option at par if rates are low. When rates are high, the issuer will normally satisfy its sinking-fund obligation by delivering bond certificates obtained by open market purchase rather than calling bonds at par. The issuer may purchase bonds several years before the sinking-fund date. The designation option creates opportunities for an issuer to reduce its cost of debt by actively prepurchasing bonds and designating them to satisfy its highest-cost sinking-fund obligations or retaining them to deter accumulators.

Managing a high-coupon sinking-fund issue is complicated because of the interaction of the sinking-fund and call provisions. The impact of any acceleration provision must also be considered, although evidence indicates that its incremental value may be small because it overlaps with the conventional call option. In general, the most profitable refunding strategy when interest rates are low will entail partial calls—that is, calling some bonds at a premium by invoking the optional redemption provision and leaving the rest outstanding to be called at par using the sinking fund

The chapter also reviewed the factors that can make it profitable for a firm to refund discounted debt and developed an analytical framework for evaluating opportunities to refund such debt. The net advantage of refunding discounted debt is very sensitive to tax factors, in particular, the tax treatment accorded the gain. In general, such refundings are not profitable to shareholders when the gain is taxed immediately at ordinary income tax rates unless the bonds can be used to satisfy sinking-fund obligations.

Chapter 13

Other Types of
Bond Refundings

This chapter considers five special cases of bond refunding: refunding floating-rate debt, advance refunding of municipal debt through legal defeasance, advance refunding of corporate debt, refunding under rate base regulation, and refunding tax-exempt corporate bonds.

Refunding Floating-Rate Debt

A borrower from a bank or an issuer of floating-rate debt may wish to refund it with a new issue of floating-rate debt to take advantage of a reduction in the required interest rate margin. Alternatively, it may wish to refund it with fixed-rate debt in order to lock in a fixed interest rate, much as a homeowner does when refinancing a variable-rate mortgage with a fixed-rate mortgage when interest rates drop.

Floating-for-Floating Refunding

If an issuer's credit standing improves, the credit spread that lenders require will shrink. A lower interest rate spread in turn lowers the total interest rate and, just like a general decline in interest rates, may create a profitable refunding opportunity.

Most corporate floating-rate debt is bank debt, which is usually prepayable without penalty. Therefore, the net advantage is given by equation 10.4 with $P = D$:

$$NA = \sum_{n=1}^{N} \frac{(1-T)(r-r')D}{[1+(1-T)r']^n} - E \qquad (13.1)$$

When both the new debt and the old debt specify interest rates that are tied to the same base rate (prime rate or one of the LIBORs), the difference in interest rates, $r - r'$, is simply the difference in interest rate spread. Although the actual interest rates will move up or down with interest rates generally, the difference in interest rates will not change.

Fixed-for-Floating Refunding

A firm replaces floating-rate debt with fixed-rate debt to reduce its interest rate risk exposure. This reduction in risk exposure conveys a benefit that is distinct from the net advantage calculated in chapter 10. In addition, the incremental cash flow, $(r - r')D$, varies from period to period, so that equation 10.4 no longer provides a comprehensive measure of the net advantage of the refunding. A negative value might be more than offset by lower interest rate risk exposure. We recommend basing the decision as to whether to replace floating-rate debt with fixed-rate debt on whether the transaction is consistent with the company's overall risk management policies rather than base it on a net advantage calculation (which assumes debt service parity).

One further consideration is important. We described interest rate swaps in chapter 7. A firm can refund floating-rate debt with fixed-rate debt to fix the interest rate, or it can engage in an interest rate swap. Swapping is usually cheaper unless a firm also wants to achieve some other objective at the same time, such as lengthening the maturity of its debt or eliminating troublesome covenants. A firm should select the least-cost alternative.

Defeasance

Defeasance refers to a debt issuer's release from a debt obligation through the irrevocable pledge of securities in an amount sufficient to discharge the liability. With an *in-substance defeasance,* a debtor placed cash or "qualifying securities" (U.S. government bonds, certain qualifying federal agency securities, or any other assets bondholders consented to) in an irrevocable trust whose cash flows exactly matched the cash flows of the outstanding issue. Once the trust was in place, the outstanding issue was extinguished for financial reporting purposes. In 1996, Statement of Financial Accounting Standards No. 125 voided this accounting treatment of in-substance defeasance.[1] In the 1980s and 1990s, corporations used in-substance defeasance as a way to avoid the tax on the accounting gain from eliminating discounted debt. Today municipal debt issues can still be legally defeased according to provisions in the bond indenture.

Legal Defeasance

The traditional form of defeasance, *legal defeasance*, is governed by the bond indenture. If the indenture does not include a defeasance provision, bondholders must agree to accept the defeasance portfolio as collateral for their bonds and release the bond issuer from the covenant restrictions. Thus, once a legal defeasance has been effected, the debt issuer is no longer bound by the covenant restrictions. The issuer must defease the entire issue because anything less will leave the covenant restrictions in place.

Legal defeasance has been practiced for many years by municipalities. Before enactment of the Tax Reform Act of 1969, municipalities and other tax-exempt borrowers had an incentive to defease because they could arbitrage their position by lending funds (buying U.S. government securities for the defeasance portfolio) at a higher yield than it cost to defease the outstanding debt. By arbitraging, a municipality could, for instance, buy a dollar's worth of defeasance securities for, say, ninety-five cents' worth of municipal securities. Although this type of arbitrage is forbidden today, legal defeasance still offers an economic advantage when interest rates drop significantly during the period of noncallability. In recent years, many firms have included defeasance provisions in their bond indentures. Thus, legal defeasance of corporate debt is also possible (subject to any restrictions contained in the bond indenture).

A legal defeasance of high-coupon debt can be profitable because of the opportunity to call the outstanding bonds at an option price below the present value of the liabilities. As with a traditional bond refunding, the economic effect is by no means identical with the financial reporting effect, which is simply an accounting recognition of a change in the market value of the defeased debt. The accounting treatment is not meant to measure the profitability of the defeasance.

We assume that the defeasance is intended as a refunding; therefore, the operation should be viewed as a combined defeasance and refunding. We develop an analytical framework to measure the net advantage of defeasing-refunding, both absolutely and in relation to other forms of refunding. The analysis shows that defeasance-refunding can benefit municipalities when interest rates are expected to rise between the legal defeasance and the call dates.

Motivations for Defeasance

The motivations for defeasance fall into four categories:

- *Cost savings.* Refunding high-coupon debt can increase shareholder wealth or, in the case of municipalities, decrease the taxpayers' burden.

- *Eliminating onerous covenants.* Once debt is issued, the issuer is bound by its covenants. As circumstances change, those covenants may become overly restrictive. Defeasing-refunding the old bonds opens the way to write more favorable covenants into the new bonds' indenture. Only a legal defeasance of the entire debt issue can accomplish this objective.

- *Restructuring debt service.* A debtor may be unable to meet debt service requirements—for example, if cash flow from a project falls short of expectations. A defeasance can be used to extend debt maturity, thereby reducing the debt service payments to a more manageable level.

- *Improving financial reporting position.* In the case of a pure defeasance (one not followed by a refunding), legal defeasance can be used to reduce reported debt in the issuer's financial structure. Defeasance should be used, however, only if the debtor's financial structure is too highly leveraged. Great care should be taken when corporate debt is involved, since transactions designed to reduce leverage tend to reduce shareholder wealth.[2]

All debt-extinguishment techniques involve securing the bond-holders' consent to retire the outstanding issue, in the form of either an indenture provision or a specific agreement to allow the exchange or sale of the bonds back to the issuer. Defeasance avoids having to get bondholders to agree to a sale or exchange of their bonds. Once the qualifying assets have been placed with the trustee, the outstanding debt is extinguished, and the debtor never has to contact the bondholders. Such an opportunity can be as economical as it is convenient. For example, sometimes even a small-scale effort to repurchase a thinly traded issue will drive the issue's price up swiftly.

Advance Refunding of Municipal Debt

Because interest income from municipal bonds is exempt from taxation and municipalities themselves are tax-exempt entities, municipalities are in a unique position to earn a tax arbitrage profit. Having access to the capital markets as both borrower and lender, municipalities can borrow at below-taxable-market rates (the yield on a tax-exempt municipal issue is typically lower than that of a U.S. Treasury issue of the same maturity) and invest the proceeds in taxable securities at higher market rates. Because of this ability to borrow cheaply and reinvest in U.S. government securities for the defeasance portfolio, municipalities have a tax incentive to defease-refund.

The Tax Reform Act of 1969 and subsequent legislation restrict tax-exempt borrowers in arbitraging their borrowing position. Under the most recent rules promulgated under the Internal Revenue Code, municipalities may not invest the proceeds of a refunding issue in assets with yields that are "materially higher" than the yield of the refunding issue; otherwise, the refunding issue may lose its tax-exempt status.[3]

If the municipality has any difficulty acquiring securities with a yield that is not materially higher than the refunding issue, the Treasury Department will make available specially issued state and local government securities (SLGS). In the analysis that follows, we assume there is no difference in yield between the refunding issue and the defeasance portfolio—that is, all the securities in the defeasance portfolio are SLGS.

Despite the elimination of significant arbitrage opportunities, municipalities continue to defease their outstanding debt profitably, but only their outstanding high-coupon debt.[4] Municipalities can use legal defeasance to get the benefit of the call option even before the option is exercisable, which is why this technique is known as *advance refunding*. In an advance refunding, a trustee is responsible for making all debt service payments before the call date and at the call date must pay off all remaining principal, interest, and any premium.

Calculating the Net Advantage of Advance Refunding

As previously, r is the old (to be defeased) bond's coupon rate, r' is the new issue coupon rate (of like maturity), and D is the face amount of the debt. N is the number of periods until the old issue matures, C is the transaction expense, and p is the call premium. Defeasing the old issue frees up enough debt service to support NI of new debt:

$$NI = \sum_{n=1}^{N} \frac{rD}{(1 + r')^n} + \frac{D}{(1 + r')^N} \qquad (13.2)$$

The cost of the advance refunding defeasance portfolio, R, has two components: interest payments until the call date, denoted M, and principal plus premium at the call date, so that

$$R = \sum_{n=1}^{M} \frac{rD}{(1+r')^n} + \frac{(1+p)D}{(1+r')^M} \tag{13.3}$$

The advance refunding portfolio lasts only until the outstanding bond's call date. At the call date, the cash flow from the defeasance portfolio pays any remaining principal plus the call premium. The net advantage of advance refunding is

$$NA = NI - R - C = \sum_{n=1}^{N} \frac{rD}{(1+r')^n} + \frac{D}{(1+r')^N}$$

$$- \left\{ \sum_{n=1}^{M} \frac{rD}{(1+r')^n} + \frac{(1+p)D}{(1+r')^M} \right\} - C \tag{13.4}$$

The larger N is, the longer the stream of interest savings is, and hence the greater the net advantage of advance refunding. The smaller the premium p is, the greater is the net advantage. The smaller M is, the sooner the outstanding issue can be called and the greater the net advantage is. Finally, as always, the greater $(r - r')$ is, the greater is the net advantage.

Examples of Advance Refunding

A municipality is advance refunding a $1,000 14 percent bond with ten years remaining to maturity. The current coupon rate for a new issue is 9 percent, and the old bonds can be called in five years at a call price of 103. Discounting the debt service stream for the old issue at the new issue rate provides the amount of new debt the municipality can issue: $1,321 per old bond. The cost of the defeasance portfolio (ignoring transaction expenses) is $1,214 per bond. This cost equals the present value of the interest payments due on the old bonds until the call date, plus the present value of the call price. The net advantage of advance refunding is $107 per bond. As with corporate debt, the profitability of refunding high-coupon municipal debt depends mainly on the opportunity to call the bonds at a price below the present value of the future payment stream.

Table 13.1 illustrates the net advantage calculation in the multi-issue case. The total issue consists of a series of separate issues.

Table 13.1 Net Advantage of the Advance Refunding of a Municipal Debt Issue

| Years Remaining to Maturity | Outstanding Issue | | | New Issue Rate | New Issue Proceeds | Cost of Defeasance Portfolio | Difference |
	Date	Principal	Coupon				
1	6/1/86	$ 1,235,378.84	11.0%	8.0%	$ 1,269,694.92	$ 1,269,694.92	0.00
2	6/1/87	1,395,978.09	11.5	8.5	1,470,151.20	1,470,151.20	0.00
3	6/1/88	1,577,455.25	12.0	9.0	1,697,245.37	1,697,245.37	0.00
4	6/1/89	1,782,524.43	12.5	9.5	1,953,886.40	1,953,886.40	0.00
5	6/1/90	2,014,252.60	13.0	10.0	2,243,320.67	2,074,680.18	$ 168,640.49
6	6/1/91	2,276,105.44	13.0	10.0	2,573,496.42	2,344,388.61	229,107.81
7	6/1/92	2,571,999.15	13.0	10.0	2,947,646.22	2,649,159.12	298,487.10
8	6/1/93	2,906,359.04	13.0	10.0	3,371,515.37	2,993,549.81	377,965.56
9	6/1/94	3,284,185.71	13.0	10.0	3,851,596.83	3,382,711.29	468,885.54
10	6/1/95	3,711,129.86	13.0	10.0	4,395,228.45	3,922,463.75	572,764.70
11	6/1/96	4,193,576.74	13.0	10.0	5,010,702.84	4,319,384.04	691,318.80
12	6/1/97	4,738,741.71	13.0	10.0	5,707,391.48	4,880,903.97	826,487.52

(continued)

Table 13.1 (continued)

Years Remaining to Maturity	Outstanding Issue			New Issue Rate	New Issue Proceeds	Cost of Defeasance Portfolio	Difference
	Date	Principal	Coupon				
13	6/1/98	$ 5,354,778.14	13.0%	10.0%	$ 6,495,885.03	$ 5,515,421.48	$ 980,463.55
14	6/1/99	6,050,899.30	13.0	10.0	7,388,151.81	6,232,426.27	1,155,725.54
15	6/1/2000	6,837,516.20	13.0	10.0	8,397,716.96	7,042,641.69	1,355,075.27
16	6/1/2001	7,726,393.31	13.0	10.0	9,539,864.81	7,958,185.11	1,581,679.70
17	6/1/2002	8,730,824.44	13.0	10.0	10,831,867.65	8,992,749.17	1,839,118.48
18	6/1/2003	9,865,831.62	13.0	10.0	12,293,244.14	10,161,806.57	2,131,437.58
19	6/1/2004	11,148,389.73	13.0	10.0	13,946,051.41	11,482,841.42	2,463,209.99
20	6/1/2005	12,597,680.39	13.0	10.0	15,815,215.04	12,975,610.80	2,839,604.23
		$100,000,000.00			$121,199,873.03	$103,219,901.18	$17,979,971.85

Less Present Value of Interest Due at the Call Date $7,588,357.87

Net Advantage of Advance Refunding $10,391,613.98

Call date: 6/1/90   Call price: 103

Municipal debt issues are often structured this way. Notice that each of the principal amounts and most of the coupon rates differ. As a result, equations 13.2 and 13.3 are applied separately to each series. Defeasing the total outstanding issue of $100 million frees up a cash flow stream able to support the issuance of $121,199,873 of new debt. The total cost of the defeasance portfolio, including interest due at the call date, is $110,808,259, giving a net advantage of advance refunding of $10,391,614.

Timing Considerations

If interest rates are expected to decline, it may be better to postpone refunding. The considerations involved in deciding whether to refund now or wait are virtually identical to those explained in chapter 11.

Advance Refunding of Corporate Debt

Advance refunding of nonredeemable high-coupon debt can be profitable when bondholders hold out and refuse to sell their bonds to the issuer at a reasonable, near-market price.[5] Bondholders might require a high price because of tax considerations, such as incurring a large capital gains tax because of a low tax basis in their bonds. In 1989, the Tennessee Valley Authority (TVA) advance refunded $6.9 billion of its outstanding nonredeemable high-coupon bonds held by the Federal Financing Bank (FFB), which had refused for policy reasons to let the TVA redeem them prior to the initial call dates.

The TVA's Advance Refunding

In July 1989, the TVA announced its intention to issue approximately $8 billion face amount of long-term debt to use primarily for an in-substance defeasance of approximately $6.7 billion of outstanding bonds held by the FFB, plus approximately $200 million of short-term debt owed to the FFB. The TVA had identified nineteen high-coupon debt issues that would become callable within between six months and four and a half years, which it intended to refund.

Net Advantage of an Advance Refunding of High-Coupon Debt

The TVA hoped to reduce its interest expense and avoid having to increase its electricity rates, implying that the benefits of the refunding would be passed through to its electricity customers. Accordingly, the net advantage of the defeasance is calculated from the standpoint of the TVA's ratepayers, unlike refundings by nonregulated private firms for which the net advantage accrues to the shareholders.

Applying the debt service parity principle, the net advantage, *NA*, of an advance refunding is

$$NA = NI - P_g - E \tag{13.5}$$

where P_g is the price paid to acquire bonds for the defeasance portfolio, *NI* is the new issue proceeds, and *E* is the expense connected to the refunding transaction.

For the TVA's advance refunding, *NI* should be calculated separately for each defeased issue by discounting the amount of debt service it will free up at the new issue rate:[6]

$$NI = \left\{ \sum_{n=1}^{N} \frac{rD}{(1 + r')^n} + \frac{D}{(1 + r')^N} + frD \right\} / (1 + r')^f \tag{13.6}$$

where

> f = fraction of the current interest period that remains until the next interest payment date for the defeased bonds,
> D = face amount of bonds to be defeased,
> r = coupon on the defeased bonds,
> r' = new issue rate,
> N = maturity of the defeased bonds (whole number of periods from the next interest payment date),
> M = first call date of the defeased bonds (whole number of periods from the next interest payment date), and
> p = call premium on the first call date.

Debt that is scheduled to mature after *N* periods will be redeemed after *M* periods, where $0 < M < N$, and will be retired at *M* for price $(1 + p)D$, where *p* is the call premium. The issuer purchases a portfolio of Treasury securities with the new issue proceeds. The portfolio costs P_g and is selected to generate enough cash flow to cover the interest payments of *rD* per period for *M* periods and the cost of redeeming the issue on the call date, $(1 + p)D$.

The cost of the defeasance portfolio, P_g in equation 13.5, should be calculated separately for each defeased issue by discounting the debt service stream to be defeased at the yield to maturity *g* on outstanding Treasury notes or bonds that mature on the first call date:

$$P_g = \left\{ \sum_{n=1}^{M} \frac{rD}{(1+g)^n} + \frac{(1+p)D}{(1+g)^M} + frD \right\} / (1+g)^f \qquad (13.7)$$

where the variables are as defined previously.

Equation 13.7 assumes that the old debt will be redeemed on the respective first possible call dates. Equations 13.6 and 13.7 explicitly take into account that the TVA defeased most of the issues during, rather than at the end of, an interest period.[7]

Net Advantage of the TVA's Advance Refunding

Table 13.2 contains an economic analysis of the TVA's advance refunding. The defeasances occurred in two phases, which correspond to the two sets of debt issues the TVA sold in October 1989 and November 1989.

The cost of a new issue is the yield the market would require on noncallable debt in order to reflect the exercise of the one-time call option. Two of the refunding issues, the 8¾ percent issue maturing in 2019 (thirty-year maturity) and the 8⅝ percent issue maturing in 2029 (forty-year maturity), both contain call provisions, whereas the other three refunding issues are noncallable. Consequently, the cost of noncallable thirty-year and forty-year TVA debt had to be estimated from the cost of the noncallable five-year, seven-year, and ten-year TVA debt issues and the yields at which other longer-term noncallable (non–full faith and credit) government agency issues were trading.[8]

The advance refunding of the nineteen debt issues produced a net advantage for the TVA's ratepayers amounting to $1,420 million. The debt issues defeased with the net proceeds of the October 17 issue were generally the more profitable refundings. The net advantage of each defeasance is positive, although several of the debt issues refunded with the net proceeds of the November 17 issue were only marginally profitable.

Timing Considerations

None of the debt issues in table 13.2 was immediately callable. The first call dates would occur as early as January 31, 1990 (for the Series 1980A issue) and would occur sequentially for the other issues over the following four years. Advance refunding effectively allowed the TVA to accelerate the first call dates. Achieving this acceleration required the TVA to pay an "acceleration premium" equal to the difference between (1) the present value of the interest payment stream

Table 13.2 Net Advantage of the TVA's Advance Refunding

| Issue | Amount (millions) | Coupon | Maturity | First Call | | Estimated Cost of New Issue | NI (millions) | Treasury Yield | P_g (millions) | $NI - P_g$ (millions) |
				Date	Price					
1980A[b]	$ 500	11.225%	1/31/05	1/31/90	106.64%	8.47%	$ 617	7.72%	$ 536	$ 81
1980B[a]	500	12.955	3/31/05	3/31/90	107.67	8.50	690	8.06	547	143
1980C[b]	500	10.475	6/30/05	6/30/90	106.20	8.47	586	7.87	538	48
1980D[b]	500	10.890	8/31/05	8/31/90	106.45	8.47	604	7.80	541	63
1980E[b]	500	12.425	11/30/05	11/30/90	107.35	8.47	672	7.78	556	116
1981A[a]	500	12.735	3/31/11	3/31/91	108.42	8.50	707	7.98	569	138
1981B[a]	500	12.925	4/30/11	4/30/91	108.54	8.50	717	7.92	573	144
1981C[a]	500	13.255	6/30/11	6/30/91	108.76	8.50	734	7.90	580	154
1981E[a,c]	550	13.035	12/31/11	12/31/91	108.62	8.50	797	7.89	645	152
1981E[b,c]	100	13.035	12/31/11	12/31/91	108.62	8.47	145	7.75	117	28

1982A[a]	700	13.565	4/30/12	4/30/92	108.97	8.50	1,053	7.87	841	212
1982B[a]	150	13.575	5/31/12	5/31/92	108.97	8.50	226	7.96	180	46
1982D[b]	100	11.945	9/30/12	9/30/92	107.90	8.47	135	7.79	117	18
1982E[b]	200	10.725	11/30/12	11/30/92	107.09	8.47	245	7.81	226	19
1983A[b]	150	10.575	1/31/13	1/31/93	106.99	8.47	182	7.79	170	12
1983B[b]	150	10.575	3/31/13	3/31/93	106.99	8.47	182	7.82	170	12
1983C[b]	100	10.425	5/31/13	5/31/93	106.89	8.47	120	7.83	113	7
1983D[b]	250	11.685	8/31/13	8/31/93	107.72	8.47	332	7.86	295	37
1983E[b]	150	11.905	1/31/14	1/31/94	107.87	8.47	203	7.82	180	23
1984A[b]	100	12.055	1/31/14	1/31/94	107.97	8.47	137	7.82	121	16
Total	$6,700						$9,084		$7,615	$1,469

Underwriting Costs and Miscellaneous Expenses 49

Net Advantage of Advance Refunding $1,420

Source: John D. Finnerty, "The Advance Refunding on Nonredeemable High-Coupon Corporate Debt Through In-Substance Defeasance, *Journal of Financial Engineering* 1 (September 1992), p. 156.

[a]Defeasance financed with proceeds of October 17, 1989 issue.
[b]Defeasance financed with proceeds of November 17, 1989 issue.
[c]The debt issue was defeased with portions of each debt issue.

up to and including the first call date plus the present value of the redemption price, with discounting at the appropriate Treasury yield, and (2) the present value of the same debt service stream, with discounting at the appropriate new issue rate. The first is simply the cost of the defeasance portfolio so the acceleration premium, denoted A, is

$$A = P_g - \left\{ \sum_{n=1}^{M} \frac{rD}{(1 + r')^n} + \frac{(1 + p)D}{(1 + r')^M} + frD \right\} / (1 + r')^f \qquad (13.8)$$

The acceleration premium the TVA paid is $71 million ($7,615 million – $7,544 million). Thus, if the TVA's refunding rates were to remain constant through each successive first call date and if the TVA were to exercise each call option on the first call date, the aggregate net advantage of refunding, in 1989 dollars, would be $1,491 million ($1,420 million + $71 million).

TVA effectively gave up $71 million (4.8 percent) of the hypothetical savings it would have realized in a constant-interest-rate environment by accelerating the refunding. If the TVA had instead waited until the initial call dates, the net advantage could have been greater or smaller, depending on the course of interest rates. The dynamic programming approach outlined in chapter 11 can also be used to calculate the efficiency of the TVA's advance refunding.

Tax Rationale for Advance Refunding Nonredeemable High-Coupon Corporate Debt

As noted with the TVA case, advance refunding can be a profitable way of refunding debt held by low-tax-basis bondholders who for tax reasons refuse to sell their bonds to the firm at a reasonable near-market price.[9]

Issuer's Indifference Condition

If debt is not immediately callable and there are debtholders with different reservation prices, there generally exists a break-even cash repurchase price below which bonds should be repurchased from investors and above which the bonds should be defeased. At the break-even price, the net advantage of refunding is the same whether by cash repurchase or advance refunding.

First consider cash repurchase. The issuer pays P_b for the debt. If the firm's tax basis in the bonds, B_0, is less than P_b, the issuer realizes a tax benefit equal to $T(P_b - B_0)$. With transaction costs via repurchases E_p, the total after-tax cost is $P_b - T(P_b - B_0) + E_p$.

The break-even price, P_b, thus satisfies the equation

$$P_b = (P_g - X + E_d - E_p - TB_0)/(1 - T) \qquad (13.9)$$

where

$$X = T \left\{ \sum_{n=1}^{M} \frac{rD - I_g(n)}{[1 + (1 - T)r']^n} + \frac{(1 + p)D - B_N}{[1 + (1 - T)r']^M} \right\} \qquad (13.10)$$

is the NPV of the incremental tax effects associated with defeasing the debt (versus no action), $I_g(n)$ is the stream of taxable income received from the defeasance portfolio, and E_d is the after-tax transaction costs of defeasance.

The price P_b is the maximum price the firm could afford to pay for the bonds before it becomes more profitable to defease. P_r is the cash repurchase price the firm offers bondholders. The firm will offer to repurchase bonds for cash only at prices P_r for which $P_r \leq P_b$. If the net advantage of refunding is positive but bondholders hold out for a higher price than P_b, the firm would be better off defeasing rather than repurchasing.

Bondholders' Indifference Conditions

If the bonds are nonredeemable, the firm cannot compel bondholders to sell their bonds. Holders will sell voluntarily only if it is profitable for them. One of the main advantages of defeasance is that it does not require any bondholder action; the issuer controls the process. Nevertheless, there may be circumstances in which bondholders would find defeasance more advantageous than a cash repurchase for tax reasons.

The ith bondholder will be indifferent between selling the bonds for cash and continuing to hold them provided

$$P_i = (P_m - t_i B_i)/(1 - t_i) \qquad (13.11)$$

where P_m is the market price of the bonds just before the repurchase offer announcement, P_i is the ith bondholder's hold-versus-sell indifference price, t_i is the ith bondholder's marginal tax rate on capital gains, and B_i is the ith bondholder's tax basis in the bonds. At prices below P_i, the ith bondholder will refuse to sell the bonds. At prices above P_i, assuming no collusion, bondholders will voluntarily sell their bonds to the firm.

The ith bondholder will be indifferent between selling the bonds to the firm and having the firm defease them provided

$$P_d = (P_g - t_iB_i)/(1 - t_i) \qquad (13.12)$$

where P_d is the ith bondholder's defeasance-versus-selling indifference price. If the defeasance portfolio has zero bankruptcy risk, the defeased bonds will be equal in value to the defeasance portfolio.[10] In such a case, the value of the defeased bonds will rise to P_g, and bondholders will receive an increase of $P_g - P_m$ in their wealth at the expense of the firm's stockholders. In-substance defeasance has no tax consequences for the bondholder, whereas selling the bonds triggers a capital gain $(P_r > B_i)$ or loss $(P_r < B_i)$. At prices above (below) P_d, bondholders will prefer selling (defeasance). Comparing equations 13.11 and 13.12, it is obvious that $P_d > P_i$ since $P_g > P_m$. Assuming no collusion among bondholders, at an in-between price P_r, such that $P_i < P_r < P_d$, bondholders will sell their bonds, although they would be better off if the bonds were defeased. If there were just one bondholder or if a group of bondholders were to act together, they might refuse to sell in an effort to get the firm to defease the bonds.

Conditions Under Which Defeasance Is Mutually Advantageous

For any particular price P_r, equations 13.9, 13.11, and 13.12 determine whether (1) repurchase is profitable $(P_r < P_b)$, (2) any bondholder would be better off with a defeasance rather than selling $(P_r < P_d)$, and (3) particular bondholders would be willing to sell their bonds, assuming they cannot collude and force defeasance $(P_r > P_i)$. Figure 13.1 illustrates these conditions.

In figure 13.1, there are two regions where $P_b \leq P_r \leq P_d$ and in-substance defeasance is better than repurchase for both the bondholders and the firm:

- The black triangle region within which $P_b \leq P_r \leq P_i$ where defeasance is the only mutually agreeable outcome because bondholders would be unwilling to sell their bonds to the firm.

- The dark-shaded trapezoidal region within which $P_i \leq P_r \leq P_d$. Although they would prefer defeasance, particular bondholders would be willing to sell their bonds, assuming they cannot collude and force defeasance.

Figure 13.1 Defeasance Versus Cash Repurchase of High-Coupon
Debt for Taxable Bondholders

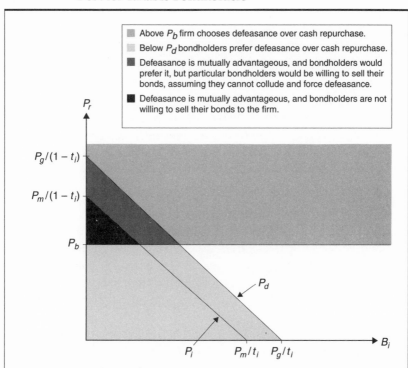

Implications for Corporate Debt Management

Taxable bondholders with relatively high tax bases in the bond
may also sell voluntarily, but inducing those with lower tax bases to
sell generally requires higher offering prices to compensate them for
their tax liability. Advance refunding is an effective way to retire nonredeemable high-coupon debt when taxable bondholders have tax bases
in the bonds so low that their required selling price would be more
costly to the issuer than defeasing the bonds. Advance refunding can
be a profitable complement to cash repurchase in certain situations.
The issuer can repurchase for cash as many bonds as it can acquire
profitably in the open market or through a tender offer and then
advance refund the balance of the issue, provided it is profitable.

Refunding Under Rate Base Regulation

So far we have assumed that refunding does not affect the firm's
revenue stream. As long as this is the case, it is appropriate to measure

the profitability of a refunding solely in terms of the present value of the incremental debt service stream. In regulated industries, however, the revenue a firm is allowed to collect depends on its cost of capital generally and its cost of debt in particular. Refunding affects both expenses and revenues, and a refunding analysis must take into account the interaction. The regulatory rationale is that because customers pay the firm's capital costs, they are the ones who ultimately should benefit from reduced interest charges. A complicating factor arises when refunding is at a premium or a discount from par. In the case of refunding at a premium, the firm must receive a satisfactory return on the premium in order to ensure that the firm's stockholders are not subsidizing the transaction.

Refunding by Regulated Firms

Firms such as investor-owned public utilities (telephone, gas, electric, and water companies) are subject to rate base regulation. Public utilities are among the largest issuers of long-term corporate debt, mainly bonds that are normally refundable after five years for a substantial premium over par. Proper treatment of the premium is therefore an important practical consideration.

In several other industries, a restructuring of the firm's liabilities indirectly affects its revenues. One example is the privately held health care industry, whose expenses, including capital costs, are partially reimbursed by the insurer, Medicare. In the financial services industry, the volume of business a firm is allowed to conduct usually depends on the amount of its capital, principally its common equity. Retiring debt at a premium reduces common equity, thereby ultimately constraining revenue. This is a relevant consideration for commercial banks. These are but a few examples of the complex accounting and cash flow interactions that may be important in a refunding for a regulated firm.

Rate Base Regulation

Federal or state regulatory commissions consider both the operating expenses and capital costs of the public utilities they regulate when setting allowable revenues. The interest rate on debt issues and allowed return on common equity jointly determine the overall cost of capital. However, the firm does not recover its capital costs dollar for dollar on the basis of the direct underlying liabilities. The firm is allowed to earn a return on its physical assets, called the *rate base*, based on its average cost of capital. The precise definition of the rate base varies from jurisdiction to jurisdiction, but essentially it consists of depreciated plant in service.

A debt refunding alters a regulated utility's cost of capital. For example, calling and refunding high-coupon debt decreases the average interest rate and simultaneously changes the firm's capital structure, increasing the amount of debt relative to equity. Because the cost of equity is higher than the cost of debt, the cost of capital may decline. But the transaction leaves the rate *base* unchanged, so the revenue requirement declines along with interest payments.

Under traditional regulatory treatment, the reduction in revenue requirements exceeds the reduction in interest payments. Therefore, some of the benefit to consumers comes at the expense of the stockholders. In the absence of corporate income taxes, the revenue decline equals the cost of capital times the reacquisition premium.[11]

Example of Refunding Under Rate Base Regulation

Before the refunding, a regulated firm's capitalization is $60 million of 14 percent debt and $40 million of common equity. The debt is repurchased for $70 million (a $10 million reacquisition premium) and funded by new 12 percent debt. The cost of equity is 16 percent. Under traditional regulatory treatment, the cost of capital k is 13.45 percent:

$$k = \frac{40}{40 + 70}(0.16) + \frac{70}{40 + 70}(0.12) = 13.45 \text{ percent}$$

The initial-year decline in revenue requirements is $1.345 million (13.45 percent of $10 million).

To preserve shareholder wealth, the traditional regulatory treatment must be modified. Stockholders can be fully compensated by either including the premium in the rate base or subtracting the premium from the book value of outstanding debt. However, including financial assets in the rate base would be unusual. Leaving the rate base unchanged and adjusting the cost of capital seems more compatible with traditional rate base regulation. Reduce the book value of outstanding debt by subtracting the unamortized call premium, which reduces the debt ratio and simultaneously increases the embedded cost of debt. Each of these changes increases the cost of capital, and their combined effect preserves shareholder wealth.

Under either treatment, the premium is usually amortized (recovered by the firm) over several years. As the premium amortizes, current revenue requirements increase by the amount amortized. The present value of the revenue requirements, discounted at the cost of capital, does not depend on the method of amortization.[12]

Case 1: The Amortization Period of the Premium Is One Year

During the year following the refunding, the cost of debt for rate-making purposes is 14 percent ([70/60][0.12]). The debt ratio is 60 percent, and the cost of capital is 14.8 percent ([0.4][0.16] + [0.6][0.14]). At the end of the first year, the premium is recovered, the book value of the debt becomes $70 million, the debt ratio becomes 63.64 percent (70/[70 + 40]), and the cost of capital becomes 13.45 percent ([0.3636][0.16] + [0.6364][0.12]). Thus, the revenue requirements associated with capital would amount to $24.8 million ($14.8 million + $10 million) during the first year and $13.455 million thereafter.

Case 2: The Premium Is Never Recovered (No Amortization)

The cost of capital for regulatory purposes remains 14.8 percent, and the annual revenue requirement amounts to $14.8 million each year. The resulting cash flows are shown in table 13.3. The present value of the difference at the true cost of capital (13.45 percent) is zero.

Refunding Tax-Exempt Corporate Bonds

Most tax-exempt bonds are issued by state and local governments and municipal authorities. However, investor-owned firms also issue tax-exempt *private activity bonds* to finance projects deemed to serve the

Table 13.3 Discounted Cash Flow Analysis of Alternative Regulatory Treatments (dollar amounts in millions)

Year	Recovery in First Year	No Recovery	Difference	PV @ 13.45%
1	$24.800	$14.800	+$10.000	$8.81
2	13.455	14.800	−1.345	−1.04
3	13.455	14.800	−1.345	−0.92
4	13.455	14.800	−1.345	−0.81
•	•	•	•	•
•	•	•	•	•
•	•	•	•	•
Total				$0

public good, such as waste disposal projects and certain energy projects. The bonds, whose tax exemption provides an important financial incentive for issuing them, are actually issued by a public authority on behalf of the investor-owned firm.

Tax-exempt corporate bonds have complex tax attributes. Investors receive interest income tax free, and the firm is able to deduct the interest cost in the usual manner. When an investor sells tax-exempt bonds, the difference between the sale price and the investor's tax basis gives rise to capital gain or loss. When a firm repurchases some of its tax-exempt bonds, the difference between its repurchase price and its tax basis gives rise to ordinary income or expense.

Firms can refund tax-exempt bonds—for example, when interest rates drop after issuance. However, corporate tax-exempt bonds cannot be advance refunded, and any premium paid in excess of par value must be funded with taxable debt. Also, the maturity of the new bonds usually cannot exceed the maturity of the old bonds. Tax-exempt corporate bonds usually become refundable after ten years at a call price that is close to par. The only feasible method of repurchasing a significant amount of bonds is through a tender offer because the bonds are usually widely held by individual investors.

Standard Methods of Tendering for Outstanding Bonds

There are three standard methods of tendering for outstanding bonds: fixed-price tender, reverse Dutch auction tender, and fixed-spread tender. A fixed-price tender offer is the least flexible method of the three because the issuer cannot retract the offer. In essence, the firm distributes put options to bondholders. If interest rates rise during the tender offer period, the firm must buy the bonds for a price above their fair market value.

To lessen the issuer's interest rate risk, Salomon Brothers developed the *reverse Dutch auction* technique in 1987. In a reverse Dutch auction, bondholders submit their offer prices before the end of the tender offer period. At the close of the period, the firm selects a cutoff price, and all offers at or below this price receive the cutoff price. The firm is not obligated to buy any bonds if it does not find any of the offer prices acceptable.

In a fixed-spread tender, a technique developed in the early 1990s, there is a tender price formula, equal to a fixed interest rate spread plus the yield of a specified Treasury security that matures around the outstanding bonds' initial call date. The tender price varies with the yield of the benchmark Treasury.

Tax Considerations

A firm must consider how repurchasing debt will affect bondholders. Taxes can increase the premium needed to repurchase high-coupon bonds because tax-exempt bonds are usually held by taxable investors, who must pay capital gains tax on any premium they get. As a result, bondholders may demand a tender price that is significantly above the fair market value of an otherwise identical newly issued bond.[13]

The Florida Power & Light Reverse Dutch Auction Tender

Florida Power & Light (FPL) held a reverse Dutch auction tender in May 1992.[14] It tendered for $60 million face amount of its 11⅜ of 2019 two years before their first call date (twenty-seven years before maturity) and bought $14 million at 118 percent of par. Its new issue rates were 6.5 percent for twenty-seven-year tax-exempt debt and 8.5 percent for taxable debt. With an 18 percent premium and a 38 percent income tax rate, the after-tax redemption premium was 11.16 percent ($18[1 - 0.38]$).

We can use equations 10.4 and 10.5 to calculate the net advantage of refunding. FPL could refinance the $14 million face amount at the tax-exempt rate, 6.5 percent, and the repurchase premium at the taxable rate, 8.5 percent. The 18 percent repurchase premium is tax deductible, so FPL had to borrow only $1,562,400 ($14,000,000[0.18]$[1 - 0.38]$) at the taxable rate. Therefore, the weighted average new issue rate is 6.7232 percent.[15] To simplify, assume $P = B$, $C = U = $280,000$, and $OI = 0$ in equation 10.5.[16] Thus

$$E = C - T(U) = (1 - 0.38)\$280,000 = \$173,600$$

and equation 10.4 gives $NA = \$4,770,731$:

$$NA = \sum_{n=1}^{54} \frac{(1 - 0.38)[(0.11375/2) - (0.067232/2)]14,000,000}{[1 + (1 - 0.38)(0.067232/2]^n}$$

$$- (1 - 0.38)(2,520,000) - 173,600$$

Applying equation 11.1, the refunding efficiency is 90.5 percent:[17]

$$\text{Efficiency} = 4,770,731/5,271,140 = 90.5 \text{ percent}$$

The FPL Dutch auction tender offer, and in particular the cutoff price FPL selected, achieved the 90 percent efficiency we recommend in chapter 11. Table 13.4 shows how the efficiency of the refunding

Table 13.4 The Tender Offer Price and Refunding Efficiency

Tender Offer Price	Net Advantage of Refunding	Efficiency[a]
132.00	$3,648,824	69.2%
126.00	4,132,657	78.4
120.00	4,603,122	87.3
119.00	4,683,874	88.9
118.00	4,763,416	90.4
117.00	4,844,851	91.8
116.00	4,925,338	93.3
111.63	5,278,000	100.0
110.00	5,409,235	100.0
104.00	5,893,482	100.0

Source: A. J. Kalotay, G. O. Williams, and A. I. Pedvis, "Refunding Tax-Exempt Corporate Bonds in Advance of the Call," *Financier* 1 (February 1994), p. 78.

[a]The forfeited option value is $5,271,140 (37.7 percent of par) assuming a 9% yield volatility.

depends on the tender offer price. Efficiency would reach 100 percent at a tender offer price of about 111.63.

Taxes play a significant role in the profitability of any refunding. FPL's refunding benefited from its ability to deduct the redemption premium and the interest payments and to amortize the other expenses. In the absence of income taxes, a cutoff price of 116 would have been required to achieve a refunding efficiency of 90 percent, and the actual 118 would be only 85 percent efficient. Figure 13.2 shows how the refunding efficiency varies with FPL's income tax rate.

Conclusion

This chapter discussed five special cases of refunding: refunding floating-rate debt, advance refunding of municipal debt through legal defeasance, advance refunding of corporate debt, refunding under rate base regulation, and refunding tax-exempt corporate bonds.

Floating-for-floating refundings are easy to analyze when the base interest rate is the same. The difference in interest rate margins determines the interest savings, and the standard formulas apply with only slight modifications. Fixed-for-floating refundings are different. They should be evaluated in the light of the firm's overall risk management policies.

Figure 13.2 The Effect of Income Taxes on Refunding Efficiency

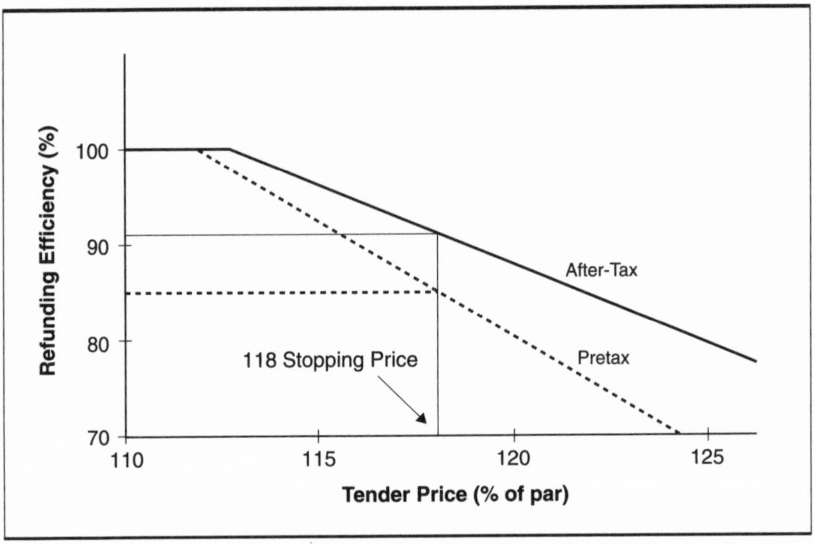

Source: A. J. Kalotay, G. O. Williams, and A. I. Pedvis, "Refunding Tax-Exempt Corporate Bonds in Advance of the Call," *Financier* 1 (February 1994), p. 79.

An advance refunding is a form of legal defeasance that permits a debtor (typically a municipality) to accelerate the benefits of an in-the-money call option. This operation can be particularly advantageous if interest rates are expected to rise between the proposed advance refunding date and the first call date. Under certain circumstances, an advance refunding can serve as a profitable strategy for refunding nonredeemable high-coupon corporate debt for tax reasons. Although it is unlikely to replace cash repurchases as the primary method of refunding nonredeemable high-coupon corporate debt, it can nevertheless serve either as a useful complement to cash repurchase when some of the high-coupon debt is held by low-tax-basis investors or as a useful substitute for cash repurchase in situations like the TVA faced when a debtholder refuses to sell its bonds.

In certain regulated industries, such as public utilities, health care, and financial services, the revenue a firm is allowed to collect from its customers depends on its cost of capital. As a result, bond refunding affects both the future stream of expenses and the future stream of revenues, and bond refunding at a premium reduces shareholder wealth. The size of this loss depends on the redemption premium, its rate of amortization, and the cost of capital. The loss in wealth could be eliminated by including the unamortized premium in the rate base or adjusting both the debt ratio and the cost of debt to reflect the unamortized premium.

Firms can issue tax-exempt bonds for certain approved purposes. Refunding such debt is restricted by the tax code. In general, the standard formulas for analyzing the net advantage of refunding high-coupon debt can be modified to handle these restrictions.

Finally, investment bankers frequently develop new bond-refunding strategies and techniques, usually designed to reduce tax liabilities and transaction costs. Reverse Dutch auction tenders and fixed-spread tenders are examples of recently introduced bond repurchase techniques.

Chapter **14**

Preferred Stock and Preference Stock

P*referred stock* and *preference stock* are hybrid securities that combine features of common stock and debt. They rank senior to common stock, and junior to debt, in claims on the firm's operating income and on its assets in the event of liquidation. For example, dividends must be paid in full on preferred and preference stock before the firm can pay any dividends on its common stock. The only significant difference between preferred stock and preference stock is subordination. Preferred stock is senior; dividends must be paid in full on the preferred stock before the company can pay dividends on its preference stock. Because of their similarity, this chapter refers simply to preferred stock.

Main Features of Preferred Stock

Preferred stock has the following key features:

- A *par value* or *stated value*, generally $25, $50, or $100 per share. Issues that are to be sold mainly to institutional investors are usually given a $100 par value. Issues targeted to individual investors are usually given a $25 par value, so that a round lot (100 shares) would cost $2,500.

- A stated *dividend rate*. Preferred stock pays dividends quarterly, like common stock, but at a stated rate, like debt. The dividends are not deductible for tax purposes. Also, preferred stock issues usually have a *cumulative dividend feature*. That is, missed dividends are accumulated. This cumulative amount must be paid in full before any cash dividends can be paid on common stock.

- An *optional redemption provision*. Preferred stock usually includes a call option similar to those found in debt issues.

- *Redeemability*. Preferred stock may be redeemable or nonredeemable. *Redeemable preferred stock* contains sinking-fund provisions similar to those found in sinking-fund debentures. *Nonredeemable preferred stock* is perpetual, like common stock.

- *Voting rights*. Preferred stock often carries one vote per share and allows the preferred stockholders to vote on the same issues as common stockholders. However, not all preferred stock conveys the same voting rights as common stock, and many preferred stocks allow voting rights only in special circumstances. These special circumstances usually include the right to elect separate directors to represent their interests if the issuer misses a specified number of dividend payments.[1] In some cases, they may even be entitled to elect a majority of the directors.

- *Liquidation rights*. If involuntary liquidation occurs, holders of preferred stock are usually entitled to receive the stated value of their shares plus a stated *liquidation premium*. If voluntary liquidation occurs, they are usually entitled to receive the optional redemption price. They must receive this price before the common stockholders can receive anything.[2]

Preferred stock's stated value is just like the principal amount of a bond. Its stated dividend rate (or *dividend rate formula*) is just like the coupon rate (or *interest rate formula*) of a bond. Preferred stock's optional redemption (or call) provision is just like a bond's, and many preferred stock issues have a mandatory redemption (or sinking-fund) provision and stated term to maturity just like a bond. All of these features make preferred stock similar to debt. In general, the shorter the average life of the preferred stock issue, the more debt-like it is. However, firms also issue perpetual preferred stock, which never has to be redeemed. In contrast, debt must have a final maturity (or the holders must have a put option) in order for interest to be tax deductible in the United States, as we noted in chapter 6.

Most issuers of preferred stock treat it like a debt obligation. They plan to make regular dividend payments. However, they reserve the right not to pay dividends—for example, if they should encounter financial distress. If the issuer makes the dividend payments and all required sinking-fund payments on time, the cash flow pattern is just like that of a bond. Understandably, such a preferred stock instrument can be valued like a bond.

Financing with Preferred Stock

Why do companies issue preferred stock? Sinking-fund preferred stock is like debt except that the dividend payments are not tax deductible. However, missing a scheduled dividend payment does not constitute default.

Preferred stock dividends paid to other corporations may qualify for the 70 percent dividends-received deduction, which explains why preferred stock yields are usually lower than comparable debt yields. If a corporation does not have taxable income, preferred stock can cost less than debt. Thrifts and commercial banks have been the heaviest issuers of floating-rate preferred stock.

There is another rationale for issuing preferred stock: preferred stock dividends are a cost that regulated utilities can pass through to their customers, which gives them an incentive to issue preferred stock instead of common stock. In fact, utility companies have been the heaviest issuers of fixed-dividend-rate preferred stock, representing between 10 percent and 15 percent of an electric utility company's capitalization.

Valuing Preferred Stock

In view of the similarity between preferred stock and debt, preferred stock can be valued using the debt valuation techniques developed in chapter 9. The main adjustment concerns the timing of dividend payments. They are usually made quarterly, whereas interest is usually paid semiannually.

Redeemable Preferred Stock

A credit analysis will establish a preferred stock's credit rating just as it will for a bond. Preferred stock issues with similar terms and the same credit rating help gauge the appropriate discount rate, also like a bond.

Perpetual Preferred Stock

Perpetual preferred stock has no maturity. Its dividend yield is calculated by dividing the annual dividend rate by the market price:

$$\text{Dividend yield} = \text{Annual dividend rate}/\text{Price} \qquad (14.1)$$

To calculate the value of a perpetual preferred stock issue, determine its credit rating. Then find one or more perpetual preferred stock issues with the same credit rating. Calculate their dividend yields and average them.[3] The price of the issue being valued can be estimated by rearranging equation 14.1,

$$\text{Price} = \text{Annual dividend rate}/\text{Dividend yield} \qquad (14.2)$$

and substituting the annual dividend rate for the preferred stock being valued and the dividend yield estimated from the comparable preferred issues.

For example, the annual dividend rate for a perpetual preferred stock issue with a stated value of $100 per share is $8. Perpetual preferred stock issues with the same credit rating provide a 10 percent yield. Thus, the value of a share is $80.00 (8.00/0.10).

Preferred Stock Innovations

Preferred stock offers a tax advantage over debt to corporate investors in the United States because U.S. corporations are permitted to deduct from their taxable income 70 percent of the dividends they receive from unaffiliated corporations. This tax advantage offers corporations an incentive to purchase preferred stock rather than commercial paper or other short-term debt instruments, the interest on which is fully taxable. Nontaxable corporate issuers find preferred stock cheaper than debt because corporate investors are willing to pass back part of the value of the tax arbitrage by accepting a lower dividend rate.

Managing Interest Rate Risk with Preferreds

Purchasing long-term preferred stock with a fixed dividend rate, however, exposes the purchaser to the risk that rising interest rates could lower the value of the preferred stock and more than offset the tax saving. A variety of preferred stock instruments have been designed to deal with this problem (see table 14.1).

Adjustable-rate preferred stock was designed to reduce principal risk by adjusting the dividend rate as interest rates change. The dividend rate adjusts according to a formula specifying a fixed spread over Treasuries. But at times the spread that investors have required to value the securities at par has differed significantly from the fixed spread specified in the formulas, causing the value of the security to deviate significantly from its face amount.[4]

Convertible adjustable preferred stock (CAPS) was designed to eliminate this deficiency by making the security convertible on each dividend payment date into enough shares to make the security worth par.

Table 14.1 Selected Preferred Stock Innovations

■ Security □ Distinguishing Characteristics ● Enhanced Liquidity ○ Reduction in Transaction Costs	■ Year First Issued □ Risk Reallocation ● Reduction in Agency Costs ○ Tax and Other Benefits	■ Number of Issues	■ Aggregate Proceeds ($billions)
■ **Adjustable-Rate Monthly Income Preferred Securities (Adjustable-Rate MIPS)**	■ 03/21/96	■ 2	■ 0.5
□ Dividend rate resets each quarter based on a specified fraction of the highest of the 3-month T-bill, 10-year, or 30-year Treasury rates. Dividends paid monthly to appeal to retail investors. Really parent-company subordinated debt repackaged as preferred stock.	□ Issuer bears more interest rate risk than a fixed-rate preferred would involve. Investors bear more credit risk than a conventional subordinated debt issue would involve.		
● Security is designed to trade near its par value.	○ Issuer can deduct the interest payments on the underlying subordinated debt, giving rise to tax deductible "capital" securities.		
■ **Adjustable-Rate Preferred Stock**	■ 05/11/82	■ 141	■ 11.6
□ Dividend rate resets each quarter based on maximum of 3-month T-bill, 10-year, or 20- year Treasury rates plus or minus a specified spread.	□ Issuer bears more interest rate risk than a fixed-rate preferred would involve. Lower yield than commercial paper.		
● Security is designed to trade near its par value.			
■ **Auction-Rate Preferred Stock (MMP/DARTS/AMPS/STAR)**	■ 08/27/84	■ 685	■ 48.8
□ Dividend resets by Dutch auction every 49 days. Dividend is paid at the end of each dividend period.	□ Issuer bears more interest rate risk than a fixed-rate preferred would involve. Lower yield than commercial paper.		
● Security is designed to provide greater liquidity than convertible adjustable preferred stock.	● Dividend rate each period is determined in the marketplace, which provides protection against deterioration in issuer's credit standing.		
■ **Convertible Adjustable Preferred Stock**	■ 09/15/83	■ 11	■ 0.7
□ Issue convertible on dividend payment dates into number of issuer's common shares, subject to cap, equal in value to par value of preferred.	□ Issuer bears more interest rate risk than a fixed-rate preferred would involve. Lower yield than commercial paper.		
● Security is designed to provide greater liquidity than adjustable-rate preferred stock (due to the conversion feature).			

(continued)

Table 14.1 (continued)

■ Security □ Distinguishing Characteristics ● Enhanced Liquidity ○ Reduction in Transaction Costs	■ Year First Issued □ Risk Reallocation ● Reduction in Agency Costs ○ Tax and Other Benefits	■ Number of Issues	■ Aggregate Proceeds ($billions)
■ **Fixed-Rate/Adjustable-Rate or Auction-Rate Preferred** □ Fixed-dividend-rate preferred stock that automatically becomes adjustable-rate or auction-rate preferred after a specified length of time. ● Security is designed to trade near its par value once the adjustment or auction period begins.	11/16/84 □ Once the adjustment or auction period begins, issuer bears more interest rate risk than a fixed-rate preferred would involve.	15	1.8
■ **Indexed-Floating-Rate Preferred Stock** □ Dividend rate resets quarterly as a specified percentage of 3-month LIBOR. ● Security is designed to trade closer to its par value than a fixed-dividend-rate preferred.	10/01/85 □ Issuer bears more interest rate risk than a fixed-rate preferred would involve. Lower yield than commercial paper.	3	0.2
■ **Monthly Income Preferred Securities (MIPS)** □ Preferred stock issued by a trust or special-purpose company that purchases cash-matching long-term subordinated debt of the parent firm. Really parent-company subordinated debt repackaged as preferred stock.	10/27/93 □ Investors bear more credit risk than a conventional subordinated debt issue would involve. ○ Parent company can deduct the interest payments on the underlying subordinated debt, giving rise to tax deductible "capital" securities.	155	33.1
■ **Remarketed Preferred Stock (SABRES)** □ Perpetual preferred stock with a dividend rate that resets at the end of each dividend period to a rate the remarketing agent determines will make the preferred stock worth par. Dividend periods may be of any length, even 1 day. Different shares of a single issue may have different periods and dividend rates. ● Security is designed to trade near its par value.	06/27/85 □ Issuer bears more interest rate risk than a fixed-rate preferred would involve. Lower yield than commercial paper. ○ Remarketed preferred stock offers greater flexibility in setting the terms of the issue than auction-rate preferred stock, which requires a Dutch auction for potentially the entire issue once every 49 days.	90	5.2

Single-Point Adjustable-Rate Stock   ■ 12/13/85   ■ 2   ■ 0.2

□ Dividend rate reset every 49 days as a specified percentage of the high-grade commercial paper rate.

● Security is designed to trade near its par value.

○ Security is designed to save on recurring transaction costs associated with auction-rate preferred stock.

□ Issuer bears more interest rate risk than a fixed-rate preferred would involve. Lower yield than commercial paper.

Step-Up Preferred Stock   ■ 06/30/97   ■ 4   ■ 0.3

□ Long-term preferred stock with a dividend rate that steps up if the issue is not called on a specific date, in one case 10 years after issue.

□ Step up in dividend rate at least partially compensates investors if the issuer's credit standing falls and the issuer fails to redeem the preferred stock.

Variable Cumulative Preferred Stock   ■ 07/07/88   ■ 8   ■ 0.5

□ At start of dividend period issuer can select between auction method and remarketing method to reset dividend rate at beginning of next period.

● Security is designed to trade near its par value.

○ Saves on transaction costs the issuer would otherwise incur if it wanted to change from auction reset to remarketing reset or vice versa.

□ Issuer bears more interest rate risk than a fixed-rate preferred would involve. Lower yield than commercial paper.

● The maximum permitted dividend rate increases according to a specified schedule if the preferred stock's credit rating falls.

○ Security is designed to give the issuer the flexibility to alter the method of rate reset.

Source: John D. Finnerty, "An Overview of Corporate Securities Innovation." *Journal of Applied Corporate Finance* 4 (Winter 1992), p. 34; Thomson Financial Securities Data.

[a] All preferred stock innovations except MIPS are designed to enable short-term corporate investors to take advantage of the 70 percent dividends-received deduction.

But although CAPS have traded closer to par than adjustable-rate preferred stocks, there have been only eleven CAPS issues, perhaps because of convertibility, which could force the issuer to issue common stock or raise a large amount of cash on short notice.

Auction-rate preferred stock carried the evolutionary process a step further. The dividend rate is reset by Dutch auction every forty-nine days, which represents just enough weeks to meet the forty-six-day holding period required to qualify for the 70 percent dividends-received deduction.[5] There are various versions of auction-rate preferred stock that are sold under different acronyms (e.g., MMP, money market preferred; AMPS, auction market preferred stock; DARTS, Dutch auction-rate transferable securities; STAR, short-term auction-rate) coined by the different securities firms offering the product. Although the names differ, the securities are the same.[6]

Two attempts have been made to refine the adjustable-rate preferred stock concept further, but only one was successful. Single-point adjustable-rate stock (SPARS) has a dividend rate that adjusts automatically every forty-nine days to a specified percentage of the sixty-day high-grade commercial paper rate. The security is designed to provide the same liquidity as auction-rate preferred stock, but with lower transaction costs since no auction need be held. The problem with SPARS, however, is that the fixed-dividend-rate formula introduces a potential agency cost. Because the dividend formula is fixed, investors will suffer a loss if the issuer's credit standing falls. Primarily for this reason, there have been only two SPARS issues.

Remarketed preferred stock, by contrast, pays a dividend that is reset at the end of each dividend period to a rate that a specified remarketing agent determines will make the preferred stock worth par. Such issues permit the issuer considerable flexibility in selecting the length of the dividend period (it can be as short as one day). Remarketed preferred also offers greater flexibility in selecting the other terms of the issue. In fact, each share of an issue could have a different maturity, dividend rate, or other terms, provided the issuer and holders so agree. Remarketed preferred has not proved as popular with issuers as auction-rate preferred stock.

Variable cumulative preferred stock was born out of the controversy over whether auction-rate preferred stock or remarketed preferred stock results in more equitable pricing. This variation effectively allows the issuer to decide at the beginning of each dividend period which of the two reset methods will determine the dividend rate at the beginning of the next dividend period.

Other Preferred Stock Innovations

In view of the similar structures for debt and preferred stock, a variety of preferred stock instruments are understandably adaptations of debt innovations. One of the more interesting examples is gold-denominated preferred stock. Commodity-linked preferred stock is just like the commodity-linked bonds discussed in chapter 8.

Freeport-McMoRan Copper & Gold Inc. raised $233 million in 1993 by issuing gold-denominated preferred stock. Table 14.2 summarizes the issue's terms. The issue price, quarterly dividend, and redemption value at maturity are all tied to the price of gold.[7] Several mutual funds that were unable to own physical gold were among the investors in the new issue, which embodied a ten-year forward contract on gold.[8] Freeport-McMoRan Copper & Gold designed the issue as a forward sale of 600,000 ounces of gold ([6,000,000]0.10), hedging some of its gold price risk exposure. It chose to issue preferred stock rather than arrange a more traditional gold loan because it wanted a relatively long-dated security that did not require any amortization of principal and did not have the restrictive loan covenants usually found in gold loans.[9]

Refunding Preferred Stock

Refunding preferred stock can be analyzed in a parallel manner to refunding debt, since the two instruments are so similar in structure.

Table 14.2 Summary of Freeport-McMoRan Copper & Gold's Gold-Denominated Preferred Stock

Issued	August 1993
Number of shares	6,000,000
Issue price per share	$38.77
Method of pricing	Value of $\frac{1}{10}$ of an ounce of gold
Price of gold on issue date	$387/ounce
Quarterly dividend rate	Value of 0.000875 of an ounce of gold
Annual dividend yield	3½%
Maturity	10 years (2003)
Redemption value at maturity	Value of $\frac{1}{10}$ of an ounce of gold
Sinking fund	None
Optional redemption	None
Listing	New York Stock Exchange

This section takes advantage of this similarity to develop expressions for the net advantage of refunding preferred stock.[10]

Some important distinctions first must be made between debt and preferred stock:

- Refunding preferred stock generally has no tax consequences for the issuer. Even expenses associated with retiring the old issue and marketing the new issue cannot be deducted currently or amortized for tax purposes.

- Corporate preferred stockholders qualify for a 70 percent dividends-received deduction, which reduces the effective tax rate on dividend income for a corporate holder from 35 percent to 10.5 percent ([0.35]0.30).[11] The dividends-received deduction gives rise to the possibility of refunding discounted preferred stock profitably.

- Preferred stock involves no default risk, because a missed dividend payment does not constitute default. But provisions typically permit preferred stockholders, voting as a separate class, to elect one or more directors after the issuer fails to make a half-dozen or so consecutive dividend payments. A viable business enterprise will almost always do everything possible to pay its preferred stock dividends on time.

- Preferred stock may be issued in perpetual form, while bonds, under the Internal Revenue Code, must have a stated maturity. The analysis of refunding perpetual preferred stock thus requires a special framework.

- Preferred stock dividends are payable quarterly, and, to be precise, calculations should be made on that basis. In practice, the simplification of annual dividends is often used.

Profitability of Refunding Preferred Stock

Preferred stock obligations treated like debt obligations are referred to as *quasi-debt obligations*. Neutralizing financial structure side effects in a proposed preferred stock refunding involves maintaining what may be termed *quasi-debt service parity*, which is perfectly analogous to the debt service parity (DSP) concept discussed in chapter 10.

A simple one-period model illustrates the rationale for refunding high-dividend-rate preferred stock when quasi-debt service parity is maintained and indicates the impact of the dividends-received deduction.

A firm has $50 million of 10 percent preferred stock outstanding that matures in a lump sum in one period. Assume the firm could issue new 8 percent preferred stock at par. To maintain quasi-debt service parity, the company can issue $62.5 million ($50 million[0.10/0.08]) of new preferred stock. Suppose the redemption premium is 5 percent, or $2.5 million, and the expenses of refunding amount to $200,000. Refunding the 10 percent issue with the 8 percent issue would provide a net advantage of $9.8 million ($62.5 million – $50.0 million – $2.5 million – $0.2 million).

Next, consider the low-dividend-rate case. Suppose instead the new issue preferred stock dividend rate is 12 percent. The firm can repurchase the outstanding preferred stock at a price of $49,107,143 ([$50 million]1.10/1.12), which is identical to the amount of new preferred stock it can issue. Because of the transaction costs of a refunding, it is generally not profitable to refund discounted preferred stock without special tax advantages.

Dividends-Received Deduction

Let us see how the dividends-received deduction affects the profitability of refunding. Consider a corporate investor with tax rates of 35 percent on ordinary income and 28 percent on capital gains. This corporation would be indifferent between the existing discounted 10 percent issue and a new par value 12 percent issue only if the new issue has the same value and offers the same after-tax returns. Table 14.3 shows that this price is $48.918298. Therefore, the net advantage of refunding is positive if the refunding costs are less than $188,845 ($49,107,143 – $48,918,298).

When the preferred stockholders at the margin are fully taxable corporations, refunding discounted preferred stock can be advantageous. Such an operation substitutes for the existing payments stream a new stream of preferred stock payments that contains a greater proportion of dividend payments, which are taxed at a lower rate than capital gains to a fully (or nearly fully) taxable corporate preferred stockholder. The greater the dividends-received deduction is, the greater is the net advantage of refunding discounted preferred stock. But as this example illustrates, such refundings are at best only marginally profitable. In any case, because the refunding of discounted preferred stock substitutes dividend income for capital gain for the investor, such refundings can be profitable only if the marginal investor's investment time horizon is relatively short. The more distant the horizon is, the less valuable is the substitution of dividend income

Table 14.3 Illustration of the Profitability of Refunding Discounted Preferred Stock

	10 Percent Preferred	12 Percent Preferred
I. Value of Preferred Stock		
Stated value per share	$50	P
Number of shares	1,000,000	1,000,000
Dividend rate	10%	12%
Effective dividend tax rate	10.5%	10.5%
Dividend income per share:		
Pretax	$5.00	0.12 P
After-tax	4.475	0.1074P
Market price	P	P
Capital gain:		
Pretax	50 − P	−
After-tax	0.72 (50 − P)	−
After-tax proceeds at maturity	P + 0.72 (50 − P)	P
Total after-tax income	4.475 + P + 0.72 (50 − P)	1.1074 P
II. Indifference Price		
4.475 + P + 0.72 (50 − P) = 1.1074 P		
P = 48.918298		
Total price = 1,000,000 × $48.918298 = $48,918,298		
III. Profitability of Refunding		
New issue proceeds[a]	$49,107,143	
Repurchase price	48,918,298	
Difference	$ 188,845	

[a]Calculated as $50 million × 1.10/1.12.

for capital gain on a present-value basis. Consequently, it is generally not profitable for a corporation to refund discounted perpetual preferred stock.

General Analytical Framework

Equation 10.4 can be modified to reflect the nondeductibility of preferred stock dividends and refunding expenses and provide an expression for the net advantage of refunding high-dividend-rate non-sinking-fund bullet maturity preferred stock:

$$NA = \sum_{n=1}^{N} \frac{(d - d')D}{(1 + d')^n} - (P - D) - E \tag{14.3}$$

where

N = number of quarters until the old preferred stock was scheduled to mature,

d = quarterly dividend rate on the old preferred stock,

D = face amount of the old preferred stock that is refunded,

d' = quarterly dividend rate on the new preferred stock,

P = cost of reacquiring the old preferred stock, and

E = expenses associated with the refunding.

The expenses E can be broken down further as

$$E = C + F + (P - B) + OI \tag{14.4}$$

where C is the underwriting commissions and other new issue expenses; F is the out-of-pocket expenses of the refunding operation, which are generally not tax deductible; $P - B$ is the difference between the redemption price P and the market price of the old preferred stock, B; and OI is any net overlapping dividends cost, which equals the extra dividend payments from selling the new issue before retiring the old one minus any after-tax income earned from investing the surplus funds during the overlap period.

Note that setting $E = 0$ in equation 14.3 would provide a useful back-of-the-envelope formula, analogous to equation 10.6.

Here is an example. A firm proposes to refund its 12 percent cumulative preferred stock issue with a new 9 percent issue, of which $60 million stated value is outstanding. The old issue has a bullet maturity, is scheduled to mature in fifteen years, and is redeemable at a premium of 5 percent over its $100 par value. The issuance expenses associated with a new issue are estimated to be 1.5 percent of the value of the issue: $900,000. Refunding leads to quarterly dividend savings of $450,000 but requires an aggregate redemption premium of $3 million. Substituting these values into equation 14.3, the net advantage of refunding is

$$NA = \sum_{n=1}^{60} \frac{450{,}000}{(1.0225)^n} - 3{,}000{,}000 - 900{,}000 = \$10{,}837{,}029$$

Perpetual Preferred Stock

For perpetual preferred stock, the discounted cash flow model 14.3 simplifies to

$$NA = (d - d')\, D/d' - (P - D) - E \tag{14.5}$$

If the 12 percent issue in the preceding example were instead perpetual, the $450,000 quarterly savings from refunding would go on forever and produce a present value of $20 million. This would then result in a net advantage of $16.1 million ($20 million – $3.9 million).

Timing

The timing issue—whether to wait or refund now by calling, market purchase, or tender offer—can be analyzed using the techniques developed in chapter 11. For the special case of a perpetual preferred stock issue, the break-even annual dividend rate, e, is

$$e = dD/(P + E) \tag{14.6}$$

For example, the break-even dividend rate for refunding the 12 percent perpetual issue just considered is 11.268 percent; the net advantage will be positive so long as the annual dividend rate of the new issue is below 11.268 percent.

Impact of a Sinking Fund

The net advantage of refunding a preferred stock issue with a sinking fund can be analyzed using the framework developed in chapters 10 and 12. Treat the sinking-fund issue as a serial obligation and calculate the net advantage for each sinking-fund payment using the new issue dividend rate on preferred stock of that payment's maturity. Use the binomial model to determine the optimal choice for each payment: wait or refund now using a call, market purchase, or tender offer.

Discounted Preferred Stock

Under certain circumstances, as we have seen, a firm can refund discounted preferred stock profitably. Refunding discounted preferred stock fully with a new issue of par value preferred stock with a finite maturity would increase the quarterly preferred stock dividend expense but decrease the principal repayment obligation. Equation 14.3 can be used to calculate the net advantage of the refunding. The analytical procedure developed in chapter 12 can be used in conjunction with the framework for preferred stock developed in this chapter to handle preferred stock sinking-fund management.

Altering Capital Structure

Firms repurchase preferred stock for reasons other than to replace it with a new lower-cost issue: (1) to alter the firm's capital structure;

(2) to substitute debt for preferred stock that was issued when the firm did not have sufficient income against which it could claim interest tax deductions; and (3) to eliminate potentially bothersome charter restrictions imposed by the preferred stock. We provide an example of each situation.

Eliminating Preferred Stock from the Capital Structure

In April 1995, General Motors (GM) launched a $2.3 billion tender offer designed to eliminate three entire issues of preference stock. GM had issued the preference stock several years earlier when it needed to raise equity capital; operating losses and recognition of a huge liability for retiree health care costs had depleted much of its common equity and depressed its common stock price.[12] However, GM earned a combined $7.4 billion in 1993 and 1994, its stockholders' equity more than doubled to $12.8 billion, and its cash and marketable securities had grown to $16.1 billion by year-end 1994.

GM decided that with the increase in its common equity, it could eliminate the preference stock. Also, the dividend rates on the preference stock were far in excess of the after-tax yields on GM's liquid assets. GM tendered for the preference stock because none of the issues was yet callable. GM tendered at prices between 5 percent and 6 percent above its preference shares' market prices. It bought back 57 percent of the shares, spending $1.2 billion, making it the largest preferred stock tender offer to date.[13]

GM's issuance and repurchase a few years later of preference shares illustrates how firms have used preferred stock as a temporary means of replenishing their stockholders' equity.

Substituting Debt for Equity

We explained in chapter 6 how firms have issued fixed-rate capital securities because they are considered debt for income tax purposes but the rating agencies consider them to be a close substitute for preferred stock. As you might expect, several firms have issued fixed-rate capital securities and used the funds to retire a portion of their preferred stock. Others have issued junior subordinated debt or conventional debt to replace preferred stock, in some cases offering preferred stockholders the opportunity to exchange their shares for newly issued debt.

Substituting debt for preferred stock generally elicits a favorable stock market reaction.[14] There is both a favorable signaling effect, because interest is a fixed obligation and preferred stock dividends are not, and a favorable tax effect due to the tax deductibility of interest.

We conjecture that because of the five-year interest-deferral feature, the signaling effect of issuing fixed-rate capital securities is less favorable than issuing straight debt, although still positive.

For example, in June 1995, McDonald's offered to exchange up to $450 million aggregate principal amount of its 8.35 percent subordinated deferrable interest debentures due 2025 for up to 18 million shares of its 7.72 percent cumulative preferred stock. The debentures were offered in minimum denominations of $25 to match the stated value of each preferred share.[15] The debentures make quarterly payments, also like preferred stock; allow McDonald's to defer interest payments for up to twenty consecutive quarters; mature in a lump sum; and were redeemable at par beginning in December 1997 when the preferred stock also was scheduled to become redeemable, also at par.

The thirty-year debentures were scheduled to mature in a lump sum, just as the preferred stock could be redeemed for par in thirty years. Thus, it seems reasonable to estimate the net advantage of the exchange by calculating the present-value cash flow savings over this thirty-year period. We can estimate the net advantage of refunding the entire $450 million principal value by adapting equations 10.4 and 14.3.

With a 35 percent tax rate, the quarterly after-tax savings are $0.4825 ([0.0772/4]$25) per share on 18 million shares minus 2.0875 percent (8.35/4) interest on $450 million principal:

$$\text{Quarterly savings} = \$0.4825(18,000,000) - 0.020875(\$450,000,000)(1 - 0.35)$$
$$= \$2,579,062.50$$

The after-tax cost of the new debt is 1.36 percent ([1.0 − 0.35][8.35/4]). The total expenses amounted to up to $11,250,000 in dealer fees for retiring the preferred stock plus $1,000,000 in other expenses associated primarily with issuing the new debt (which are tax deductible).[16] The maximum possible net advantage of the exchange is approximately[17]

$$NA = \sum_{n=1}^{N} \frac{[d - (1 - T)r']D + TC/N}{[1 + (1 - T)r']^n} - E \qquad (14.7)$$

$$NA = \sum_{n=1}^{120} \frac{2,579,062.50 + (0.35)(1,000,000/120)}{(1.0136)^n} - 12,250,000 = \$140,067,690$$

The exchange offer met with limited success; only 26 percent of the preferred stockholders exchanged their shares. The lower-than-expected response rate was attributed to the higher-than-expected percentage of corporate holders, who could claim the 70 percent dividends-received deduction, which would be lost with the debt.[18] In general, a debt-for-preferred exchange would not be profitable if the interest rate had to compensate preferred stockholders fully for the loss of the dividends-received deduction.[19]

Eliminating Potentially Bothersome Restrictions

Preferred stock often imposes restrictions. Like bond covenants, they are designed to protect the economic interest of the preferred stockholders. Also like bond covenants, a firm can find them too costly and decide to try to amend or eliminate some of them. It can get permission from the security holders by obtaining *consents*, or it can repurchase a large enough portion of the issue to ensure that it will have sufficient votes to make the desired changes.

For example, in February 1997, Texas Utilities Company offered to purchase for cash all the outstanding shares of preferred stock (representing twenty issues and an aggregate cost of up to $562.5 million) of its wholly owned subsidiary, Texas Utilities Electric Company. It planned to use its bank lines to finance the repurchase. The repurchase was aimed at amending limitations on the subsidiary's ability to issue unsecured debt or additional preferred stock or to repurchase junior equity securities. Texas Utilities also wanted to increase to six from four the number of consecutive missed dividend payments that would trigger the preferred stockholders' right to elect directors and reduce to a simple majority from a two-thirds majority the number of preferred shares needed to eliminate certain other restrictions.

When a firm wants to eliminate bothersome restrictions on preferred stock that is currently callable and selling above par, the simplest and probably least costly strategy is to call it.[20] The issuer may have to call it if the change requires unanimous consent, because even one holdout can block the desired change in that case. If the preferred stock is not callable or has a below-market dividend rate, then repurchasing it is likely to be less costly.

As with debt, we recommend analyzing the elimination of the restrictions within the refunding framework. Calculate the net advantage of refunding the old preferred stock with new preferred that does not have the restrictions. If the net advantage is negative, then the issuer must decide whether the change is worth this cost. In any case, when senior debt will permanently replace the preferred stock, it is important to consider the capital structure change as a separate decision.

Conclusion

The principal differences between debt and preferred stock from the issuer's viewpoint are that preferred stock dividends and issuance expenses are not tax deductible and missing a dividend payment does not constitute default, and so does not expose the issuer to the risk of bankruptcy. But preferred stock and debt have similar financial structures, particularly when the preferred stock issue provides for a sinking fund. This similarity allows us to use the available debt structures to design preferred stock issues. It also enables us to apply the general analytical bond refunding frameworks to analyze the profitability of refunding preferred stock.

Chapter 15

Convertible Securities

A *convertible security* includes a valuable option that allows its owner to convert the security into a predetermined number of the firm's common shares, which are newly issued at the time of conversion. The conversion features of *convertible bonds* and *convertible preferred stock* are very similar.

Convertible Security Features

Most of the features of a convertible security are like those of other nonconvertible securities. For example, a convertible bond will have a coupon rate, a maturity date, and probably a redemption option. In addition to such common features, a convertible security has the following features associated with conversion:

- Each security is convertible at any time prior to maturity into common stock at a stated *conversion* (strike) *price*. At the time the security is issued, the strike price usually is set to exceed the market value of the shares into which it is convertible. In other words, the conversion option is normally issued *out-of-the-money*. That is, the security's value as a bond is greater than its value as stock, generally by between 10 percent and 20 percent. Dividing the face amount of the convertible security by the conversion price gives the *conversion ratio*, which is the number of shares of common stock into which each security can be converted. The conversion terms are normally fixed for the life of the issue, although some convertible securities provide for one or more step-ups (increases) in the conversion price over time.

- The conversion price is usually adjusted for stock splits, stock dividends, or rights offerings that have a discounted offering price. It is also adjusted when the firm distributes assets (other than cash dividends) or indebtedness to its shareholders.

- Security holders who convert do not receive accrued interest or preferred dividends. Therefore, security holders rarely convert voluntarily in the time just before such a payment is due.

- If the securities have a redemption option and are called by the firm, the security holders' conversion option will expire just before (usually between three and ten days before) the redemption date.

Exchangeable Debentures

Firms have also issued *exchangeable debentures*, which are bonds that are exchangeable for the common stock of another firm.[1] The debentures are in effect "convertible" into the common stock of the other firm. But in all other respects, they are like conventional convertible bonds. Exchangeable debentures may be attractive to a firm that owns a block of another firm's common stock when it would like to raise cash and intends to sell the block eventually. The firm may want to defer the sale, because it believes the shares will increase in value or because it wants to defer the capital gains tax liability.

Interpreting the Bond Conversion Option

A convertible bond is typically described as a *security package* made up of a "straight" bond plus a call option to buy a predetermined number of the firm's (newly issued) common shares. But a convertible bond also can be viewed in another way. In option valuation theory, there is a concept called *put-call parity*. For any security package that includes a call option, put-call parity says there is an alternative security package that includes a put option (instead of a call option). In this case, the alternative security package is shares of common stock plus a put option to sell the shares for a fixed price.

In the typical bond-call view, convertible bondholders own a bond, but they can choose to exercise their call option and convert their bond into shares of stock. However, because convertible bondholders can convert into shareholders any time they choose, they are in effect already shareholders. Using this fact, the alternative stock-put view is that convertible bondholders own shares of stock, but they can choose to exercise their put option and convert their shares into a bond. Using the put option is attractive when the shares are not worth very much;

they can instead sell their security as a bond. Using the call option in the bond-call view is attractive when the shares are worth a lot; the security holders can instead sell their security as shares of stock.

Consider a simple illustration: a convertible bond that is worth $1,000 but can be converted into fifty shares of the firm's common stock. Let us say the stock is currently worth $30 per share, so the security package is worth $1,500 as stock and $1,000 as a bond. Now suppose the stock's value drops to $10 per share, so that the security package is worth only $500 as stock. Of course, the security package is still worth $1,000 as a bond. The important point is that the convertible bond's "optionality" allows us to view the security package as either a bond that could be stock or as stock that could be a bond. Of course, the market value of the security package will reflect whichever value is greater: bond or stock. If the stock is at $30, convertible bondholders will view themselves as stockholders and will not sell their security for less than its $1,500 value as stock. Otherwise they would convert it into shares and sell the shares for $1,500. Similarly, if the stock's value is $10 per share, convertible bondholders will view themselves as bondholders and certainly not sell their security for $500. The interest payments and par value at maturity make the bond worth $1,000.

The illustration skips over the complexities (which can be explored in other work).[2] Our purpose here is to provide the intuition underlying the equivalence of these alternative security packages. We use this equivalence to aid our explanation of some of the additional aspects of convertible bonds.

Why Firms Issue Convertible Securities

There are a number of plausible explanations for why a firm might want to issue convertible securities. In this section, we discuss the more prominent ones.

Deferred Sale of Common Shares

Convertible securities are typically issued out-of-the-money, but with the expectation that the stock's value will increase and the security will ultimately be worth more as stock than it is as a nonconvertible security. Therefore, they are issued with the expectation that they will ultimately become shares of common stock and will no longer be a debt or preferred stock obligation. Because of this, convertible bonds are sometimes referred to as *backdoor equity*.[3]

Reduced Interest Cost

Because the conversion option is valuable, investors accept a lower fixed payment rate on a convertible security than they require on an otherwise identical nonconvertible security. It is important to understand that the value of the conversion option is equal to the value of the reduction in fixed payment rate. However, for some firms, especially young ones, reducing their fixed cost financing cash flow is an attractive exchange for an equal-value option that requires no immediate cash flow.

Equity Kicker

The conversion option is sometimes referred to as an *equity kicker* or *sweetener*. Although the option and reduced fixed payment rate are of equal value, the equity feature intensifies the investors' relationship with the firm. It benefits the convertible security holders if the firm's common stock price rises above the conversion price. That is, convertible security holders are, in effect, both nonconvertible security holders and stockholders.

Reduced Impact of Differences in Risk Perceptions

When a firm and its investors disagree in their perceptions of the risk of the firm's operations, convertible securities can reduce the impact of the disagreement.[4] Risk affects security value, but not in the same way for every security. In fact, risk affects the values of the components of a convertible security, straight debt and a call option, in opposite ways.

On the downside, higher risk in a firm's operations provides more chances that the firm will do poorly. On the upside, however, higher risk in a firm's operations also provides more chances that the firm will do well. Debtholders are concerned about the downside because they can be hurt by poor firm performance. They are not concerned about the upside because they do not get any more than what is contractually promised, no matter how extraordinarily well the firm does. Therefore, higher perceived risk of a firm's operations creates a lower value for a straight bond.

The risk of a firm's operations has the opposite effect on the value of a call option on the firm's stock. Call option holders are concerned about the upside because they get more if the firm does well. They are less concerned about the downside because no matter how poor the firm's performance is, their loss is truncated when their option becomes worthless. Therefore, higher perceived risk of a firm's operations creates a higher value for a call option.

This means that when investors believe a firm's operations are riskier than the firm believes them to be, investors will place a lower value (require a higher interest rate) on straight debt than what managers think is reasonable. At the same time, investors will place a higher value on a call option on the firm's stock than what managers believe is correct. Because a convertible bond is a combination of straight debt and a call option, it is a diversified investment portfolio that has lower variation than that of its components as a result of good outcomes canceling out bad outcomes. Therefore, a difference in the perception of the risk of a firm's operations does not create nearly as large a disparity in the perceived value of a convertible security as it does for straight bonds and common stock. A firm and its investors are more likely to agree on the terms of convertible securities than they are for the individual securities that combine to make up the convertible security.

Reduced Agency Costs

Because convertible security holders are, in effect, already stockholders, they are not subject to some of the conflicts of interest that naturally arise between other security holders and the stockholders.[5] For example, consider the so-called *asset-substitution problem*. If a firm has a large proportion of debt and is approaching insolvency, managers have an incentive to undertake excessively risky investments, on the chance of saving the firm. In such a case, managers and stockholders would be, in effect, betting the debtholders' money on these risky projects. This is because the stockholders and managers have little more to lose at this point. In contrast, the debtholders get whatever is left, so they stand to lose the rest of their value. At the same time, they would not share in the gain if the risky project is successful. (This problem was widely observed in the savings and loan crisis of the 1980s.) Convertible debt helps control this incentive because the convertible debtholders are, in effect, already shareholders and would therefore at least share in the gain if the risky project is successful. As a result, convertible bonds have lower agency costs than comparable nonconvertible bonds do.[6]

Valuing Convertible Bonds

A convertible bond has to be worth at least whichever is greater: its value as stock or its value as a bond. But unlike the firm's other shares or its other bonds, this security also has an option and, because of this optionality, it is normally worth even more than the greater of the two values. How much more depends primarily on the remaining maturity, which is the time until the option expires.

Another complicating factor in valuing a convertible bond is the stockholders' limited liability, which is the option to default. When the stock value is low, investors rely on the security's value as a bond. However, if the stock's value is extremely low because the firm is doing very poorly, there is the possibility that the firm will default on its bond payments.

The factors just noted, along with others, make convertible bond valuation very complicated. Figure 15.1 shows the value of a convertible bond as a function of the market value of a share of the firm's stock. The diagonal 45-degree line is the security's stock value. In the portion denoted by the solid line, where the stock value exceeds the bond value, the stock value is the basis for the convertible security's value. In the portion denoted by the dashed line, where its stock value is less than its bond value, the bond value is the basis for the convertible security's value. Again, because of the optionality, the convertible security's actual value exceeds whichever is the basis for its value. And all else equal, the greater the remaining maturity is, the more this optionality is worth.

The security's bond value is also shown in figure 15.1. In the portion denoted by the solid line, where it exceeds the stock value, it is the

Figure 15.1 Value of a Convertible Bond

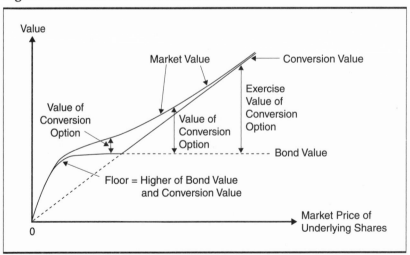

basis for the convertible security's value. In the portion denoted by the dashed line, where it is less than the stock value, the stock value is the basis for the convertible security's value. Note that the line is horizontal when the firm is healthy and there is almost no chance of default. However, when the firm is doing very poorly and the stock price falls, the chance of default increases, and the bond value also falls. In the extreme and exceedingly unlikely event that the firm's assets are totally worthless, both the stock and the bonds would be worthless.

Forced Conversions

Just like many other bonds, convertible bonds are normally callable according to a schedule of fixed redemption (strike) prices that decline over the life of the issue. This call provision allows the issuer to force holders to convert the debt into common stock whenever the conversion value exceeds the call price. Most convertible bond indentures require the issuer to notify bondholders of the call prior to the redemption date, usually thirty days in advance. Security holders can convert at any time during this notice period.

How Forced Conversion Works

The market value of a convertible bond always exceeds its conversion value unless the conversion option is about to expire. The difference between the market and conversion values reflects the conversion option's time premium. If the underlying common stock does not pay a dividend, convertible bondholders would never convert voluntarily, no matter how high the conversion value becomes. This is because they can always realize greater value by selling the bond. Even when the underlying common stock is paying cash dividends, convertible bondholders do not voluntarily convert if the after-tax dividends they would receive after conversion are less than the after-tax interest they receive now.

Suppose the market value of the underlying common stock exceeds the call price. Calling the convertible issue motivates holders to convert, because converting provides more value than tendering the bonds for cash redemption. A firm should follow the forced conversion strategy that maximizes shareholder wealth. If the firm calls convertible bonds when their conversion value is less than the effective call price, the bonds will not be converted, and wealth will be transferred from shareholders to bondholders. If the firm calls convertible bonds when the conversion value exceeds the call price, bondholders will simply convert. The forced-conversion strategy that maximizes shareholder wealth is the one that minimizes bondholder value. In a perfect capital market, a firm should call convertible bonds when their conversion value reaches the *effective call price* (optional redemption price plus accrued interest).[7]

Timing a Forced Conversion

Judged by the standards of a perfect capital market, most firms appear to wait "too long" to call their convertible bonds. They usually wait until the conversion value exceeds the call price by a seemingly wide margin.[8] However, we and others disagree. One article argues that (1) there is no significant call delay; (2) given the period of call protection, most are called as soon as possible; (3) for those that are not, there are significant cash flow advantages to delaying; (4) the median call delay is just four months; and (5) the desire to have a safety premium explains most of the delay.[9]

Investment bankers actually recommend that a firm have a *safety premium* (also called a *redemption cushion*) of at least 20 percent before it tries to force conversion by calling. Why do they recommend this, and why do firms behave this way? We agree with the explanation that it is a combination of potential transaction costs and agency costs.

Actual capital markets are not perfect. If the market price of the issuer's common stock falls—and remains—below the conversion price during the thirty-day notice period, the cash redemption value will exceed the conversion value and bondholders will surrender their bonds for cash rather than convert. In that case, the firm may have to raise enough cash to cover the cash redemption value on very short notice. That could involve significant transaction costs. In addition, a failed attempt is highly embarrassing for the firm's executives and could even lead to termination of employment. This possibility, of course, tends to bias managers toward waiting for an even larger margin and creates an agency cost because managers may be making suboptimal decisions to avoid any personal risk connected with trying to force conversion. To eliminate any chance of a failed conversion, managers engage the services of investment bankers to underwrite the redemption in most cases.[10] The investment banker agrees to purchase any shares of common stock that fail to be claimed by the conversion because security holders instead choose to take the cash. Understandably, the investment banker's fee is higher the smaller is the safety premium.

Example of a Forced Conversion

Time Incorporated called its Series C $4.50 cumulative convertible preferred stock for redemption at a price of $54.9375, including accrued dividends. Time used the services of investment bankers to underwrite the call. The issue was convertible into 1.5152 shares of Time common stock at a conversion price of $33.00 per share. The market price of the common stock was $46.375, representing a 40.5 percent premium over the conversion price. Time was paying dividends on its common stock at the rate of $1.00 per share per year. A holder who converted at that time would suffer a decrease in pretax annual security income amounting to $2.98 ($4.50 − (1.5152)[$1.00]) per preferred share. Consequently, few holders had converted voluntarily.

The market value of the common stock provided a redemption cushion over the redemption price amounting to 27.9 percent.[11] This cushion gave holders a strong incentive to convert when Time called the issue. With the assistance of investment bankers, the entire issue was converted.

Convertible Preferred Stock

The main buyers of convertible securities are either entirely tax-exempt investors or those who cannot benefit directly from the corporate 70 percent dividends-received deduction. Consequently, under most market conditions, issuers of convertible securities have been able to obtain essentially the same terms (interest or dividend rate and conversion premium) whether they issued the convertible security as debt or as preferred stock.

Convertible preferred stock is similar to convertible debt; it is preferred stock that is convertible at the holder's option into shares of the issuer's common stock. Issuers who are in a tax-paying position and expect to remain so for a number of years find it cheaper to issue convertible debt than convertible preferred stock. Interest payments are tax deductible, whereas preferred stock dividend payments are not. The tax deductions reduce the cost of capital. Interest deductions are much less valuable to issuers who do not expect to be in a tax-paying position for a number of years. They are worthless if the issuer will never be able to claim them for tax purposes. Thus, in either case, non-tax-paying firms that wish to issue convertible securities issue convertible preferred stock.

Convertible preferred stock is usually perpetual, whereas convertible debt has a stated maturity and usually has a sinking fund. The rating agencies view perpetual convertible preferred stock as "true" equity for credit rating purposes.

Convertible Securities Innovations

The rapid pace of securities innovation in the past few decades has brought about an explosion in the financial instruments available to financial managers and investors. In chapter 8 we discussed bond innovations. Many of the other innovations in the explosion involve convertible securities, apparently in large measure because of financial contracting considerations. For example, convertible bonds reduce agency costs arising from possible conflicts of interest between stockholders and other security holders, such as the problems of *asset substitution* (noted earlier), *underinvestment*, and *claim dilution*. Table 15.1 describes some of the innovations in convertible securities.

Convertible reset debentures provide for an adjustment in the coupon rate to a current market rate on a specified future date, which protects bondholders against deterioration in the issuer's credit standing prior to the reset date. Such deterioration could result from actions that managers take to increase stockholder value. Certain *puttable convertible bonds* reduce agency costs by giving bondholders the right to put the bonds back to the issuer if there is a change in control of the firm or if the firm increases its leverage above some stated threshold.

Preferred Equity Redemption Cumulative Stock

Preferred equity redemption cumulative stock (PERCS) is a form of convertible preferred stock whose conversion feature differs from a traditional convertible preferred stock. Conversion of PERCS into common stock is mandatory, not voluntary, and the option is European, not American. It is initially at the money because PERCS convert share for share. However, there is a cap on the payoff. The issuing firm can call them for redemption prior to maturity, and the holder must surrender them for the cash redemption price, even if the price of the common stock exceeds the redemption price.

The issuing firm holds the option, and conversion is ultimately mandatory. Therefore, referring to PERCS as a convertible security is actually somewhat of a misnomer. The contract is in fact more like a futures contract for common stock from a PERCS holder's viewpoint. The PERCS holder has essentially purchased the common stock to be delivered at a future (but not absolutely certain) date.

PERCS pay a higher dividend rate than the underlying common stock. Investors must decide whether the extra dividend amount adequately compensates for the cap on the payoff.[12] Later we describe how PERCS have been used to reduce the disruptive effects of a dividend cut.

Table 15.1 Selected Convertible Debt and Preferred Stock Innovations

Security □ Distinguishing Characteristics ● Enhanced Liquidity ○ Reduction in Transaction Costs	■ Year First Issued □ Risk Reallocation ● Reduction in Agency Costs ○ Tax and Other Benefits	■ Number of Issues	■ Aggregate Proceeds ($billions)
■ **ABC Securities** □ Non-interest-bearing convertible debt issue on which the dividends on the underlying common stock are passed through to bondholders if the common stock price rises by more than a specified percentage (typically around 30%) from the date of issuance.	■ 02/06/91 ○ If issue converts, the issuer will have sold, in effect, tax deductible common equity. If holders convert, entire debt service stream is converted to common equity.	■ 2	■ 0.4
■ **Adjustable-Rate Convertible Debt** □ Debt with interest rate that varies directly with the dividend rate on the underlying common stock. No conversion premium at issuance.	■ 04/18/84 ○ Effectively, tax deductible common equity. Security has since been ruled equity by the IRS. Portion of each bond recorded as equity on the issuer's balance sheet.	■ 3	■ 0.4
■ **Cash-Redeemable LYONs** □ Non-interest-bearing convertible debt issue that is redeemable in cash for the value of the underlying common stock, at issuer's option.	■ 06/20/90 ○ If issue converts, the issuer will have sold, in effect, tax deductible common equity. Issuer does not have to have its equity ownership interest diluted through conversion.	■ 1	■ 0.9
■ **Cash-Settled Convertible Notes** □ Issuer pays the value of the underlying common stock in cash when the holder tenders shares for exchange. ○ Holders save on the cost of having to sell their common stock when they want cash.	■ 07/13/89	■ 8	■ 2.7
■ **Conversion Price Reset Notes/Premium Adjustable Notes** □ The conversion price adjusts downward on one or more specified dates if the market price of the underlying common stock is below the conversion price. It cannot be adjusted upward but is subject to a floor.	■ 07/13/88 □ The reset feature at least partially protects investors if the managers take actions that diminish the firm's value. Cutting the strike price restores (part of) the value of the conversion option.	■ 3	■ 0.8

(continued)

Table 15.1 (continued)

■ Security	■ Year First Issued	■ Number of Issues	■ Aggregate Proceeds ($billions)
□ Distinguishing Characteristics	□ Risk Reallocation		
● Enhanced Liquidity	● Reduction in Agency Costs		
○ Reduction in Transaction Costs	○ Tax and Other Benefits		

■ **Convertible-Exchangeable Preferred Stock** — 12/15/82 — ■ 180 — ■ 16.4

□ Convertible preferred stock that is exchangeable, at the issuer's option, for convertible debt with identical rate and identical conversion terms.

○ Issuer can exchange debt for the preferred when it becomes taxable with interest rate the same as the dividend rate and without any change in conversion features. Appears as equity on the issuer's balance sheet until it is exchanged for convertible debt.

○ No need to reissue convertible security as debt—just exchange it—when the issuer becomes a taxpayer.

■ **Convertible Interest-Rate-Reset Debentures** — 10/13/83 — ■ 8 — ■ 0.6

□ Convertible bond with an interest rate that must be adjusted upward, if necessary, 2 years after issuance by an amount sufficient to give the debentures a market value equal to their face amount.

○ Investor is protected against a deterioration in the issuer's credit quality or financial prospects within 2 years of issuance.

■ **Convertible Monthly Income Preferred Securities (MIPS)** — 03/22/94 — ■ 27 — ■ 5.5

□ Long-term convertible subordinated debt is issued to a trust or a special-purpose company wholly owned by the parent. This entity issues cash-matching convertible preferred stock that pays dividends monthly. The parent can defer interest payments for up to 5 years without triggering a default, but interest compounds during the deferral period.

□ Investors bear more credit risk than a conventional subordinated debt issue would involve but the issuer gets some "equity" credit from the rating agencies.

○ Parent company can deduct the interest payments on the underlying subordinated debt.

■ **Debt with Mandatory Common Stock Purchase Contracts** — 04/22/82 — ■ 4 — ■ 0.7

□ Notes with contracts that obligate note purchasers to buy sufficient common stock from the issuer to retire the issue in full by its scheduled maturity date.

○ Notes provide a stream of interest tax shields, which (true) equity does not. Commercial bank holding companies have issued it because it counted as "primary capital" for regulatory purposes.

■ **Dividend-Enhanced Convertible Stock (DECS)/PRIDES** — 06/30/93 — ■ 59 — ■ 12.0

□ Preferred stock that pays a cash dividend significantly above that on the underlying common stock's capital appreciation potential in return for an enhanced dividend rate. Differs from PERCS because there is no cap on the upside potential.

□ Investor trades off a portion of the underlying common stock's capital appreciation potential in exchange for a conversion option and a requirement to convert no later than 4 years after issuance.

Equity-Commitment Notes
■ N/A ■ N/A

□ The bank or bank holding company issuer commits to refund the notes with securities that qualify as primary capital.
  ○ At one time, the notes were treated as bank capital for regulatory purposes. The bank (or parent) realized tax deductible capital.

Equity-Contract Notes
■ 02/21/96 ■ 4 ■ 0.3

□ Notes that obligate investors contractually to convert the notes into the bank's or its parent's common stock.
  ○ The issuer avoids the equity market risk inherent in waiting to issue common stock.
  ○ The issuer saves the transaction costs of issuing the common stock in a separate transaction.
  ○ At one time, the notes were treated as bank capital for regulatory purposes. The bank (or parent) realized tax deductible capital.

Equity-Index-Linked Notes/Upside Note Securities
■ 10/22/92 ■ 18 ■ 2.0

□ The interest payments or principal payments, or both, are indexed to a specified equity index or basket of equity securities. The dividend rate can exceed the blended dividend rate of the underlying equities.
  ○ Securities reduce the investors' risk exposure by furnishing part of the return as enhanced dividends, diversifying the equity risk, and providing downside protection in the form of principal repayment.
  ○ The securities provide some diversification and downside protection more cheaply than retail investors could achieve it on their own.
  ○ The structured notes enable investors who cannot invest directly in the underlying equity securities to invest indirectly.

Exchangeable Auction-Rate Preferred Stock/Remarketed Preferred Stock
■ 02/12/88 ■ 8 ■ 0.4

□ Auction-rate preferred stock or remarketed preferred stock that is exchangeable on any dividend payment date, at the option of the issuer, for auction-rate notes, the interest rate on which is reset by Dutch auction every 35 days.
  ○ Issuer bears more interest rate risk than a fixed-rate instrument would involve.
  ○ Issuer can exchange notes for the preferred when it becomes taxable. Appears as equity on the issuer's balance sheet until it is exchanged for auction-rate notes.
● Security is designed to trade near its par value.
  ○ Issuance of auction-rate notes involves no underwriting commissions.

Liquid Yield Option Notes (LYONs)/Zero-Coupon Convertible Debt
■ 04/12/85 ■ 154 ■ 46.7

□ Non-interest-bearing convertible debt issue.
  ○ If issue converts, the issuer will have sold, in effect, tax deductible equity. If holders convert, entire debt service stream converts to common equity

Preferred Equity Redemption Cumulative Stock (PERCS)/Mandatory Conversion Premium Dividend Preferred Stock
■ 06/26/91 ■ 45 ■ 14.9

□ Preferred stock that pays a cash dividend significantly above that on the underlying common stock in exchange for a conversion option that has a capped share value and requires conversion no later than 3 years after issuance.
  ○ Investor trades off a portion of the underlying common stock's capital appreciation potential in return for an enhanced dividend rate.

(continued)

Table 15.1 (continued)

■ Security ■ Distinguishing Characteristics □ Enhanced Liquidity ○ Reduction in Transaction Costs	■ Year First Issued □ Risk Reallocation ● Reduction in Agency Costs ○ Tax and Other Benefits	■ Number of Issues	■ Aggregate Proceeds (\$billions)
■ **Puttable Convertible Bonds** □ Convertible bond that can be redeemed prior to maturity, at the option of the holder, on certain specified dates at specified prices.	■ 07/21/82 ● Issuer is exposed to risk that the bonds will be redeemed early if interest rates rise sufficiently or common stock price falls sufficiently. Investor has one or more put options, which provide protection against deterioration in credit quality.	■ 1,444	■ 133.8
■ **Synthetic Convertible Securities** □ Issuer sells units consisting of subordinated discount notes and warrants that have the same risk-return characteristics as a conventional convertible bond. The synthetic convertible securities may be either coupon bearing or zero coupon.	■ N/A □ Investors can sell the debt and warrants separately, or they can alter the mix of debt and warrants to tailor the package to suit their individual preferences. ○ The structure enables the issuer to realize larger interest expense deductions than a traditional convertible because the discount can be amortized for income tax purposes. The ability to separate the debt and warrants appeals to a broader market than traditional buyers of convertibles, resulting in better pricing.	■ N/A	■ N/A
■ **Zero-Premium Exchangeable Notes** □ Notes that are exchangeable for another firm's common stock, at the holder's option, without any conversion premium. Interest can be deferred for up to five years without triggering default, but interest compounds during the deferral period. Holders can put the notes to the issuer at 95% of the market value of the underlying shares. ● Put option could improve liquidity.	■ 09/15/99 ○ Under the tax regulations pertaining to contingent-payment debt instruments, the issuer can claim interest deductions based on the (much higher) "comparable yield" at which it could sell conventional fixed-rate straight debt. A firm can use a stock investment it does not want to sell immediately to support a long-term debt issue at a relatively low interest rate.	■ 1	■ 1.0

Source: John D. Finnerty, "An Overview of Corporate Securities Innovation," *Journal of Applied Corporate Finance* 4 (Winter 1992), p. 36; Thomson Financial Securities Data.

Convertibles and Taxes

Many of the convertible security innovations involve a form of tax arbitrage because 80 percent to 90 percent of convertible bond investors are tax-exempt. The tax motive is especially clear in the case of *convertible-exchangeable preferred stock*. This security is attractive to corporations that are not currently in an income tax–paying position but may be in the future. It starts out as convertible perpetual preferred stock, but the issuer has the option to exchange the preferred for an issue of convertible subordinated debt with the same conversion terms and an interest rate that equals the dividend rate on the convertible preferred. Preferred stock dividends are not a tax deductible expense, whereas interest payments on debt are tax deductible. The exchange feature, then, enables the issuer to reissue the convertible preferred stock as convertible debt should the firm reach sufficient profitability to begin paying income taxes. Not surprisingly, a large volume of such securities have been issued by firms that were not at the time paying federal income taxes. Similarly, *exchangeable auction-rate preferred stock* permits the issuer to exchange auction-rate notes for auction-rate preferred stock on any dividend payment date.

Adjustable-rate convertible debt was a thinly disguised attempt to package equity as debt. The coupon rate varied directly with the dividend rate on the underlying common stock, and there was no conversion premium (at the time the debt was issued). After just three issues, the IRS ruled that the security is equity for tax purposes, thereby denying the interest deductions. Not surprisingly, the security has not been issued since that ruling.

Zero-coupon convertible debt, which includes *liquid yield option notes* (LYONs) and *ABC securities*, represents a variation on the same theme. If the issue is converted, both interest and principal are converted to common equity, in which case the issuer will have effectively sold common equity with a tax-deductibility feature.

Debt and warrants (exercisable into the issuer's common stock) can be combined to create *synthetic convertible debt,* with features that mirror those of conventional convertible debt.[13] Synthetic convertible debt has a tax advantage over a comparable convertible debt issue because, in effect, the warrant proceeds are deductible for tax purposes over the life of the debt issue.

Meeting Regulatory Restrictions

Banks have issued *capital notes* because they can be substituted for equity (subject to certain restrictions) for regulatory purposes while still generating the normal interest tax deductions provided by debt. For example, prior to the passage of the Financial Institutions Reform, Recovery and Enforcement Act of 1989, banks issued interest-deductible debt with mandatory common stock purchase contracts (which qualified as primary capital for regulatory purposes because conversion was mandatory).[14]

An Example Using a Securities Innovation

One innovative security we have described, PERCS, was created to help a corporation deal with the otherwise disruptive effects of reducing its dividend payout. At the same time the firm announced a reduction of its dividend payout, stockholders were offered the alternative of exchanging their shares for PERCS. Since then, the security has been used in similar situations by other corporations.

Dividend Policy

The impact of dividend policy on firm value has been extensively examined, especially since Miller and Modigliani's demonstration of its irrelevance in a perfect capital market environment.[15] As with other aspects of financing, three broad categories of imperfections can cause dividend policy to affect firm value: asymmetric information, asymmetric taxes, and transaction costs. Among these, asymmetric information—specifically the information content of a dividend announcement—is generally believed to have the potential for causing the largest impact on a firm's market value. This is because the so-called *clientele effect* may be able to mitigate much of the impact of asymmetric taxes and transaction costs.

In equilibrium, investors sort themselves into various clientele groups that invest in firms that follow the dividend policy most favorable to the clientele group in terms of taxes and transaction costs. When a firm changes its dividend policy, investors in that group may be forced to incur transaction costs and tax liabilities as they sell their stock in that firm and purchase new shares in firms that have the dividend policy that is best for them.

Corporate dividend policies are notoriously stable, reflecting management's well-known reluctance to cut the dividend. This reluctance has been attributed primarily to two factors: the possible misinterpretation of the information content of a dividend cut and the potential tax liability and transaction costs that those investors incur when they are forced to sell their stock and purchase shares in other firms. But what can a firm do if it believes that cutting its cash dividend payout is a shareholder-wealth-maximizing decision? How can it communicate such a belief most accurately and at the lowest cost? If the dividend cut is perceived negatively, current shareholders would suffer a loss of wealth if they sell shares for less than their true value during the time it takes the market to see that the dividend cut is not negative after all.

Combining a PERCS-for-common exchange offer with a dividend cut can reduce the disruptive effects of a dividend cut for the following reasons:

- It sends a credible positive signal to market participants about the firm's longer-run prospects.

- It offers the option of continued capital gains tax deferral to shareholders who might otherwise sell their common shares and trigger a tax liability.

- It offers the option of lower transaction costs to shareholders who choose to maintain their cash dividend income by exchanging for the PERCS rather than selling their common shares and reinvesting in higher-dividend-paying shares of other firms.

Cutting the Dividend Payout

When a firm cuts its cash dividend payments, it reduces the rate of cash flow from the firm to the shareholders. But a simultaneous PERCS-for-common exchange offer can be structured so as to provide shareholders with the option to continue to receive the same cash dividend payments, at least during the life of the PERCS. If management believes the dividend cut is in the best interest of its shareholders but some shareholders do not agree and do not want the firm to cut their cash dividend payments, those shareholders can opt to have their cash dividend payments continue by exchanging their common shares for PERCS.

With the exchange offer, the firm is offering to buy a call option on the firm's stock. The call option price the firm is offering the exchanging shareholders is the continuation of the higher dividend rate. By making this offer, management is signaling its belief that the call option is worth *at least* the incremental dividends that they are paying for it—and perhaps more. Such a positive signal when management offers shareholders the choice can help reduce the extent of the market's negative reaction to the dividend cut.

A dividend cut may be a significantly more disruptive event than previously thought. Research has found evidence of significant "price recovery" following calls of convertible bonds and dividend cuts.[16] Such findings imply that investors who sell early in the conversion period bear significant "liquidity cost" by selling at what are seen later to be temporarily depressed prices.

Turning to those shareholders who would sell their shares to preserve their dividend income stream, a PERCS-for-common exchange can also lower direct shareholder transaction costs, including capital gains tax liabilities. As a practical matter, some shareholders will choose to sell their shares following the announcement of a dividend cut for reasons such as tax considerations (e.g., the 70 percent dividends-received deduction), legal or policy considerations (e.g., restrictions that limit discretionary spending to current income), cash flow management considerations (e.g., specific future cash timing needs), or (perhaps irrational) individual dividend preference. When a firm cuts its dividend rate, some shareholders will sell their stock and reinvest the funds in other high-dividend-yielding stocks, thereby incurring direct transaction costs. Offering shareholders the opportunity to exchange their common shares on a tax-free basis for PERCS that pay cash dividends at the former common stock dividend rate enables the exchanging shareholders to continue to postpone both sale and reinvestment transaction costs and any capital gains tax liability.

A PERCS-for-Common Exchange Offer

A PERCS-for-common exchange offer can be designed as a non-zero-sum game because of taxes and transaction costs. In particular, the terms can be tailored so as to make exchanging more attractive than selling for at least some shareholders.

A PERCS-for-common exchange offer improves what might be called the "tax efficiency" of the dividend cut by giving taxable shareholders who have a sufficiently low tax basis in their shares and would otherwise sell those shares the opportunity to continue to postpone their capital gains tax liability by exchanging their common shares for PERCS on a tax-free basis. The difference in value between the PERCS and the common shares will determine how the potential tax benefit will be allocated between exchanging and nonexchanging shareholders.

The value of a share of PERCS can be expressed as (1) the value of a share of common stock (for which the PERCS is redeemable on the PERCS maturity date); plus (2) the present value of the stream of incrementally higher dividends the PERCS will provide; minus (3) the value of the call option on the underlying common share (which the issuer has effectively purchased from the PERCS holder). There are two important conditions to meet in this situation. First, the terms must make the value of a PERCS share less than the value of a common share. Otherwise all shareholders would want to exchange, thereby negating the dividend cut. Second, the terms must make the value of the PERCS sufficiently high that a significant number of the shareholders who would otherwise sell their shares are enticed to exchange them instead.

The Avon Case

On June 3, 1988, Avon announced three events simultaneously:

1. A 50 percent reduction in the annual dividend rate on its common stock to $1.00 per share from $2.00 per share (which had prevailed since 1983).

2. An offer to exchange up to 18 million shares of PERCS (which would have a 3.25-year life and pay a $2.00 per share dividend) for shares of its common stock on a share-for-share basis (at the time, Avon had approximately 71 million common shares outstanding, so Avon was offering to exchange PERCS for approximately 25 percent of its common stock).

3. Plans to sell off its subacute health care business and its senior citizen residence business.

The expressed purpose of the exchange offer was "to provide those shareholders whose primary objective is current income with a yield-oriented security."[17] The PERCS were to pay an annual dividend rate of $2.00 per share, the old dividend rate on Avon's common stock. In return for receiving the larger dividend, exchanging shareholders would give Avon a call option on their shares. The call price on the option would be set initially at $34.75 and decline by $0.25 per quarter over the subsequent 3.25 years to $31.50. Avon's common stock was trading at about $24.00 per share at the time of the announcement.

Before the Announcement

Avon's payout ratio was 90 percent in 1986, 89 percent in 1987, and forecasted to be approximately 87 percent in 1988.[18] Although doubts had been raised about whether it would continue to sustain the $2.00

dividend rate, Hicks Waldron, chairman of Avon, had continued to insist publicly, as late as Avon's annual shareholders' meeting held on May 5, 1988, that the $2.00 cash dividend rate was secure.[19] In the light of Avon's announced cut in its dividend rate less than a month later, it seemed that the credibility of Avon's public statements would be suspect. In such an environment and given the empirically observed market reaction to dividend cut announcements by other firms, it would seem likely that Avon's dividend cut announcement would be perceived as significantly negative new information about Avon's future prospects.

Reaction

The two-day announcement period return relative to the S&P 500 index was minus 2.22 percent. Although negative, this decline was significantly smaller in magnitude than what would have been expected if Avon's dividend reduction had not been accompanied by the PERCS exchange offer.[20] Approximately 19 million out of 71 million shares were tendered in response to the exchange offer. Avon then issued 18 million shares of PERCS on a pro rata basis, which began trading on the New York Stock Exchange on July 5, 1988. Clearly the offer was attractive to many Avon shareholders (more than 25 percent of them). For those who wanted to exchange, the tax and transaction cost benefits were attractive. At the same time, the overwhelming majority of Avon common stockholders elected not to exchange. Apparently for them, the call option was worth more than the added dividends.

Life of the Issue

Avon's common stock traded between a low price of 18¾ on November 28, 1988, and a high price of 46⅝ on April 4, 1991. On April 5, 1991, Avon announced a redemption call for the PERCS and redeemed them on June 3, 1991. Avon common stock closed at 46⅝ on April 4, 1991, and at 44¾ on June 3, 1991.

Conclusion

A convertible security is a package of a conventional (nonconvertible) security and an option. Most of its features are like those of the conventional security. In addition, it includes features that make up its option component. The package can be viewed as a debt security plus a call option or, equivalently, as shares of stock plus a put option. Usually the shares are common stock in the issuing firm. Exchangeable debentures are an exception, wherein the shares to be converted into are the common stock of another firm.

Convertible securities may be issued for several different reasons, such as to reduce the impact of differences in risk perceptions, to reduce agency costs, as a deferred sale of common shares, to reduce interest cost, and as an equity kicker. They are typically issued with the option out-of-the-money, but with the expectation that ultimately they will be converted into equity. Firms often force their conversion into equity after the security's market value as stock has risen significantly above (usually by 20 percent or more) its market value as a straight debt security. Conversion is forced by calling the issue.

A number of the many securities innovations in the past few decades have involved convertible securities, apparently in large measure because of considerations involving financial contracting.

Chapter **16**

The Future of
Debt Management

*P*revious chapters have covered the two phases of debt management: (1) the new-issue design decision, that is, design decisions made before the debt is issued and (2) the refunding decision, that is, managerial decisions made after the debt has been issued. Having read this book, we hope you can now appreciate just how multifaceted debt management is and how important effective debt management is for the corporation's financial health and the value of its shareholders' investment. We also hope we have given you some useful insights into how a firm can cost-effectively manage its debt. We are confident the analytical tools we have explained will help you manage your firm's debt.

Debt management is continually evolving. Investment bankers churn out a steady stream of new securities and regularly develop new refunding strategies. You may be involved, or you may become involved, in this process. If you work for a debt issuer, your challenge may be to determine whether one of these new securities or strategies can enable your firm to reduce its cost of debt. Since "new" securities are not always truly innovative and "new" strategies are not always more cost-effective than existing ones, you should evaluate these opportunities critically. Embrace a new security or strategy only if you are comfortable that it will increase shareholder wealth.

Fortunately, this task has become a little easier because the quality of information available in the debt market has improved enormously in recent years, and the cost of obtaining the information you need to apply the techniques discussed in this book has diminished. Data vendors have improved their databases, and the Internet has made an enormous variety of financial and economic data and analytical models more accessible at reasonable cost (although at times we have found the voluminous amount of information almost overwhelming). The problem confronting fixed-income analysts used to be one of finding any information that might help solve a problem. Today it is more likely to be one of sorting through all the available information and separating what is useful from what is not. The insights we have provided in this book should enable you to make that determination.

The Future of Debt Markets

The U.S. Treasury market continues to shrink. The one-year Treasury bill will be retired in 2001, under recently approved legislation, and the issuance of two-year notes and thirty-year bonds will be curtailed sharply. Bond market participants will have to find new pricing benchmarks when the Treasury benchmarks are no longer available. Building on recent developments, we believe that the electronic revolution will continue to have an important impact on the fixed-income market. The electronic marketplace has already arrived. In fact, lots of them have! A recent Bond Market Association report listed thirty-nine separate electronic transaction systems for U.S. fixed-income securities as of November 1999.[1] More have been introduced since that report was written. Corporations, municipalities, and their bankers auction new issues of bonds and commercial paper over the Internet.[2] Similarly, various broker-dealers have begun marketing bonds or commercial paper over the Internet, often in response to pressure from investors who wanted more efficient trading systems.[3] The electronic issuance and trading systems reduce transaction costs, which should improve market liquidity and pricing efficiency.

We believe the electronic revolution will speed up the information revolution, and bond pricing will become more transparent. We do not think it is too far-fetched to think that the bond market will eventually have a consolidated tape, probably electronic, like the one in the equity market, to report transaction prices for the most actively traded bonds.[4] Pricing transparency will improve market efficiency.

The trends we observe domestically—electronic trading, cheaper and more readily available information, pricing transparency, and so on—are proceeding at a rapid pace globally as well. This trend is due in part to the global nature of the information highway. Also, the development of the euro zone has integrated the national European bond markets. The issuance of bonds denominated in euros has exploded, and the euro fixed-income market is growing so fast that it could reach the size of the U.S. bond market in five years.[5] This market provides large firms with the opportunity to sell bonds globally and is a viable alternative to issuing bonds denominated in U.S. dollars.

We also expect that the emerging markets will spawn new local debt markets just as they have spawned the development of local equity markets. These local markets grow as the economies develop and wealth builds; they reallocate capital (locally) from savers to investors. Viable corporate fixed-income markets already exist in Brazil, India, Korea, Mexico, Trinidad and Tobago, and several other emerging-market countries. More will develop.

The Future of Securitization

The securitization of a diverse array of asset cash flow streams has been one of the most significant innovative forces shaping the capital markets over the past three decades. Securitization has transformed residential and commercial mortgages and home equity loans into mortgage-backed bonds; automobile, truck, and credit card receivables into asset-backed bonds; and lease payments, franchise fees, music royalties, and a variety of other nontraded cash flow streams into tradable bonds. Such securitization can enhance liquidity, permit better portfolio diversification, and facilitate more efficient risk allocations. As we have noted, investment bankers are continually on the lookout for new assets or liabilities to securitize, so we expect this trend to continue.

The most readily securitizable assets have been securitized, and the markets for securitized residential mortgages, home equity loans, automobile and truck loans, and credit card receivables have matured. And securitization has spread globally. Nevertheless, there are undoubtedly additional asset classes that can be securitized. For example, in 1992, securitization spread to property catastrophe insurance as a means of deepening the pool of risk capital available to the property and casualty reinsurance industry. The development of property catastrophe securitization instruments began with the property catastrophe options that are currently traded on the Chicago Board Options Exchange. They were followed by private, and then public, issues of catastrophe bonds (also called act-of-God bonds), which were followed next by contingent surplus notes, and finally by property catastrophe swaps.[6] The evolution of this class of reinsurance products suggests that there may be additional types of insurance that can be securitized.

Securitization will also develop further outside the United States. Securitization in the foreign markets has generally lagged behind the

United States because investment bankers have discovered that differences in the structure of assets (such as U.K. mortgages as compared to U.S. mortgages) or unfavorable local laws (such as French laws that discouraged the securitization of residential mortgages and for a time prohibited the securitization of credit card receivables) have required significant financial reengineering of products or changes in law before securitization could take place.[7] As these hurdles are overcome, securitization will spread to new asset classes and new markets.

The Future of Securities Innovation

Investment bankers find it profitable to develop new securities and new derivative instruments. It is easier to secure the underwriting mandate when the banker has developed an innovative security that a firm is interested in issuing. In addition, new products tend to permit wider profit margins than established products. Thus, investment bankers have a strong financial incentive to innovate.

Prospective debt issuers are often bombarded with new securities ideas. How can a firm decide whether a new design is better than existing alternatives? A new security may be different, but is it really better for the issuer's shareholders?

Here is a checklist of important considerations for corporate treasurers in evaluating the issuance of new bonds (or preferred stock):

- How do the new bond's features differ from the features of the most closely comparable conventional fixed-income securities?

- How will interest (or dividend) and principal payments vary under different interest rate conditions? If the interest (or dividend) or principal payments depend on exchange rates, commodity prices, or some other general economic variable, how do the debt service requirements vary under different scenarios?

- Under what circumstances might the holders be able to force redemption to their advantage and the issuer's disadvantage? Will the issuer be adequately compensated for bearing the early redemption risk?

- Under what circumstances might the issuer be able to force redemption to its advantage and the investors' disadvantage? Is such a call option worth more or less to the issuer than what investors will charge for it? Alternatively, will the new security limit the issuer's flexibility more than conventional securities—

and if so, will it reduce the issuer's cost sufficiently to compensate for the reduced flexibility?

- Are there any unusual covenants or other restrictions on the issuer's operating or financial flexibility relative to conventional securities? If so, will the issuer be fully compensated?

- Does the new security entail any sort of risk shifting when compared to conventional fixed-income securities? If so, does this risk shifting work to the issuer's advantage? For example, does it appreciably reduce the risk of financial distress, and if so, are investors charging a lower interest rate to reflect this reduced risk?

- Does the new security enhance investors' liquidity by making it publicly marketable or by broadening the base of investors? And if so, does the reduction in interest costs resulting from greater liquidity outweigh the expected cost of the resulting reduction in the firm's ability to reorganize its more dispersed claims in the event of financial distress?

- How do the underwriting spread and other issuance costs compare to the cost of issuing conventional fixed-income securities?

- Does the new security confer tax benefits or impose tax liabilities on either the issuer or investors as compared to conventional fixed-income securities? If there is a significant net tax advantage, does it involve significant risk that the IRS will disallow the intended tax treatment?

- Are there any significant regulatory benefits or costs?

- Are there accounting considerations? Will such considerations benefit shareholders?

- On balance, will issuing the new security add sufficiently more to shareholder value than the available alternatives to justify the risk inherent in issuing an unfamiliar security? Or can comparable benefits be obtained by using a simpler, more conventional securities design?

The Future of Fixed-Income Derivatives and Hedging

While the asset-backed securities markets were developing, investment bankers were introducing a variety of new currency, interest rate, commodity, equity, credit, weather, energy, and other derivative instruments. Additional classes of derivatives are undoubtedly under development. New derivative instruments create additional opportunities for hedging different types of risk. Such instruments have the potential to alter fundamentally how these risks are priced; they allow the financial markets to reallocate risk exposures to market participants who are best equipped to handle them; and they permit investors to diversify their risk exposures more efficiently.

Among the fastest-growing derivatives markets is the market for credit derivatives, which approximated $1 trillion in outstanding notional amount at year-end 2000. These are especially difficult instruments to price because the underlying quantity is not the price of a traded security or the value of an index based on such prices. Better credit information, improved valuation technology, and the recent availability of standardized documentation from the International Swaps and Derivatives Association have significantly reduced transaction costs and spurred the growth of this market.

Derivatives use will continue to grow. These instruments are very useful financial tools, and their variety will expand as market participants identify additional risks they wish to hedge and as investment bankers respond to this market demand by crafting new and more effective hedging vehicles.

The Future of Innovative Corporate Finance Strategies

Investment bankers, tax lawyers, and accountants have been almost relentless in their search for more tax-efficient refunding strategies. As the tax laws or accounting rules change and eliminate one strategy, the search for the next-generation strategy is often already under way. The history of strategies designed to refund discounted debt without triggering income tax on the gain and then strategies for refunding high-coupon debt without triggering a loss for financial reporting purposes illustrates this regulatory dialectic.

The Importance of Active Debt Management

Active debt management is important. A corporation can lower its cost of debt and increase shareholder wealth by managing its debt obligations effectively. This process includes identifying and exploiting profitable opportunities to (1) call and refund outstanding high-coupon debt (as well as preferred stock) issues, (2) reacquire and refund discounted debt issues, (3) increase the amount of sinking-fund payments when that option is available, and (4) prepurchase future sinking-fund requirements at a discount.

The profitability of refunding high-coupon debt stems chiefly from the call option, which entitles the issuer to call the bonds away from holders at a fixed price, and from the tax deductibility of the reacquisition premium (by call or market repurchase). The profitability of refunding discounted debt, on the other hand, results from increasing the proportion of debt service payments that are tax deductible. In both cases, the basic analytical approach to evaluating the refunding opportunity is the same: discount the change in after-tax debt service payments at the after-tax cost of money for a comparable new debt issue, and subtract the after-tax costs and expenses associated with the refunding.

Under certain circumstances, refunding discounted debt can enhance shareholder wealth through a form of tax arbitrage. Refunding a corporation's discounted debt obligations can benefit both bondholders and shareholders by reducing their aggregate tax liability when the corporation and its bondholders pay income tax at different marginal rates. However, bondholders and shareholders will realize these benefits only if the value of the reduction in aggregate tax liability exceeds the costs of the refunding, including any tax liability on the gain. Repeated changes in federal tax law have made it increasingly difficult to refund discounted debt profitably, at least in the United States.

The existence of a sinking fund makes the refunding analysis more complex but creates profitable opportunities for the issuer. Debt issues generally do not have to be called in their entirety, and publicly held debt issues typically give the corporation a valuable delivery option. When interest rates are comparatively low, it may be more profitable for a corporation to call only part of an issue and retire the balance through the sinking fund. When interest rates are comparatively high, it may be more profitable for the issuer to buy bonds at a discount in anticipation of future sinking-fund requirements rather than wait until the sinking-fund date to buy bonds or redeem them at par. Active sinking-fund management involves elements of both option strategy and game theory, making it one of the more challenging aspects of corporate financial management.

Regulation of the issuer adds further complexity. A regulated firm undertaking a refunding should ensure that those who will benefit from it—its rate payers—also will bear all the costs of refunding.

Unfortunately, under traditional rate base regulation, shareholders subsidize the refunding. Such subsidization can be mitigated by either including the unamortized premium in the firm's rate base or appropriately adjusting both the debt ratio and the cost of debt to reflect the unamortized premium.

Defeasance is a relatively new form of debt extinguishment available to taxable issuers. Municipalities have long used legal defeasance to refund high-coupon debt by effectively accelerating the benefits of a fixed-price call option. In the 1980s, in-substance defeasance emerged as a means of extinguishing discounted corporate debt, although the debt was extinguished for financial reporting purposes only. In-substance defeasance enabled an issuer to avoid the tax liability to which a cash repurchase of the debt or a stock-for-debt swap would give rise. Although the accounting rules have changed and in-substance defeasance no longer produces the favorable accounting treatment that made it popular, a similar strategy can be used to advance refund corporate debt in special situations where bondholders refuse to sell their bonds at an acceptable price.

Any proposed debt refunding should be analyzed on an after-tax basis, with all financial structure side effects neutralized. Certain refunding transactions are desirable principally because of their tax advantages. The recently developed par-for-par debt exchange is one such example. To determine whether a proposed refunding would truly benefit the firm's shareholders, you must understand its tax consequences and assess its true profitability, as distinct from the purely accounting benefits. The analytical frameworks developed in this book will enable you to make such determinations.

The Future of Fixed-Income Valuation

Fixed-income valuation technology has undergone significant improvements in recent years. Financial engineers have developed new valuation models that accommodate the jump processes and fat tails we observe empirically in bond rate of return probability distributions. Improved models are also being developed to handle default risk and mortgage prepayment risk more accurately. The former class of models will help promote the fast-growing market for credit derivatives.

The electronic revolution has three important modeling implications. First, the greater availability—and reliability—of data facilitates model development because models can be tested more thoroughly. Second, the greater availability of real-time prices enables market participants to calibrate their models more accurately and more regularly. Third, the Internet significantly improves access to the latest valuation technology because much of it is posted on university or vendor Web sites.

We believe that valuation technology will continue to improve, although many of the most sophisticated models are likely to remain proprietary to securities firms. A successful modeler can earn substantial arbitrage profits if a new model identifies significant mispricing. The large broker-dealers try to spot these opportunities in their proprietary trading activities. This opportunity to earn an arbitrage profit provides a strong incentive that drives the search for better valuation models.

A Final Word

With the fast pace of change taking place in the fixed-income market, we think that it is a good place to be if you are looking for exciting challenges and potentially rewarding opportunities.

Notes

Chapter 1

1. F. Norris, "After 114 Years, It's Payday," *New York Times,* July 1, 1995, p. 33, recounts the history of the bonds.

2. The bondholders nearly got a windfall, however. Like virtually all other bonds issued at the time, the Atchison, Topeka and Sante Fe 4s of 95 were gold bonds, which promised to pay in "gold coin of the United States of the present standard of weight and fineness, or its equivalent." The "present standard" in 1895 valued gold at just $20.67 per ounce. The price of gold in July 1995 was about $385.00 per ounce, making each bond worth $18,626, or more than eighteen times its face amount. Unfortunately for the bondholders, Congress declared gold payment contractual obligations invalid in 1933, and the U.S. Supreme Court upheld the decision in a five-to-four vote in 1935. But for one vote the bonds would have been worth a lot more than their face amount.

3. Some foreign countries permit perpetual bonds to qualify for interest tax deductions. As discussed in chapter 6, Congress has considered eliminating the tax deductibility of interest payments for bonds with very long maturities. Also, bonds can satisfy the fixed-maturity requirement by giving the bondholders the right to force the issuer to redeem the bonds (a put option) on a specified date rather than requiring an unqualified repayment.

4. As of this writing, final regulations under Section 385 of the Internal Revenue Code have yet to be issued.

5. There were five-year issues in U.S. dollars, Japanese yen, German marks, and euros; ten-year issues in dollars and euros; and thirty-year issues in dollars and marks. The mix of maturities and currencies was designed to appeal to a clientele large enough to buy $14.6 billion in bonds.

6. In addition, states with income taxes usually exclude from state income taxation the interest on bonds issued by local governments and their agencies located within the state.

7. We do not discuss bond investment strategies but there are other good books on the subject. For example, see F. J. Fabozzi, *Bond Markets: Analysis and Strategies,* 4th ed. (Upper Saddle River, NJ: Prentice Hall Business Publishing, 2000).

8. Banks must maintain capital equal to 8 percent of their total assets. The so-called risk-based capital rules risk-weight each bank's loans and other assets according to their riskiness (as perceived by the bank regulators). A loan to a corporation carries a 100 percent risk weighting, which means that the bank must hold capital equal to $8 for every $100 of such loans. Mortgage loans carry a 50 percent risk weighting ($4 for every $100), federal agency mortgage-backed securities a 20 percent risk weighting, loans to high-grade banks a 20 percent risk weighting, and Treasury securities or

a loan to an Organization for Economic Cooperation and Development member government a zero risk weighting.

9. See S. McGee, "Corporate Bonds Set to Blossom in a New Europe," *Wall Street Journal*, July 22, 1998, pp. C1, C23.

10. See M. R. Sesit, "Olivetti Plans Big Bond Issue to Fund Bid for Telecom," *Wall Street Journal*, May 11, 1999, p. A17.

11. See M. R. Sesit, "Euro Secures Big Role in International Finance Despite Weakness Against the Dollar and Yen," *Wall Street Journal*, January 4, 2000, p. A17.

12. In September 1999, Ecuador became the first Brady bond issuer to default.

13. See G. Zuckerman, "Bond Dealers Set Up Interdealer-Broker Venture," *Wall Street Journal*, June 25, 1999, p. C19.

14. *Bond Markets: Beta Test Set for Corporate Bond Price Transparency Product* (New York: Bond Market Association, March 16, 1999).

15. See *The 1998 Review of Electronic Transaction Systems in the U.S. Fixed Income Securities Markets* (New York: Bond Market Association, 1998), and *eCommerce in the U.S. Fixed Income Markets: The 1999 Review of Electronic Transaction Systems* (New York: Bond Market Association, November 1999).

16. See G. Zuckerman, "Trading Bonds Online Slowly Catches On," *Wall Street Journal*, April 26, 1999, pp. C1, C18.

17. Ibid.

18. Ibid.

19. Ibid.

Chapter 2

1. APY stands for *annual percentage yield,* the legal term for what was commonly called the effective annual rate of return. The term *APY* was coined in 1993 in the so-called Regulation Z.

2. It used to be the interest rate that banks charged their largest, most creditworthy customers. Currently, however, banks often lend to their best customers at below prime rate.

3. A credit swap is a form of insurance. A bank can buy a credit swap and transfer the risk of such things as default or a rating downgrade to some other entity. A credit swap is an example of a class of derivative instruments known as credit derivatives. Credit derivatives are described in J. D. Finnerty, *Credit Derivatives: Introduction to the Mechanics* (New York: PricewaterhouseCoopers LLP, 1999).

4. In a leasing agreement that was later highly publicized, the U.S. Navy leased a fleet of oil tankers instead of getting congressional approval to finance them.

5. NAIC-2 generally corresponds to a Moody's rating of Baa and an S&P rating of BBB. NAIC-1 generally corresponds to debt rated A or higher. S&P used to have a separate rating system for private debt placements but recently phased it out; it now uses the same rating system for public and private debt.

6. A qualified institutional buyer (QIB) is a financial institution (e.g., an insurance company or a bank) that invests for its own account (or for the account of other QIBs) on a discretionary basis at least $100 million ($10

million in the case of registered securities dealers) in qualifying securities (generally consisting of money market instruments, Treasury securities, and publicly traded stocks and bonds of other firms with which it is not affiliated). Individuals are not eligible as QIBs. There are roughly 150 reasonably active QIBs in the United States that trade more than $100 billion of unregistered corporate debt securities each year.

7. A sale in compliance with Rule 144A must satisfy four basic criteria. See J. P. Forrester, "Terms and Structure of Debt Instruments Issued to Finance Infrastructure Projects," in *Innovative Financing for Infrastructure Roundtable* (Washington, D.C.: Inter-American Development Bank, October 23, 1995). Most important, the securities can be offered for sale only to QIBs.

8. The securities laws in jurisdictions outside the United States generally require less extensive disclosures than do the U.S. securities laws.

9. See G. Zuckerman, "Privately Placed Junk Bonds Pass Public Offerings," *Wall Street Journal*, November 18, 1996, pp. C1, C16.

10. Ibid.

11. The Employee Retirement Income Security Act (ERISA) is intended to ensure that employees receive the pension and other benefits promised by their employers. ERISA requires pension fund managers to make "prudent" investments.

Chapter 3

1. The Securities Act of 1933 (the 1933 Act) and its related rules regulate interstate issues of securities. All the states have their own laws to regulate intrastate securities issues. An offering limited to one state only is registered with the state securities department rather than the SEC. In addition, each state's "blue sky" laws regulate the sale of any securities (including SEC registered) within that state.

2. There are some exemptions from this requirement. Note 1 mentioned the intrastate exemption. There is a commercial paper exemption for notes that will mature within 270 days of issue. There is also a small-issue exemption. Regulation A under the 1933 Act provides for an abbreviated offering statement when the issue will raise no more than $1.5 million.

3. AT&T Capital Corporation, $500,000,000 8.25 Percent Senior Public Income NotES (PINES^SM) due 2028, prospectus, November 4, 1998.

4. See C. Valenti, "Corporate Issues Tailored to Individual Investors Prove Popular, and Profitable, in Tough Times," *Wall Street Journal*, November 12, 1998, p. C19.

5. Ibid.

6. See S. Biswas, "Benchmark Notes Become Popular with Investors, Offering Another Alternative to Treasury Bonds," *Wall Street Journal*, March 9, 1998, p. C19.

7. Early indications are favorable. Ibid. Investors appear to accept benchmark notes and similar securities as reasonably close substitutes for Treasury bonds for benchmarking purposes.

8. See G. Zuckerman, "Ford Motor Credit to Become a Regular Issuer of Corporate Bonds, Cutting the Costs of Its Debt," *Wall Street Journal*, June 4, 1999, p. C17.

9. D. S. Allen, R. E. Lamy, and G. R. Thompson, "The Shelf Registration of Debt and Self-Selection Bias," *Journal of Finance* 45 (1990): 275–288.

10. D. W. Blackwell, M. W. Marr, and M. F. Spivey, "Shelf Registration and the Reduced Due Diligence Argument: Implications of the Underwriter Certification and the Implicit Insurance Hypotheses," *Journal of Financial and Quantitative Analysis* 25 (1990): 245–259; A. Sherman, "Underwriter Certification and the Effect of Shelf-Registration on Due Diligence," *Financial Management* 28, no. 1 (1999): 5–19.

11. L. Shayam-Sunder, "The Stock Price Effect of Risky versus Safe Debt," *Journal of Financial and Quantitative Analysis* 26 (1991): 549–558.

12. Allen, Lamy, and Thompson, "The Shelf Registration of Debt and Self-Selection Bias," and Blackwell, Marr, and Spivey, "Shelf Registration and the Reduced Due Diligence Argument."

13. The agent in a private placement does not actually purchase and resell the securities.

14. C. W. Smith, Jr., "Investment Banking and the Capital Acquisition Process," *Journal of Financial Economics* 15 (1986): 3–29.

15. C. W. Smith, Jr., and J. B. Warner, "On Financial Contracting: An Analysis of Bond Covenants," *Journal of Financial Economics* 7 (1979): 117–161.

16. S. H. Szewczyk and R. Varma, "Raising Capital with Private Placement of Debt," *Journal of Financial Research* 14 (1991): 1–14; L. P. Fields and E. L. Mais, "The Valuation Effects of Private Placements of Convertible Debt," *Journal of Finance* 46 (1991): 1925–1932; and K. H. Wruck, "Equity Ownership Concentration and Firm Value: Evidence from Private Equity Financings," *Journal of Financial Economics* 23 (1989): 3–28.

17. S. C. Gilson, K. John, and L. H. P. Lang, "Troubled Debt Restructuring," *Journal of Financial Economics* 27 (1990): 315–353.

18. P. Asquith, R. Gertner, and D. Scharfstein, "Anatomy of Financial Distress: An Examination of Junk-Bond Issuers," working paper, MIT Sloan School of Management, 1991.

19. Gilson, John, and Lang, "Troubled Debt Restructuring."

20. Asquith, Gertner, and Scharfstein, "Anatomy of Financial Distress."

21. R. G. Rajan, "Insiders and Outsiders: The Choice Between Informed and Arm's-Length Debt," *Journal of Finance* 47 (1992): 1367–1400.

22. J. C. Easterwood and P. Kadapakkam, "The Role of Private and Public Debt in Corporate Capital Structure," *Financial Management* 20, no. 3 (1991): 49–57.

23. D. W. Blackwell and D. S. Kidwell, "An Investigation of Cost Differences Between Public Sales and Private Placements of Debt," *Journal of Financial Economics* 22 (1988): 253–278.

24. Blackwell and Kidwell's study (ibid.) predates by several years the widespread usage of the shelf registration procedure, which began in 1992. Their sample consists of 293 public utility bond issues sold between June 1979 and December 1983. To the extent the shelf registration procedure reduces transaction costs, we would expect greater reliance on public offerings after this procedure became available.

25. Citigroup Inc., $750,000,000 5.80 Percent Notes due 2004 and $750,000,000 6.20 Percent Notes due 2009, prospectus, March 26, 1999.

Chapter 4

1. M. S. Fridson, *Extra Credit: The Journal of Global High Yield Bond Research* (New York: Merrill Lynch, January–February 2000), has excellent updates on the high-yield market.
2. Ibid., p. 60.
3. Telecommunications debt made up more than 17 percent of the high-yield bond market as of year-end 1999. Ibid.
4. The bond indenture often permits a special call if the issuer raises common equity capital. This "equity clawback" feature usually allows the firm to call some portion of the bonds (usually between one-quarter and one-third) during the call grace period but requires a steep call premium.
5. PIK securities are frequently issued by firms emerging from bankruptcy. The PIK period usually lasts three to five years.
6. In this regard, PIK securities are similar to preferred stock, which is discussed in chapter 14.
7. The IRNs have a basic flaw. The increasing-rate feature can increase the investors' default risk exposure because the higher interest rate makes it harder for the firm to meet its interest obligations. If the refinancing cannot take place, for example, because the firm's prospects failed to improve as expected, the IRNs can intensify the firm's problems. As a result, IRNs have virtually disappeared from the market.
8. In many cases, a specified set of investment banks were given responsibility for determining the fair market interest rate.
9. If the reset notes are designed like IRNs but with the interest rate increase based on dealer quotes instead of by formula, reset notes can intensify a firm's credit problems even faster than IRNs. Because of this, few high-yield extendable or reset notes remain outstanding.
10. QIBs are financial institutions that have $100 million or more invested in securities. They can freely trade unregistered securities with each other.
11. This process could take four weeks for a below-investment-grade debt issue. As an alternative to registering the securities, the issuer often commits to exchange them for registered securities as soon as it can effect registration.
12. Fridson, *Extra Credit*, p. 14.
13. Ibid., p. 17. Fridson cites data produced by Edward I. Altman of the Salomon Center at New York University. See also W. B. Hickman, *Corporate Bond Quality and Investor Experience* (Princeton, NJ: Princeton University Press, 1958).
14. E. I. Altman, "Measuring Corporate Bond Mortality and Performance," *Journal of Finance* 44 (September 1989): 909–922; P. Asquith, D. W. Mullins, Jr., and E. D. Wolff, "Original Issue High Yield Bonds: Aging Analyses of Defaults, Exchanges and Calls," *Journal of Finance* 44 (September 1989): 923–952; and R. Cheung, J. C. Bencivenga, and F. J. Fabozzi, "Original Issue High-Yield Bonds: Historical Return and Default Experiences, 1977–1989," *Journal of Fixed Income* (September 1992): 58–75.
15. Altman, "Measuring Corporate Bond Mortality and Performance," p. 5, found that the average recovery on defaulted issues was 40.19 percent between 1978 and 1999. See also E. I. Altman, *Default Risk, Mortality Rates,*

and the Performance of Corporate Bonds (Charlottesville, VA: Research Foundation of the Institute of Chartered Financial Analysts, 1989).

16. Altman, "Measuring Corporate Bond Mortality and Performance," p. 5.
17. See J. V. Amato, "The High-Yield Bond Market," in F. J. Fabozzi, ed., *The Handbook of Fixed Income Securities,* 5th ed. (Chicago: Irwin, 1997), pp. 307–326, and Fridson, *Extra Credit,* pp. 3, 13–14. This issue seems to us worthy of further investigation. Do investors systematically underestimate the risk and the severity of defaults, or is there some other explanation for the two studies' surprising finding?
18. Fridson, *Extra Credit,* p. 12.
19. J. Tripp Howe, "Credit Considerations in Evaluating High-Yield Bonds," in Fabozzi, *Handbook of Fixed Income Securities,* pp. 405–413.
20. Securities analysts' research reports are a good source to check for lists of comparable firms and summaries of their financial data. We used the September 12, 2000, issue of *Merrill Lynch's High Yield Energy Review* in preparing table 4.3.
21. Moody's and Standard & Poor's reached somewhat different conclusions regarding Pogo's credit standing, with Moody's at the lower end and Standard & Poor's at the upper end of the Ba/BB range.
22. The bankruptcy reorganization process and the valuation of distressed securities are described in D. DiNapoli, ed., *Workouts and Turnarounds II: Global Restructuring Strategies for the Next Century* (New York: Wiley, 1999).
23. The debtor-in-possession needs to get court approval for all major decisions, including how to repay its debts.
24. Even stockholders have gotten recoveries, although these are usually limited to between zero and 10 percent of their claims.
25. The program was named for Nicholas Brady, former U.S. Treasury secretary.
26. See P. Druckerman and T. T. Vogel, Jr., "Ecuador Misses Deadline, Defaults on Brady Bonds," *Wall Street Journal,* October 1, 1999, p. A13.
27. See J. Brauer and D. Chen, *Brady Bonds: A Decade of Volatility* (New York: Merrill Lynch, December 15, 1999).
28. Ibid.

Chapter 5

1. However, there are exceptions. For example, a sinking fund (discussed in this chapter) might begin to operate even before the period of call protection expires. Second, some bonds require mandatory redemption if certain events occur. These provisions can apply throughout the life of the issue, triggering a redemption during the call provision's grace period.
2. Sinking-fund payments are a fixed obligation from the issuer's viewpoint but not from the bondholder's. The bonds to be repaid in a given year are chosen by lottery, so any particular bondholder does not know her bond will be repaid until just before it happens. Of course, this is the opposite of the typical lottery: In this case, you win by not being picked!
3. A long-term call option written by a corporation on shares of its own common stock is called a *warrant.* A *convertible bond* is a bond with warrants attached.

4. When a corporate bond and a Treasury security are identical in all respects except for credit quality, the yield spread between them is referred to as a *credit spread*.

5. Such restrictions, called *event-risk protection*, prohibit the issuer from issuing new bonds without first paying off the old bonds, or raising the coupon, or otherwise protecting current bondholders, if issuing the new bonds would trigger a rating downgrade. Event-risk protection seems to have declined within the past few years.

6. A leveraged restructuring is like an LBO without new owners.

7. P. Asquith and T. A. Wizman, "Event Risk, Covenants, and Bondholder Returns in Leveraged Buyouts," *Journal of Financial Economics* 27 (1990): 195–213.

8. D. O. Cook, J. C. Easterwood, and J. D. Martin, "Bondholder Wealth Effects of Management Buyouts," *Financial Management* 21, no. 1 (1992): 102–113.

9. L. Crabbe, "An Analysis of Losses to Bondholders and 'Super Poison Put' Bond Covenants," *Journal of Finance* 46 (1991): 689–706.

10. More than any other single event, the RJR Nabisco LBO, which occurred in late 1988, led to demands for the type of event-risk protection that the super poison put covenant provides.

11. The M&R requires a certain percentage of revenues (or percentage of fixed assets) to be spent on plant maintenance or else pledging additional property and depositing cash with the trustee. This cash can be used to redeem bonds, often at or near par value. The first time this happened, the bonds were selling at about $1,130.00, the call price was $1,016.50, and the grace period had more than two years left.

12. G. Laber, "Bond Covenants and Managerial Flexibility: Two Cases of Special Redemption Provisions," *Financial Management* 19, no. 1 (1990): 82–89.

13. In at least two cases, investors sued the firm, claiming the redemptions were improper. The courts ultimately ruled against the investors.

14. G. Laber, "Bond Covenants and Forgone Opportunities: The Case of Burlington Northern Railroad Company," *Financial Management* 21, no. 2 (1992): 71–77.

15. The bonds were issued in 1896 in connection with the reorganization of a predecessor railroad. They were scheduled to mature in 1997 in one case and 2047 in the other. It is certainly understandable that the drafters of the indenture in 1896 could not foresee the problems that would develop ninety years later.

16. M. E. Iskandar-Datta and D. R. Emery, "The Role of Indenture Provisions in Determining Bond Ratings," *Journal of Banking and Finance* 18 (1994): 93–111.

17. M. J. Barclay and C. W. Smith, Jr., "The Maturity Structure of Corporate Debt," *Journal of Finance* 50 (1995): 609–631.

18. S. C. Myers, "Determinants of Corporate Borrowing," *Journal of Financial Economics* 5 (1977): 147–175, and A. Barnea, R. A. Haugen, and L. W. Senbet, "A Rationale for Debt Maturity Structure and Call Provisions in the Agency Theoretic Framework," *Journal of Finance* 35 (1980): 1223–1234.

19. Barclay and Smith, "The Maturity Structure of Corporate Debt."

20. D. W. Blackwell and D. S. Kidwell, "An Investigation of Cost Differences Between Public Sales and Private Placements of Debt," *Journal of Financial Economics* 22 (1988): 253–278.

21. C. M. James, "Some Evidence on the Uniqueness of Bank Loans," *Journal of Financial Economics* 19 (1987): 217–235.
22. C. W. Smith, Jr., "Investment Banking and the Capital Acquisition Process," *Journal of Financial Economics* 15 (1986): 3–29.
23. C. W. Smith, Jr., and J. B. Warner, "On Financial Contracting: An Analysis of Bond Covenants," *Journal of Financial Economics* 7 (1979): 117–161.
24. M. Berlin and J. Loeys, "Bond Covenants and Delegated Monitoring," *Journal of Finance* 43 (1988): 397–412.
25. R. M. Stulz and H. Johnson, "An Analysis of Secured Debt," *Journal of Financial Economics* 14 (1985): 501–521.
26. T. S. Y. Ho and R. F. Singer, "Bond Indenture Provisions and the Risk of Corporate Debt," *Journal of Financial Economics* 10 (1982): 375–406.
27. M. J. Flannery, "Asymmetric Information and Risky Debt Maturity Choice," *Journal of Finance* 41 (1986): 19–37, and J. R. Kale and T. H. Noe, "Risky Debt Maturity Choice in a Sequential Equilibrium," *Journal of Financial Research* 13 (1990): 155–165.
28. D. W. Diamond, "Debt Maturity Structure and Liquidity Risk," *Quarterly Journal of Economics* 106 (1991): 709–737, and D. W. Diamond, "Seniority and Maturity of Debt Contracts," *Journal of Financial Economics* 33 (1993): 341–368.
29. I. E. Brick and S. A. Ravid, "On the Relevance of Debt Maturity Structure," *Journal of Finance* 40 (1985): 1423–1437, and I. E. Brick and S. A. Ravid, "Interest Rate Uncertainty and the Optimal Debt Maturity Structure," *Journal of Financial and Quantitative Analysis* 26 (1991): 63–82.
30. C. Kim and D. C. Mauer, "Corporate Debt Maturity Policy and Investor Tax-Timing Options: Theory and Evidence," *Financial Management* 24, no. 1 (1995): 33–45.
31. D. M. Chance, "Default Risk and the Duration of Zero Coupon Bonds," *Journal of Finance* 45 (1990): 265–274.
32. F. A. Longstaff, "Pricing Options with Extendible Maturities: Analysis and Applications," *Journal of Finance* 45 (1990): 935–957.
33. K. Mitchell, "The Call, Sinking Fund, and Term-to-Maturity Features of Corporate Bonds: An Empirical Investigation," *Journal of Financial and Quantitative Analysis* 26 (1991): 201–222, and J. R. Morris, "Factors Affecting the Maturity Structure of Corporate Debt," working paper, University of Colorado at Denver, 1992.
34. Mitchell, "Call, Sinking Fund, and Term-to-Maturity Features."
35. J. Guedes and T. Opler, "The Determinants of the Maturity of Corporate Debt Issues," *Journal of Finance* 51 (1996): 1809–1833.
36. Diamond, "Debt Maturity Structure and Liquidity Risk," and Diamond, "Seniority and Maturity of Debt Contracts."
37. Bond investors may also require a large premium in yield to compensate for the substantial fixed costs of researching the speculative-grade issuer's credit quality, which would discourage short-term speculative-grade issues.
38. Y. C. Kim and R. M. Stulz, "The Eurobond Market and Corporate Financial Policy: A Test of the Clientele Hypothesis," *Journal of Financial Economics* 22 (1988): 189–205.
39. C. Kao and C. Wu, "Sinking Funds and the Agency Costs of Corporate Debt," *Financial Review* 25 (1990): 95–114.

40. Mitchell, "Call, Sinking Fund, and Term-to-Maturity Features."
41. Laber, "Bond Covenants and Managerial Flexibility." The funnel, or aggregate, sinking-fund provision gives the option to retire the debt from one or more of the firm's other outstanding debt issues rather than being from that specific debt issue.
42. J. D. Finnerty, "Indexed Sinking Fund Debentures: Valuation and Analysis," *Financial Management* 22, no. 2 (1993): 76–93.
43. S. A. Ravid and O. H. Sarig, "Financial Signalling by Committing to Cash Outflows," *Journal of Financial and Quantitative Analysis* 26 (1991): 165–180, and Y. K. Kim, I. E. Brick, and M. Frierman, "Precommitting Cash Outflows to Stockholders and Bondholders and the Value of the Firm: Theory and Evidence," working paper, Rutgers University Graduate School of Business, 1992.
44. Bankers Trust Corporation, $500,000,000 Global Floating Rate Notes due 2003, prospectus, April 24, 1998.

Chapter 6

1. For a discussion of these changes, see T. S. Sims, "Long-Term Debt, the Term Structure of Interest and the Case for Accrual Taxation," *Tax Law Review* 47 (Winter 1992): 313–326, and J. Strnad, "The Taxation of Bonds: The Tax Trading Dimension," *Virginia Law Review* 81 (February 1995): 47–116.
2. Technically the test is based on the redemption price at maturity. But since this redemption price is normally face amount, we will simplify the discussion by assuming that the redemption price at maturity is the face amount. A market discount generally results from a rise in interest rates. Alternatively, the bond's rating might decline, reflecting an increase in the bond's riskiness and causing the required return to rise.
3. This tax deferral conveys an obvious advantage. It could be eliminated by taxing market discount in the same manner as OID. However, such tax treatment might be administratively burdensome for bondholders, who would have to accrue the market discount period by period, including fractional periods. President Clinton's last budget included a proposal to tax market discount like OID.
4. More complete discussions of the discount and premium amortization rules are contained in other work. For example, see Strnad, "Taxation of Bonds."
5. The present value at 10 percent of $80.00 per year for ten years plus an additional $1,000.00 at the end of the ten years is $877.11.
6. The formula is easily adjusted to handle semiannual interest payments. When an OID bond is sold during an interest period, OID is allocated by the fraction of the period the bond was held.
7. If the yield curve remained flat and stationary, the bond's price would track the amounts reported for the end-of-year tax basis in table 6.1. The investor's total return each year would be the same 10 percent, with 8 percent in cash interest and the remaining 2 percent in capital appreciation.
8. The bond's tax basis equals the original issue price plus OID accrued through the date of sale.

9. The new "original issue discount" is 25 (1,000 – 975). It is fully allocated to years 6 through 10 by applying equation 6.1: 4.10, 4.50, 4.95, 5.45, and 6.00, which sum to 25.

10. The original OID amortization schedule applies because the investor paid less than the OID tax basis when she bought it. Alternatively, the investor can elect to accrue market discount on a straight-line basis.

11. Strnad, "Taxation of Bonds," assumes a twenty-year maturity for the par value bonds and a twelve-year maturity for the discount and zero-coupon bonds.

12. The Treasury Department estimated in 1995 that eliminating the tax deduction for interest on supermaturity bonds could raise $6.5 billion over seven years. Others predicted that firms would simply stop issuing supermaturity bonds. As predicted, with the proposed tax change in 1995, Monsanto immediately cancelled its previously announced plans to issue $200 million face amount of hundred-year bonds. See S. Strom, "Citing Tax Proposal, Monsanto Drops Plan for 100-Year Bonds," *New York Times*, December 9, 1995, p. 37.

13. S. B. Land, "Recent Tax Developments Affecting Fixed Income Derivative Securities," in J. D. Finnerty and M. S. Fridson, eds., *The Yearbook of Fixed Income Investing 1995* (Chicago: Irwin, 1996), pp. 381–399, describes these four sets of proposed regulations.

14. The underlying instrument does not have to be identical, but it should be substantially similar.

15. Under the Internal Revenue Code, the gain should be allocated to assets in the following order of decreasing priority: (1) assets securing the bonds, (2) assets other than those securing the bonds that were purchased with the bond's proceeds, and (3) other depreciable assets.

16. "Interest on Receivables and Payables," *Accounting Principles Board Opinion No. 21* (New York: American Institute of Certified Public Accountants, 1971).

17. "Accounting for Certain Investments in Debt and Equity Securities," *Financial Accounting Standard No. 115* (Stamford, CT: Financial Accounting Standards Board, May 1993).

18. A. Fliegelman, "Changes in Fixed-Income Securities Accounting: The Portfolio Management Effects on a Financial Institution," in Finnerty and Fridson, *The Yearbook of Fixed Income Investing 1995*, pp. 418–439.

19. Financial institutions responded to FAS 115 by restructuring their fixed-income portfolios to reduce price volatility, reducing the portion of their portfolios consisting of securities available for potential sale, increasing their investments in nonsecuritized fixed-income instruments that fall outside FAS 115's scope, increasing their use of derivatives and reverse repurchase agreements in order to cut back on the need to sell securities prior to maturity, and altering their capital structures in order to minimize FAS 115's impact on their reported financial positions. Ibid., p. 419.

20. If a financial institution securitizes residential mortgage loans and continues to hold the securitized mortgages, it must report the securitized mortgages in accordance with FAS 115. Also, FAS 140 requires that interest-only strips, retained interests in securitizations, and certain other financial assets should be accounted for as debt available-for-sale or trading under FAS 115.

21. One study found that insurance companies were classifying 78.92 percent of their debt securities assets as AFS, 19.60 percent as HTM, and only 1.49 percent as trading securities. Ibid., pp. 419, 431–434.

22. "Disclosures About Fair Value of Financial Instruments," *FASB Statement No. 107* (Stamford, CT: Financial Accounting Standards Board, December 1991).

23. "Accounting for Derivative Instruments and Hedging Activities," *FASB Statement No. 133* (Stamford, CT: Financial Accounting Standards Board, 15 June 1998).

24 . "Early Extinguishment of Debt," *Accounting Principles Board Opinion No. 26* (New York: American Institute of Certified Public Accountants, October 1972).

25. "Reporting Gains and Losses from the Early Extinguishment of Debt," *Statement of Financial Accounting Standards No. 4* (Stamford, CT: Financial Accounting Standards Board, March 1975).

26. Many studies have called for such a change. One of the earliest is D. S. Shannon and W. P. Stevens, "How Debt Refunding Can Cause Decision Conflicts," *Management Accounting* 65 (December 1983): 40–44.

27. J. Agudelo and J. M. Harmon, "Debt Defeasance: Its Impact on Corporate Financial Reporting," *Ohio CPA Journal* 43 (Spring 1984): 61–65. FAS 119 represents an important step in this direction.

28. Payments cannot be made on junior subordinated debentures until all required payments have been made on the issuer's "senior" obligations and all other conditions in the indenture have been met. Junior subordinated debenture holders rank ahead of preferred and common shareholders.

29. During the deferral period, income continues to accrue for income tax purposes, and the investor is liable for income tax on the deferred income, although the investor does not receive any cash payments. An investor could avoid such a tax liability by holding the securities in a tax-deferred retirement account. At the end of the deferral period, the issuer must pay all deferred distributions in cash.

30. Such a disallowance was proposed in 1995 but never enacted into law.

Chapter 7

1. Understanding these complex instruments is critical to using them properly. Misuse of complex derivatives has led to several highly publicized embarrassing situations and attracted closer regulatory monitoring. See J. Overdahl and B. Schachter, "Derivatives Regulation and Financial Management: Lessons from Gibson Greetings," in J. D. Finnerty and M. S. Fridson, eds., *The Yearbook of Fixed Income Investing 1995* (Chicago: Irwin, 1996), pp. 199–219.

2. Futures contracts were created to deal with the default risk inherent in forward contracts.

3. Similarly, in a currency swap, the cash flows are determined by the interest rates in two different currencies.

4. See C. W. Smithson, C. W. Smith, Jr., and D. S. Wilford, *Managing Financial Risk* (Burr Ridge, IL: Irwin, 1995), chap. 2.

5. Traders often refer to a cap as a "call option on LIBOR," to buy LIBOR for the cap rate. The seller is "delivering" LIBOR in exchange for the fixed rate. Describing a cap as a call on LIBOR versus a put on a Eurodollar time deposit is simply semantic preference.

6. Analogous to a cap, traders often like to refer to a floor as a "put option on LIBOR."

7. The FRN floor is the minimum coupon on the FRN. Suppose LIBOR is 4 percent on a reset date. The FRN floor is 5 percent. The unrestricted FRN and the annuity provide 4.50 percent combined, and the floor contract pays 0.50 percent. Similarly, the FRN cap is the maximum coupon on the FRN (10 percent).

8. The notional principal amount of the swap, the floor, and the cap match the face value of the FRN. Also, the swap and the two notes are par value instruments.

9. Transaction costs affect the pricing of fixed-income instruments, such as swaps, caps, floors, and collars. Because of bid-ask spreads, the collared FRN and the synthetic collared FRN will yield identical returns, but their prices may differ.

10. J. P. Ogden, "An Analysis of Yield Curve Notes," *Journal of Finance* 42 (1987): 99–110, and D. J. Smith, "The Pricing of Bull and Bear Floating Rate Notes: An Application of Financial Engineering," *Financial Management* 17, no. 4 (1988): 72–81, describe and analyze this instrument.

11. They are not perfectly equivalent, however, because the inverse FRN's coupon rate cannot fall below zero. Equivalence requires adding fixed-rate notes and a cap to the mix.

12. For example, Sallie Mae's first inverse FRN issue had a five-year maturity and a reset formula of 17.2 percent – LIBOR. Albert Lord, the chief financial officer, remarked that Sallie Mae's resulting cost of funds, including the cost of the cap, was below the five-year Treasury rate.

13. L. E. Crabbe and J. D. Argilagos, "The Anatomy of the Structured Note Market," *Journal of Applied Corporate Finance* (Fall 1994): 73–84, and K. C. Brown and D. J. Smith, "Structured Swaps," in Finnerty and Fridson, *Yearbook of Fixed Income Investing 1995*, pp. 137–156, describe the development of the market for structured products.

14. The Statement of Financial Accounting Standards No. 133, "Accounting for Derivative Instruments and Hedging Activities" (FAS 133), which was issued in June 1998, requires each counterparty to treat derivatives as assets or liabilities, whether they are standing alone or are embedded in structured products. FAS 133 essentially eliminates the pure accounting rationale for preferring structured swaps over structured notes.

Chapter 8

1. This chapter is based on J. D. Finnerty, "Financial Engineering in Corporate Finance: An Overview," *Financial Management* 17, no. 4 (1988): 14–33, and J. D. Finnerty, "An Overview of Corporate Securities Innovation," *Continental Bank Journal of Applied Corporate Finance* (Winter 1992): 23–39. See also D. J. Smith, "The Arithmetic of Financial Engineering," *Journal of*

Applied Corporate Finance (Winter 1989): 49–58, C. W. Smithson, C. W. Smith, Jr., and D. S. Wilford, *Managing Financial Risk* (Burr Ridge, IL: Irwin, 1995), and P. Tufano, "Financial Innovation and First-Mover Advantages," *Journal of Financial Economics* 25 (1989): 213–240.

2. Some securities innovations are designed to circumvent provisions of the tax or regulatory code. Merton Miller likened the role of regulation in stimulating innovation to that of the grain of sand in the oyster. And since few things in this world are as mutable as the current tax code or a set of regulations, securities intended to overcome such obstacles are likely to disappear along with the tax or regulatory quirk that gave rise to them. M. Miller, "Financial Innovation: The Last Twenty Years and the Next," *Journal of Financial and Quantitative Analysis* 21 (1986): 459–471.

3. See J. C. Van Horne, "Of Financial Innovations and Excesses," *Journal of Finance* 40 (1985): 621–631. See also R. C. Merton, "Financial Innovation and Economic Performance," *Continental Bank Journal of Applied Corporate Finance* (Winter 1992): 12–22, and S. A. Ross, "Institutional Markets, Financial Marketing, and Financial Innovation," *Journal of Finance* 44 (1989): 541–556.

4. Ross, "Institutional Markets, Financial Marketing, and Financial Innovation," emphasizes this aspect of financial innovation.

5. The U.S. Treasury responded to this activity, and the profits that securities dealers were making from it, by issuing registered Treasury STRIPS (Separate Trading of Registered Interest and Principal of Securities), which permitted the coupon payments and principal to be registered and traded separately. The Treasury hoped to realize the benefits of coupon stripping for itself.

6. The securities are often issued in a senior-subordinated structure. The senior class of securities, which is sold to investors, has a prior claim to the cash flows from the underlying collateral pool. The issuer typically retains the subordinated interest.

7. See F. J. Fabozzi, ed., *The Handbook of Mortgage-Backed Securities*, 4th ed. (Chicago: Probus, 1995), and F. J. Fabozzi, ed., *Advances and Innovations in the Bond and Mortgage Markets* (Chicago: Probus, 1989).

8. The introduction of these securities also enhanced market completeness because of their duration and convexity characteristics. The apparent failure to understand fully the riskiness of these securities led to a substantial and highly publicized financial loss in 1987 by a major brokerage house. For an account, see J. Sterngold, "Anatomy of a Staggering Loss," *New York Times*, May 11, 1987, pp. D1ff.

9. For a more detailed consideration of hybrid debt securities designed to manage commodity and exchange rate risks, see Smithson, Smith, and Wilford, *Managing Financial Risk*.

10. Still, the issuer often retains a subordinated interest in the underlying collateral pool so that a large portion of the yield reduction results from the investors' senior claim on the pool's cash flows. Asset securitization, in a sense, involves carving out a firm's highest-quality assets and selling them on a stand-alone basis. Any measure of overall cost reduction must account for the effect on the firm's other liabilities and the riskiness of the firm's equity.

11. A variant of reset notes, known as *remarketed reset notes*, includes a put option that protects investors against the possibility that the issuer and the remarketing agent will conspire to set a below-market coupon rate. It also provides a flexible interest rate formula (in the event the issuer and the remarketing agent cannot agree on a rate) that provides for a higher interest rate should the issuer's credit standing decline.

12. These securities, however, have a potentially serious flaw: The interest rate adjustment mechanism will tend to increase the issuer's debt service burden just when it can least afford it—when its credit rating has fallen, presumably as a result of diminished operating cash flow.

13. The increasing-rate feature can have a perverse effect. In the extreme, the feature might require such a large jump in the interest rate that the issuer would be forced into bankruptcy. For example, Hillsborough Holdings conducted an exchange offer in anticipation of an interest rate reset that would have raised the interest rate on its debt to more than 20 percent. When the exchange offer failed, Hillsborough Holdings was forced into bankruptcy. See J. Greiff, "Hillsborough Holdings Files for Chapter 11," *St. Petersburg Times,* December 28, 1989, p. 1E.

14. Variable-coupon renewable notes were given a nominal maturity of one year, the maximum maturity permitted money market mutual fund investments. Also, because of the weekly rate reset, these notes were permitted to count as 7-day assets in meeting the 120-day upper limit on a money market mutual fund's dollar-weighted average portfolio maturity.

15. Historically, financial institutions, such as thrifts, issued short-term or intermediate-term debt and invested in long-term fixed-rate mortgages. The resulting asset-liability mismatch bankrupted many thrifts when interest rates rose sharply in the 1970s and early 1980s. This led to two innovations to reduce lenders' risk exposure: variable-rate mortgages and mortgage securitization.

16. See L. S. Hayre and C. Mohebbi, "Mortgage Pass-Through Securities," in Fabozzi, *Advances and Innovations,* pp. 259–304.

17. B. Roberts, *The Frontiers of Asset Securitization* (New York: Bear, Stearns & Co., September 30, 1991), describes the evolution of asset-backed securitization in the international capital markets. D. C. Bonsall, ed., *Securitisation* (London: Butterworths, 1990), and C. Stone, A. Zissu, and J. Lederman, eds., *Asset Securitisation: Theory and Practice in Europe* (London: Euromoney Books, 1991), provide in-depth analyses of asset securitization in Europe.

18. See P. P. Boyle, "Valuing Canadian Mortgage-Backed Securities," *Financial Analysts Journal* (May–June 1989): 55–60.

19. See S. Din, "Commercial Property," in Stone, Zissu, and Lederman, *Asset Securitisation,* pp. 193–206, and I. Falconer, "Asset Securitisation in the United Kingdom," in Stone, Zissu, and Lederman, *Asset Securitisation,* pp. 493–512, and N. Shah, "2000 Year in Review and 2001 Outlook: ABS Markets Post Record-Breaking Number of Deals in Europe, the Middle East and Africa, with More Growth to Come," New York: Moody's Investors Service, January 11, 2001.

20. See J. D. Smallman and M. J. P. Selby, "Asset-Backed Securitisation," in Bonsall, *Securitisation,* pp. 242–264.

21. See C. David, "Securitisation in France," in Stone, Zissu, and Lederman, *Asset Securitisation*, pp. 257–272, and M. Quéré, "Securitisation in France: Titrisation," in Bonsall, *Securitisation*, pp. 265–287. *Titrisation* translates to *securitization.*

22. Because the French government did not wish to promote "credit card mania," the 1988 law limits asset securitization to those assets that amortize, which excludes credit card receivables.

23. The CMO market in the United States was given a major boost in 1986 when the U.S. Congress authorized real estate mortgage investment conduits (REMICs) for multiclass mortgage pass-through securities. The new law greatly enhanced issuers' flexibility in structuring multiclass mortgage pass-through securities. Essentially any corporation, partnership, trust, or segregated pool of mortgages that elects REMIC status becomes transparent for income tax purposes. This ensures that the risk-reallocation structure does not give rise to tax liabilities that might offset the benefits of prepayment risk reallocation.

24. The PSA Standard Prepayment Model assumes that mortgages prepay at the annualized rate of 0.2 percent during the first month, the prepayment rate steps up in increments of 0.2 percent each month until month 30, and prepayments remain constant at 6 percent per year for all succeeding months.

25. See S. D. Perlman, "Collateralized Mortgage Obligations: The Impact of Structure on Value," in Fabozzi, *Advances and Innovations*, pp. 417–436.

26. Asset Backed Securities Corporation, Asset Backed Obligations, Series 4, prospectus, July 29, 1987. See "First Boston Unit's Loan-Backed Issue Has New Structure," *Wall Street Journal*, July 29, 1987, p. 25.

27. M. Waldman, M. Gordon, and K. J. Person, "Interest Only and Principal Only STRIPs," in Fabozzi, *Advances and Innovations*, pp. 401–416, provide an in-depth analysis of these securities.

28. PO STRIPS are recognized as "bullish" investments because a decrease in interest rates, which benefits bond prices generally, tends to boost prepayments and hence PO STRIP prices. IO STRIPS are recognized as "bearish" investments because their prices move in the opposite direction. The riskiness of trading and investing in IO/PO STRIPS has been highlighted by some large financial losses that securities firms have experienced trading these instruments. See, for example, Sterngold, "Anatomy of a Staggering Loss," and "J.P. Morgan Had $50 Million in Losses in Trading Mortgage-Backed Securities," *Wall Street Journal*, March 10, 1992, p. A4.

29. Waldman, Gordon, and Person, "Interest Only and Principal Only STRIPs."

30. See A. K. Bhattacharya and P. J. Cannon, "Senior-Subordinated Mortgage Pass-Throughs," in Fabozzi, *Advances and Innovations*, pp. 473–483.

31. Ibid.

Chapter 9

1. Treasury bonds pay interest on the basis of the actual number of days elapsed in a 365-day year. In equation 9.3, the numerator is the actual number of days between the settlement (or closing) date and the next

coupon payment date. Count the settlement date but not the coupon payment date (money is borrowed overnight). The denominator is the number of days in the interest period, which may be 181, 182, 183, or 184, depending on the bond. This information is provided in the bond contract. Corporate bonds usually pay interest on the basis of a 360-day year, and each month is treated as having 30 days (including February). Count the actual number of days elapsed in each partial month.

2. The floater can trade above or below par between coupon reset dates. If the cap or floor is reached, however, the floater will trade more like a bond with a fixed interest rate.

3. Note that the effective margin is 100 basis points, the same as the stated spread, when the loan is selling at par.

4. There are actual market-traded zero-coupon Treasury securities, called U.S. Treasury STRIPS, with a maturity greater than one year. They are not issued by the U.S. Treasury but are created by securities dealers from coupon Treasury securities. You would think that the observed yields on these zero-coupon Treasury securities could be used to construct the actual spot-rate curve. However, there are some technical problems with this approach. First, many of the STRIPS are relatively illiquid. Second, there are some maturity sectors of the STRIPS market that attract certain investors who may be willing to trade off pretax yield in return for an attractive tax feature associated with that particular maturity sector. Both factors tend to distort the term structure relationship.

5. If the one-year Treasury was a zero-coupon instrument, no further calculation would be required. Its yield would be the one-year spot rate.

6. More precisely, the binomial model assumes that interest rates evolve over time according to what is known as a *lognormal random walk*. This version of the model also assumes the U and L branches have the same probability. Other versions allow for unequal probabilities (but require, of course, that they sum to one).

7. Bond pricing services such as Bloomberg LP calculate the historical volatility and the implied volatility for a variety of interest rates. For more on calculating implied interest rate volatility, see J. C. Hull, *Options, Futures, and Other Derivatives*, 4th ed. (Upper Saddle River, NJ: Prentice Hall, 2000), pp. 545–546.

8. This value is the same as when we discounted at the spot rates and the one-period forward rates. We get exactly the same result because the bond is option-free. This example demonstrates that the binomial model is consistent with the standard approaches for valuing an option-free bond.

9. An important question not addressed here is the rule for determining when the issuer will call the bond. Chapter 11 addresses this timing issue.

Chapter 10

1. W. G. Lewellen and D. R. Emery, "On the Matter of Parity Among Financial Obligations," *Journal of Finance* 36 (March 1981): 97–111; K. D. Reiner, "Financial Structure Effects of Bond Refunding," *Financial Management* 9

(Summer 1980): 18–23; J. D. Finnerty, *An Illustrated Guide to Bond Refunding Analysis* (Charlottesville, VA: Financial Analysts Research Foundation, 1984); J. D. Finnerty, "Refunding Discounted Debt: A Clarifying Analysis," *Journal of Financial and Quantitative Analysis* 21 (March 1986): 95–106.

2. Overlapping interest expense arises because the refunding bonds are usually issued before the refunded bonds are retired. In such a case, the firm invests the proceeds of the refunding issue in the interim, and the overlapping interest expense is the interest expense minus the income.

3. J. S. Ang, "The Two Faces of Bond Refunding," *Journal of Finance* 30 (June 1975): 869–874, and "The Two Faces of Bond Refunding: Reply," *Journal of Finance* 33 (March 1978): 354–356; H. Bierman, "The Bond Refunding Decision," *Financial Management* 1 (Summer 1972): 27–29; T. H. Mayor and K. G. McCoin, "Bond Refunding: One or Two Faces?" *Journal of Finance* 33 (March 1978): 349–353; E. Schwartz, "The Refunding Decision," *Journal of Business* 40 (October 1967): 448–449; J. B. Yawitz and J. A. Anderson, "The Effect of Bond Refunding on Shareholder Wealth," *Journal of Finance* 32 (December 1977): 1738–1746, and "The Effect of Bond Refunding on Shareholder Wealth: Reply," *Journal of Finance* 34 (June 1979): 805–809; R. S. Harris, "The Refunding of Discounted Debt: An Adjusted Present Value Analysis," *Financial Management* 9 (Winter 1980): 7–12; G. Laber, "Repurchases of Bonds Through Tender Offers: Implications for Shareholder Wealth," *Financial Management* 7 (Summer 1978): 7–13, "Implications of Discount Rates and Financing Assumptions for Bond Refunding Decisions," *Financial Management* 8 (Spring 1979): 7–12, and "The Effect of Bond Refunding on Shareholder Wealth: Comment," *Journal of Finance* 34 (June 1979): 795–799; O. D. Bowlin, "The Refunding Decision: Another Special Case in Capital Budgeting," *Journal of Finance* 21 (March 1966): 55–68; Finnerty, *An Illustrated Guide*, and "Refunding Discounted Debt"; R. Johnson and R. Klein, "Corporate Motives in Repurchases of Discounted Bonds," *Financial Management* 3 (Autumn 1974): 44–49; A. J. Kalotay, "On the Advanced Refunding of Discounted Debt," *Financial Management* 7 (Summer 1978): 14–18; Lewellen and Emery, "On the Matter of Parity"; Reiner, "Financial Structure Effects"; and A. R. Ofer and R. Taggart, Jr., "Bond Refunding: A Clarifying Analysis," *Journal of Finance* 32 (March 1977): 21–30.

4. Lewellen and Emery, "On the Matter of Parity"; Reiner, "Financial Structure Effects."

5. Lewellen and Emery, "On the Matter of Parity."

6. Ibid. M. Livingston, "Measuring the Benefit of a Bond Refunding: The Problem of Nonmarketable Call Options," *Financial Management* 16 (Spring 1987): 38–40, argues that assuming noncallable new debt overstates the true net advantage to the extent that the call option on the refunded issue has any remaining time premium. This suggests that the call option on the refunding issue should have a value equal to the call option's remaining time premium on the old debt. D. R. Emery and W. G. Lewellen, "Shareholder Gains from Callable-Bond Refundings," *Managerial and Decision Economics* 11, no. 1 (1990): 57–63, show that this remaining time premium equals the difference between the old debt's call price and its market value just before the call announcement. To deal with

the possible overstating of the net advantage of refunding, Emery and Lewellen recommend *subtracting* the option's time premium from the net advantage of refunding calculated based on noncallable new debt.

7. Also, $T' = T$ in the high-coupon case and usually also in the low-coupon case. We distinguish between them so that our equations will be as general as possible and apply to all high- and low-coupon refundings.

8. W. M. Boyce and A. J. Kalotay, "Tax Differentials and Callable Bonds," *Journal of Finance* 34 (September 1979): 825–838.

9. The overlapping interest expense is the interest cost of the new bonds during the period of overlap when the interest savings are computed from the date of retiring the old bonds and the interest cost of the old bonds during the period of overlap when the savings are computed from the date of issuing the new bonds. Subtract the interest earned on the investment of the funds during the overlap period. See D. R. Emery, "Overlapping Interest in Bond Refunding: A Reconsideration," *Financial Management* 7 (Summer 1978): 19–20.

10. Because of these benefits, a bond refunding could be worthwhile even if $NA < 0$.

11. Lewellen and Emery, "On the Matter of Parity."

12. W. M. Boyce and A. J. Kalotay, "Optimum Bond Calling and Refunding," *Interfaces* 9 (November 1979): 36–49.

13. A. Kalotay and L. Abreo, "Premium Debt Swaps: The Best of Both Worlds?" *Financial Management* 27 (Autumn 1998): 83–86, analyzes one such debt swap and explains the tax and accounting aspects of the exchange.

14. Ibid., 84–85.

15. Bond market participants refer to bond prices in this manner, which they understand to mean a percentage of the $1,000 face amount. For example, a price of 123.76 means $1,237.60.

16. The cost of debt service is the present value of the after-tax cash flows, discounted at the after-tax rate on the new debt, for both the old and new debt.

17. J. D. Finnerty, "Evaluating the Economics of Refunding High-Coupon Sinking-Fund Debt," *Financial Management* 12 (Spring 1983): 5–10.

18. Certain expenses, such as printing costs and lawyers' and accountants' fees, will be incurred regardless of the number of bonds called for redemption. Because these fixed costs do not affect the refunding decision at the margin, you can ignore them until you determine the number of bonds that maximizes the increase in shareholder wealth.

19. R. W. Masulis, "The Effects of Capital Structure Change on Security Prices: A Study of Exchange Offers," *Journal of Financial Economics* 8 (June 1980): 139–178; and R. W. Masulis, "The Impact of Capital Structure Change on Firm Value: Some Estimates," *Journal of Finance* 38 (March 1983): 107–126.

Chapter 11

1. See J. D. Vu, "An Empirical Investigation of Calls of Non-Convertible Bonds," *Journal of Financial Economics* 16 (June 1986): 235–265.

2. C. D. Howard and A. J. Kalotay, *Efficiency and Optimal Bond Refunding* (New York: Salomon Brothers, March 1987), recommend selecting as the target refunding rate the new issue rate that will achieve 85 percent efficiency. See also A. J. Kalotay, "No-Brainer Refinancing," *Treasury and Corporate Risk Management* (Spring 1992): 4.

3. H. Bierman, Jr., "The Bond Refunding Decision as a Markov Process," *Management Science* 12 (August 1966): 545–551; E. J. Elton and M. J. Gruber, "Dynamic Programming Applications in Finance," *Journal of Finance* 26 (May 1971): 473–505; B. A. Kalymon, "Bond Refunding with Stochastic Interest Rates," *Management Science* 18 (November 1971): 171–183; A. Kraus, "The Bond Refunding Decision in an Efficient Market," *Journal of Financial and Quantitative Analysis* 8 (December 1973): 793–806; H. M. Weingartner, "Optimal Timing of Bond Refunding," *Management Science* 13 (March 1967): 511–524; and W. M. Boyce and A. J. Kalotay, "Optimum Bond Calling and Refunding," *Interfaces* 9 (November 1979): 36–49.

4. Note, however, that investor income taxes can still affect the interest rate tree because they can affect the shape of the par value yield curve, as we discussed in chapter 6.

5. To be precise, the gain is the repurchase price minus the bond's tax basis, which may be different from 100 because of issue expenses and discount or premium. Still, $100 - P_{ij}$ is a useful approximation of the forgiveness-of-indebtedness income. As discussed in chapter 12, it is sometimes possible to defer at least a portion of this tax liability, in which case the equivalent present value tax rate T' should replace T in equation 11.4.

6. D. R. Emery and W. G. Lewellen, "Refunding Noncallable Debt," *Journal of Financial and Quantitative Analysis* 19 (March 1984): 73–82.

7. This statement assumes that the tax rate on the gain (the forgiveness-of-indebtedness income) equals the tax rate on the loss (the call premium).

8. If the OAS varies with maturity, as it usually does, calibrate the tree to a set of noncallable corporate bonds. Use the procedure described to create figure 9.5, but use a set of bonds with the same credit rating as the target bond.

9. The market price is 101.833 ($1,018.33 per bond), or an after-tax cost of 101.191. The issuer can afford to pay up to 101.203, or a pretax price of 101.851, which is a premium of only $0.18 ($1,018.51 – $1,018.33) per $1,000 bond over the current market price.

10. To simplify, treat the call premium and out-of-pocket expense as being immediately tax deductible, making the after-tax redemption cost 103.6 $(100 + 0.6[5.0 + 1.0])$.

11. To be precise, the swaption's notional amount should have decreases that match the declines in the bond's call price schedule.

Chapter 12

1. More generally, in computing the optimal refunding rates, we must also take into account that short-term interest rates are more volatile than long-term rates. This feature creates an additional incentive for waiting. We provide more on this point later in the chapter.

2. J. D. Finnerty, "Refunding Discounted Debt: A Clarifying Analysis," *Journal of Financial and Quantitative Analysis* 21 (1986): 95–106.

3. J. D. Finnerty, *An Illustrated Guide to Bond Refunding Analysis* (Charlottesville, VA: Financial Analysts Research Foundation, 1984); Finnerty, "Refunding Discounted Debt."

4. When the firm is not a taxpayer, the net advantage of refunding discounted debt is negative because of transaction costs. See T. H. Mayor and K. G. McCoin, "Bond Refunding: One or Two Faces?" *Journal of Finance* 33 (1978): 349–353. They tried to generalize from that; however, because they ignored the role of income taxes, they incorrectly concluded that refunding discounted debt could not be profitable.

5. Finnerty, "Refunding Discounted Debt"; R. Johnson and R. Klein, "Corporate Motives in Repurchases of Discounted Bonds," *Financial Management* 3 (1974): 44–49; and A. J. Kalotay, "On the Advanced Refunding of Discounted Debt," *Financial Management* 7 (1978): 14–18.

6. Through a series of changes in tax law during the 1980s, Congress gradually eliminated virtually all the strategies firms had adopted to achieve a tax-free gain when extinguishing discounted debt. However, strategies may exist that will work in other tax jurisdictions. See A. J. Kalotay and B. Tuckman, "A Tale of Two Bond Swaps," *Journal of Financial Engineering* 1 (1992): 325–343.

7. Finnerty, *An Illustrated Guide;* Finnerty, "Refunding Discounted Debt."

8. The issuer reacquires the bonds by paying the market price; thus, $P = B$.

9. K. Dunn and C. Spatt, "A Strategic Analysis of Sinking Fund Bonds," *Journal of Financial Economics* 13 (1984): 399–423; and A. J. Kalotay, "On the Management of Sinking Funds," *Financial Management* 10 (1981): 34–40.

10. A. Kalotay and B. Tuckman, "Sinking Fund Prepurchases and the Designation Option," *Financial Management* 21 (1992): 110–118, found that firms were, on average, about two to three sinking-fund payments ahead of schedule.

11. Although most sinking-fund bond indentures grant a designation option for prepurchased bonds, bond indentures differ as to the treatment of optionally redeemed bonds. You should check the bond indenture before undertaking a sinking-fund-management study.

12. For example, when interest rates are high, it will designate repurchased bonds to the nearest sinking-fund payments. If interest rates drop sharply, it might redesignate them to the most distant sinking-fund obligations.

13. This comparison is meaningful only if the C_j are first expressed on a per-bond basis when the sinking-fund amounts (S_j) differ.

14. F_i, the face amount remaining to be paid, may be positive but less than S_i, the originally scheduled sinking-fund amount, if the firm's treasury lacked sufficient bonds to designate a sinking-fund obligation in full.

15. A. J. Kalotay and G. O. Williams, "The Valuation and Management of Bonds with Sinking Fund Provisions," *Financial Analysts Journal* 48 (1992): 59–67.

16. You may be wondering how long the firm should wait to reconsider the redeem-or-repurchase-or-wait decision. There is no hard and fast rule. We recommend reconsidering the decision no later than a date that is far

enough in advance of the next sinking-fund date that the firm would be able to repurchase bonds and deliver them to the bond trustee if that is the most profitable strategy. We also recommend reconsidering the decision if there is a significant movement up or down in interest rates, say, more than 100 basis points.

17. This case study is based on A. J. Kalotay, F. M. Saldanha, and G. O. Williams, "The Management of Sinking Funds: The World Bank Experience," *Journal of Fixed Income* 3 (1993): 32–38.
18. Ibid., 34.
19. Ibid., 34–35.
20. Ibid., 37. The forfeited option value consists of $836,000 for the delivery options and $543,000 for the call option.

Chapter 13

1. "Accounting for Transfers and Servicing of Financial Assets and Extinguishments of Liabilities," in *Statement of Financial Accounting Standards No. 125* (Stamford, CT: Financial Accounting Standards Board, June 1996), superseded *Statement of Financial Accounting Standards No. 76* and extinguished what had become a highly controversial accounting technique.
2. R. W. Masulis, "The Effects of Capital Structure Change on Security Prices: A Study of Exchange Offers," *Journal of Financial Economics* 8 (June 1980): 139–178; and R. W. Masulis, "The Impact of Capital Structure Change on Firm Value: Some Estimates," *Journal of Finance* 38 (March 1983): 107–126.
3. Generally a materially higher yield is at least 12.5 basis points above the yield of the new debt issue. The Tax Reform Act of 1986 also fundamentally altered the rules with respect to advance refunding of municipal bonds. Bonds sold before January 1, 1986, may be advance-refunded at most twice, and the bonds sold on or after that date only once while the original issue is still outstanding. In addition, since lower marginal tax rates have narrowed the spread between tax-exempt and taxable bond yields, negative arbitrage, arising when earnings on the escrowed funds are less than the interest cost of the new bond issue, is likely to occur more often than it did in the past.
4. As we discussed in chapter 12, the benefit of refunding low-coupon debt is derived from a debt issuer's opportunity to increase the proportion of debt service that is tax deductible. Defeasing low-coupon debt is at best a break-even proposition for a nontaxpayer.
5. This section is based on J. D. Finnerty, "The Advance Refunding of Nonredeemable High-Coupon Corporate Debt Through In-Substance Defeasance," *Journal of Financial Engineering* 1 (September 1992): 150–173.
6. The TVA is a wholly owned corporate agency of the United States, but its debt is not a full-faith-and-credit obligation of the U.S. government. The TVA is not subject to federal income taxes or to taxation by any states or their subdivisions. It makes payments to the states and counties in which it operates in lieu of taxes. But these payments are calculated as 5 percent of gross revenues from the sale of power and hence are not affected by

changes in interest payments. Accordingly, income taxes do not enter into the analysis of the TVA defeasance.

7. The same parameter f appears in both equations to take into account the amount of interest for the balance of the current interest period, which must also be defeased.

8. The estimated cost of noncallable thirty-year TVA debt was 8.50 percent, which is 62 basis points less than the actual cost of funds for the thirty-year callable issue. The estimated cost of noncallable forty-year TVA debt was 8.47 percent, which is 60 basis points less than the actual cost of funds for the forty-year callable issue. According to the financial staff of the TVA, the underwriters had estimated that including a call provision would increase the required yield in each case by approximately 60 basis points. The thirty-year Treasury issue is used as the pricing benchmark for the forty-year TVA issue because the U.S. Treasury does not issue forty-year debt.

9. Ibid., 160–170.

10. In order for bankruptcy risk to be completely eliminated, the defeasance trust must be insulated from all events of bankruptcy by the issuer.

11. A. J. Kalotay, "Bond Redemption Under Rate Base Regulation," *Public Utilities Fortnightly* 1 (March 1979): 68–69.

12. Ibid.

13. The capital gain tax issue is much less important for taxable bonds because a large proportion of those bonds are held by pension funds, which do not pay income taxes.

14. A. J. Kalotay, G. O. Williams, and A. I. Pedvis, "Refunding Tax-Exempt Corporate Bonds in Advance of the Call," *Financier* 1 (February 1994): 74–79, list eight such tender offers for a total of $1 billion of debt that attracted between 21.67 percent and 56.14 percent of the issues, with an average of 37.69 percent.

15. This is 11.16 percent (1,562,400/14,000,000) at the 8.5 percent new issue rate and 88.84 percent (100.00 – 11.16 percent) at the 6.5 percent new issue rate.

16. The underwriting and other expenses amounted to 2 percent of the $14 million face amount. Ibid.

17. Ibid., 78.

Chapter 14

1. For example, in February 1996, holders of USAir Group Inc.'s publicly traded Series B convertible preferred stock became eligible to elect two directors to represent their interests on the airline's board because USAir had failed to pay dividends on the preferred stock for six consecutive quarters. When the airline encountered financial difficulties, it first suspended its common stock dividends in 1990 and then its preferred stock dividends in 1994. See "USAir Group Holders of Preferred Name Two to Be Directors," *Wall Street Journal*, June 12, 1996, p. B5.

2. For example, if the stated value is $25.00 per share and the liquidation premium is 10 percent, or $2.50, the preferred stockholders must receive

$27.50 for each share before the issuer can distribute anything to common stockholders.

3. However, it is important to exclude from this calculation any issues that have a put option feature or unusual call or other features that might make them poor comparables.

4. This result increases the volatility of the security's rate of return. One study documents the high volatility of adjustable-rate preferred stock holding-period returns relative to those of alternative money market instruments. See B. J. Winger, C. R. Chen, J. D. Martin, J. W. Petty, and S. C. Hayden, "Adjustable Rate Preferred Stock," *Financial Management* 15 (Spring 1986): 48–57.

5. A Dutch auction accepts the highest bid, the next highest bid, and so on, until a market-clearing price is found for which all the securities offered for sale will be purchased. All the sales then take place at the market-clearing price.

6. At least one study has documented the tax arbitrage that auction-rate preferred stock affords under current tax law. See M. J. Alderson, K. C. Brown, and S. L. Lummer, "Dutch Auction Rate Preferred Stock," *Financial Management* 16 (Summer 1987): 68–73.

7. Freeport-McMoRan Copper & Gold used the proceeds of the issue to help fund the expansion of one of the largest gold mines in the world: its Grasberg mine in Irian, Jaya, Indonesia.

8. The investors purchased the shares for $38.77 each. At maturity, each investor will receive the value of one-tenth of an ounce of gold for each share, whether the price of gold is higher or lower than $387.00 per ounce. In effect, the investor will trade the stated value of $38.77 per share at maturity for the cash value of one-tenth of an ounce of gold, profiting if the price of gold is above $387.00 per ounce and losing if it is below.

9. See *Gold-Denominated Preferred Offers Benefits to Issuer and Investors* (New York: Lehman Brothers, September 1993): 8–9.

10. J. D. Finnerty, "Preferred Stock Refunding Analysis: Synthesis and Extension," *Financial Management* 13 (Autumn 1984): 22–28.

11. The Revenue Act of 1987 reduced the dividends-received deduction to 70 percent from 80 percent. At times, Congress has considered reducing it further.

12. The cumulative effect of accounting changes involved a charge of $20.9 billion in 1992 and resulted in a loss for that year of $23.5 billion. As a result, GM's stockholders' equity at year-end 1992 declined to just $6.2 billion, while total assets were $190.2 billion. See General Motors Corporation, "Offer to Purchase," April 25, 1995.

13. T. Pratt, "Merrill Wraps Up Biggest-Ever Preferred Stock Tender Offer," *Investment Dealers' Digest*, May 29, 1995, pp. 13, 20.

14. R. W. Masulis, "The Effects of Capital Structure Change on Security Prices: A Study of Exchange Offers," *Journal of Financial Economics* 8 (June 1980): 139–178, and R. W. Masulis, "The Impact of Capital Structure Change on Firm Value: Some Estimates," *Journal of Finance* 38 (March 1983): 107–126.

15. The preferred stock issue consisted of 20 million shares. McDonald's wanted to leave outstanding at least 2 million shares, representing $50 million of stated value, to ensure reasonable liquidity for the remaining

shareholders. See McDonald's Corporation, "Offer to Exchange," June 5, 1995. The debentures were structured as fixed-income capital securities known in the market as quarterly income debt securities (QUIDS).

16. Ibid.

17. Equation 14.7 is the adaptation of equations 10.4 and 14.3. The cost of the old issue is the preferred stock dividends, and the new issue cost is the after-tax debt cost. In equation 10.4, the term for the amortized cost of issuing the new debt, TC/N, is embedded in the present value of the after-tax new issue expense, E (equation 10.5). In equation 14.7, it is included in the summation instead of being embedded in E.

18. T. Pratt, "McDonald's 'QUIDS' Exchange Bombs as Only 26% Accept," *Investment Dealers' Digest*, July 10, 1995, p. 11.

19. Since the dividends are taxed at a 10.5 percent effective rate after allowing for the 70 percent dividends-received deduction whereas interest income is taxed at the full 35 percent rate.

20. For example, in May 1993, General Motors spent $265 million to redeem two series of preferred stock, issued in 1930 and 1946, that restricted its ability to sell receivables.

Chapter 15

1. See C. Ghosh, R. Varma, and J. R. Woolridge, "An Analysis of Exchangeable Debt Offers," *Journal of Financial Economics* 28 (1990): 251–264.

2. See A. Barnea, R. A. Haugen, and L. W. Senbet, *Agency Problems and Financial Contracting* (Upper Saddle River, NJ: Prentice Hall, 1985).

3. See J. C. Stein, "Convertible Bonds as Backdoor Equity Financing," *Journal of Financial Economics* 32 (1992): 3–22.

4. See M. J. Brennan and E. S. Schwartz, "The Case for Convertibles," *Journal of Applied Corporate Finance* 1 (Summer 1988): 55–64.

5. For a detailed examination of sources of such conflicts of interest, see chapter 9 of D. R. Emery and J. D. Finnerty, *Corporate Financial Management* (Upper Saddle River, NJ: Prentice Hall, 1997).

6. At the same time, convertible securities are subject to other agency costs. For example, when a firm exercises its call option on convertible preferred stock (thereby forcing security holders to choose between accepting a cash call price or the shares of stock), they sometimes use the technical wording of the contract to avoid paying the last dividend. See T. Pratt, "BankAmerica Applies 'Screw' as Convert Holders Cry Foul," *Investment Dealers' Digest*, May 22, 1995, p. 12.

7. This decision rule assumes that the convertible security's value as stock exceeds its value as a bond at the time of the call. However, suppose interest rates decline following the bond's issuance but the underlying share price also falls, causing the conversion option to have little value. The convertible bond will then behave like a nonconvertible bond. In such cases, the decision rule for refunding the convertible bond is the same as the decision rule for refunding a nonconvertible bond.

8. Jonathan Ingersoll found that firms wait, on average, until the conversion value exceeds the call price by 44 percent, behavior later confirmed by

Wayne Mikkelson. See J. E. Ingersoll, Jr., "An Examination of Corporate Call Policies on Convertible Securities," *Journal of Finance* 32 (1977): 463–478, and W. H. Mikkelson, "Capital Structure Change and Decreases in Stockholders' Wealth: A Cross-Sectional Study of Convertible Security Calls," in B. M. Friedman, ed., *Corporate Capital Structures in the United States* (Chicago: University of Chicago Press, 1985), 265–296.

9. P. Asquith, "Convertible Bonds Are Not Called Late," *Journal of Finance* 50 (1995): 1275–1289.

10. See A. K. Singh, A. R. Cowan, and N. Nayar, "Underwritten Calls of Convertible Bonds," *Journal of Financial Economics* 29 (1991): 173–196.

11. The redemption cushion equals the difference between the conversion value of $70.2674 ([1.5152]$46.375) and the $54.9375 redemption price, divided by the redemption price, which equals 27.9 percent ([$70.2674 − $54.9375]/$54.9375).

12. In response to some investor-voiced objections to the cap on PERCS, securities dealers created dividend-enhanced convertible stock (DECS) and PRIDES, which are similar. Conversion of DECS is also mandatory, but the conversion feature is initially out of the money, and the payoff is not capped. See T. Pratt, "Salomon Unveils New Hybrid with PERCS-like Features," *Investment Dealers' Digest*, June 28, 1993, p. 12.

13. See J. D. Finnerty, "The Case for Issuing Synthetic Convertible Bonds," *Midland Corporate Finance Journal* (Fall 1986): 73–82.

14. The Financial Institutions Reform, Recovery and Enforcement Act (FIRREA) of 1989 established new minimum capital standards for financial institutions. Previously, banks could include mandatory convertible debt in primary capital up to 20 percent of the sum of the other elements of primary capital. FIRREA excludes mandatory convertible debt from "core capital," which is the new definition of what was formerly called primary capital.

15. See M. H. Miller and F. Modigliani, "Dividend Policy, Growth, and the Valuation of Shares," *Journal of Business* 34 (October 1961): 411–433.

16. See M. A. Mazzeo and W. T. Moore, "Liquidity Costs and Stock Price Response to Convertible Security Calls," *Journal of Business* 65 (1992): 353–369; and J. R. Woolridge and C. Ghosh, "Dividend Cuts? Do They Always Signal Bad News?" *Midland Corporate Finance Journal* (Summer 1985).

17. See Avon Products, "Offer to Exchange," p. 1.

18. See L. Sachar, "Avon's Fall Guy CFO," *Financial World*, August 9, 1988, pp. 22, 23, 25.

19. Ibid.

20. See D. R. Emery and J. D. Finnerty, "Using a PERCS-for-Common Exchange Offer to Reduce the Costs of a Dividend Cut," *Journal of Applied Corporate Finance* 7 (Winter 1995): 77–89.

Chapter 16

1. *eCommerce in the U.S. Fixed Income Market: The 1999 Review of Electronic Transaction Systems* (New York: Bond Market Association, 1999).

2. See "Pittsburgh Bonds to Sell on Internet," *Wall Street Journal*, October 12, 1999, p. C1, "Web Helps World Bank Sell $3 Billion in Debt; U.S. Treasury's

Weakness, Yield Inversion Persist," *Wall Street Journal*, January 21, 2000, p. C19, and "World Bank Drops Fidelity Investments from E-Bond Deal," *Wall Street Journal*, January 21, 2000, p. A2.

3. See "Upstart Firm Rolls Out Commercial Paper on Web," *Wall Street Journal*, April 21, 2000, p. C1, and "Bond Traders Seek More, Better Online Services," *Wall Street Journal*, October 25, 1999, pp. C1, C19.

4. In January 2001, the Securities and Exchange Commission approved Trace, the Trade Reporting and Comparison Entry Service, a system that will for the first time collect and report information on transactions in the corporate bond market. See "SEC Clears System to Collect, Distribute Bond-Trading Data," *Wall Street Journal*, January 23, 2001, p. C23.

5. See "Bond Issuance in Euro Zone Is Exploding," *Wall Street Journal*, December 1, 1999, pp. C1, C25.

6. S. Borden and A. Sarkar, "Securitizing Property Catastrophe Risk," *Federal Reserve Bank of New York Current Issues in Economics and Finance* 2 (August 1996): 1–6, and N. A. Doherty, "Financial Innovation in the Management of Catastrophe Risk," *Journal of Applied Corporate Finance* 10 (Fall 1997): 84–95, describe the evolution of property catastrophe securitization instruments.

7. See J. D. Finnerty, "Sources of Value Added from Structuring Asset-Backed Securities to Reduce or Reallocate Risk," in C. Stone, A. Zissu, and J. Lederman, eds., *The Global Asset Backed Securities Market* (Chicago: Probus, 1993), pp. 27–60.

Suggested Additional Readings

Asquith, Paul, and David W. Mullins, Jr. "Convertible Debt: Corporate Call Policy and Voluntary Conversion." *Journal of Finance* 46, no. 4 (1991): 1273–1290.

Black, Fischer, Emanuel Derman, and William Toy. "A One-Factor Model of Interest Rates and Its Application to Treasury Bond Options." *Financial Analysts Journal* 46, no. 1 (1990): 33–39.

Cowan, Arnold R., Nandkumar Nayar, and Ajai K. Singh. "Underwriting Calls of Convertible Securities: A Note." *Journal of Financial Economics* 31, no. 2 (1992): 269–278.

———. "Calls of Out-of-the-Money Convertible Bonds." *Financial Management* 22, no. 4 (1993): 106–116.

Crabbe, Leland E., and Jean Helwege. "Alternative Tests of Agency Theories of Callable Corporate Bonds." *Financial Management* 23, no. 4 (1994): 3–20.

Diamond, Douglas W. "Monitoring and Reputation: The Choice Between Bank Loans and Directly Placed Debt." *Journal of Political Economy* 99, no. 4 (1991): 689–721.

Easterwood, John C., and Palani-Rajan Kadapakkam. "The Role of Private and Public Debt in Corporate Capital Structures." *Financial Management* 20, no. 3 (1991): 49–57.

Emery, Douglas R., J. Ronald Hoffmeister, and Ronald W. Spahr. "The Case for Indexing a Bond's Call Price." *Financial Management* 16, no. 3 (1987): 57–64.

Fabozzi, Frank J., ed. *The Handbook of Mortgage Backed Securities.* 4th ed. Chicago: Probus, 1995.

———. *Bond Markets: Analysis and Strategies.* 4th ed. Upper Saddle River, NJ: Prentice Hall, 1999.

———, ed. *The Handbook of Fixed Income Securities.* 6th ed. New York: McGraw-Hill, 2000.

Ferreira, Eurico J., Michael F. Spivey, and Charles E. Edwards. "Pricing New-Issue and Seasoned Preferred Stocks: A Comparison of Valuation Models." *Financial Management* 21, no. 2 (1992): 52–62.

Ho, Thomas, and Ronald F. Singer. "The Value of Corporate Debt with a Sinking-Fund Provision." *Journal of Business* 57, no. 3 (1984): 315–336.

Houston, Joel F., and S. Venkataraman. "Optimal Maturity Structure with Multiple Debt Claims." *Journal of Financial and Quantitative Analysis* 29, no. 2 (1994): 179–197.

Hsueh, L. Paul, and David S. Kidwell. "Bond Ratings: Are Two Better Than One?" *Financial Management* 17, no. 1 (1988): 46–53.

Hull, John C. *Options, Futures, and Other Derivatives.* 4th ed. Upper Saddle River, NJ: Prentice Hall, 2000.

James, Christopher, and Peggy Wier. "Borrowing Relationships, Intermediation, and the Cost of Issuing Public Securities." *Journal of Financial Economics* 28, no. 1/2 (1990): 149–172.

Jarrow, Robert, and Stuart Turnbull. *Derivative Securities*. Cincinnati, OH: South-Western, 1996.

John, Kose. "Managing Financial Distress and Valuing Distressed Securities: A Survey and a Research Agenda." *Financial Management* 22, no. 3 (1993): 60–78.

Kalotay, Andrew J., George O. Williams, and Frank J. Fabozzi. "A Model for the Valuation of Bonds and Embedded Options." *Financial Analysts Journal* 49, no. 3 (1993): 35–46.

Kaplan, Steven N., and Jeremy C. Stein. "How Risky Is the Debt of Highly Leveraged Transactions?" *Journal of Financial Economics* 27, no. 1 (1990): 215–246.

Longstaff, Francis A., and Eduardo S. Schwartz. "A Simple Approach to Valuing Risky Fixed and Floating Rate Debt." *Journal of Finance* 50, no. 3 (1995): 789–819.

Myers, Stewart C., and Nicholas J. Majluf. "Corporate Financing and Investment Decisions When Firms Have Information That Investors Do Not Have." *Journal of Financial Economics* 13, no. 2 (1984): 187–222.

Ogden, Joseph P. "Determinants of the Relative Interest Rate Sensitivities of Corporate Bonds," *Financial Management* 16, no. 1 (1987): 22–30.

Ramaswamy, Krishna, and Suresh M. Sundaresan. "The Valuation of Floating-Rate Instruments: Theory and Evidence." *Journal of Financial Economics* 17, no. 2 (1986): 251–272.

Smithson, Charles W. *Managing Financial Risk*. 3d ed. New York: McGraw-Hill, 1998.

Standard & Poor's Ratings Group. *S&P's Corporate Finance Criteria*. New York: Standard & Poor's, 1996.

Sundaresan, Suresh. *Fixed Income Markets and Their Derivatives*. Cincinnati, OH: South-Western, 1997.

Thatcher, Janet S. "The Choice of Call Provision Terms: Evidence of the Existence of Agency Costs of Debt." *Journal of Finance* 40, no. 2 (1985): 549–561.

Tuckman, Bruce. *Fixed Income Securities: Tools for Today's Markets*. New York: Wiley, 1995.

Tufano, Peter. "Financial Innovation and First-Mover Advantages." *Journal of Financial Economics* 25, no. 2 (1989): 213–240.

Vu, Joseph D. "An Empirical Investigation of Calls of Non-Convertible Bonds." *Journal of Financial Economics* 16, no. 2 (1986): 235–265.

Walmsley, Julian. *The New Financial Instruments*. New York: Wiley, 1988.

Index

407